AF646668

EAST ASIA STRATEGIC REVIEW

China's Rising Strategic Ambitions in Asia

EAST ASIA STRATEGIC REVIEW

China's Rising Strategic Ambitions in Asia

Editor

M.S. Prathibha

idsa

INSTITUTE FOR DEFENCE STUDIES & ANALYSES
NEW DELHI

PENTAGON PRESS LLP

East Asia Strategic Review: China's Rising Strategic Ambitions in Asia
Editor: M.S. Prathibha

First Published in 2018

Copyright © Institute for Defence Studies and Analyses, New Delhi

ISBN 978-93-86618-65-8

All rights reserved. No part of this publication may be reproduced, stored in a retrieval system, or transmitted, in any form or by any means, electronic, mechanical, photocopying, recording, or otherwise, without first obtaining written permission of the copyright owner.

Disclaimer: The views expressed in this book are those of the authors and do not necessarily reflect those of the Institute for Defence Studies and Analyses, or the Government of India.

Published by
PENTAGON PRESS LLP
206, Peacock Lane, Shahpur Jat
New Delhi-110049
Phones: 011-64706243, 26491568
Telefax: 011-26490600
email: rajan@pentagonpress.in
website: www.pentagonpress.in

In association with
Institute for Defence Studies and Analyses
No. 1, Development Enclave,
New Delhi-110010
Phone: +91-11-26717983
Website: www.idsa.in

Printed at Aegean Offset Printers, Greater Noida, U.P.

Contents

Preface

China has achieved tremendous economic development in the last few decades, and has been leveraging it through its political and diplomatic presence in its neighbourhood to achieve its strategic ambitions in Asia. In fact, the depth of its economic presence in Asia has led it to underscore its cooperation through multilateral and global initiatives. From its role in helping establish new financial institutions to introducing grand initiative of One Belt and One Road (OBOR), Chinese engagement in the region is continuously increasing. As a result, China's interaction with the region's political elite has been growing so as to convince the Asian countries the benefits of tying their developmental agendas with the Chinese economic policies, and simultaneously to assure them of the benign nature of its rise.

Nowhere it is more conspicuous than in Asia, where China considers itself capable of handling more responsibilities and assuming leadership role. Thus, its relations with major countries in East Asia, Southeast Asia, South Asia, and Central Asia have expanded significantly. After the Chinese President Xi Jinping assumed office in 2012, China's diplomatic engagement has become pro-active that is witnessed in its efforts to implement its OBOR initiatives and regional economic integration. Due to its growing investments, dependence on energy supplies and securing routes, maritime security has become an important component of its policy in the South China Sea and the Indian Ocean Region. Although concerns have been raised about China's sovereignty claims in the SCS, many external powers such as the United States (US) have consistently been performing freedom of navigation patrols in the SCS. Yet, China has been so far successful in keeping ASEAN (Association for Southeast Asian Nations) from forcing the Chinese to concede on island building. Nevertheless, SCS continues to remain a source of anxiety in the Chinese minds due to the perceived threat of US naval deployments in Asia and its impact on Chinese military operations.

China's maritime interests have also impacted the way it is expanding its naval assets and has implications for the major countries in the Indian

Ocean region. Apart from the sovereignty and the territorial dispute in the SCS, the ongoing island-building and military installations are clear indications that China intends to protect its interests in SCS even it means to threaten or the actual use of force. The security dilemma in the Malacca Strait means that the Chinese access through OBOR countries into the Indian Ocean region is imperative along with the domestic legal avenues to enforce its sovereignty claims. The foreign policy of China has been adjusted to reflect these strategic objectives to support its rising ambitions by ensuring that China maximises the benefits through political and economic involvement. However, there are certain challenges that China is facing in attempting to legitimise its interest in the Asian countries. Deep mistrust in some countries, scepticism in other countries, combined with countries that are seeking to support Chinese initiatives as it provides them opportunities for investment meant that responses to Chinese role are varied and multifaceted. The risks involved in such investment or the concessions given to China has also become problematic. Nevertheless, smaller countries are opting for Chinese investment due to the complications involved in altering their economic policies and developmental models in order to procure loans from international financial institutions such as the International Monetary Fund (IMF).

Thus, China's strategic ambitions in Asia is as complex as the responses it incurs from countries in the region. However, challenges it faces to its endeavours are often entwined with concerns on the growing Chinese economic and military power in the region. The recent reforms in the Chinese military show that the leadership is keen on transforming the military into a professional force. The organisational and structural restructuring in the military and changes in the leadership were undertaken to increase efficiency and better decision-making system. These reforms have shown that China is increasing its deterrence posture that is required to enforce its strategic interests and counter any external power from challenging Chinese interests. Besides, the Chinese leadership has also been focusing on equally engaging all the armed services, and improve their contribution in the military planning. The primary reason seems to be the realisation that the type of war China is likely to fight in the future would depend on developing its joint operational capability and joint warfare. Thus, a highly integrated force structure and strengthened civil-military integration is designed towards propelling Chinese military into a more professional force.

In addition, Xi Jinping's anti-corruption campaign from 2012 has made sure that the Chinese military has been forced to reform and restructure.

Xi Jinping has been successful to a large extent in reigning the opposing forces to reform as well as his political opponents. This great transformation of China has become a point of scholarly and public debate, because the rising power not only challenges the established power and also the international system, where countries are forced to respond to Chinese rise.

Among the Asian countries, India's role in the region and how it navigates its bilateral relationship has become significant. Other countries also take cue from Indian response to Chinese rise because of India's geo-political influence. As a result, whether it is conflict or cooperation, the trajectory of the bilateral relationship affects the region and sets the tone for stability of Asia. While bilateral irritants continue to impinge on the relationship, broad consensus exists on the nature of cooperation between the two powers on a range of regional and global issues.

The transformation of China and its ambitions are of importance to Asia, and the perspectives from India offer a meaningful contribution to the ongoing debates about it. The recent debates among Indian thinkers show such diversity of thought about the role of China and the way in which it shapes the evolving regional environment.

M.S. Prathibha

List of Contributors

Dr Abanti Bhattacharya is Associate Professor at the Department of East Asian Studies, University of Delhi. She teaches courses on Chinese foreign policy, Chinese History, India-China relations, East Asian international relations and Chinese Nationalism. Prior to this, she was Associate Fellow at the Institute for Defence Studies and Analyses (IDSA). She holds a PhD from Jawaharlal Nehru University, New Delhi. As part of the government exchange programme, she pursued Chinese language course from Fudan University Shanghai. Currently, she is a member of the editorial board of India Quarterly, a flagship publication of the Indian Council of World Affairs. (ICWA). She has published extensively in national and international journals including Issues and Studies, Asia-Pacific Review, East Asia, Journal of East Asian Affairs, Strategic Analysis among others. Dr. Bhattacharya can be reached at: abantidelhi@gmail.com

Dr Amrita Jash is an Associate Fellow at Centre for land Warfare Studies. She is also the co-founder and Editor-in-Chief at IndraStra Global, New York. Her research has appeared in four edited books, International Journals such as East Asian Policy, Review of Global Politics, Strategic Analysis, Yonsei Journal, China Report and Strategic Vision. She has also published in forums such as CSIS, RSIS, Huffington Post, E-IR, Asia Times, Munk School of Global Affairs, Crawford School, ISDP, China-India Brief, IPP Review, SADF, I-A Forum, Gateway House, China Focus and others. Her research interests are China's foreign policy, Chinese military, strategic and security issues.

Dr Prashant Kumar Singh, Associate Fellow, East Asia Centre, IDSA, follows the strategic and domestic affairs of China. He is also a keen follower of state and society in Taiwan. And he has a deep interest in India's engagement with East Asia. His current research project is "Foreign Relations and Security in Xi Jinping's Chinese Dream". He is a recipient of the prestigious CCS Grant for Foreign Scholars (2016) by National Central Library (Taiwan), Taiwan Fellowship (2014) and National Huayu

Enrichment Scholarship, Taiwan (2011-12). Dr. Singh has been invited to speak at renowned institutes including Chung-Hua Institution for Economic Research (CIER), National Central Library (NCL), National Chengchi University (NCCU), National Chung Hsing University (NCHU), Council of Advanced Policy Studies (CAPS), Taiwan Think Tank and Tamkang University [all in Taiwan]; China Institute of International Studies (CIIS) in China, Asia Centre in France, and Ho Chi Minh National Academy of Politics and Thai Nguyen University in Vietnam.

Saheli Chattaraj is an Assistant Professor at the Centre for China Studies at the Academy of International Studies, Jamia Millia Islamia, New Delhi. Her basic training has been in Chinese Language and Literature and is a fluent speaker of Mandarin. She holds a Bachelors and Masters degree in Chinese Language, Literature and Cultural Studies from Jawaharlal Nehru University. She holds an M.Phil Degree in Chinese Studies from the School of International Studies, JNU. Her research interest includes contemporary India-China relations and India-Taiwan relations, politics and state and society relations in China. She had been awarded a fellowship by the Ministry of Human Resource Development under the China-India Cultural Exchange program 2010-2011 to undertake advanced studies in Chinese. She has also been awarded the Taiwan Fellowship by the Ministry of Foreign Affairs, Taiwan to conduct research on India and Taiwan. She was affiliated with the National Chung Hsing University. She has also been associated with the India-China bilateral project of the Encyclopedia of India-China Cultural Contacts, Ministry of External Affairs, Government of India. On several academic assignments she has travelled to China, Taiwan and Hong-Kong.

Cmde. Abhay Kumar Singh is a Research Fellow in the Military Affairs Centre at the Institute for Defence Studies and Analyses, New Delhi. He is an Indian Navy veteran with extensive command and staff experience spanning 27 years. A surface warfare officer with a specialisation in Missile and Gunnery Warfare, he has commanded various naval platforms which include frontline frigate, submarine rescue & deep diving vessel, and fleet auxiliary. He has also served as Director (Military Affairs) in the Disarmament and International Security Division of the Ministry of External Affairs. Cmde. Singh is an alumnus of the Naval Academy, Defence Services Staff Course and Naval War College.

Col Adarsha Verma is a Research Fellow in the Institute for Defence Studies and Analyses, New Delhi with keen interest in security issues of East Asia and the Indian Ocean region.

Dr Smruti S Pattanaik is a Research Fellow at the IDSA. Her area of specialisation is South Asia. Dr Pattanaik has been a recipient of many international fellowships. She was India Chair and Visiting Professor on ICCR's India Chair in the Centre for Contemporary Indian Studies at the University of Colombo in 2013. She is a recipient of number of international fellowships. She was a visiting Fellow at the Peace Research Institute Oslo (PRIO) in 2011, postdoctoral fellow at Centre for International Relations and Research FMSH in Paris in 2008, Visiting Asia Fellow at the Department of International Relations, Dhaka University in 2004 and 2007, Kodikara fellow of the Regional Centre for Strategic Studies; Colombo, She was Visiting Professor, Colombo University in 2013. She has lectured on India's foreign policy at Asia Centre, Paris, Warsaw University, University of Colombo, Sir John Kotelawala Defence University, Asia Centre in the University of Melbourne, University of Karachi, University of Peshawar, University of Dhaka, Jahangirnagar University, Chittagong and Rajshahi University in Bangladesh. She lectures regularly on the neighbourhood at the BSF Academy, ITBP Academy, Army War College, Mhow and College of Air Warfare, Secunderabad. She is the Coordinator of Pakistan project at IDSA. Dr Pattanaik has published more than 50 articles in various journals, has contributed more than 40 chapters in edited books.

Dr Sampa Kundu works as an Assistant Professor at the Symbiosis School of International Studies (SSIS), Symbiosis International (Deemed University), Pune, India. Her research interests include geo-strategic affairs in the Indo-Pacific with a special focus on Southeast Asia, India's relations with Southeast Asia, ASEAN and other regional cooperation initiatives and domestic and external affairs of Myanmar. She has published several book chapters, research articles and book reviews and contributed commentaries in various forums. Prior to SSIS, she worked with the Southeast Asia and Oceania Centre at the Institute for Defence Studies and Analyses, New Delhi as a Researcher. She has finished her PhD on *India and Myanmar in BIMSTEC: implications for Northeast India* from the Center for Indo-Pacific Studies, School of International Studies, Jawaharlal Nehru University, New Delhi in 2015.

Dr Vrushal T. Ghoble is an Assistant Professor in the Centre for West Asian Studies (CWAS), School of International Studies (SIS), Jawaharlal Nehru University, New Delhi, India. He pursued his M.Phil and Ph.D from CWAS/SIS. His main research pursuits are Energy security; Gulf energy market; Asian Oil Corporations; Oil industry and Corporate Social Responsibility; Energy & Environment; Maritime energy transits; Asian energy resources; Oil and Democracy; African energy; Alternative energy; Globalization.

Sana Hashmi is a Consultant in the Ministry of External Affairs, New Delhi, India. She has been associated with Centre for Air Power Studies from 2011-2016. She is the author of "China's Approach towards Territorial Disputes: Lessons and Prospects". She has published several book chapters and articles in journals, magazines, web portals. Her doctoral research is on China-Central Asia Relations with a special focus on Shanghai Cooperation Organisation.

Swati Arun was a Researcher at the East Asia Centre, IDSA. She is also a PhD scholar at East Asia Centre, Jawaharlal Nehru University. She has been working on China-US relations and Chinese foreign policy for over five years. She has worked with several think tanks and has produced research articles on China.

Supriya Sharma is a Research Scholar at the Centre for East Asian studies, School of International Studies, Jawaharlal Nehru University. Supriya has worked with IDSA and Observer Research Foundation in the past and published articles on Foreign Policy of China, Maritime Disputes of China and One Belt One Road. She is particularly interested to carry forward her research work in China's foreign policy.

M V Rappai is a Delhi based security analyst specializing in Asian Strategic issues. He worked with the Ministry of Defence, Govt. of India and later on joined the IDSA as a Research Fellow (1996 - 2002). He is currently associated with the Institute of Chinese Studies, Delhi and has published chapters in books and articles in reputed journals and newspapers. Rappai holds a P G Diploma in Chinese language from the School of Foreign Languages, Government of India, New Delhi.

1

Emerging Foreign Policy Trends Under Xi Jinping

Abanti Bhattacharya

ABSTRACT

Under Xi Jinping, Chinese foreign policy has entered a new era. The rising nationalism propelled by the China Dream slogan on the one hand, and increasing domestic challenges precipitated by Xi Jinping's economic rebalancing on the other, have arguably pushed Beijing to a belligerent foreign policy course. An analysis of foreign policy trends in China under Xi Jinping thus indicates that China is progressively trying to reshape the international environment to conform to its national interest. But while China claims not to reinvent the wheel, it puts forward a new model of international relations.

Key words: *Nationalism, China Dream, Economic Globalization, Global Governance, Peripheral Diplomacy, Rejuvenation.*

Sparked by the Chinese President Xi Jinping's slogan of the China Dream, Chinese foreign policy has entered an interesting phase, albeit a difficult one. This is because the rise in Chinese influence and the expansion of its global role has raised Beijing's stakes in supporting, and in some cases, consolidating the existing international order. Yet, the rising nationalistic aspirations of China to occupy a dominant place in international politics on the one hand and the pressures of domestic challenges, in the context of Xi Jinping's economic rebalancing on the other, are likely to push Beijing to follow a belligerent foreign policy course.

Looking at the broad spectrum of international developments, it can be seen that the Brexit issue and Donald Trump's presidency in the US, have significantly determined the course of Chinese foreign policy. Both international developments are symptomatic of a hardening of boundaries that spell the doom of globalisation. More particularly, President Trump's slogan of 'America First', that is signalling the revival of isolationism and protectionism in US foreign and economic policies, has ignited substantial worries in the Zhongnanhai. It may be observed that the US is the leading China's export partner accounting for 16.9 per cent of its exports. Therefore, the 'America First' policy is bound to impinge on China's growth story, at a time when Xi Jinping has embarked upon an economic rebalancing, characterised by the 'new normal' of economic development, which essentially involves a shift "from an economy driven by low-quality exports and public investments to an economy with a stronger role for services, domestic consumption and high-quality goods."[1] Clearly, China is at a juncture where it needs a robust global economic environment that can facilitate the absorption of the fallout of the economic rebalancing at home. Also, simultaneously, China has entered a phase where nationalism has assumed a more potent form. The 'China Dream' has evidently fuelled Beijing's great power aspirations, and thus, Xi Jinping's inauguration of the Belt and Road Initiative (BRI) in 2013 has emerged as the principal means to achieve the great rejuvenation of the Chinese nation. However, the worldwide trend of shrinking globalisation and rising nationalism is likely to place greater pressure on China. The issues of sovereignty and territorial conflicts are likely to sharpen Beijing's nationalism, spelling a further assault on globalisation and regionalism. All this would lead to a belligerent turn in Chinese foreign policy.

Given this background, this chapter is going to project the trends defining Chinese foreign policy under the leadership of Xi Jinping. In order to do so, the chapter is first going to analyse some of the important speeches and policy documents that have marked the Xi Jinping's leadership thus far. Second, the chapter will highlight the continuities and changes in Chinese foreign policy on the basis of these documents and speeches. Third, it will list and evaluate the emerging foreign policy options for China, and finally draw few inferences.

The 18th Party Congress Report

At first glance, the section on foreign policy in the 18th Party Congress Report (PCR), appears to be similar to the 17th PCR of 2007.[2] It starts with a similar reiteration of following the 'Peaceful Development' path and highlighting the growing trends towards a multipolar and globalised world. However, if the 17th PCR mentioned multi-polarity as an "irreversible" trend, the 18th PCR stated, that it is "deepening". It seems to suggest a declining enthusiasm for a multi-polar world within the Chinese leadership.

With regard to globalisation, however, both the reports mention that the trend is intensifying. But the 18th Party Report further goes on to add that "cultural diversity is increasing, and an information society is fast emerging." Furthermore, it states that emerging economies and developing countries are fast gaining strength, and therefore, they are evolving as new constituencies, supporting the global peace and stability.

Like all previous party congress reports, the 18th PCR moves on to outline in its second paragraph the problems of 'power politics' and 'hegemonism' afflicting global politics but it, in addition, mentions 'neo-interventionism for the first-time. This usage of the term, seems to be in the nature of a warning to the West, particularly the US, for its pre-emptive intervention in Syria and elsewhere. Significantly as well, the report for the first time highlights the impact of the 2008 world financial crisis and other global issues such as energy security, resource security and cyber security that are all becoming acute in the current era.

There is another new pronouncement in the latter paragraphs of the report. While the 17th PCR states that China "will continue to take an active part in multilateral affairs, assume our due international obligations, play a constructive role," the 18th PCR iterates, in a more candid and forceful manner, that China will "get more actively involved in international affairs, play its due role of a major responsible country, and work jointly with other countries to meet global challenges." The phrases "get more actively involved" and play "a major responsible role" indicate that China would not merely participate in international affairs, but rather it will assume a more responsible role, in shaping the international order. Another very notable feature of the 18th PCR is that it talks about protecting China's legitimate rights and overseas interests. It states: "We will take solid steps to promote public diplomacy as well as people-to-people and cultural exchanges, and protect China's legitimate rights and interests overseas." The question thus arises: Does this require China to interfere in the internal affairs of other countries? It is important to remember that non-interference has been a basic tenet of Chinese foreign policy and all the PCRs, including the 18th PCR, have reiterated it.

The rest of the 18th PCR reiterates those issues that are common to the previous PCRs. These are: building a harmonious world; following the five principles of peaceful coexistence; pursuing an independent foreign policy of peace; safeguarding sovereignty and territorial integrity; safeguarding security and development; respecting the diversity of civilisations; avoid seeking hegemony; and pursuing a common development and win-win programme globally.

Xi Jinping's 'Road to Rejuvenation Speech' November 2012

Right after Xi Jinping assumed the chairmanship of the Chinese Communist Party, he gave a speech at the 'Road of Rejuvenation' exhibition at the National History Museum. The opening sentence of his speech is quite telling. He said, "This exhibition reviews the yesterday of the Chinese nation, displays the today of the Chinese nation, and announces the tomorrow of the Chinese nation." By the yesterdays of the Chinese nation, he meant the humiliations that China had suffered at the hands of the colonial and imperialist forces in the late 19th and early 20th centuries. By the today of the Chinese nation, interestingly he meant, not the post -1949 Maoist era but the post-1978 reform era, when China had finally found "a correct path to realise the great rejuvenation of the Chinese nation." By the tomorrow of the Chinese nation, Xi Jinping meant that the great efforts at rejuvenation of the Chinese nation which began in 1840, would finally be achieved. His speech, then spelt out the path followed by the Chinese people to achieve rejuvenation and categorically stated that, "only development enables self-strengthening." One may recall that during 1861-1895, following its defeat in the Opium Wars the Chinese imperial government under the Qing dynasty had first adopted the self-strengthening measures that essentially meant appropriating Western technology to repel the Western menace. Therefore, President Xi reiterated the importance of the path of development for achieving the goal of rejuvenation. It was in this speech that he, for the first time, mentioned the 'China Dream', the term which gained currency in China with the publication of Liu Mingfu's book (*The China Dream: The Great Power Thinking and Strategic Positioning of China in the Post-American Era*) in 2010. He said, "We believe that realising the great rejuvenation of the Chinese nation is the greatest Chinese dream of the Chinese nation in modern times." He wrapped up his speech by setting two centenary goals: 2021, the 100th anniversary of the CCP; and 2050, the 100th anniversary of the founding of the PRC, by which time, Xi was optimistic, the great rejuvenation of the Chinese nation would be achieved.

Xi Jinping's CICA Speech May 2014

China hosted the fourth summit of the Conference on Interaction and Confidence Building Measures in Asia (CICA) in Shanghai, after taking over as chair. At this conference, Xi Jinping, for the first time, proposed a New Asian Security concept and called for creating an Asian forum for security cooperation. In fact, just as the Japanese had advocated, 'Asia for the Asians' during the Second World War, Xi also sought the creation of a security forum exclusive to the region. He said, "In final analysis, it is for the people of Asia to run the affairs of Asia, solve the problems of Asia and uphold the security of Asia." Notably, one criteria for gaining membership of the group is that at least a part of a state's territory should be in Asia. This, say critics, while a valid criterion for membership, is essentially targeted at keeping the US out. Arguably, the New Asian Security concept almost mirrors the New Security Concept advocated by Jiang Zemin in 1997. It may be recalled that in the context of growing US unilateralism, Jiang Zemin had emphasised the need for a new definition of security by the formulation of a common and cooperative security concept. In a similar vein, Xi Jinping enumerated a four-fold notion of security which encompassed a common, comprehensive, cooperative and sustainable security architecture; and called for the establishment of universal, equal and inclusive security mechanism in Asia. Clearly, through CICA China seeks, not only a regional security framework, but essentially a framework created by Asian countries alone. Most notably, Xi Jinping proposed the setting up of a non-governmental forum to establish a regional security architecture for Asia. To this end, on June 29, 2017, the CICA non-governmental forum pushed for the establishment of a regional security framework with Asian characteristics. Xi's speech also underlined the links between security and development by emphasising that, "development is the foundation of security and security is the precondition for development." Predictably, he ended his speech by harping upon building a peaceful and prosperous neighbourhood, as well as speeding up the development of the Belt and Road Initiative. In other words, the BRI was identified as the vehicle for steering development, thereby, promoting security and creating a cooperative security architecture in Asia for the Asians. Clearly then, through CICA China seeks to provide an alternative structure to the US hub and spoke security architecture.

China's Defence White Paper May 2015

The White Paper on defence is the ninth in the series that the Chinese defence ministry has been issuing since 1998. Thus far, the Chinese defence ministry had entitled their white papers as China's National Defence. But for the first time in 2015, the white paper was entitled, China's Military Strategy.[3] Thus, China for the first time revealed its military strategy, albeit selectively. Nevertheless, as some China watchers argue, this white paper was the sign of a more confident China.[4]

The opening paragraphs began by stating that China was at a critical juncture of its reform and development, and therefore, the thrust of the government was on development and peace to attain the China Dream. It then reiterated the standard position that China's defence policy is defensive in nature and that it is opposed to hegemonism and power politics. It also spelt out its decade old 'active defence' strategy, which essentially means that China would always remain strategically defensive, but not necessarily at the tactical level. It enumerated the national security situation and reiterated that the global trends of multipolarity and economic globalisation are intensifying. While accepting that the possibilities of a major war have receded, it however emphasised that new threats are arising from hegemonism, power-politics and the new interventionism. Further, it characterised the US-rebalancing strategy and Japan's overhaul of its defence and security policies as inimical to regional peace. The white paper also highlighted the South China Seas issue and how China's maritime security is under threat. It also underscored the threats emanating from the Korean Peninsula. It also said that the Taiwan factor and the challenges emanating from the 'East Turkistan independence' and 'Tibetan independence' pose grave threats to the integrity of Chinese nation.

In view of these challenges, the white paper then goes on to delineate the strategic tasks of the Chinese armed forces. The most important of these are the tasks of safeguarding "China's security and interests in new domains" and "the security of China's overseas interests." In keeping with the overall foreign policy thrust of the Xi Jinping era, these two are arguably the new thrust areas in the white paper. Thus, it states, "(I)n line with the strategic requirement of offshore waters defence and open seas protection, the PLA Navy (PLAN) will gradually shift its focus from 'offshore waters defence' to the combination of 'offshore waters defence' with 'open seas protection'."

The white paper also underscores the "four critical security domains" where China would like to focus its force development. These are: cyber space; outer space; nuclear; and maritime. It is in the fourth domain that this white paper makes a significant departure from the past white papers. It states that: "(T)he traditional mentality that land outweighs sea must be abandoned, and great importance has to be attached to managing the seas and oceans and protecting maritime rights and interests." Thus, it is clear that maritime security has acquired a pre-eminent focus in Chinese military strategy and hence the prioritisation of its navy in its modernisation plans.

The White Paper on China's Policies on Asia-Pacific Security Cooperation

Issued on January 11, 2017 this white paper is the first one to deal in regional issues.[5] But the contents do not mark a radical break from the past. Rather, there is continuity in the treatment of international and regional developments. It begins with a conceptual exposition of the concept of security, underscoring the four dimensions of common, comprehensive, cooperative and sustainable security.

The second section suggests ways to improve the regional security framework. By doing so, it actually indicates China's intentions to shape the regional order on its own terms. The first method it suggests the creation of a multi-layered, comprehensive and diversified regional system. The rationale for such a system is explained by the diversity of political systems, historical tradition, and levels of development and security concerns. It however, mentions that China does not seek to create a new architecture, but rather to build on the existing ones. The second method it proposes is the creation of a common framework by all the countries in the region. But the next sentence contradicts the former position by stating that the major powers should jointly promote a regional security framework. It seems therefore, that the white paper makes a distinction between major and lesser powers. The third method it suggests involves the creation of a framework on the basis of consensus, which can be built by moving from the easier tasks to the more difficult ones. In other words, China still prefers to keep the contentious sovereignty issues on the backburner. Fourth, it talks about creating an economic regional framework that is separate from the security framework. This again implies an economic framework in which China could and would play a decisive role and the overlooking of security issues, where China has less room for manoeuvrability.

The third section is quite intriguing. It deals with China's relations with major powers. Apart from China, the US, Russia, India and Japan are dubbed as major powers. Also interesting is the order in which the relationships are discussed, with obviously the US in the lead, followed by Russia, India and Japan. This also indicates China's notion of multipolarity. In the 1990s, when multipolarity was gaining ascendance in Chinese foreign policy, it was the European Union that was seen as a pole, but not India. In the present era, India occupies third place, indicating the growing significance of India-China relations. And perhaps this is a first document of its kind in which India gets pronounced attention.

In this section, the white paper also discusses issues relating to hotspots. It appears that it has graded the issues in terms of their impact on China's security and in terms of their distance to China. Therefore, the North Korean nuclear issue is the most pressing for China and quite rightly so. It may be recalled that it was the Korean War in 1950-53 that brought the US back into the East Asian theatre, leading to a deepening of Cold War divisions.

From then on Korea has caused a high degree of concern. North Korea's adventure with nuclear weapons and ballistic missiles, has compounded the security threat, particularly because North Korea has a close ethnic and economic dependence on the PRC. The second hotspot issue relates to anti-ballistic missiles. The US decision last year to deploy THAAD (Terminal High Altitude Area Defence) in South Korea has raised Beijing's concerns. China holds that such a deployment will vitiate the regional security balance. It may be noted that following the deployment of the US missile shield on March 7, 2017, China reacted sharply by forcing the South Korean retail giant Lotte to shut down dozens of stores in China. The Afghanistan issue occupies third place with China calling for an "inclusive reconciliation process that is 'Afghan-led and Afghan-owned'." Afghanistan is located near China's vulnerable Xinjiang Uighur Autonomous Region (XUAR) where ethnic unrest has been fermenting since the 1990s. It is little wonder, therefore, that China, without making a distinction between good Taliban and bad Taliban, hosted the Afghan Taliban delegation on March 7, 2017 with the aim of including the militant group in the peace process of war-torn Afghanistan. The fourth is the counter-terrorism issue. Apparently, China has borrowed from India the idea of opposing the 'double-standard' in fighting terrorism, even as ironically, its record in the Masood Azhar case, has become a major irritant in its relations with India. The fifth in the list of hotspot issues is maritime cooperation. Quite predictably, China claims indisputable sovereignty over the Nansha Islands and its adjacent waters and warns against any internationalisation of the issue. It has also issued a warning that "China is forced to make necessary responses to the provocative actions which infringe on China's territorial sovereignty and maritime rights and interests, and undermine peace and stability in the South China Sea."

There is a major focus on multi-lateralism in the fifth section of the white paper where China-ASEAN is given a priori attention followed by the ASEAN plus Three mechanism, China-Japan-ROK Cooperation, East Asia Summit (EAS), ASEAN Regional Forum (ARF), ASEAN Defence Ministers' Meeting Plus, the Lancang-Mekong Cooperation, the Shanghai Cooperation Organisation (SCO) and CICA. Quite notably, in all these multilateral initiatives China prevails over others through its bilateral mode of interaction on contentious territorial issues. Significantly, the US is not a part of any of these forums.

The last section deals with China's role in non-traditional security cooperation wherein China is following a multilateral path and assuming a leadership role, as for instance, in the Paris Agreement on climate change.

The white paper concludes by highlighting China's primary goal of realising the 'China Dream'. It claims that the 'China Dream' will provide "greater opportunities" and "benefits for development and cooperation" in the Asia-Pacific region. The concluding line is quite telling. It talks about building a new model of international relations, although this refrain is not a novel one. It can be traced to Deng Xiaoping's idea of a New International Political and Economic Order. But what is novel in this is, China's fast rising confidence in emerging as a new alternative to the US. And the white paper is basically gearing up China to attain this goal.

Xi Jinping's Davos Speech January 2017

In his speech at the World Economic Forum at Davos on January 17, 2017, Xi Jinping came across as the avowed champion of globalisation and a staunch advocate of free trade principles.[6] Indeed, the speech reflected China's desperation to uphold globalisation and prevent protectionism. At the outset, therefore, he made the case that the ills plaguing the world today, such as the refugee waves from the Middle East and North Africa or the global financial downturn are not the consequences of economic globalisation, but are the consequences of the lack of reform and development, inadequate global economic governance, and unequal global development. In other words, he defended and advocated, economic globalisation. He put forward four solutions for the ills: an innovation-driven growth model; open and win-win cooperation; fair and equitable governance; and balanced, equitable and inclusive development. It appears that at this juncture when the US has turned its back on globalisation, China has come to fill the void. His speech not only sought to reassure the world about China's adherence to globalisation path but also seemed to suggest a better model for the world to adopt. His speech ended by offering a promising picture of China's continuing economic growth and assuring the world of its role in enhancing and consolidating the fruits of globalisation. He particularly assured the world community that China would not devalue its currency and more importantly, he hailed the BRI launched in 2013, as the lynchpin of China's model of globalisation. He announced that in May 2017 that China would be hosting the Belt and Road Forum for International Cooperation in Beijing.

However, the speech did not lay out any substantial steps for promoting globalisation. It was also silent on the deregulation of the Chinese market. In fact, the speech was dotted with concerns. According to Xi, the rising US protectionism and the 'America First' policy is going to not only hurt Chinese growth, but also end the free ride that China has been enjoying since the 1972 China-US rapprochement.

China Government Work Report of March 2017

Chinese Premier Li Keqiang presented the Government Work Report at the opening session of the National People's Congress on March 5, 2017.[7] The report included major announcements related to domestic economy, environment, housing, defence and foreign policy issues.

On the foreign policy issue, Li Keqiang said, "As a major country, China has made outstanding achievements in its diplomacy with distinctive features over the past year." The achievements included: the visits made by President Xi Jinping and other Chinese leaders, to foreign countries; participation in 24th APEC Economic Leaders Meeting; the Shanghai Cooperation Organisation Summit; the BRICS Leaders Meeting; the Nuclear Security Summit; high-level meetings during the 71st session of the UN General Assembly; the Asia-Europe Meeting; and the East Asian Leaders meeting on cooperation. His speech also highlighted China's first ever Lancang–Mekong Cooperation Leaders Meeting. Apart from these, he spoke about China's active role in reforming and improving the global governance system, particularly China's success in putting into force the Paris Agreement.

After outlining the achievements, his speech moved on to listing the tasks that needed to be fulfilled, in view of the 19th Party Congress in October. On economic issues his forecast was rather grim, as according to him the, "world economic growth remains sluggish, and both the deglobalisation trend and protectionism are growing. There are many uncertainties about the direction of the major economies' policies and their spill-over effects." He goes on to say that "China is at a crucial and challenging stage in its own development endeavours."

On foreign policy, the Work Report mentions the "actively expanding China's opening up to the world." This is telling, given the wider trend of 'deglobalisation' in the West. It enumerates four- steps to achieve this target. First, making "solid efforts to pursue the Belt and Road Initiative". In this respect, it categorically states that China would accelerate the building of overland economic corridors and maritime cooperation hubs and would promote the export of Chinese equipment, technologies, standards, and services. Second, China would ensure that "foreign trade continues to pick up and register steady growth." Third, China would make "big moves to improve the environment for foreign investors," and fourth, that China would "promote the liberalisation and facilitation of international trade and investment." Here, the report again highlights the importance of economic globalisation and China's adherence to the multilateral trading regime as the main channel of international trade. It is noteworthy that the report seeks to amend the Framework on Comprehensive Economic Cooperation between China and ASEAN and to advance the development of the Free Trade Area of the Asia-Pacific.

Additionally, on defence issues, China pledged to strengthen maritime and air defence systems, as well as border controls, to safeguard the stability and security of the country. The report is also significant in terms of highlighting the Hong Kong and Taiwan issues. It pledged to uphold the Basic Law of the Hong Kong Administrative region and the One-China principle and the 1992 Consensus related to the Taiwan issue. More importantly, the Work Report also laid stress on improving mechanisms and capacity "for protecting China's rights and interests overseas."

Above all, in the concluding paragraphs, in consonance with the white paper, the report reiterates China's goal of building "a new type of international relations based on cooperation and mutual benefit and make new contribution to building a community of shared future for all humankind." The report concludes by reiterating the goal of realising the "Chinese dream of national rejuvenation."

Xi Jinping's Speech at the BRI Forum, May 2017

In his keynote speech at the Belt and Road Forum on May 14, 2017, Xi Jinping hailed the ancient Silk Route as an embodiment of the spirit of peace and cooperation, openness, inclusiveness, mutual learning and mutual benefit. He said that the same features inform the BRI under his leadership. Speaking about the present global situation that is marked by multipolarity, economic globalisation, digitisation, and cultural diversification, he reiterated that global interdependence and aspirations for peace and development are growing world-wide. Alluding to the ancient Chinese saying, "Peaches and plums do not speak, but they are so attractive that a path is formed below the trees," he claimed more than a hundred countries and international organisations were participating in the BRI.

His speech then, defined the BRI as essentially a multi-dimensional "policy connectivity" project in four respects: infrastructure, trade, finance and people-to-people contact. He then delineated the five guiding principles of the BRI. It was: a road for peace; a road of prosperity; a road for opening-up; a road for innovation; and a road connecting different civilisations. Underpinning these principles was China's need for an open and free trade environment that supports its "new normal" of economic development as, "China has reached a new starting point in its development endeavours. Guided by the vision of innovative, coordinated, green, open and inclusive development, we will adapt to and steer the new normal of economic development and seize opportunities it presents."

He enumerated the steps China would take for the successful implementation of the BRI namely: enhance friendly cooperation with countries participating in the BRI on the basis of the five-principles of peaceful co-existence; enter into practical cooperation agreements with the countries concerned; scale up financial support by contributing an additional RMB 100 billion to the Silk Road Fund; build win-win business partnerships; enhance cooperation on innovation with countries joining the BRI, by providing assistance worth RMB 60 billion to the developing countries and international organisations participating in the BRI; and put in place institutional mechanisms to boost belt and road cooperation. He concluded his speech by reiterating that the BRI was rooted in the ancient Silk Road and as such, it was a win-win for all the participating countries.

Continuity and Changes in Chinese Foreign Policy

From the above speeches and documents, one can identify the continuities and changes in China's foreign policy in the present era. First, the preeminent feature that under girds almost all the policy documents and White Papers is the continuing emphasis on multipolarity and globalisation. However, there is an interesting caveat here. While in the 18th Party Congress Report, globalisation is seen to be a growing trend, the Defence White Paper of 2015 prefixes economics with globalisation. Thereafter globalisation is mentioned in all the speeches and documents, thus marking a difference in China from the general notion of globalisation commonly held world-wide. The second major continuity is China's repeated stance of opposing force and hegemonism in global politics. This is indicative of China's intention to project itself as a different kind of power, or rather, a better alternative to the US. Third, continuity is observed on the issue of development, which has been a running theme in Chinese foreign policy since the 1978 reform and opening up. But significantly, development is being increasingly clubbed with the notion of security. This is evident from Xi Jinping's CICA speech where he said that "development is the fundamental of security and security is the precondition for development." Further, security has acquired a more comprehensive meaning under Xi Jinping, as seen in his four-pronged notion of security, i.e. common, comprehensive, cooperative and sustainable security. A fifth continuity can be witnessed in China's objective of creating an alternative security architecture, the germ of which was already present in Jiang Zemin's New Security Concept. But under Xi Jinping, this goal has found decisive and concrete expression in the CICA forum, when he identified the BRI as the principal vehicle for steering the creation of a cooperative security architecture in Asia. Finally, the Five Principles of Peaceful Co-existence that were the hallmarks of Mao Zedong's foreign policy in the 1950s, have invariably undergirded all the Chinese foreign policy speeches and documents, along with the running theme of safeguarding China's sovereignty and territorial integrity.

However, there have also been quite a few significant departures and changes in Chinese foreign policy, under Xi Jinping. For instance, the term 'new interventionism' finds mention for the first time in the 18th Party Congress Report along with multipolarity and globalisation being seen as rising global trends. The second most prominent departure is the emphasis on maritime security. Thus, phrases like protecting China's legitimate rights and interests overseas finds increasing mention in the 18th Party Congress Report and thereafter in the White Papers on Defence and Asia Pacific Cooperation. The third and most significant departure associated with Xi Jinping's leadership is the slogan 'China Dream'. Though in terms of meaning and significance, it signifies nationalism that has been the running theme of Chinese foreign policy, since the 1990s, yet in terms of intent and purpose, as encapsulated in the idea of rejuvenation, the China Dream has acquired a central place in China's foreign policy under Xi Jinping. It marks a decisive turning point in the history of China's economic growth story, as well as national rejuvenation.

Chinese Foreign Policy Options

A closer analysis of the abovementioned documents, reveals the foreign policy options that China has increasingly adopted in view of the challenges that confront it in the current era. The challenges are shrinking globalisation and rising protectionism. Arguably, China's rise could not have been possible without the liberal capitalist order created by the US in the post-War era. At present, when China is grappling with economic rebalancing at home and pursuing its BRI abroad, it more than ever, requires an open economic world order that is free from protectionism. The second challenge for China is the securing of its overseas interests including the security of its maritime claims in the South China Sea region. As China's influence and interests expand beyond its shores, the need for securing these resources and assets is becoming necessary. The third challenge emanates from power-politics, hegemonism and neo-interventionism, all of which are attributed to the US. The US remains a principal challenge for China, and Trump's policy uncertainty has deepened the mistrust in US-China relations. Also, notably, most Chinese academics and policy think-tanks identify the US 'rebalancing to Asia,' as the major rationale for Xi Jinping's BRI. The fourth challenge is associated with China's internal cohesion and social stability, in view of the ongoing problems of separatism and ethnic conflict. In fact, the Chinese leadership believes that external challenges tend to heighten China's internal security concerns. This is delineated in the 2015 Defence White Paper[8] that states:

> ...(W)ith the growth of China's national interests, its national security is more vulnerable to international and regional turmoil, terrorism, piracy, serious natural disasters and epidemics, and the security of overseas interests concerning energy and resources, strategic sea lines of communication (SLOCs), as well as institutions, personnel and assets abroad, has become an imminent issue.

Given the present nature of challenges, the Chinese leadership has opted for four foreign policy tools: selective multilateralism; peripheral diplomacy; military diplomacy; and nationalism.

Selective Multilateralism not Multipolarism

Multilateralism appears to be a more effective tool than multipolarism in China's foreign policy. Multipolarism is related to power politics and zero-sum competition that are not conducive to win-win cooperative security objectives. Therefore, China places a premium on multilateralism as a principal foreign policy tool.[9] Thus, China advocates the notion of economic globalisation, whereby China can opt for a multilateral trading regime as the main channel of international trade.

An article in the *Journal of Chinese Political Science* has identified four distinct strategies in Chinese multilateral diplomacy: watching; engaging; circumventing; and shaping.[10] Drawing from the article, it could be argued that China has moved well beyond simply watching and has chosen to engage, circumvent and shape multilateral institutions. However, while engaging still remains the overall norm as exemplified by China's role in the UNSC or the UNHRC, circumventing and shaping are also fast gaining currency. China's role in the SCO is a clear example of circumventing the Western led multilateral organisations. The SCO has, however, not emerged as an alternative structure to undermine the existing collective security organisations such as the NATO, but mainly seeks to work around them. But the formation of BRICS (Brazil, Russia, India, China), the founding of the AIIB (Asian Infrastructure Investment Bank) are clear instances of China's initiatives in shaping new multilateral institutions. Though the White Paper on Asia-Pacific Cooperation insists that China will not create new regional frameworks but rather work within the existing ones, the AIIB is certainly an economic structure alternative to the International Monetary Fund and the World Bank, but unlike them, it does not make lending conditional to political considerations. Also, the vote share of China, about 26 per cent compared to India's 7.5 per cent, is indicative of Beijing's dominance in the multilateral body. Furthermore, the Chinese leadership has recently proposed expanding the 57-country AIIB to include 25 new member countries, which again signals China's over all influence in deciding the composition of the body.

While multilateralism remains the norm, China prefers to operate on a bilateral basis. The 2017 Work Report mentions China's preference for making a distinction between economic and security multilateral bodies. In security-oriented multilateral structures, like the SCO or the ARF, China works on a bilateral basis for resolving contentious issues of territory and sovereignty. The basic rationale for China is to retain its claim of sovereignty over the disputed territories and yet call upon the other claimants to jointly work together on lesser conflicting non-territorial issues. Thus, this is China's strategy to wait for the opportune moment to settle the issue on its terms. The Chinese sovereignty claims on the Nansha islands, as highlighted in the White Paper on Asia-Pacific Cooperation, is a case in point. Clearly, this explains China's selective multilateral approach. Yuan Jindong of the US based, Monterey Institute of International Studies, has aptly described China's multilateralism as "thinking unilaterally, pursuing issues bilaterally and posturing multilaterally."[11]

Peripheral Diplomacy

Under Xi Jinping, periphery diplomacy has emerged as the number one foreign policy strategy of China.[12] In 2013, right after the announcement of the BRI, a conference on Diplomatic Work toward Neighbouring Countries was held in Beijing on October 24 and 25. Highlighting the importance of the conference, Xi Jinping stated that "doing well in the diplomatic work with neighbouring countries is out of the need to realise the two 'centenary goals' and achieve the great rejuvenation of the Chinese nation." He further averred that, "China needs to work with its neighbours to hasten interconnectivity and establish a Silk Road economic belt and a maritime silk road for the 21st century" and thereby "create a new pattern of regional economic integration". This conference categorically spelt out the significance of the periphery in Xi Jinping's foreign policy formulation. More importantly, his speech indicated how the periphery is deeply linked with the rejuvenation of the Chinese nation.

It may be noted that periphery diplomacy has been a running theme in Chinese foreign policy. The 'Lean to One Side' under Mao Zedong; 'Good Neighbourly Policy' (mulin zhengce) under Deng Xiaoping; the 'Western Development Strategy and Multilateralism' under Jiang Zemin; the Peaceful Rise and Harmonious Development policy under Hu Jintao; and currently the BRI under Xi Jinping, all speak of periphery as a predominant factor in the shaping of China's foreign and domestic policies. What makes periphery diplomacy critical for China at this juncture is the need for peaceful and prosperous neighbourhood to support and absorb the fallout from economic rebalancing strategy under Xi Jinping.

The Action Plan of March 2015, in fact, indicated the importance of the periphery for China's economic and foreign policy goals. It categorises the peripheral and underdeveloped regions of China as—northeastern, northwestern, southwestern, and inland—and enumerates their comparative advantages in order to systematically integrate them with the economies of the surrounding countries. Thus, Xinjiang would serve as a window for the westward opening up with Central, South, and West Asia; Inner Mongolia would establish links with Russia and Mongolia; Heilongjiang, Jilin, and Liaoning would connect with Russia's Far East; and the Guangxi Zhuang Autonomous Region would link up with the ASEAN countries. By linking the periphery with the economies of contiguous countries, China seeks, not only to develop and integrate the periphery regions, but essentially strives to expand its geopolitical role. In 2012, a noted Chinese scholar, Wang Jisi had talked about the need for a 'March West' policy in order to counter the US threat. China thus responded by devising the BRI, which is essentially meant to fulfil its two broad national goals: (1) to usher in economic prosperity and combat security threats in its backward and vulnerable peripheral regions and thereby meet the demands of the slowing economy; and (2) to spread its geopolitical influence in Eurasia and de-centre the US from Asia and thereby fulfil the China Dream. Consequently, the BRI is meant to keep the US out.

Military Diplomacy

Military diplomacy forms an essential part of Xi Jinping's China Dream that includes "making China world's dominant power" and "a stronger nation with a strong military."[13] China routinely conducts joint military exercises, participates in multilateral military diplomacy like the UN Military Staff Committee and peacekeeping operations, and also participates in International Arms Control and Disarmament activities.[14] It also imports arms and technology along with exporting arms, technology and providing military assistance to other countries. Besides, the PLA has greatly expanded its role in humanitarian assistance and disaster relief operations. One of the most significant PLAN (People's Liberation Army Navy) events was the visit of PLAN to Sri Lanka in 2014, which was the first port of call abroad by a Chinese submarine. Further, in November 2014, China Military Sciences Society (CMSS) held the fifth round of Xiangshan Forum. In this round, it elevated the meet from Track 2.0 to Track 1.5 level by inviting the defence chiefs of South Korea, North Korea and Japan and by including representatives from 57 countries. This upgrade is seen as a Chinese attempt to compete with the Shangri-La Dialogue that is held annually in Singapore. Clearly, this is an indication of China, not only displaying its military power, but attempting to emerge as a military leader. The objectives of military diplomacy are three: maintaining a favourable security environment; achieving modernisation of armed forces; and establishing influence in other countries.[15]

In the current era, maritime security has emerged as a principal element of its military diplomacy. To this end, in 2016, China acquired its first overseas military base at Djibouti. The deal ensures China's military presence in the country up to 2026, with a contingent up to 10,000 soldiers.[16] Undoubtedly, Djibouti serves as a strategic cog in the Maritime Silk Route (MSR) project as well. Further, China's growing naval capability would not only help in protecting its interests overseas but also assist in resolving the South China Seas dispute in its favour. Consequently, the Yulin Naval Base on Hainan Island is "fast emerging as the most strategically important military base in the South China Sea."[17] This is closer to the Indian Ocean Region (IOR), and therefore, it also signals a greater Chinese foray into the Indian Ocean.

Nationalism

Xi Jinping's speech at the National Museum's 'Road to Revival' exhibition laid out the significance of nationalism to China. It was from this platform that for the first time he gave the slogan of 'China Dream'. The exhibition essentially projected the Chinese suffering and humiliation at the hands of the colonial powers. His speech underlined the fact that "to realise the great renewal of the Chinese nation is the greatest dream for the Chinese nation in modern history."[18] From a foreign policy perspective, Xi's China Dream essentially underscored the twin aspects of China's loss in history: the loss of territory and the loss of leadership role in East Asia. Therefore, the China Dream evoked the unrelenting quest for retrieving lost lands and greatness, and thereby, fulfilling the goal of Chinese nationalism.

Under Xi Jinping, it appears that nationalism has acquired a new momentum, and this has been variously explained. Gideon Rachman holds that the "dislocating effects of global capitalism including mass migration and the 2008 financial crisis" have all increased the "nostalgic appeal of a more-stable, homogeneous and nation-centred past."[19] According to another authoritative study by Filippo Fasulo, the China Dream is the result of a need for a new narrative. He argues that "China is in transition and its leader needs a narrative to make his political agenda a success." Quite inevitably, there is an intensification of party control over history and ideology. In 2016 November, Xi Jinping used the 80th anniversary of the Long March to rally the people and Chinese youth to create a 'New Long March' and build a prosperous and a more powerful China.

It may be noted that China uses nationalism as a foreign policy tool to further its national interests. More particularly, it appropriates nationalism for claiming sovereignty rights over disputed territories. It has therefore selectively used history to make territorial claims and posit China's sovereignty as a core interest. In other words, when nationalism is enmeshed with strategic interest, the combination is lethal and possibilities for resolution of territorial disputes become remote.

Inferences

A few inferences can be drawn with regard to emerging Chinese foreign policy trends by sieving through these policies and documents. First, it is apparent that for China, globalisation is a prerequisite for its growth and prosperity. However, the retreat of globalisation in the West, has the Chinese leadership worried. It fears that liberal internationalism that has so long aided China's rise, is shrinking. This spells doom for its BRI that has been envisaged to not only meet the demands of a slowing economy, but to expand its global footprint and thereby, fulfil the China Dream. Arguably in China, nationalism is critical for enhancing party legitimacy which in turn is contingent on economic development; and economic development, in turn, is dependent on globalisation and the liberal international order. In other words, the paradox of China's growth story is, that globalisation supports nationalism. Therefore, externally China has intensified its call for economic globalisation at almost all the international fora, and internally, it has intensified the China Dream rhetoric to mobilise the people behind the party. However, as a consequence, the paradoxical pulls of globalisation and nationalism have given a belligerent turn to its foreign policy. Notably, the China Dream slogan rests upon the nationalistic calls for regaining China's lost territories and past greatness. Therefore, on issues relating to territorial disputes, Beijing leaves no room for negotiation. Inevitably thus, under Xi Jinping bellicosity and territorial conflicts have increasingly acquired a sharper focus.

The second inference that can be drawn from these speeches and documents is, that China is progressively trying to reshape the international environment to conform to its national interest. In this context, it is seeking to reform the global governance system and calling for greater participation of the global south in international affairs. However, as noted in the documents and speeches, China is not seeking to change the existing international order but reform it. This is evident, for instance, in China's role in the ratification of the Paris Agreement on climate change. Likewise, China took on a leadership role at the 2016 APEC Economic Leaders' Meeting by suggesting the establishment of a Free Trade Area in the Asia-Pacific. In the BRICS, it has called for an expansion of membership. With regard to China-Africa Cooperation, the Chinese government has taken the lead in implementing the major cooperation deals signed in 2015. It has also taken a leading role in the functioning of the AIIB. Moreover, now that the US has scrapped the Trans-Pacific Partnership Agreement, China is likely to emerge as the new champion of free trade and to this end, the Regional Comprehensive Economic Partnership (RCEP) is likely to gain pre-eminence. What is evident is that China is likely to take on "more responsibilities in global governance".[20] But it also alerts the world that it would not "fill the void left by the West, as it is still a developing country."[21] Therefore, China supports economic globalisation and is promoting the BRI to achieve this objective. Xi in his BRI forum speech said, it "is not meant to reinvent the wheel" but "to complement the development strategies of countries involved by leveraging their comparative strengths." Hence, the Eurasian Economic Union of Russia, the Master Plan on ASEAN Connectivity, the Bright Road initiative of Kazakhstan, the Middle Corridor initiative of Turkey, the Development Road initiative of Mongolia, the Two Corridors, One Economic Circle initiative of Vietnam, the Northern Powerhouse initiative of the UK and the Amber Road initiative of Poland are all about building on the existing structures and not about creating new ones.

The above point leads us to the third inference that while China claims not to reinvent the wheel, it however, puts forward a new model of international relations as evidenced in the Xi Jinping's CICA and Davos speeches and the White Paper on Asia-Pacific Cooperation. China, thus, proposes an alternative model, shorn of power politics, hegemonism and the zero-sum game that had characterised the US liberal hegemonic order. It may be argued that this alternative model has long been in the making. It evidently began under Jiang Zemin with the formulation of the New Security Concept (NSC). The NSC was a blueprint for a counter-hegemonic response to contain the US unilateralism and hegemonism in the 1990s.

Apparently, Xi Jinping reiterated the NSC's principles—mutual trust, mutual benefit, equality, and coordination—when he called for an Asian security architecture in his CICA speech. This theme also underscored the concept of harmonious world under Hu Jintao's leadership that essentially sought to engender a Chinese idea of global governance by its emphasis on the democratisation of international relations, the principles of justice and common prosperity, of diversity and tolerance, and the peaceful resolution of international conflicts. Also, during Hu's leadership, the debates on *Tianxia* had informed the Chinese discourse. The *Tianxia* debate sought to echo China's tributary system and claimed to offer an alternative international model based on a win-win cooperative strategy. Xi Jinping's China Dream reflects the same conceptual continuity and offers a normative economic and political model based on mutual security and common development. This can be gleaned from Xi Jinping's speech at the BRI Forum. He said, "China has reached a new starting point in its development endeavours. Guided by the vision of innovative, coordinated, green, open and inclusive development, we will adapt to and steer the new normal of economic development and seize opportunities it presents." The BRI, thus, essentially epitomises China's recipe for an alternative model of global governance.

NOTES

1. Filippo Fasulo, 'Waking from the China Dream,' in Alessia Amighini (ed.), ISPI Report, *China Dream: Still Coming True*, July 2016.
2. Full Text of Hu Jintao's report at 18th Party Congress, *Xinhua.net*, November 11, 2012, http:// news.xinhuanet.com/English/special/18cpcnc/2012-11/17/c_131981259.htm
3. Dennis J. Blasko, 'The 2015 Chinese Defence White Paper on Strategy in Perspective,' The Jamestown Foundation, *China Brief*, Vol 15, Issue 12, June 19, 2015, https://jamestown.org/program/the-2015-chinese-defense-white-paper-on-strategy-in-perspective-maritime-missions-require-a-change-in-the-pla-mindset/
4. Felix K. Chang, 'Strategic Intentions: China's military strategy white paper,' *FPRI*, May 27, 2015, https://www.fpri.org/2015/05/strategic-intentions-chinas-military-strategy-white-paper/
5. Full Text: China's Policies on Asia-Pacific Security Cooperation, *Xinhua.net*, January 11, 2017, http://news.xinhuanet.com/english/china/2017-01/11/c_135973695.htm
6. President Xi's speech to Davos in full, *World Economic Forum*, January 17, 2017, http://www.google.co.in/amp/
7. Full Text: *Report on the Work of the Government*, Delivered at the Fifth Session of the 12th National People's Congress of the People's Republic of China, March 5, 2017, *Xinhua*, http://googleweblight.com/

8. China's Military Strategy, *The State Council Information Office of the People's Republic of China*, May 2015, Ministry of National Defence, The People's Republic of China, http://eng.mod.gov.cn/Database/WhitePapers/index.htm
9. Leif-Eric Easley, 'Multilateralism, not multipolarity should be goal,' *The China Post*, March 29, 2008, http://m.chinapost.com.tw
10. Joel Wuthnow, Xin Li and Lingling Qi, 'Diverse Multilateralism: Four Strategies in China's Multilateral Diplomacy,' *Journal of Chinese Political Science*, Vol. 17, No. 3 (September 2012), DOI: 10.1007/s11366-012-9202-6
11. Keith R. Krause, *Culture and Security*, London: Frank Cass Publishers, 1999, p. 97.
12. This section is drawn from my study on "Conceptualizing the Silk Road Initiative in China's Periphery Policy," *East Asia: An International Quarterly*, Vol. 33, No. 4, December 2016: 309-328.
13. Kenneth Allen, 'The Top Trends in China's Military Diplomacy,' *China Brief*, Vol. 15, Issue 9, The Jamestown Foundation, May 1, 2015, https://jamestown.org/program/the-top-trends-in-chinas-military-diplomacy/
14. Matsuda Yasuhiro, 'An Essay on China's Military Diplomacy: Examination of Intention in Foreign Strategy,' *NIDS Security Reports*, No. 7, December 2006, pp. 1-40. http://www.nids.mod.go.jp/english/publication/kiyo/pdf/bulletin_e2006_ 2_Matsuda.pdf
15. Shannon Teizzi, '3 Goals of China's Military Diplomacy,' *The Diplomat*, January 30, 2015, http://thediplomat.com/2015/01/3-goals-of-chinas-military-diplomacy/
16. Francois Dube, 'China's Experiment in Djibouti,' *The Diplomat*, October 05, 2016, http://thediplomat.com/2016/10/chinas-experiment-in-djibouti/
17. Damen Cook, 'China's most important South China Sea military base,' *The Diplomat*, March 09, 2017, http://thediplomat.com/2017/03/chinas-most-important-south-china-sea-military-base/
18. *Xinhua*, Xi pledges great renewal of Chinese nation, *Xinhuanet.com*, November 29, 2012. http://news.xinhuanet.com/english/china/2012-11/29/c_132008231.htm
19. Gideon Rachman, 'Trump, Putin, Xi and the rise of nostalgic nationalism,' *Financial Times*, January 2, 2017, https://www.ft.com/content/198efe76-ce8b-11e6-b8ce-b9c03770f8b1
20. Pang Zhongying, 'What is China's role in global governance?' *China Daily*, December 21, 2016,
21. Ibid.

2

China's Japan Challenge: Regional Ambitions and Geopolitics of East Asia

Amrita Jash

ABSTRACT

Since the dawn of the 21st Century, there has been a shift in the strategic architecture of the Asian balance of power, wherein the dominant 'counterbalancing' intra-regional behaviour is causing instability. The re-emergence of Asia in the global political scenario, mainly driven by the rise of China, has redefined the power dynamic in the Asian theatre. The United States (US) is gradually losing its grip on Asia, but more importantly, the regional flux is orchestrated by China and Japan, the two key and strong players in the region. The ambition and quest for regional leadership by China and Japan, has turned the Asian region into a volatile theatre of power politics. This paper explores China's growing ambitions in Asia. It will also examine as to how Beijing's ambitions encounter the Japan challenge. Furthermore, the chapter examines the power dynamics between Beijing and Tokyo, in view of their strong aspirations for regional leadership in Asia.

Key words: *China, Japan, East Asia, Regionalism*

Introduction

On January 1, 2017, China's Ministry of Foreign Affairs published its first ever White Paper on *China's Policies on Asia-Pacific Security Cooperation*—clearly hinting at its intentions of playing a dominant role in the Asian theatre. Unlike the previous White Papers that mainly stated China's military and national defence policies, this specific document focused on China's role in ensuring security in the Asia-Pacific region that included North East and South East Asia as well as the United States and India. The

White Paper stated: "China is fully aware that its peaceful development is closely linked with the future of the region. China has all along taken the advancement of regional prosperity and stability as its own responsibility".[1] China's motive is to dislodge US influence in Asia and in addition, project itself as the defender of the post -war regional order. The White Paper clearly mentioned that, "Old security concepts based on the Cold War mentality, zero-sum game, and stress on force are out-dated given the dynamic development of regional integration".[2] Furthermore, China's ambitions of expanded regional leadership are exemplified by the recommendations in the White Paper. In Beijing's perspective, as the White Paper notes, peace and stability in the Asia-Pacific region can be attained by: promoting regional development and laying a solid economic foundation; building partnerships and strengthening the political foundation; improving the existing regional multilateral mechanisms and strengthening the framework for regional peace and stability; promoting rule-setting and improving institutional safeguards; intensifying military exchanges and cooperation and; resolving differences and disputes, and maintaining a sound environment.[3] These suggestions are indicative of China's objective of altering the longstanding US-dominated security architecture.

In view of this, China's concept of a new Asian regionalism that excludes the US, could be traced back to President Xi Jinping's speech at the Conference on Interaction and Confidence-Building Measures in Asia (CICA) on May 21, 2014. In this speech Xi put forward proposals for, "the people of Asia to run the affairs of Asia, solve the problems of Asia and uphold the security of Asia. The people of Asia have the capability and wisdom to achieve peace and stability in the region through enhanced cooperation".[4] It can, therefore be argued that unlike the US, China's ambition is to attain regional rather than global supremacy, by outpacing the US and its alliance partnerships. Given China's surging regional ambitions, it becomes imperative to understand as to how Beijing 'perceives' its dominance in Asia. The key assumption here is that China's leaders aim, not only to expand their capabilities and influence, but to "establish their country as East Asia's preponderant power".[5] China believes that its 'preponderance' or dominance would not: require the elimination or complete subjugation of other East Asian powers; second, China's pre-eminence would manifest itself primarily in political terms; third, it would require a substantial diminution, if not the outright elimination, of America's regional presence.[6]

This suggests that China is reshaping the Asian strategic space and thus, compelling other actors in the region to re-calibrate their ties with

China as well. It is well known that the US remains the key challenger to China's great power ambitions; however, what cannot be dismissed is Japan's challenge to China's aspirations of taking the lead in Asia. For China, Japan acts as the significant 'other' in counter-balancing China's economic, diplomatic and military might in the region. In addition, China's concerns regarding a resurgent Japan is drawn heavily from its historical consciousness. This is validated by Beijing's unwillingness to accept the looming transformation of Japan into a so-called 'normal country'. Besides, Japan's counter balancing of China's regional aspirations is manifested in East China Sea, South China Sea and Belt and Road Initiative (BRI). The China-Japan contest in the Asian region can be defined in the context of the old Chinese proverb that states: "One mountain cannot contain two tigers" (*Yīshānbùrónggèrhǔ*). However, due to the complex dynamics involving, Beijing and Tokyo in the Asian region, Michael Yahuda suggests that "China and Japan are two tigers of Northeast Asia, [who] will have to learn how to share the same mountain".[7] In this context, the paper explores China's growing ambitions in Asia. More specifically, it examines the challenge posed by Japan to Beijing's regional aspirations.

China and Japan: Two Tigers on the Same Mountain in Asia

China's Dream (*Zhongguo Meng*) (中国梦), of the "rejuvenation of great Chinese nation" manifests in its thinking of itself as a great rising nation, and being proactive and confident in the exercise of its great power capabilities. Moreover, China's self-perception in the changing international order, has been influenced by two forces: the old identity formed between 1949 and 1979, and the new identity it has acquired since the 1980s have shaped and formed China's current international identity.[8] As a result, China predominantly views itself as a 'developing country' and feels obligated to promote the interests of the developing world; at the same time, China aspires to be a major regional and even global power and hence, works closely with developed countries. That is to suggest, China's role in Asian regionalism has been transformed.

In view of this, the central issue is: 'Can China really attain to regional dominance in Asia?' What makes this a tough calculation is that China's ambitions are facing a Japanese challenge, since both are competing to acquire regional dominance. The most striking features of post-Cold War East Asia are: China and Japan are both becoming strong and affluent at the same time, along with the growing rivalry between the two.[9] In this regard, what makes a 'stagnating Japan' a strong countervailing force to a 'rising China' can be explained in the following ways:[10]

First, following three decades of rapid economic growth, China, in 2010, replaced Japan as the second largest economy in the world after the US—elevating itself from Communist isolationism to the status of a global power. But, China's growing economic clout has failed to overshadow Japan's long held economic prowess. Japan's temporary fiscal weakness, as compared to China's robust economic growth, does not guarantee its demise as a strong economic player. Rather Japan's, comparative advantage lies in its highly developed economy based on advanced technology and a strong capacity for scientific and technological innovation- which makes it a more robust manufacturing economy than China.

Secondly, with regard to the security aspect, both China and Japan possess significant military capabilities, that make each a strong player in the East China Sea dispute. While Japan maintains administrative control over the contested islands, China asserts its strategic supremacy by heightened maritime patrolling. The most significant counter to Japan's terra nullius policy and later nationalisation of the islands followed by China's unilateral establishment of the East China Sea Air Defence Identification Zone (ADIZ)—illustrates the existing parity between the two countervailing forces in the region. Most significantly, Japan is trying to become a 'normal' power as it recently passed new security laws-abandoning its 70 year old policy of pacifism and legalising its exercise of the right to collective self-defence. Thus, Japan's unfolding military posture raises concerns relating to the re-militarisation of Japan's foreign policy-thereby, acting as a strong deterrent to China's aggressive military power.

Thirdly, China and Japan's aspirations are also reflected in ideational terms, wherein, the 'self' versus the 'other' provides a competitive impetus. For China, the core threat is from a resurgent Japan and this draws heavily on a historical consciousness; while for Japan it is the burden of acting as a responsible power unlike its erstwhile imperial image. For instance, take the issue of Yasukuni Shrine. On the one hand, China harbours old resentments against the enshrined Class-A war criminals, while on the other hand, the Japan leadership defies this Chinese sensitivity by making high profile visits to the Shrine. For example, Japanese prime ministers from Junichiro Koizumi to Shinzo Abe have constantly tested China's patience by visiting the controversial Shrine. Besides, Japan has also repeatedly challenged China's condemnation by revising history text books, and disputing the comfort women issue. This attitude on both sides is further testimony that neither wants to submit to the other in the power hierarchy.

These factors manifest the competition between China and Japan for regional influence in Asia, and also exemplify China's transformation from being a dormant power to an active stakeholder in the region. This reason for this 'action-reaction dynamic' between China and Japan for regional influence in Asia, according to John J. Mearsheimer, is because "the mightiest states attempt to establish hegemony in their own region while making sure that no rival great power dominates another region. [As] the ultimate goal of every great power is to maximise its share of world power and eventually dominate the system".[11] In view of this, and given the shifting balance of power in Asia, it is widely argued that the rise of China and the stagnation of Japan will put the two countries on a collision course that will also drag the US into its orbit.

For China, Japan is the 'Significant Other'

Another aspect that shapes the China-Japan regional equation is the ideational factor. Allen Whiting suggested that: "Provocative events in Japan associated with the war, trigger an automatic response in China that combines anger over the past with apprehension about the future".[12] To suggest, that rising nationalism, disputed histories and conflictual identities are the main causal factors, further complicates the competition between China and Japan. According to Qin Yaqing, the role of identity as an essential factor of China's regional aspirations can be explained, as follows:" A state's attitudes towards international society and its international behaviour are rooted in its identity. States with different identities have different world-views, which, in turn, make different impacts upon its foreign policies and strategies".[13]

The core of China's 'Self' is directly related to China's encounters with the Western and later the Japanese 'Others'. That is, for China, the historical memory as a 'victim' who has constructed the identity of a 'victimised state', which plays a crucial role in determining Chinese psyche in international politics. In addition it is argued that Japan's emergence as an 'Other' in China's identity is a by-product of China's attempts to assert its 'victimhood' and regain its social and moral legitimacy within international society.[14]

Moreover, Japan is a more 'significant other' than other foreign invaders as China did not adjust its image of Japan by "recategorising it as a *waiguoren* (foreign) state, rather it perceived itself as an "un-Japanese" state".[15] Thus China's historical consciousness of Japan's aggression during 1931-1945, serves as a common link in the collective post war identity of the Chinese that distinguishes them from the Japanese 'Other'. The 'othering' of Japan plays a strong role as it gives a positive thrust to China's identity in relation to Japan. Because of this identity clash, the notion of the "potential resurgence of Japanese militarism dominates Chinese perception"[16]—as witnessed in case of Diaoyu/Senkaku islands dispute, Taiwan and others—which shows that wartime history has become a leading factor in determining China's attitude towards Japan. The image of Japan as a "modern, friendly neighbour" that was formed in the 1980s quickly gave way to one of a remorseless, vexatious, and stubborn "small man" that is still defined in the early 21st century, in terms of its wartime history of aggression against China.[17]

The distrustful image of Japan translates into a 'constructed fear' that an unrepentant Japan is bound to repeat its past aggression, echoing the widespread historical deterministic idea of many Chinese, that a country which does not acknowledge its past misdeeds "correctly" is bound to repeat them.[18] This makes the beliefs about the shared past a reason for viewing it as a threat in the present and future foreign policy preferences, since empirical findings suggest that "security and insecurity in Northeast Asia are not just a question of the balance of economic and military power in the region, but also hinge on the impact that beliefs about the shared past have on the perception of threat".[19] In this regard, Chinese perceptions and beliefs about the Japanese threat, based on the events of history, impact China's present assessment of Japan.

Given the identity rationale, China's aspirations of playing a dominant role in Asia projects the sense of becoming "a responsible big country".[20] To achieve this goal, it becomes imperative for China to ensure long-term moral superiority over Japan. However, China's notion of "a responsible big country" vis-à-vis Japan has a dual meaning:[21] First, it shows that China, based on its own sense of being a big country, will live up to its commitment to act magnanimously, by overlooking relatively trivial issues (or considered to be trivial, such as history textbook distortion, the Yasukuni Shrine tribute, etc.). And secondly, at the same time, it will make up excuses for its possible strong reaction in future contingencies. However, it is important to note that in the process of acting responsible, China's regional behaviour has become increasingly assertive.

China and Japan's Entangled Aspirations for Asian Regionalism

It remains undisputed that China's quest is to gain regional supremacy as Asia's leader. However, this ambition is heavily weighed down by Japan, as a strong countervailing force. This has manifested into a regional rivalry between Beijing and Tokyo.

(I) Competition in the East China Sea

The fierce China and Japan regional rivalry is witnessed in their territorial contest over the Diaoyu/Senkaku islands, and maritime rights in the East China Sea. On the sovereignty issue, Japan claims the islands under terra nullius, while China makes its claims on the basis of historical records. Beijing argues that the islands have always been Chinese territory as they were "first discovered, named and used by the Chinese as early as the 14th century".[22] China negates Japan's claims in the basis of the principle of "discovery occupation" as the islands were not terra nullius. China's 2012 White Paper on "Diaoyu Dao" strongly claims that "Diaoyu Dao and its affiliated islands are an inseparable part of the Chinese territory. Diaoyu Dao is China's inherent territory in all historical, geographical and legal terms, and China enjoys indisputable sovereignty over Diaoyu Dao."[23] Unlike Japan, Beijing acknowledges the sovereignty dispute over the islands and thus, wants to establish its own jurisdiction in the East China Sea by challenging Japan's administrative control over the islands and the surrounding waters.[24]

Secondly, on the issue of maritime rights, the dispute revolves around the demarcation of the sea boundary and the different interpretations of the UNCLOS in the East China Sea, thus, causing them to clash over the overlapping Exclusive Economic Zones (EEZs) between China and Japan. China argues that its zone extends to the edge of the continental shelf, while Japan says that it should stop at the midpoint between the two nations—thus, resulting in overlapping claims over nearly 81,000 square miles.[25] In addition, the East China Sea dispute is also driven by calculated material interests of both sides because of the presence of rich hydrocarbon reserves. This has further exacerbated their assertive behaviour and hard-line positions.

Given these conflicting interests, Japan nationalised the islands in 2012, which triggered China's hard-line response in the form of patrols along the islets and a unilateral declaration of the ADIZ in 2013. Since then the tensions over territoriality and maritime rights have significantly heightened as seen in the rising military shadowboxing between China and Japan in the East China Sea. China is rapidly militarising by deploying Chinese coast guard vessels and armed navy frigates into the contiguous zone of the disputed Diaoyu/Senkaku islands as well as making fighter jet incursions into the Japanese airspace. Japan responds by counter militarisation through an increased fleet presence and heightened intelligence gathering and reconnaissance by means of its radar installations etc.[26] Such military muscle flexing by Beijing and Tokyo has contributed to regional instability.

China and Japan have thus pushed the regional security index to dangerous levels. This has raised significant concerns regarding the risks involved. The risks are mainly three-fold.[27] first, the risk of an accidental and unintended military confrontation between China and Japan given the heightened emotions and their operational activities at close proximity. Secondly, there is the risk of a political miscalculation in their efforts to demonstrate sovereign control which can lead to an armed conflict. This can be caused by a misunderstanding of the other's motives and actions. And third, the risk involves deliberate action to forcibly establish control over the islands, which largely remains unlikely, but the possibilities cannot be ruled out. Hence, these risks have increased the volatility in the East China Sea, thus, affecting the Asian regional stability.

(II) Competition over Asian Infrastructure

Apart from their conflict over sovereignty and maritime rights, China and Japan's quest for regional competition is also witnessed in Asia's infrastructure build-up. Asia's growing infrastructure investment gap has become an important regional concern. According to the Asian Development Bank (ADB) 2017 report titled "Meeting Asia's Infrastructure Need",[28] infrastructure development in the Asia-Pacific region will require in excess of $22.6 trillion through 2030, or $1.5 trillion per year. Given its surging needs, the Asian region currently invests about $881 billion per annum in infrastructure (for 25 economies with adequate data, comprising 96 percent of the region's population).[29] The reason for this regional concern is the infrastructure investment gap, as the difference between investment needs and current investment levels- stands at 2.4 percent of the projected GDP for the 5-year period from 2016-2020, based on climate-related adjustments.[30] This 'investment gap' has prompted China and Japan to strengthen their regional leadership by undertaking proactive measures to meet the investment needs. That is, both Beijing and Tokyo are competing with each other for providing public goods and services in Asia. The competition can be seen between China's 'Belt and Road Initiative' which runs parallel to Japan's 'Quality Infrastructure Investment'.

The competition is also apparent in the way that China and Japan are taking initiatives to expand their regional space through infrastructure build up. It was with this objective, that China under the leadership of President Xi Jinping, launched the grand initiative of "One Belt, One Road" (OBOR). The plan is to build the 'Silk Road Economic Belt' and the '21st Century Maritime Silk Road'—thereafter, officially translated as "Belt and Road Initiative". As the 2015 "Vision" document notes: The "need [is] to improve the region's infrastructure, and put in place a secure and efficient network of land, sea and air passages, lifting their connectivity to a higher level".[31] It goes on to say that: Facilities connectivity is a priority are for implementing the Initiative. [...] [wherein] countries along the Belt and Road should improve the connectivity of their infrastructure construction plans and technical standard systems, jointly push forward the construction of international trunk passageways, and form an infrastructure network connecting all sub-regions in Asia, and between Asia, Europe and Africa, step-by-step.[32]

In addition, China has followed up on its quest for regional leadership by setting up the Asian Infrastructure Investment Bank (AIIB) in 2015, which aims to fund infrastructure projects in the Asian region. The AIIB began operations in 2016, with a $100 billion capital and disbursed $1.7 billion in loans in the very first year of its operations. China's BRI got further traction with 21 Asian countries signing the "Memorandum of Understanding on Establishing Asian Infrastructure Investment Bank"[33] as founding members on October 24, 2014 in Beijing,[34] which extended to 57 Prospective Founding Members (PFMs) in 2016. AIIB's strategic priorities are three-fold.[35] (i) Sustainable infrastructure—to promote green infrastructure and support countries to meet their environmental and development goals; (ii) Cross-country connectivity- to build cross-border infrastructure, ranging from roads and rail, to ports, energy pipelines and telecom infrastructure across Central Asia, and the maritime routes in South East and South Asia, and the Middle East, and beyond; (iii) Private capital mobilisation—to devise innovative solutions that catalyse private capital, in partnership with other MDBs, governments, private financiers and other partners. With the objective of infrastructure investment, China-led AIIB has approved loans of $1.73 billion to support nine infrastructure projects in seven countries.[36] In addition, China also established a $40 billion Silk Road Fund in December 2014, to "promote common development and prosperity of China and other countries and regions involved in the Belt and Road Initiative", which was primarily dedicated to "supporting infrastructure, resources and energy development, industrial capacity cooperation and financial cooperation."[37]

In response to China's BRI, Japan too has ramped up its infrastructure activities in Asia. In 2015, Japanese Prime Minister Shinzo Abe launched the "Partnership for Quality Infrastructure" (PQI) initiative, with the aim of building "high-quality and innovative infrastructure throughout Asia, with a long-term view".[38] Abe proposed that "Japan will, in collaboration with the ADB [Asian Development Bank], provide Asia with innovative infrastructure financing at a scale of $110 billion dollars i.e. 13 trillion yen—

over five years".[39] This has been increased to $200 billion in 2016—higher than the founding capital of AIIB.

Japan's policy is seen as a counter to the China-led AIIB, and the amount of money proposed by Japan is slightly higher than the founding capital of that of AIIB.[40] On December 1, 2016, Japan's private companies announced another new vehicle, the "Japan Infrastructure Initiative",[41] which reveals Japan's plans to increase public-private partnership in project development by setting up a special fund for the purpose. Wherein, the joint venture aims to provide a total of around 100 billion yen ($878 million) in investment and loans to support private-sector infrastructure exports, for projects including power plants and railways in Asia, Europe and the United States.[42] Moreover Japan has also refrained from joining the AIIB—thus, raising the ante against China. This also exhibits Tokyo's departure from its past Official Development Assistance (ODA) policy, as it now seeks to add a strategic dimension to its overseas infrastructure development.

There are overlapping interests between China and Japan that inject a competitive edge into the relationship. The escalating competition between the two countries and their tit-for-tat strategies are impacting Asia's regional peace and stability. Both are involved in a win-lose competition as witnessed in their clashing over sovereignty claims and maritime rights in the East China Sea that impacts the security architecture as well as their growing interests and active participation in economic regionalism. As the stakes involved are high for both sides, the competition between the two countries is likely to intensify over time.

Conclusions

China and Japan are at loggerheads in their quest for regional leadership in Asia. China's great power ambitions are fuelled by the dreams of becoming the Asian leader by dislodging the US from Asia. Most importantly, China's stakes are at risks given Japan's regional counter-balance that significantly checks Beijing's growing ambitions. As witnessed in the East China Sea, Beijing and Tokyo are constantly testing each other's resolve. Both are vying for power through the BRI and PQI as orchestrated by AIIB and ADB. This has already vitiated the geopolitical and geo-economic architecture of Asia.

Given these opposing forces, the Asian regional dynamic is far from being stable. There is a heightened risk of the status-quo changing with China taking the lead. But the fact of Japan becoming 'normal' will further widen the gulf in Asia. This makes the Asian region the key theatre for 21st Century great power politics, as the two tigers are determined to sit on the same mountain. But how long will they be able to sit on the same mountain is difficult to predict.

NOTES

1. Ministry of Foreign Affairs of the People's Republic of China, "China's Policies on Asia-Pacific Security Cooperation", January 11, 2017, at http://www.fmprc.gov.cn/mfa_eng/zxxx_662805/t1429771.shtml (Accessed August 10, 2017).
2. Ibid.
3. Ibid.
4. Ministry of Foreign Affairs of the People's Republic of China, "New Asian Security Concept For New Progress in Security Cooperation", May 21, 2014, http://www.fmprc.gov.cn/mfa_eng/zxxx_662805/t1159951.shtml (Accessed August 10, 2017).
5. Aaron L. Friedberg, "China's Strategic Ambitions in Asia", April 2007, pp. 4, http://carnegieendowment.org/files/Friedberg_paper.pdf (Accessed August 5, 2017).
6. Ibid., pp. 4-5.
7. Michael Yahuda, *Sino-Japanese Relations after the Cold War: Two Tigers Sharing a Mountain*, Oxon, Routledge, 2014, pp. 1.
8. Da Wei, "A Partnership for Collective Emergence: BRICS in China's International Strategy," in Francis A. Kornegay Jr. and Narnia Bohler-Muller (eds.), *Laying the BRICS of a New Global Order: From Yekaterinburg 2009 to eThekwini 2013*, Pretoria, Africa Institute of South Africa, 2013, pp. 38.
9. Bhubhindar Singh et. al, "Rising Sino-Japanese competition: perspectives from South-East Asian elites," *Australian Journal of International Affairs*, 71(1), 2017, pp. 105-120.
10. Amrita Jash, "China and Japan: Two Tigers on the same Mountain", *IndraStra Global*, October 22, 2015, http://www.indrastra.com/2015/10/FEATURED-China-and-Japan-Two-Tigers-on-Same-Mountain-by-Amrita-Jash-0335.html (Accessed August 5, 2017).
11. John J. Mearsheimer, "Better to be Godzilla than Bambi", *Foreign Policy*, 146, January/February 2005, p. 47.
12. Allen Whiting, *China Eyes Japan*, Berkeley, University of California Press, 1989, pp. 41.
13. Qin Yaqing, "Struggle for Identity: A Political Psychology of China's Rise," in Brantly Womack (ed.), *China's Rise in Historical Perspective*, New York, Rowman & Littlefield, 2010, p. 265.
14. Suzuki Shogu, "The importance of 'Othering' in China's national identity: Sino-Japanese relations as a stage of identity conflicts," *The Pacific Review*, 20(1), 2007, pp. 24.
15. Shih Chih-Yu, "Defining Japan: The Nationalist Assumption in China's Foreign Policy," *International Journal*, 50(1), 1995, pp. 544.
16. Zhao Quansheng, "Sino-Japanese relations in the context of the Beijing-Tokyo-Washington strategic triangle," in Marie Soderberg (ed.), *Chinese-Japanese Relations in the Twenty-first Century: Complementarity and Conflict*, London, Routledge, pp. 41-44.

17. Caroline Rose, *Sino-Japanese Relations: Facing the past, looking to the future?*, New York, Routledge, 2005, pp. 15.
18. Reinhard Drifte, *Japan's Security Relations with China since 1989: From Balancing to Bandwagoning*, London, Routledge Curzon, 2003, pp. 15.
19. Peter H. Gries et. al, "Historical beliefs and the perception of threat in Northeast Asia: colonialism, the tributary system, and China-Japan-Korea relations in the twenty-first century," *International Relations of the Asia-Pacific*, 9(2), 2009, pp. 263.
20. Choi Jiyoung, "Chinese nationalism in Sino-Japanese Relations," in Guy Faure (ed.), *New Dynamics between China and Japan in Asia: How to Build the Future from the Past?*, Singapore, World Scientific, 2010, pp. 44.
21. Ibid.
22. Ibid., p. 38.
23. "Diaoyu Dao, an Inherent Territory of China", White Paper, State Council Information Office of the People's Republic of China, 25 September 2012, http://english.gov.cn/archive/white_paper/2014/08/23/content_281474983043212.htm
24. "Competition and Confrontation in the East China Sea and the Implications for U.S. Policy", A Roundtable Report by Laura Schwartz, *The National Bureau of Asian Research*, February 2014, p. 3.
25. Teshu Singh, "China & Japan: Tensions in the East China Sea," *IPCS Issue Brief*, No. 129, http://www.ipcs.org/issue-brief/east-asia/china-japan-tensions-in-east-china-sea-198.html (Accessed August 11, 2017).
26. Amrita Jash, "China, Japan and the East China Sea Conundrum", *IndraStra Global*, August 19, 2016, http://www.indrastra.com/2016/08/FEATURED-China-Japan-and-East-China-Sea-Conundrum-002-08-2016-0031.html (Accessed August 15, 2017).
27. Sheila A. Smith, "A Sino-Japanese Clash in the East China Sea," *Contingency Planning Memorandum* No. 18, April 2013, http://www.cfr.org/japan/sino-japanese-clash-east-china-sea/p30504 (Accessed August 15, 2017).
28. "Meeting Asia's Infrastructure Needs", Asian Development Bank, 2017, https://www.adb.org/sites/default/files/publication/227496/special-report-infrastructure.pdf (Accessed August 15, 2017).
29. Ibid.
30. Ibid., pp. xi.
31. National Development and Reform Commission, Ministry of Foreign Affairs, and Ministry of Commerce of the People's Republic of China, "Vision and Actions on Jointly Building Silk Road Economic Belt and 21st-Century maritime Silk Road," March 28, 2015, http://en.ndrc.gov.cn/newsrelease/201503/t20150330_669367.html (Accessed August 12, 2017).
32. The State Council of the People's Republic of China, "Action plan on the belt and Road Initiative", March 30, 2015, http://english.gov.cn/archive/publications/2015/03/30/content_281475080249035.htm (Accessed August 12, 2017).
33. *Xinhuanet*, "21 Asian countries sign MOU on establishing Asian Infrastructure Investment Bank," October 24, 2014, http://news.xinhuanet.com/english/business/2014-10/24/c_133740149.htm (Assessed August 12, 2017).
34. The 21 countries are Bangladesh, Brunei, Cambodia, China, India, Kazakhstan,

Kuwait, Laos, Malaysia, Mongolia, Myanmar, Nepal, Oman, Pakistan, the Philippines, Qatar, Singapore, Sri Lanka, Thailand, Uzbekistan and Vietnam.

35. Asia Infrastructure Investment Bank, *Strategies,* https://www.aiib.org/en/policies-strategies/strategies/index.html#goals (Accessed August 10, 2017).
36. Ibid.
37. Silk Road Fund, URL: http://www.silkroadfund.com.cn/enweb/23775/23767/index.html#homezd (Accessed Online 8 March 2017).
38. Speeches and Statements by the Prime Minister", Prime Minister of Japan and His Cabinet, May 21, 2015, http://japan.kantei.go.jp/97_abe/statement/201505/0521foaspeech.html (Accessed August 14, 2017).
39. Ibid.
40. Justyna Szczudlik, "Many Belts and Many Roads: The Proliferation of Infrastructure Initiatives in Asia", *PISM Policy Paper* No. 7 (148), February 2016, pp. 4.
41. This Joint Infrastructure Initiative is made up of Mitsubishi UFJ Lease & Finance and Hitachi Capital, each having a stake of 47.55 per cent and Bank of Tokyo-Mitsubishi UFJ having a stake of 4.9 per cent.
42. "Japanese companies team up to fund infrastructure exports," *Nikkei Asian Review,* December 1, 2016, http://asia.nikkei.com/Business/Companies/Japanese-companies-team-up-to-fund-infrastructure-exports (Accessed August 15, 2017).

3

Resurfacing of Divergence in India-China Relations

Prashant Kumar Singh

ABSTRACT

The resurfacing of strategic divergence in India-China relations after 2013 underscores the mistrust that pervades the relationship. This serves, yet again, as a reminder of the limitations of the modus vivendi of 'plucking the low hanging fruit first'. The strategic divergence that appears to have taken precedence over convergence in recent times, stems from their seemingly incompatible grand strategic schemes. It is also a consequence of the assertive nationalisms of both Narendra Modi and Xi Jinping that they are unable to negotiate on core issues. In a significant development, India has conveyed to China that it cannot let its (China's) growing economic and security convergence with Pakistan grow at the expense of India's security concerns. Finally, the recent Doklam military crisis between them (June-August 2017) has underlined the assumption, that aggression can be confined to diplomacy, and will not lead to a simultaneous armed conflict, may prove to be a misnomer for both countries. Therefore, the complexities of the current situation demand sincere efforts for a breakthrough to be achieved. This chapter discusses the antecedents of the divergence between the two countries by focusing on the personality of the leaders and the associated political and ideological contexts, and how these have contributed to redefine structural factors shaping the relations.

Key words: *India-China; Belt and Road Intiative; Strategic divergence; Xi Jinping; Narendra Modi*

Given their long history of strategic mistrust, India and China, since the normalisation of relations in 1988, have essentially focused on managing the relationship. They have "managed" it by ensuring that strategic mistrust and bilateral irritants do not impact normal bilateral trade, economic and cultural relations. Prime ministers Atal Bihari Vajpayee (1998-2004) and Dr. Manmohan Singh (2004-14), whose tenures coincided with that of Presidents Jiang Zemin (1993-2003) and Hu Jintao (2003-2013) in China, supported this understanding, and adopted it as a strategy. Between 2003 and 2014, the two sides established approximately three dozen dialogue mechanisms and signed several Memoranda of Understanding (MOUs). The strategic objective of this approach could be described as preferring 'stability' in the overall relations in general and 'tranquility' on the border in particular.[1]

The shared premise was that *cooperation can prevail over friction.* In particular, during Vajpayee's visit to China in 2003, it was "envisaged as a way to enhance India-China economic relations by emphasising complementarities rather than competitiveness between the two countries."[2] A similar spirit was evident before Vajpayee's visit when both countries signed the *Agreement on the Maintenance of Peace and Tranquility along the Line of Actual Control in the India-China Border Areas* (1993) and the *Agreement on Confidence Building Measures in the Military Field Along the Line of Actual Control in the India-China Border Areas* (1996). However, after 2000, amidst fast growing bilateral, economic and other interactions both countries have translated the spirit into an appropriate strategy. As a result, the dialogue mechanisms and CBMs between 2003 and 2014 stressed on creating interdependence between India and China for reducing mutual mistrust. The oft repeated dictum—*this world has enough space for both to grow together*, became the mantra of the Manmohan Singh-Hu Jintao era and was indicative of the pragmatism of both sides.[3] This was relatively successful in keeping mistrust and friction under check, for approximately a decade or so. In fact, after the India-China diplomatic spat in the wake of India's nuclear tests in 1998,[4] no significant destabilising row took place, until the stand-off between the Indian Army and the People's Liberation Army (PLA) in Depsang, Ladakh in April 2013.[5] From April 2013 onwards, however, the relationship began moving in an uncertain direction, bringing strategic divergence between the two to the fore.[6]

Highlighting the Change

The last five years have witnessed a worsening of bilateral relations. This short period has seen political-diplomatic stand-offs over: the Chinese technical hold on India's application in the UNSC 1267 Sanctions Committee relating to Pakistan-based terrorists; the China-Pakistan

Economic Corridor (CPEC) passing through Pakistan-Occupied Kashmir (POK); and China's opposition to India's entry into the Nuclear Suppliers Group (NSG). Besides, the same period has witnessed a series of unprecedented military stand-offs in Depsang, Ladakh in April 2013; Chumar, Ladakh in September 2014; and in the India-Bhutan-China border tri-junction region in June-September 2017.[7]

The Political-Diplomatic Stand-Offs

China's technical hold on India's listing application in the UN Sanctions Committee has left India wondering about China's motivations behind the action. India moved resolutions to sanction three individuals who are based in Pakistan: the Jaish-e-Mohammed chief Masood Azhar in March 2016; the Hizbul Mujahideen chief and the head of the United Jihad Council Syed Salahuddin in May 2015; and Zakiur Rehman Lakhvi, the mastermind of the 2008 Mumbai attacks, in June 2015. China, as a veto-wielding permanent member of the UNSC, has been putting technical holds on these resolutions; the last veto was used in February 2017 on the Masood Azhar issue. India has been holding discussions with higher-level officials in China to ameliorate the situation, including during Prime Minister Narendra Modi's personal interaction with President Xi Jinping at the Shanghai Cooperation Organisation (SCO) Summit in Ufa, in July 2015. Foreign Minister Sushma Swaraj also discussed it with her counterpart, Wang Yi, at the International Donors Conference in Kathmandu in June 2015. Moreover, in response to China's explanation that it placed the hold on India's resolution because of insufficient evidence, the then Foreign Secretary S. Jaishankar clarified India's stand on the issue, during his visit to China in February 2017. He said that Masood Azhar's "actions were 'well-documented'". He made it known to the Chinese audience that the case against Azhar, "was pursued by other countries too, not India alone..." He was referring to the US application against Azhar in the UNSC, which was supported by countries like France. However, the issue between the two countries remains unresolved.[8]

Further, to make matters worse, the CPEC Agreement, signed in April 2015, has emerged as a fresh bone of contention between India and China as the corridor passes through the POK. The territory is part of the larger Kashmir dispute between India and Pakistan. There have been continuous reports relating to China's civilian and military presence in the POK, predating the Modi-Xi years,[9] which the Indian establishment has taken note of, in its security calculations.[10] China has justified its presence as being only for humanitarian and commercial purposes. The CPEC has however changed the nature of this presence. For instance, previously China could justify its presence on the basis of random activities. But, in India's perception, the CPEC, as an international bilateral agreement formalises Chinese presence, which in turn renders China's professed neutrality on Kashmir irrelevant. It calls into question the 1963 Boundary Agreement between China and Pakistan, wherein China had formalised its neutrality.[11] Voicing these concerns, at the Raisina Dialogue, in New Delhi, Modi said that, "regional connectivity corridors should not 'override or undermine the sovereignty' of nations."[12] Giving a detailed explanation of India's opposition to the CPEC because of the violation of its sovereignty, S. Jaishankar said:

> "There has been overall broadening of ties with China, especially in areas of business and people-to-people contact, but they have been overshadowed by differences on certain political issues..." "...both countries should show sensitivity to each other's sovereignty...China is a country, which is very sensitive on matters concerning its sovereignty. So we would expect that they would have some understanding of other people's sensitivity on their sovereignty... The CPEC passes through a "piece of land that we call Pakistan-occupied Kashmir which is territory [belonging] to India and which is illegally occupied by Pakistan"... "the project has been undertaken without consultation with India and its sensitivity and concerns towards it are natural."[13]

On this basis, India declined the Chinese invitation to participate in its Belt-and-Road Initiative (BRI) international conference in May 2017. India's absence could be termed as a boycott of the conference. Moreover, India released an official statement citing its grievance over the CPEC and in addition, its reservations against the economic and environmental implications of BRI projects.[14]

Apart from the issue of terrorism, India and China locked horns in 2016, over China's open opposition to India's application for NSG membership. This convinced many, perhaps, of China's discomfort in sharing a leadership position with India in international bodies that are of strategic significance.[15] In response, India has openly acknowledged China as the major hurdle. For instance, Sushma Swaraj informed the Lok Sabha (Lower House of the Indian Parliament): "I am saying it today on the floor of the House that China introduced procedural hurdles, the main being on whether a non-NPT state can have NSG status... It is true that this was the reason for the non-decision on India's application."[16]

These ongoing and recurring diplomatic face-offs created acrimony between the two governments and mark the first serious downturn in India-

China relations since the diplomatic spat after India's 1998 nuclear tests. These issues are grave to the extent that top Indian leaders and officials namely Modi, Sushma Swaraj, S. Jaishankar—have all spoken vociferously on these and made them part of the talks held with their Chinese counterparts.

The Military Stand-offs

The April 2013 stand-off, on the eve of Premier Li Keqiang's India visit broke the pattern of peace and tranquility on the border. From the 1962 war until April 2013, the border had seen only two major military incidents—a short, geographically limited, isolated, but an intense armed clash at Nathu la pass in Sikkim, which took place only a few years after the 1962 war, in 1967,[17] and a military standoff in 1987 in the Sumdorong Chu valley in the Arunachal Pradesh border region.[18] The 1987 standoff, in a way, was the backdrop for the full normalisation of relations and was followed by Prime Minister Rajiv Gandhi's visit to China. However, the April 2013 military standoff was different; it was the beginning of a phase which was to be marked by divergence, mistrust and hostility in the relationship. The Border Defence Cooperation Agreement (BDCA) signed in October 2013, following the April 2013 military standoff, could not prevent the repeat of another equally significant stand-off in September 2014, right in the midst of President Xi Jinping's India visit.[19] The two incidents in quick succession came as a reminder that the existing CBMs were insufficient for reducing border tensions. These two standoffs indicated how competitive infrastructure-building and capability augmentation by the two countries that have brought their troops in close proximity with each other have given rise to these renewed border tensions. More importantly, although the exact causes of the incident remain in the realm of speculation, the September 2014 stand-off intensified the security dilemma in India vis-à-vis China, raising suspicions about the sincerity of the Chinese intentions, as the PLA intruded into Indian territory during Xi's visit to India.[20]

Bilateral relations further worsened as the two countries witnessed heightened military tensions from June-August 2017, in Doklam at the India-Bhutan-China tri-junction, adjacent to the Sikkim sector of India's border with China. At this time, troops from both sides were eyeball-to-eyeball with each other. This stand-off will be remembered in history as a watershed event in bilateral relations. War seemed imminent, but eventually better sense prevailed. This period witnessed unprecedented sabre-rattling and heightened anti-India polemics in the Chinese media, which was reminiscent of the period leading up to the 1962 war. Tensions rose when the Indian troops came down from their posts on the ridge-line to stop the Chinese troops from extending an existing Chinese road, through a patch of land that was disputed between Bhutan and China ("a motorable road from Dokola in the Doklam area towards the Bhutan Army camp at Zompelri"[21]).[22]

The road, if completed, would have brought India's narrow Siliguri Corridor under Chinese surveillance. The corridor, also known as the Chicken's Neck, is located in Indian territory to the north of West Bengal, between Bangladesh and Nepal, and is the only land connection between India's Northeast and the rest of India.

The Chinese contention was that even though the road construction site was a disputed area, it was in its possession and its dispute was with Bhutan. It argued that the 1890 Convention between British India and Imperial China relating to Tibet and Sikkim (the Calcutta Convention) had settled the boundary between India and China in this area. Therefore, India had transgressed by crossing the international boundary to halt Chinese construction activity. The Indian point of view was that the Convention had settled the boundary in principle, but the demarcation on the map and alignment on the ground, in the tri-junction area is yet to be completed. Therefore, the Chinese actions if not checked, would change the status quo, complicating the demarcation and alignment process. The extension of the road by the Chinese would continue to be perceived as a threat to India's security till such time the demarcation and alignment is finalised. Moreover, India argued that it had an obligation to support Bhutan as it was committed to ensure Bhutan's security under various bilateral instruments. The stand-off was finally resolved after hectic diplomacy in the run up to the 9th BRICS Summit, held in China, in September 2017.

We can only speculate about the Chinese motives behind undertaking road construction. These range from China not anticipating India's reaction to its road construction, overcoming its (China's) perceived military operational disadvantage in the Chumbi Valley (Tibet), driving a wedge between India and Bhutan as part of its larger political strategy for the Himalayas, and teaching India a lesson before its (China's) advantage is eroded.[23] It was also argued that the Chinese motives were guided by the general situation of bilateral relations. There is speculation that the construction activity and the resultant crisis was nothing more than an ego issue for General Zhao Zongqi, commander of the Chinese Western Theatre Command.[24] However, what attracted international attention was India's pre-emptive approach and its demonstrable resolve to stand up to China, something which China had not been accustomed to in its neighbourhood in recent history.[25]

Even though the two sides formally disengaged and withdrew their troops from the site of the confrontation in end-August 2017, the situation, at the time of writing, is still ambiguous. The latest media reports and the official statements from the two sides give out conflicting accounts, indicating that the issue remains potentially destabilising.[26] The announcement of the disengagement in August 2017 was not followed by any formal agreement unlike the resolution of the 2013 and 2014 stand-offs, when agreements "explicitly stating that status quo ante as on a date preceding the crisis would be restored"[27] were signed. Signing a formal agreement to end the Doklam crisis and prevent any such incidents in the region in future, was difficult, because the existing bilateral mechanisms could not have been applied to the disputed territory in question since the dispute primarily involved Bhutan and China.[28]

The Heart of the Matter: The All-Weather Friendship Crosses India's 'Redline'

Presently, the three main contentious issues in India-China relations—the Chinese response to Indian resolutions against terrorists in the UNSC 1267 sanctions committee; the China-Pakistan Economic Corridor (CPEC); and its stand on India's NSG membership—have a clear Pakistan dimension. This requires a proper assessment of the role of the Pakistan factor in shaping India-China relations in recent times.

Highlighting the India reference in China-Pakistan relations does not take away from Pakistan's historical importance for China in terms of facilitating the Sino-US rapprochement and China's relations with West Asia. However, the following discussion highlights the fact that historically India has perhaps been the single most influential factor in China-Pakistan relations. The China-Pakistan *all-weather friendship*, in popular parlance, has all along been perceived as being guided by the balance of power approach towards India. The two signed the China-Pakistan Boundary Agreement in 1963 in the wake of heightened tensions between India and China in the late 1950s and early 1960s, which culminated in the 1962 war. Pakistan was China's only non-communist friend, that was not "publicly criticised during the Cultural Revolution."[29] China supported Pakistan during the Indo-Pak wars of 1965 and 1971, and on Kashmir. Chinese support for Pakistan's nuclear and missile and conventional military weapon programmes is well recorded. Incidentally, China, 1979 onwards, gradually adopted the stance of formal neutrality vis-à-vis the contentious issues between India and Pakistan—a hallmark of Deng Xiaoping's policy of moderation in the post-Mao era. This process started with the then

Foreign Minister Atal Bihari Vajpayee's visit to China in 1979, which was the first such political contact after the War. But, instructive in this regard is the fact that China continued to maintain the core military-security and strategic substance of the friendship.[30] It is important to note that the *all-weather friendship* had little economic substance for decades, except for China's arms exports to Pakistan, making it a unique political/strategic relationship, justifiably interpreted as China's balancing of India in South Asia.[31]

The Redefining Developments

In recent times, the relationship has acquired three new redefining features. First, Pakistan's strategic value for China has increased as global Islamist terrorism has further aggravated China's security concerns in the province of Xinjiang, which has been restive for decades.[32] Secondly, geographically, Pakistan is almost indispensable for China with its vision for overland connectivity with the energy sources in West Asia. This desired connectivity reduces the distance, which otherwise traverses South East Asian waters and the Indian Ocean, to reach the energy-rich region of West Asia. The connectivity through Pakistan also addresses China's Malacca dilemma, relating to the perceived vulnerability of its sea lanes that pass through the choke point of the Malacca Strait in South East Asia. China's investment in the Gwadar Port in Pakistan's Balochistan province, has been made precisely for this purpose. The port will act as a terminus for land transport, coming down from China from the Northern Himalayan direction, and maritime transport, towards West Asia.[33] Thirdly, the US$ 46 billion investment announced under the CPEC Agreement in 2015 made Pakistan formally a part of China's Belt-and-Road Initiative (BRI), injecting the long-missing financial muscle into the relationship. The investment was later hiked up to US$ 62 billion in early 2017.[34] At present, the CPEC-BRI appears to have subsumed the pre-existing Chinese connectivity and other infrastructure projects in Pakistan within its framework.

China Shields Pakistan in the UNSC: Perhaps, what perturbs India most is China's determination to support Pakistan in the UNSC in the face of India's determined efforts to ensure international action against the terrorists based in Pakistan. India, which faces grave threats to its national security from terrorism and the protracted insurgency in many regions, has serious disagreements with Pakistan because Pakistan-based agencies fuel the turmoil in Kashmir and they have had a hand in the terrorist violence in India. These concerns have been further aggravated by the rise of ISIS in West Asia, and the possible organisational or inspirational links between the Islamist terrorist groups active in India and other parts of South Asia are actively investigated.[35] Thus, anti-terror international cooperation has become an important pillar of India's anti-terror efforts in recent years. It has inked several agreements, MOUs and pledges with various countries, of which Bangladesh, the UAE, Israel, Russia, Saudi Arabia, Tajikistan and the US are some prominent examples. Anti-terror cooperation figures in all of India's major bilateral interactions. Hence, the Chinese stand on the Indian resolutions in the UNSC, in a way, undermines India's policy to link international counter-terrorism efforts to national security policy. In fact, many commentators have been blunt. They believe that China colludes with Pakistan to undermine India's national security and sovereignty, and consider the anti-terror cooperation such as the Hand-in-Hand counter terror exercises between the two countries as futile. No doubt, China has put its reputation at stake by supporting Pakistan on the issue. This stand is criticised by many, even within China.[36]

Geo-Economics Enhances Pakistan's Geopolitical Value for China: China's disregard for India's objections to the CPEC are seen in India as Chinese double standards on sovereignty-related issues and its insensitivity to India's sentiments. Even though the prospects of the success of the CPEC are debatable, it had initially kindled hopes that the China-Pakistan relationship was taking off independently of the India factor, and that this new-found development and prosperity orientation would eventually de-hyphenate India and Pakistan in the Chinese calculus. However, as the BRI is seen as having both geo-economic and geo-political designs, the same is true of the CPEC. China's technical hold on India's resolutions in the UNSC in fact, proves that Pakistan's new-found geo-economic importance, also buttresses its longstanding geo-strategic significance for China. It does not matter whether this aspect of the CPEC is intended or unintended, but clearly, there are implications and consequences for India.

The CPEC faces objections from India for three reasons. First, although India has not militarily pursued the retrieval of the POK since 1947-48 when Pakistan occupied this territory, India remains constitutionally committed to it. In February 1994, the Indian Parliament passed a resolution reiterating India's claim over the territory.[37] The word POK also evokes a strong nationalist reaction among certain sections in India. The frequency of statements by Indian leaders highlighting and drawing the international community's attention to India's claim over the POK has increased under the Modi government.[38] Therefore, even though India may appear to be grudgingly reconciled to the reality of it being a 'lost territory', the CPEC reveals a lack of sensitivity for India's concerns and sentiments, on the part of China, particularly when it is so demanding of respect for its sovereign claims on Tibet and Taiwan. Jaishankar's statement that, "we would expect that they would have some understanding of other people's sensitivity on their sovereignty" echoes this sentiment. The CPEC is yet another reminder for many Indians, who argue that India's goodwill towards China always goes unrequited.[39] Secondly, as argued above, India perceives that China's actions in relation to the CPEC will not only render China's formal neutral position irrelevant, they could also potentially make China a stakeholder in the disputed region. As China has been consolidating its western periphery towards Pakistan by infrastructure development, the CPEC would further increase its security focus in the region. Thirdly, the enhanced connectivity under CPEC, which will give China and Pakistan greater geographical contiguity in the Himalayas, becomes a serious concern for India, from the military point of view as well.[40]

In view of this, the argument that India is not justified in opposing the CPEC—which is a developmental programme for the welfare of the people living in the POK and other parts of Pakistan—would appear to many in India as lacking in credibility. The view that India should not oppose the CPEC just as China does not oppose India's economic and cultural relations with Taiwan[41] may not be a fitting analogy. The more appropriate example would be China's reaction if India were to undertake maritime explorations in the Diaoyu Tai/Senkaku Islands with Japan—a territory under Japanese possession, that is contested by China.

China Preserves the Balance of Power in South Asia: The primary function and objective of NSG membership for India is to gain parity with other legitimate nuclear powers. However, the Modi government's spirited pursuit of the membership has also underscored India's quest for a place in such elite clubs. This has underlined the aspirational aspect of Modi's foreign policy, which is at cross-purposes with the Chinese understanding of the issue. It was perceived that China's opposition to India's claim is being guided by its concerns for Pakistan, without denying its larger strategic motivations. China supports and demands a criteria-based approach with regard to membership for non-NPT members. However, it is not known whether China has actually offered any criteria for the purpose. Although the NSG proceedings are confidential, based on the views of the other NSG members that are in the public domain, it could be assumed that while some other member states may also want to offer the membership to India upon it meeting some conditions, it is unlikely that they are as rigid as China over the issue.[42] No country, including China, has come forward with any criteria, which would prevent India's entry into the NSG. China's willingness to take the blame for stalling India's entry into the NSG in 2016 by vetoing and openly airing its rigid opposition seemed to be guided by political and strategic considerations.[43] Strategically, China appeared to have opposed India's application because India's membership of the NSG would affect the balance of power in South Asia, since Pakistan is not a member. More importantly, it might also have conveyed a message to the US that if the US cannot accommodate China's rise because of its concerns about its allies such as Japan and the Philippines, China too has an ally in Pakistan, which it has to stand by.[44]

Sources of Intractability of the Situation

The unwelcome course of bilateral relations could be attributed to the following reasons: First, the political power of the two neighbouring giants has been rising almost simultaneously. China has grown and so has India, although at a slower pace. While their interests are seen to be converging on global developmental issues, the interests are diverging on core strategic issues. Thus, there needs to be careful mutual accommodation. The lack of accommodation is bound to produce aberrations such as the differences over the CPEC and the Chinese vetoes against the Indian resolutions in the UN Sanction Committee or India's application for the NSG membership. Secondly, the ideological predispositions and the personality factors in the leadership styles of the two countries appear to be playing a role in their aggressive diplomatic stances.

Xi and Modi: Not on the Same Page?

Xi and Modi have ushered in certain changes in their countries' domestic politics that could be attributed to their ideological predispositions and leadership styles, which are also reflected in their foreign policies. For example, they have conducted themselves as *strongmen* with a firm grip over power and decision-making; they seem to be utterly dissatisfied with the state of affairs they had inherited; they appear to believe in a fierce nationalism, and aggressively pursue what they consider to be their countries' best interests; they have taken a deep personal interest in foreign policy and believe in a strong link between domestic development and foreign and security policies. The following discussion on their ideological predispositions, politics and personality, captures how these factors seem to have led the interactions between their governments to heightened friction.

Xi's Chinese Dream and India: The 18th Party Congress of the Communist Party of China (CPC) in October 2012 saw the rise of Xi Jinping to the helm of the party and government affairs. Since then, China has witnessed ideological and political changes of far-reaching significance under his leadership. The sum of it is that China has seen the emergence of a politically strong leadership, without a parallel in the post-Mao period. Xi's leadership possesses a transformatory zeal. He has his own understanding of China's rightful place in the international community. Xi's quest for what he perceives to be China's rightful destiny is attributed to have led to its increased assertions in the neighbouring regions, particularly in the South China and the East China Seas. This has also had an impact on bilateral relations with India. China's India policy under Xi has been perceived as non-accommodative.

- *Tight Grip of the Strong Leader:* Xi Jinping, who became the General Secretary of the CPC in October 2012 and then President of the PRC in March 2013, ushered in a new phase of politics and foreign policy. His tenure can be considered as the antithesis of the Hu Jintao era (or Hu Jintao-Wen Jiabao [Hu-Wen] era), which was perceived as being relatively permissive with regard to freedom, civil and political rights and inner party democracy. It was also the era of consensual politics based on collective leadership. However, it saw the continuing presence in politics of the former President, Jiang Zemin. Jiang's influence was seen as the main reason for the intense factional politics of the era and for the rising corruption, inefficiency, and poor governance at the time. In contrast, Xi's anti-corruption drive has highlighted his will to govern. The fall from grace of giant political opponents such as the former Politburo Standing Committee (PSBC) member Zhou Youkang and President Hu's close confidante Li Jinhua as well as scores of other Communist Party leaders and civil and military officers in the anti-graft campaign, is evidence of his grip over power. The fact that President Hu Jintao's retirement from the presidency as well as the chairmanship of the Central Military Commission (CMC) was simultaneous, unlike Jiang Zemin's in 2002—who retained the CMC chairmanship till 2004—served as a powerful indicator of Xi's authority. At present, his authority within the Party is perceived to be unchallenged. Xi is reported to have restored, what many would argue, the Party's authority in the classic Leninist way of democratic centralisation with an emphasis on socialist values, the Party's authority and discipline and the rejection of the so-called Western values, such as the Western-style democracy or the rule of law.[45]

- *The BRI as the "New Organising Principle" of Politics and Foreign Policy:* Xi's Chinese Dream, a hold-all and catch-all formula aimed at appealing to the nationalist sentiments of the Chinese, seeks the *great rejuvenation of the Chinese nation*. His strategy for realising the dream or rejuvenating the nation seeks to redesign domestic politics in the above-mentioned manner, and economically transform China to make it 'a moderately prosperous society' by 2021 and a 'moderately developed country' by 2049.[46] In foreign policy, he envisages a New Type of Major Power Relations that involves a greater role for China in the world affairs.[47] The BRI is in keeping with this vision and ensures his political consolidation in the economic realm. It also promotes top-down planning, and is geared towards transforming China from a manufacturing and trade-led economy to a services and investment (overseas Chinese foreign direct investment [OFDI])-led economy, thus linking China's domestic development with the international community, particularly with the developed markets of Europe. The BRI corridors that will link China with Europe through a cross-continental transport and infrastructural connectivity network require huge amounts of money, thereby, projecting China as a stakeholder in global economic development. The BRI has, thus, emerged as the new organising principle of Chinese foreign policy. It provides a new framework for Chinese foreign policy to project China's image as a responsible power that is interested in peace and development and is willing to assume greater international responsibility towards this end, thus carrying forward Hu Jintao's theme of China's Peaceful Rise.[48] Therefore, India's "boycott" of the BRI will understandably disappoint China as it is keen for all the major powers and countries to be on board the BRI so that it can successfully sell this grand initiative to the international community. India's "boycott" might not have gone down well with China.

Parenthetically, the BRI is a means for the Chinese economy to overcome stagnation by economic reforms and restructuring. This is a political challenge for the Chinese leadership because of the vested interests of various bureaucratic and business lobbies who had been benefitting from the existing economic model. This challenge has led Xi Jinping to consolidate and accumulate the political power necessary to push reforms, as envisaged by him. In turn, this has pushed China under Xi Jinping to curb domestic dissent to ensure that the party's authority is unchallenged. Internationally, particularly in the neighbourhood, a general hardening of China's approach for safeguarding its interests has been observed. China's "unilateral" and "without any consultation with neighbours" declaration of the Air Defence Identification Zone (ADIZ) in the East China Sea (ECS) in November 2013; its outright rejection of the legitimacy of the Permanent Court of Arbitration at The Hague, and its ruling in 2016 that upheld the Philippines' contention against Chinese activities in the South China Sea (SCS); and its vigorous military-infrastructure building in the SCS, point to this change in attitude. In the disputed maritime regions, China, in fact, has appeared to be opposing the United Nations Convention on the Law of the Sea (UNCLOS), which it had signed and ratified.[49] Also, its forceful push of its contested historical claims appears to be at variance with modern international law. Thus, China's recent actions under Xi Jinping with regard to disputed maritime claims raise questions about Xi's lofty vision, such as his Three Communities—Shared Interests; Common Destiny; and Shared Responsibilities—along with the concept of common, comprehensive, cooperative and sustainable security in Asia.[50] On the one hand, this hardening appears to not only stem from Xi's own notions of China's historical place in the international community, but appears to be also useful to buttress his credentials as a strong nationalist leader in domestic politics, on the other. China's unrelenting approach towards India over the CPEC, terrorists and NSG issues, is, in a way, reflective of this general hardening of attitude on the issues of national interest under Xi Jinping.

- *The CPEC in the BRI and Pakistan's Primacy over India:* CPEC, the thorny issue between India and China, is one of the six main BRI corridors. In addition to this, the carrot and stick interpretation of Xi's neighbourhood diplomacy (also known as peripheral diplomacy) promotes a China-centric Asia and *Asianism*.[51] Pakistan, which is classified as sub-regional secondary great power (SSGP) in this interpretation, is pivotal for the BRI. On the other hand, cooperation with India, classified as a sub-regional great power (SGP), is important, but a favourable balance of power needs to be maintained because it is regarded as one of the major countries, which have an ambivalent attitude towards China's rise.[52] Thus, there have been suggestions that India has only an incidental place in China's grand strategy. This is confirmed by China not yielding to India's repeated remonstrations over the CPEC and the terrorists issue. Besides, there are doubts whether India has the same critical geographical significance as Pakistan, for the success of the BRI connectivity projects, even though the pre-existing Bangladesh, China, India and Myanmar Corridor (BCIM) is officially a part of the BRI.[53]

Modi's Ideological Predisposition and Leadership: China's attitude towards terrorism in India, in general, predates the phase under discussion.[54] So does its presence in the POK,[55] and its perceived discomfort with sharing leadership space with India in the international and regional order.[56] These had begun figuring in India-China relations even during the Manmohan Singh-Hu Jintao era and the repeated Chinese vetoes were unlikely to go unchallenged, whatever the leadership in India. Besides, it may also be legitimately queried whether India's present assertiveness vis-à-vis China could be attributed to other factors as well. For example, could it not be explained by the Realism of International Relations theory? Or, could India's longstanding Look and Act East Policy not explain its deepening strategic engagement, with a perceived hedging vis-à-vis China, in Asia-Pacific under Modi? (An issue to be discussed subsequently). There has been a structural continuity in India's growing assertiveness vis-à-vis China in order to safeguard its national interests. Weapons, physical military infrastructure and enhanced deployment in the border regions of Ladakh and Arunachal Pradesh to bolster India's assertive stand towards China, have been built over decades, by successive governments. Similarly, the hawkish sections within the Indian strategic community (academics, experts and public intellectuals in the security and defence fields) have also gained prominence, independent of their political ideologies along with the demands for squarely taking on China on issues related to India's strategic and security interests. However, maintaining the balance of power and alliance-building—key features of Realism—are inadequate for explaining certain changes, developments and events, in the Modi government's foreign policy. These include: Repeated reiterations of India's claim on the POK; the raising of the Balochistan issue by Modi in his Independence Day address in 2016; demanding that China reciprocate India's support for China's One-China policy by supporting the One-India idea; the perceived playing of Tibet-card; and the passionate quest for NSG membership and flagging China's role in vetoing India's application. These examples can be considered as diplomatic quid pro quo or commonsensical tit-for-tat tactics. However, Realism does not explain the motivation behind these changes. These changes are by and large attributable to the choices and preferences of the leadership of the day.[57] Thus, it is difficult to ignore Modi's style of engaging with the world in pushing India's national interests by standing up to China on the issues discussed in the previous sections. This approach stems from his persona and his government's political-ideological positioning.[58] The point here is that India under Modi has refused to take Xi's non-accommodation in its stride.

• *Modi's Ideological Location:* Modi and the ruling Bharatiya Janata Party (BJP), occupies the *Hindutva* space in Indian politics,[59] which is trenchantly opposed to the Nehruvian legacy of secularism and socialism in domestic politics and non-alignment in foreign policy. This political stream does not shun alliance-building unlike the non-aligned foreign policy espoused by Nehru. In fact, it opposed India's tilt towards erstwhile USSR and had questioned Nehru's and the successive Congress governments' non-aligned claims. The *Hindutva* political stream has criticised Nehruvian foreign policy as lacking in great-power ambition, and not being tough enough, particularly with reference to China and Pakistan. However, despite its criticisms of the established foreign policy culture, *Hindutva* politics is yet to provide a well-structured alternative foreign policy framework. It only demonstrates a different ideological orientation and foreign policy polemic. Even so, the new ideological orientation and foreign policy rhetoric informs Modi's foreign policy in general and his China policy in particular, and explains them to us.[60] The author's objective here is to highlight and capture the change, without subjectively endorsing any particular type of politics.

➤ *Modi's Attempts to Break Away from the Past:* Since Modi became prime minister in May 2014, his government has strived to convey the message that in foreign policy matters, it would like to tread a path that differs from conventional understanding, both in style as well as substance. It closed down the office of the United Nations Military Observer Group in India and Pakistan (UNMOGIP), a virtually defunct legacy of the Nehru government, which had sought UN mediation for the Kashmir dispute, in July 2014.[61] Modi's reluctance for a non-aligned foreign policy became clear when he did not attend the 17th Non-Aligned Movement (NAM) Summit in Venezuela in September 2016. This change does not necessarily imply that India has abandoned strategic autonomy, which was the core objective of NAM. However, it may be seen as a signal that the Modi government was not too concerned about being perceived as being partial to alliances in international politics.[62] The Modi government also initiated high-level political visits to Israel, moving away from India's longstanding consideration for West Asia's Islamic countries.[63] It has made it a point to convey that it will not shy away from resorting to tough, and even unconventional, measures to protect national interest. It called off the then Foreign Secretary Sujatha Singh's visit to Pakistan in August 2014 following the Pakistan High Commissioner in India Abdul Basit's meeting with the Hurriyat Conference leader Shabir Shah.[64] The well-publicised 'surgical strike', which though not first of its kind, across the Line of Control (LOC) in September 2016 was intended to convey a tough military posture towards Pakistan on the issue of terrorism. Earlier "surgical strikes" were closely guarded security affairs.[65] These examples, and the aforementioned examples of including the issue of POK in the discourse, India's questioning of the BRI and its proactive actions in Doklam, bear out the assertion that Modi's foreign policy style greatly differs from India's conventional foreign policy style, and to the extent possible, in substance as well.

• *China in "Modi's World":* The *Hindutva* disaffection with Nehru's China policy, started in the 1950s with an attack on Nehru's policy on Tibet and

Formosa and the subsequent border dispute. The Hindutva parties at that time, the Jan Sangh (BJP's predecessor) and the Hindu Mahasabha, along with the socialist parties, and the pro-free market Swatantra Party joined hands to protest against Nehru's foreign policy decisions. The Hindutva parties accused Nehru and the succeeding governments of the weak handling of China. They were critical of India's unreciprocated support for the PRC's One-China Policy, and wanted India to join the international anti-communist alliance to contain China. The present ruling BJP and Modi come with this ideological legacy. When BJP became a powerful opposition in the latter years, especially during the Congress-led United Progressive Alliance (UPA) government under Manmohan Singh (2004-14), they criticised the government for not taking suitable steps to counter the PLA's border incursions and described its China policy as weak.[66] In keeping with the ideological legacy, the Modi government has repeatedly conveyed direct or subtle messages that India expects reciprocity for its longstanding support for the PRC's One-China policy.

It should be noted that notwithstanding his ideological predisposition, Modi adopted a pragmatic attitude towards China when he took over as prime minister in May 2014.[67] In his developmental vision, he saw China as an important source of foreign direct investment for India. He had come to appreciate this during his tenure as chief minister of Gujarat (2002-14), when he made several visits to China scouting for investment for his state. During President Xi's visit to India in September 2014 and later his own visit to China in May 2015, the promotion of economic and people-to-people ties dominated the agenda. During his visit, Modi espoused the view that India and China could play a critical role in realising the Asian Century and that China could play a pivotal role in his plan for reviving and restoring cultural connectivity with East Asia by drawing on their common Buddhist heritage.[68] In fact, he was reported to be throwing his weight behind liberalising the visa regime for the Chinese in spite of the reservations of the security-intelligence agencies.[69] However, as Modi emerges as the spokesperson of India's aspirational and assertive foreign policy, India has come face to face with China's own scheme for expanding and safeguarding its national interests. Here, Modi's foreign policy intent is not to be perceived as willingness to compromise on India's strategic interests (CPEC, the terrorists, the NSG and the territorial issues) in return for cooperation.[70]

➢ *"One India" Speaks Up:* The new orientation was very clear in Sushma Swaraj's pointed question to the visiting Wang Yi in June 2014: If China wants India's support for its One-China policy, what about China's policy with regard to One India? At that time Swaraj's articulation appeared to be more emotional rather than well-defined. However, over the last four years or so, the idea has acquired some clarity, though it is far from becoming the general policy. Thus, anything that does not take into consideration India's sovereignty or nationalistic sentiments[71] amounts to opposing the idea of "One India". The support for India's fight against Pakistan-sponsored terrorism in India; respect for India's position on the POK; and recognising Arunachal Pradesh as Indian territory seem to have become the three main points of reference for "One India". As already mentioned, the idea will have to cover a lot of distance before it becomes an official and universal policy.[72] But the idea has, indeed, got a China-specific context in which India appears to be demanding reciprocity for its support for the One-China policy. China's support for Pakistan in the UNSC on the terrorists issue, and the CPEC are contrary to the Modi government's expectations of respect for its One-India idea.

➢ *"One India's" Leverages:* The Dalai Lama's well-publicised visit to Tawang in Arunachal Pradesh in April 2017[73] and the renaming/respelling of six places in Arunachal Pradesh by China's ministry of civil affairs immediately after the visit,[74] yet again indicated the deepening divergence in the relations. The unavailability of Wang Yi for the Russia-India-China (RIC) trilateral meeting in April 2017,[75] appeared to be China's way of conveying its displeasure over the Dalai Lama's visit. Thus, the visit may have served the purpose of conveying to China that Tibet was a possible strategic lever for India. Although the visit was not the Dalai Lama's first to the town, its high-profile nature and the media attention it received was unlike that in the past.[76] Kiren Rijiju, union minister of state for home affairs, accompanied the Dalai Lama to Arunachal Pradesh. Prema Khandu, the chief minister of Arunachal Pradesh, accompanied him to Tawang. Khandu, in fact, said, "Let me get this straight. China has no business telling us what to do and what not to do because it is not our next-door neighbour…India shares boundary with Tibet and not China."[77] Although a chief minister's statement on foreign policy issues in India is generally not of much consequence; however, in the given context, Khandu's statement raises the question whether it was a well thought-out statement, as it ran counter to the MEA's position that "the Tibet Autonomous Region is part of the territory of the People's Republic of China." The visit was also different in the backdrop of some other changes in India's approach towards the Central Tibetan Administration (CAT), the Dalai Lama and Tawang.[78] These developments may, in part, be perceived as a consequence of the "One-India" concept, as well as a willingness to accord greater respect and dignity to the Dalai Lama and the CAT, so as not to be seen as being unduly pressured by China. India's perceived manoeuvres in its dealings with the

Tibetan leadership living in India and to an extent in some instances in its relations with Taiwan and Mongolia,[79] also seem designed to send a message to China in this regard. These developments point to broader manoeuvers and counter-manoeuvers.

The discussion, thus far, makes it clear that there has been a visible change in the substance and style of India's China policy,[80] which was, till now, essentially designed to deal with the challenge of a superior power, with a sense of asymmetry on India's part.[81] How far it will succeed and what results it will yield, only time will tell as the policy is still unfolding.

Widening Divergence beyond Bilateral Context

A closer look at the India-China interactions in the Asia-Pacific—a major geo-political playground for the two countries—reveals how they have drifted further apart beyond the bilateral context. This drift and the growing divergence in bilateral relations are mutually reinforcing. From November 2014, the transformation of India's 'Look East Policy' into the 'Act East Policy' under Modi, succinctly captures this drift.[82] In keeping with this transformation, India is declaring its intent to enhance its strategic engagement with the region and establishing itself as a regional actor. Becoming a countervailing force to China in the region and offsetting its influence in South Asia is perceived to be one of the motivations behind this intent.[83] India has all along given enough signals to convey where its interests and affinities lie in this maritime region. India's advocacy of the rule-of-law and UNCLOS based-maritime regime, couched in the phraseology of Western democratic ideas, combined with its political positioning in international politics, conveys an unmistakable message about the convergence of its strategic understanding and interests with Vietnam, the Philippines and Japan and the US, which is the extra-regional security guarantor of countries like Japan and the Philippines, in regional maritime disputes. The 'Act East Policy' has given fresh impetus to this convergence.

India and the US, for the first time, expressed their concerns about peace in the SCS in their joint communiqué during Modi's US visit in October 2014.[84] The signing of the Logistics Exchange Memorandum of Agreement (LEMOA) by India and the US has been viewed with a degree of concern by China. The old and familiar refrain that *Indian foreign policy is too independent to align with any one single super-power,* found in Chinese writings and statements of Chinese scholars, finally seems to have given way to concerns over an 'India-US alliance'.[85] Modi's condemnation of expansionist tendencies during his visit to Japan was interpreted as an oblique reference to China's maritime claims.[86] Japan has its own maritime dispute with China in the ECS. India has regularised Japan's participation in its MALABAR naval exercises with the US.[87] The Modi government has renewed its push for strategic relations with Vietnam as well.[88] In an interesting development amidst the Doklam stand-off, the Vietnamese foreign ministry spokesperson appeared to have given the impression that India had finally sold BrahMos missiles to Vietnam, a claim that the Indian media reported to have been endorsed by its Vietnamese counterpart. However, Indian official sources denied the sale. Later, other conflicting reports, such as Vietnam's change of mind and willingness to buy the missiles from Russia, were also published. Incidentally, the two countries have been negotiating the deal for the missiles, which China has viewed with concern.[89]

Finally, President Trump's usage of the term Indo-Pacific, during his first visit to Asia in November 2017, came as an endorsement of the Indo-Pacific concept, which India has been pushing for, with a view to strategically integrate the Indian and Pacific Ocean regions. This along with the embryonic QUAD (US-India-Japan-Australia strategic cooperation) that came into being in the form of working/official-level meetings of these four countries ahead of the 31st ASEAN and the 12th EAS Summit in November 2017, marks the end of India's reluctance in favour of clear-cut strategic choices (also see endnote 56).[90] Thus, while China pushes its primacy in the region vigorously by challenging the US pre-eminence, India positions itself with the countervailing forces ranged against China.

Conclusion

It is difficult to deny that in the current relationship between India and China, "the overall broadening of ties, especially in business and people-to-people contacts", has been "overshadowed by differences on certain political issues".[91] The principal contradiction in the relations at present, is that while India's doubts regarding China's sincerity have multiplied, China has also become apprehensive about India reversing its China policy.

Clashing grand strategic schemes and national interests have exposed the cracks. It should be noted that the *cooperation can prevail over friction* strategy or *modus vivendi* could work well in the past because the two countries chose to avoid confrontation. However, the prevailing mood in both countries now seems to be that it is not necessary to shy away from friction for the sake of cooperation, if strategic interests are at stake. Structural factors that create the divergence exist as they did earlier. However, what cannot be denied is the influence of the leadership's preferences, which have brought these factors to the fore, in the period under discussion.

India under Modi, foregoing the diplomatic niceties, has compelled China to declare that it accords more importance to its military-security-economic strategic partnership with Pakistan than a development and prosperity-oriented strategic partnership with India. However, considering the power asymmetry i.e. an economy that is five-times larger than that of India; a defence budget that is four times larger; India's internal vulnerabilities, particularly in Kashmir and the Northeast that are susceptible to exploitation by external forces; the manoeuvring by China in international and global bodies by taking advantage of its leadership position; and finally the spectre of a joint China-Pakistan action, raises doubts as to how far India can assert itself. Whether Cold War tactics such as the playing of the Tibet, Taiwan or Mongolia cards can be effective in the present-day context, is uncertain.[92] Any government of the day is well within its rights to amend India's foreign policy as per its understanding of the national interest. However, the issue is: will reducing India-China relations to just the CPEC and the terrorist issue further solidify the China-Pakistan bond or weaken it? Also, which of the two countries among India and China has greater internal vulnerabilities? Which of the two has greater leverage to exploit the other's vulnerabilities? India needs to grapple with the answers to these questions.

On the other hand, China too, under Xi, needs to be reminded that India's rise cannot be contained by diplomatic manoeuvrings. China should realise that its unwillingness to accommodate India will only push it into the US embrace—a scenario that makes China uncomfortable. As the strands of Asian geopolitics continue to shift, China needs India's empathy for issues concerning its core national interests, such as the Tibet issue and the maritime disputes in the SCS among others. China should also realise that asymmetry does not work mathematically. It should not be oblivious to the fact that Modi's confidence in taking the Chinese bull by the horns over problematic issues, stems from India's capability enhancement in terms of weapons, deployment and other infrastructural strengths that have been acquired over the decades. This was amply demonstrated by India's resolve in the various military incidents involving the two sides, especially during the military standoff in Chumar, Ladakh, in September 2014 and in Doklam, in 2017.[93]

The lessons from India-China relations in the late 1950s and early 1960s would suggest that any assumption that diplomatic offensives will remain confined to the diplomatic arena and will not spiral out of control, may prove to be a costly mistake. The two sides need to sit down and seriously consider mutual accommodation. Since the old strategic approach of managing the relations appears to have run out of steam, the existing dialogue mechanisms it created also seem to be incapable of tackling the present divergence. Therefore, new mechanisms with a clear and strong political mandate are necessary to tackle the issues of critical divergence.

The following course could be adopted for a thaw in relations.[94] China and India could consider signing an agreement in which China—in conformity with Article 6 of the China-Pakistan Agreement of 1963, (see endnote 11) accepts that the POK is a disputed territory and the dispute is only between India and Pakistan, and China neither endorses any party's claim nor does it have any political stake in the matter, and that, it will renegotiate the CPEC-related projects whenever the dispute is resolved between the two parties. Such an agreement should also include a CBM relating to Chinese military presence in the POK. China should see reason and withdraw its technical hold on India's resolutions in the UNSC 1267 sanctions committee. It should understand that its insistence that its technical hold is not against India but because of multilateral and international compulsions, ignores the implications for India and hurts Indian interests and sensibilities. It should also realise that its open opposition to India's application for the NSG membership goes against the spirit of friendly relations. Even a partial blinking on these issues by both will reduce friction and open doors for future cooperation. However, the long-lasting bridging of the strategic divergence would be possible only if the two countries see the point made by Jaishankar, that India's "rise is not harmful to China's rise just as China's rise need not be harmful to India's rise."[95]

NOTES

1. Prashant Kumar Singh, 'An Overview of Bilateral Mechanisms', *Extraordinary and Plenipotentiary Diplomatist*, Vol. 2, Issue 6, June 2014: pp. XVIII-XX.
2. Surjit Mansingh, 'India-China Relations in the Context of Vajpayee's 2003 Visit', *The Sigur Center Asia Papers,* The George Washington University (Washington DC): p. 7, at https://www2.gwu.edu/~sigur/assets/docs/scap/SCAP21-Mansingh.pdf (Accessed April 21, 2017).
3. 'Space for Both China and India to Grow', *The Hindu*, December 16, 2010, at http://www.thehindu.com/news/Space-for-both-China-and-India-to-grow/article15595303.ece (Accessed April 21, 2017); 'Joint Communiqué of the Republic of India and the People's Republic of China', MEA, December 16, 2010, at http://mea.gov.in/bilateral-documents.htm?dtl/5158/Joint_Communiqu_of_the_Republic_of_India_and_the_Peoples_Republic_of_China (Accessed April 21, 2017).

4. N. Ram, 'What Wrong did This Man Do?', Frontline, Vol. 16, Issue 10, May 08-21, 1999, at http://www.frontline.in/static/html/fl1610/16100220.htm (Accessed April 21, 2017).
5. Manoj Joshi, 'Making Sense of the Depsang Incursion', *The Hindu*, May 07, 2013, at http://www.thehindu.com/opinion/op-ed/making-sense-of-the-depsang-incursion/article4689838.ece (Accessed April 21, 2013); V. Mahalingam, 'Daulat Beg Oldie Standoff: An Assessment', *IDSA Issue Brief*, May 22, 2013, at http://www.idsa.in/issuebrief/DaulatBegOldiestandoff_vmahalingam_220513 (April 21, 2013).
6. A quick recall of the complicated political and security issues in the bilateral ties would be helpful in understanding the present state of the relations. The issues include: the long-festering unresolved border dispute and associated bitter memories of the 1962 War; India's concerns regarding the perceived India-centric nature of China-Pakistan strategic relations; Chinese apprehensions relating to the 14th Dalai Lama's and the Central Tibetan Administration's (CTA's) continued presence in India since 1959; the supposed balance of power posturing in South Asia by China, and in East Asia by India in close coordination with other countries such as US, Japan and Vietnam; their differences over the US presence in political and security matrix of Asia; and China's apparent non-cooperation towards India's quest for greater responsibilities, with reference to the UNSC and more particularly in the Nuclear Suppliers Group (NSG). All of these issues and themes have a longstanding background. However, ambiguities and differences over these, which were minimised, or at least talked down, have alarmingly come out into the open in recent years, giving rise to apprehensions whether antagonism is becoming the defining feature of the relations. For issues and themes in India-China relations in the post normalisation and the post-Cold War era, see, Surjit Mansingh, 'India-China Relations in the Post-Cold War Era', *Asian Survey*, Vol. 34 No. 3, March 1994; pp. 285-300; Zhang Li, 'Sino-Indian Relations: An Overview of Recent History', *Asie. Visions* 34, Center for Asian Studies, September 2010, at https://www.ifri.org/sites/default/files/atoms/files/asievisions34zhangli.pdf (Accessed April 21, 2017).
7. It should be mentioned that India and China had issues of mistrust during 2003-14 too. Some specific instances include: security concerns about Chinese telecommunication company Huawei; insinuations about the Chinese hand in the flash floods in India's Himachal Pradesh in 2000; concerns over the reported plans of China damming Yarlung Tsangpo (the Brahmaputra) and diverting its course northward; the Chinese ambassador Sun Yuxi's careless statement claiming Tawang and whole Arunachal Pradesh on the eve of President Hu Jintao's India visitin 2006; China's attempt to block the Asian Development Bank's (ADB's) fund for a project in Arunachal Pradesh in 2009; and the denial of visa to Lt. Gen. B.S Jaswal on grounds that he was army commander in Jammu & Kashmir—which China considers disputed territory between India and Pakistan, and also between India and China due to China's claims in India's Ladakh region. However, except for the visa denial issue, which led to the temporary suspension of military exchanges between the two countries, the other issues remained confined to media and academic discourse. The ADB fund finally came in to India for the purpose (Jeff M. Smith, *Cold Peace: China–India Rivalry in the Twenty-First Century*, Lexington Books, 2013: p. 202). The visa issue, too, was resolved and

military exchanges resumed.

8. Press Trust of India (PTI), 'Modi Takes Up Lakhvi Issue with Xi', *The Hindu*, July 09, 2015, at http://www.thehindu.com/news/national/modi-takes-up-lakhvi-issue-with-xi/article7400568.ece (Accessed April 21, 2017); ET Bureau, 'Sushma Swaraj Meets Chinese Counterpart Wang Yi, Raises Zaki-ur-Rehman Lakhvi's Issue', *The Economic Times*, June 26, 2015, at http://economictimes.indiatimes.com/news/politics-and-nation/sushma-swaraj-meets-chinese-counterpart-wang-yi-raises-zaki-ur-rehman-lakhvis-issue/articleshow/47813137.cms (Accessed April 21, 2017); PTI, 'Case against Masood Azhar solid', *The Hindu*, February 23, 2017, at http://www.thehindu.com/news/national/case-against-azhar-solid/article17349784.ece (Accessed April 22, 2017).
9. Selig S. Harrison, 'China's Discreet Hold on Pakistan's Northern Borderlands', *New York Times*, August 26, 2010, at http://www.nytimes.com/2010/08/27/opinion/27iht-edharrison.html (Accessed April 22, 2017).
10. Indo-Asian News Service (IANS), 'Chinese Troops in POK: Indian Army Chief', *Strat Post*, October 06, 2011, at http://www.stratpost.com/chinese-troops-in-pakistani-kashmir-indian-army-chief/ (Accessed April 22, 2017).
11. Article 6 of the agreement says, 'The two Parties have agreed that after the settlement of the Kashmir dispute between Pakistan and India, the sovereign authority concerned will reopen negotiations with the Government of the People's Republic of China, on the boundary as described in Article Two of the present Agreement, so as to sign a formal Boundary Treaty to replace the present agreement.' 'The Boundary Agreement between China and Pakistan, 1963', at http://people.unica.it/annamariabaldussi/files/2015/04/China-Pakistan-1963.pdf (Accessed April 21, 2017).
12. Devirupa Mitra, 'Modi Criticises China's One Belt One Road Plan, Says Connectivity Can't Undermine Sovereignty', *The Wire*, January 17, 2017, at https://thewire.in/100803/modi-criticises-chinas-one-belt-one-road-plan-says-connectivity-corridors-cant-undermine-sovereignty/ (Accessed April 21, 2017).
13. PTI, 'India to China: Our Rise Not Harmful to Your Ascent, Sovereignty', *NDTV*, January 18, 2017, at http://indiatoday.intoday.in/story/china-india-rise-foreign-secretary-s-jaishankar-raisina-dialogue-cpec-united-nations-pakistan/1/860220.html (Accessed April 22, 2017).
14. 'Official Spokesperson's Response to A Query on Participation of India in OBOR/BRI Forum', MEA, May 13, 2017, at http://www.mea.gov.in/media-briefings.htm?dtl/28463/official+spokespersons +response +to +a +query +on +participation+of+india+in+oborbri+forum (Accessed May 31, 2017).
15. The diplomatic face-off over India's aspiration to enter the Nuclear Suppliers Group (NSG) has vindicated the view that while China would welcome cooperation with India in the multilateral forums such as the New Development Bank (formerly known as BRICS Development Bank) and the Asian Infrastructure and Investment Bank (AIIB) or cooperation on issues of common concerns such as trade issues in the WTO, when it comes to sharing the leadership space with India in international organisations, which command international strategic significance, China has a different view. The NSG episode has acted as the confirmation of old apprehensions about China being uncomfortable in sharing the leadership space with India, earlier perceived in China's reservations against India's entry into the regional forums such as the East Asia Summit (EAS) and

Shanghai Cooperation Organisation (SCO). Incidentally, it should be noted that, on its part, India too has appeared not too eager to welcome China in the South Asian Association for Regional Cooperation (SAARC). C. Raja Mohan, 'Raja-Mandala: Speak frankly with China: Delhi needs a more agile—and more open—policy to engage with Beijing', *The Indian Express*, July 5, 2016, at http://indianexpress.com/article/opinion/columns/india-china-foreign-policy-nsg-2893904/ (Accessed April 21, 2017); Ranjit Gupta, 'Where are India-China Relations Heading?: A Futuristic Outlook', in Sudhir T. Devare, Swaran Singh, Reena Marwah, *Emerging China: Prospects for Partnership in Asia*, London/New York/New Delhi Routledge, 2012.

16. Express News Service (ENS), 'Centre Names China as Country Blocking India's Entry into Nuclear Suppliers Group', *The Indian Express*, July 21, 2016, at http://indianexpress.com/article/india/india-news-india/nsg-china-blocking-india-entry-sushma-swaraj-2926704/ (Accessed April 21, 2017).
17. V.K. Singh, 'The Skirmish at Nathu La (1967)', *Scholar Warrior*, Autumn 2014, CLAWS, at http://www.claws.in/images/journals_doc/2042471866_VKSingh.pdf (Accessed April 21, 2017); Mandip Singh, 'Lessons from Somdurong Chu Incident', *IDSA Website*, April 26, 2013, at http://www.idsa.in/idsacomments/CurrentChineseincursionLessonsfromSomdurong ChuIncident_msingh_260413 (Accessed April 21, 2017).
18. Mandip Singh, 'Lessons from Somdurong Chu Incident', *IDSA Website*, April 26, 2013, at http://www.idsa.in/idsacomments/CurrentChineseincursion LessonsfromSomdurong Chu Incident_msingh_260413 (Accessed April 21, 2017).
19. The origin of the military incident during President Xi Jinping's India visit in September 2014 has remained unclear. The various cited causes include some localised border-infrastructure related issues between the locally stationed troops of the two countries, local PLA commanders' enthusiastic action, some "rogue" general's indiscipline, being the result of the domestic factional politics aligned with the PLA or even China's testing of water in relations with India and so on.
20. Prem Shankar Jha, 'How the Modi Government Spurned Friendly Overtures by China to Move Closer to the US', *The Wire*, July 25, 2016, at https://thewire.in/53677/narendra-modi-government-spurning-friendly-overtures-china-move-closer-us/ (Accessed May 9, 2017).
21. Press Release, Ministry of Foreign Affairs, Royal Government of Bhutan, June 29, 2017, at http://www.mfa.gov.bt/?p=4799 (Accessed August 1, 2017).
22. 'Recent Developments in Doklam Area', MEA, June 30, 2017 at http://www.mea.gov.in/press-releases.htm?dtl/28572/Recent_Developments_in _Doklam _Area (Accessed August 1, 2017); 'Full Text of Facts and China's Position Concerning Indian Border Troops' Crossing of China-India boundary', a Foreign Ministry of People's Republic of China (FMPRC) document, at http://www.bjreview.com/Documents/201708/t20170803_800101631_3.html (Accessed August 18, 2017).

    The Government of India did not speak to the media much and remained reticent during the course of the stand-off. The author has interpreted the Indian position and actions, and the Indian reading of the Chinese motivations on the basis of his reading of a large amount of press reportage published during that period.
23. John Garver, 'This Standoff is China Telling India to Accept Changing Realities', *The South China Morning Post*, July 16, 2017, at http://www.scmp.com/week-

asia/geopolitics/article/2102547/standoff-china-telling-india-accept-changing-realities (Accessed July 25, 2017).

24. Sushant Singh, 'Five Months on, Understanding Doklam 'Disengagement', A Few Other Issues', *The Indian Express*, January 22, 2018, at http://indianexpress.com/article/explained/five-months-on-understanding-doklam-disengagement-a-few-other-issues-india-china-5033943/ (Accessed January 23, 2017).

25. 'Press Statement on Doklam Disengagement Understanding', MEA, August 28, 2017, at http://www.mea.gov.in/press-releases.htm?dtl/28893/Press_Statement_on_Doklam_disengagement_understanding (Accessed August 30, 2017); 'Press Statement on Doklam Disengagement', Ministry of Foreign Affairs, Royal Government of Bhutan, August 29, 2017, at http://www.mfa.gov.bt/?p=4948 (Accessed August 30, 2017); 'Foreign Ministry Spokesperson Hua Chunying's Regular Press Conference', FMPRC, August 28, 2017, at http://www.fmprc.gov.cn/mfa_eng/xwfw_665399/s2510_665401/2511_665403/t1487932.shtml (Accessed September 6, 2017).

26. IANS, 'Modi, Sushma Mislead Nation on Doklam: Congress', *The Times of India*, January 18, 2018, at https://timesofindia.indiatimes.com/india/modi-sushma-mislead-nation-on-doklam-congress/articleshow/62553484.cms (Accessed January 23, 2018); 'Official Spokesperson's Response to Queries regarding the Situation in Doklam', MEA, January 18, 2018, at http://mea.gov.in/media-briefings.htm?dtl/29363/official+spokespersons+response+to+queries+regarding+the+ situation+ in+ doklam (Accessed January 23, 2018); 'Doklam Phase II will Test India More than Phase I', *Live Mint*, January 23, 2018, at http://www.livemint.com/Opinion/5ZTEKWGtdv0M6A0BWM7g1L/Doklam-phase-II-will-test-India-more-than-phase-I.html (Accessed January 23, 208); 'Will Build Doklam Infrastructure, Says Aggressive China After Satellite Pics', *NDTV*, January 19, 2018, at https://www.ndtv.com/india-news/will-build-doklam-infrastructure-says-aggressive-china-after-satellite-pics-1802180 (Accessed January 23, 2018); Sudhi Ranjan Sen, 'Chinese Army may Return to Doklam after Winter, Says General Rawat', *India Today*, January 12, 2018, at https://www.indiatoday.in/india/story/chinese-army-may-return-to-doklam-after-winter-says-general-rawat-1144210-2018-01-12 (Accessed January 23, 2018); ANI, 'Chinas Infrastructure Work in Doklam Temporary', *The Week*, January 17, 2018, at http://www.theweek.in/news/india/china-infrastructure-development-doklam-temporary.html (Accessed January 23, 2018); PTI, 'China Mum over Gen Rawat's Remarks on PLA Troop Reduction in Doklam', *The Economic Times*, January 9, 2018, at https://economictimes.indiatimes.com/news/defence/china-mum-over-gen-rawats-remarks-on-pla-troop-reduction-in-doklam/articleshow/62429550.cms (Accessed January 23, 2018); 'Foreign Ministry Spokesperson Lu Kang's Regular Press Conference', FMPRC, January 15, 2018, at http://www.fmprc.gov.cn/mfa_eng/xwfw_665399/s2510_665401/2511_665403/t1525880.shtml (Accessed January 23, 2018).

27. Sushant Singh, No. 24.

28. Ibid.

29. J.D. Armstrong, *Revolutionary Diplomacy: Chinese Foreign Policy and the United Front Doctrine*, Berkeley, University of California Press, 1980: p. 171.

30. John Garver, 'China's Kashmir Policies', *India Review*, Volume 3, No. 1, 2004: pp. 1-24; Sheldon W. Simon, 'The Kashmir Dispute in Sino-Soviet Perspective', *Asian*

Survey, Volume 7, No. 3, 1967: pp. 176-187.

31. In recent years, China-Pakistan economic relations have taken off considerably. In 2014, their bilateral trade was around US$ 16 billion which was only $ 8.66 billion in 2010. Similarly, Chinese FDI stocks have gone up to $ 3736 billion in 2014 from $1828 billion in 2010. Prashant Kumar Singh, 'China and South Asia: Deepening of Engagement', in J.P. Panda (ed.), *China Yearbook 2015*, New Delhi, Pentagon Press (ISBN 978-81-8274-907-8), 2016, p. 280 and 283.
32. Praveen Swami, 'Beijing's Terror Conundrum, *The Indian Express*, May 4, 2016, at http://indianexpress.com/article/opinion/columns/masood-azhar-un-jem-masood-azhar-india-pakistan-china-relations-2783105/ (Accessed April 21, 2017).
33. Ian Storey, 'China's "Malacca Dilemma"', *China Brief*, Vol. 6, Issue 8, April 2006, at https://jamestown.org/program/chinas-malacca-dilemma/ (Accessed April 21, 2017).
34. Shailaja Neelakantan, 'China Hikes Investment in CPEC to $62bn from $55bn', *The Times of India*, April 16, 2017, at http://timesofindia.indiatimes.com/world/pakistan/china-hikes-investment-in-cpec-to-62bn-from-55bn/articleshow/58206829.cms (Accessed April 23, 2017).
35. Tanima Biswas, 'In First Conviction of ISIS Men In India, Two Sent To Jail For 7 Years', *NDTV*, 21 April 2017, http://www.ndtv.com/india-news/in-first-conviction-of-isis-men-in-india-two-sent-to-jail-for-7-years-1684268 (Accessed April 21, 2017)
36. PTI, 'Masood Azhar is a Terrorist, China should 'Adjust' Its Stand Accordingly, Says Former Chinese Diplomat', *The Indian Express*, January 06, 2017, at http://indianexpress.com/article/world/ex-chinese-diplomat-asks-china-to-adjust-stand-on-masood-azhar-4462525/ (Accessed May 9, 2017). The PTI reported that Mao Siwei, a former Chinese diplomat at the Chinese Consulate in Kolkata, sought a "change in China's repeated efforts to block India's bid to slap a UN ban on JeM leader Masood Azhar, arguing that he is a terrorist and Beijing should 'adjust' its stand accordingly... [and] China should take advantage of India's complaint against Azhar and 'get rid of the passive diplomatic situation' between the two countries." His views appeared "in his lengthy blog on social media WeChat".
37. The resolution is available at South Asia Terrorism Portal website http://www.satp.org/satporgtp/countries/india/document/papers/parliament_resolution_on_Jammu_and_Kashmir.htm (Accessed May 09, 2017).
38. PTI, 'India Underlines Claim Over Pakistan-Occupied Kashmir, Gilgit-Baltistan', *NDTV*, April 5, 2017, at http://www.ndtv.com/india-news/india-underlines-claim-over-pakistan-occupied-kashmir-gilgit-baltistan-1677728 (Accessed April 21, 2017); "First Vacate PoK': India Slams Pakistan after Nawaz Sharif's Speech at UN', *First Post*, at http://www.firstpost.com/world/india-hits-back-after-sharif-speech-says-pakistan-prime-sponsor-of-terror-2451108.html (Accessed April 21, 2017); 'Vacate POK and End Terrorism, India Tells Pakistan at UN', *Scroll.in*, October 2, 2015, at https://scroll.in/article/759385/vacate-pok-and-end-terrorism-india-tells-pakistan-at-un (Accessed 22 April 2017). Minhaz Merchant, 'Face it: POK, not J&K, Is the Core Dispute between India and Pakistan', *Dailyo*, October 06, 2015, at http://www.dailyo.in/politics/indiapak-narendra-modi-nawaz-sharif-kashmir-kargil-pok-sushma-swaraj/story/1/6645.html (Accessed April 21, 2017).

39. Ranjit Gupta, No. 15.
40. S. Kalyanaraman, 'Rethinking India's Approach towards Pakistan-occupied Kashmir', *IDSA Comment*, May 3, 2016, at http://www.idsa.in/idsacomments/rethinking-indias-approach-towards-pakistan-occupied-kashmir_skalyanaraman_030516 (Accessed 21 April 2017).
41. Long Xingchun, 'New Delhi's Objection to CPEC in Kashmir Not to Its Own Benefit', *Global Times*, March 6, 2017, at http://www.globaltimes.cn/content/1036227.shtml (Accessed April 21, 2017).
42. Andrew Small, 'Why China is Playing a Tougher Game on the NSG This Time Around', *The Wire*, June 20, 2016, at https://thewire.in/43991/why-china-is-playing-a-tougher-game-on-the-nsg-this-time-around/ (Accessed July 24, 2017); Suhasini Haider, 'India's NSG Chances Possible but Unlikely, Says Expert', [Interview with , Mark Fitz Patrick, Nuclear Expert, The International Institute Strategic Studies], *The Hindu*, at http://www.thehindu.com/news/Indias-NSG-chances-possible-but-unlikely-says-expert/article14414715.ece (Accessed April 21, 2017).
43. Shubhajit Roy, 'No Entry in NSG: India Blames One Country (China), Others Said No Too', *The Indian Express*, June 25, 2016, at http://indianexpress.com/article/india/india-news-india/no-entry-in-nsg-india-blames-one-country-china-others-said-no-too-2874377/ (Accessed April 21, 2017).
44. Fu Xiaoqiang, 'Beijing could Support India's NSG Accession Path if It Plays by Rules', *Global Times*, June 16, 2016, at http://www.globaltimes.cn/content/988607.shtml (Accessed April 21, 2017).
45. Willy Wo-Lap Lam, *Chinese Politics in the Era of Xi Jinping: Renaissance, Reform, Or Retrogression?*, New York and London, Routledge, March 2015; Joseph Fewsmith, 'Mao's Shadow', *China Leadership Monitor* (*CLM*), Hoover Institution, (43), Spring 2014: pp. 1-9; Joseph Fewsmith, 'China's Political Ecology and the Fight against Corruption', *CLM*, (46), Winter 2015: pp. 1-26; Johnson, Christopher K., 'Thoughts from the Chairman: Xi Jinping Unveils His Foreign Policy Vision', *Freeman Report*, Centre for Strategic & International Studies (CSIS), (15), December 2014: pp. 1-15; Lin, Zhu, 'Punishing Corrupt Officials in China', *China Quarterly*, (223), September 2015: pp. 595-617; Pei, Minxin, 'In Beijing, Signs of a Major Political Power Struggle in the Offing', *Fortune* (Online), 28 March 2016. (Accessed September 12, 2016); SXH Shen, 'New Silk Road Project', *East Asia*, 32(1), March, 2015: PP. 1-5.
46. Xi, Jinping, Xi Jinping: *The Governance of China*, Beijing, Foreign Language Press, 2014.
47. Camilla T N Sorensen, 'The Significance of Xi Jinping's 'Chinese Dream' for Chinese Foreign Policy: From 'Tao Guang Yang Hui' to Fen Fa You Wei', *Journal of China and International Relations*, 3(1), 2015, pp. 53-73; Michael D. Swaine, 'Xi Jinping's Address to the Central Conference on Work Relating to Foreign Affairs: Assessing and Advancing Major Power Diplomacy with Chinese Characteristics', *CLM*, (46), Winter 2015: pp. 1-19; Wang, Zheng, 'China's Alternative Diplomacy', *The Diplomat*, January 30, 2015, at http://thediplomat.com/2015/01/chinas-alternative-diplomacy/ (Accessed April 21, 2017).
48. Gal Luft, *It Takes a Road*, Institute for the Analysis of Global Security, Potomac, Maryland (US), 2016; T. Fallon, 'China's Pivot to Europe', *American Foreign Policy Interests*, 36(3), 2014, pp. 175-182; T. Fallon, 'The New Silk Road: Xi Jinping's

Grand Strategy for Eurasia', *American Foreign Policy Interests*, 37(3), 2015, pp. 140-147.

49. Jun Osawa, 'China's ADIZ over the East China Sea: A "Great Wall in the Sky"?', *Brookings*, December 17, 2013, at https://www.brookings.edu/opinions/chinas-adiz-over-the-east-china-sea-a-great-wall-in-the-sky/ (Accessed May 09, 2017); Prashant Kumar Singh, 'The Hague Ruling on the South China Sea: Has David Taken Down Goliath', *IDSA Comment*, July 14, 2016, at http://www.idsa.in/idsacomments/hague-ruling-on-the-south-china-sea_pksingh_140716 (Accessed May 09, 2017); 'Images Show 'Significant' Chinese Weapons Systems in South China Sea', *The Guardian*, December 15, 2016, at https://www.theguardian.com/world/2016/dec/15/images-show-significant-chinese-weapons-systems-in-south-china-sea (Accessed May 09, 2016).
50. For the concepts, please see 'China's New Neighbourhood Diplomacy: Seeking Stability through Management and Planning', *CIIS Report*, No. 9, February 2016, at http://www.ciis.org.cn/english/2016-02/14/content_8570872.htm (Accessed May 09, 2017).
51. *Ibid*.
52. Xue Li and Zheng Yuwen, 'A Blueprint for China's Neighborhood Diplomacy', *The Diplomat*, March 30, 2016, at http://thediplomat.com/2016/03/a-blueprint-for-chinas-neighborhood-diplomacy/ (Accessed April 21, 2017).
53. S.L. Narasimhan, 'How Candid is China's Good Neighbourhood Policy?', *Defence Aviation Post*, January 09, 2017, at http://defenceaviationpost.com/chinas-good-neighbourhood-policy/ (Accessed May 09, 2017).
54. 'China's Reaction to Mumbai Terror Strikes: Pro-Pakistan Bias?', December 8, 2008, at https://www.c3sindia.org/archives/chinas-reaction-to-mumbai-terror-strikes-pro-pakistan-bias/ (Accessed December 15, 2017); Sutirtho Patranobis, 'Awkard [sic] China Fumbled for Reactions after 26/11 Mumbai Attacks', *Hindustan Times*, April 16, 2015, at http://www.hindustantimes.com/world/awkard-china-fumbled-for-reactions-after-26-11-mumbai-attacks/story-YJ2p5H0XU3OdwDemoFzn3H.html (Accessed December 15, 2017).
55. 'Chinese Soldiers Present in PoK: Army Chief', *The Times of India*, September 19, 2012, at https://timesofindia.indiatimes.com/india/Chinese-soldiers-present-in-PoK-Army-Chief/articleshow/16464272.cms (Accessed December 29, 2017); Bidanda Chengappa, 'Why China is Setting Up Military Bases in PoK', *DNA India*, November 15, 2011, http://www.dnaindia.com/analysis/comment-why-china-is-setting-up-military-bases-in-pok-1612612 (Accessed December 29, 2017); 'China has Never Deployed A Single Soldier in PoK: Liang', *The Hindu*, September 4, 2012, at http://www.thehindu.com/news/international/china-has-never-deployed-a-single-soldier-in-pok-liang/article3855456.ece (Accessed December 29, 2017).
56. Ranjit Gupta, No. 15.
57. A question could be raised about the validity of the ideological interpretation citing Vajpayee government's dialogue-oriented approach towards the Kashmir issue because Vajpayee was also from the same party. However, there is always a personality factor. And also, the Vajpayee government was essentially an alliance government dependent on its allies for its survival, many of whom may not have shared the BJP's ideology. The political-ideological analysis of Indian foreign policy is a time-honoured academic exercise. Nehruvian foreign policy

has been interpreted as an extension of Nehruvian socialist, secular and anti-imperial politics. In more contemporary times, the Manmohan Singh government's hesitation to further deepen relations with the US even after the Indo-US Nuclear Deal (2005) and the India-specific NSG waiver with US help in 2008 is attributed to the ideological discomfort of the sections within the Congress party with the US. Similarly, his government's move to strengthen trilateral relations—India, Japan and US— was reported to have met with stiff resistance from the Left parties, which were the ruling Congress party's allies from 2004-09, and from within the Congress party for ideological reasons. See 'India Invites Japan to be Part of Malabar Naval Exercises with the US', *The Indian Express*, January 25, 2014, at http://indianexpress.com/article/india/politics/india-invites-japan-to-be-part-of-malabar-naval-exercises-with-the-us/ (Accessed May 10, 2017); Rajat Pandit, 'India Snubs Australia, US Move to Check China', *The Times of India*, December 02, 2011 at http://timesofindia.indiatimes.com/india/India-snubs-Australia-US-move-to-check-China/articleshow/10950305.cms (Accessed May 10, 2017)). The present government's push towards strengthening relations with Japan and the US has been described as the shedding of this ideological baggage. The shedding can also be termed as Modi's breaking away from the legacy of NAM and the secularist considerations. C. Raja Mohan, 'Time for India to Move to Shed its Other 'Hesitations of History', Especially towards China, Pakistan', *The Indian Express* at http://indianexpress.com/article/opinion/columns/us-india-foreign-plicy-pakistan-china-2851090/ (Accessed June 14, 2016).

58. As can be seen that the CPEC and the terrorist issues are related to the ongoing tussle over Kashmir between India and Pakistan. Kashmir has a defining place in the ruling party's discourse on nationalism. The demand for the abolition of Article 370 in the Indian Constitution that grants special status to the state of Jammu and Kashmir (J&K) has been part its electoral agenda. The Hindutva parties, and also other voices in politics and outside, have criticised Nehru, holding him responsible for the incomplete merger of the state with India under Article 370, his approaching the UN for mediation on Kashmir between India and Pakistan and the loss of the state's territory to Pakistan in the 1948 war. The continuing tough stance of the Modi government in the ongoing phase of violence that started after the killing of Burhan Wani, a Hizbul Mujahideen commander, in the operation by security forces in July 2016 highlights the government's supposedly non-compromising and tough approach towards separatism in Kashmir, which is in line with the ruling party's political position on Kashmir. Thus, China's stand on the CPEC and the terrorists is without doubt clashing with sovereign assertion of the Modi government on Kashmir vis-à-vis Pakistan. There are opinions that suggest that its political-ideological convictions seem to have converged with the non-ideological hawkish sentiments of the influential sections of the official set-up towards the Kashmir issue, Pakistan and China (see Sushil Aaron, 'Narendra Modi is Implementing the Doval Doctrine in Kashmir', *The Hindustan Times*, September 16, 2016, at http://www.hindustantimes.com/analysis/narendra-modi-is-implementing-the-doval-doctrine-in-kashmir/story-uPZfR9aNCPwFCD3VkTnWZN.html (Accessed May 01, 2017).

59. Prime Minister Narendra Modi's and his party Bharatiya Janata Party's (BJP's) rise to power and their numerical parliamentary strength is a phenomenal

development in India. The party for the first time has wrested political power with a majority of its own. The earlier BJP governments were alliance governments. The party stands in long-standing ideological opposition to the Indian National Congress (INC), which has been in government for most years after independence in 1947. Although the implications of Modi's and the BJP's unprecedented rise for national policies, and foreign policy, are still unfolding, ignoring this changed political context in any discussion on Modi's foreign policy in general and his China policy in particular will render the discussion incomplete.

60. Mainly the present ruling party Bharatiya Janata Party (BJP), founded in 1980, to which Modi belongs, and its ideological mentor Rashtriya Swayamsevak Sangh (RSS), founded in 1925, in which Modi began his political career as a volunteer, Bharatiya Jana Sangh, founded in 1951 and from which the BJP later emerged and the Akhil Bharatiya Hindu Mahasabha, founded in 1915, represent Hinduvite politics in India. The coinage of the word *Hindutva* is attributed to V.D. Savarkar who authored *Essentials of Hindutva* in 1921-22. The present-day propagator of the term and the philosophy behind it is the BJP. It sees Bharatiyata (Indianness) and Hindutva as synonyms and defines Indian nationhood in terms of Hindu culture which is again a synonym of Indian culture for it. This understanding stands in direct opposition to the Nehruvian idea of Indian nationhood defined in terms of a composite and syncretic culture. For BJP's official position on Hindutva, please see, 'Vision Document 2004', The Bharatiya Janata Party (BJP) Website, at http://www.bjp.org/documents/vision-document?u=vision-document-2004 (Accessed April 21, 2017).

61. Shubhajit Roy, '"No relevance", Centre Asks UN Mission to Vacate Delhi Office', *The Indian Express*, July 08, 2014, at http://indianexpress.com/article/india/india-others/no-relevance-centre-asks-un-mission-to-vacate-delhi-office/ (Accessed May 09, 2017).

62. Nikita Doval, 'Narendra Modi Skips NAM Summit, the First Indian PM to Do So', *Live Mint*, September 15, 2016, at http://www.livemint.com/Politics/ectxbpHsJ2XUmRkXXqVbpL/Hamid-Ansari-leaves-for-Venezuela-to-attend-17th-NAM-summit.html (Accessed May 09, 2017). Earlier only Prime Minister Charan Singh did not attend the Havana Summit in September 1979 because at the time, his government was an interim government **as** he had resigned in August 1979.

63. Although India recognised Israel in 1950 itself, it kept the relations low-key as it was more inclined towards West Asia's Islamic countries, in keeping with the larger anti-imperial sentiments prevailing in India, which considered the creation of Israel as a Western imperial legacy in Asia, India's opposition to the creation of a state on the basis of religion, the importance of oil rich Islamic countries for energy supplies to India and the India's Muslim community's perceived sentiments against Israel. India established full-fledged ambassadorial relations as late as 1992. President Pranab Mukherjee's Israel visit in October 2015 was the first President-level visit from India. Narendra Modi became the first Indian Prime Minister to visit Israel in July 2017. Here, it should be noted that other high ranking Indian leaders and officials have been visiting Israel for long. The Israeli president and prime minister started visiting India much earlier. More importantly, India is a big buyer of Israeli defence equipment, and they have

been long sharing information and cooperating against terrorism, though such cooperation has been kept under wraps. India's cautious political engagement with Israel has been a legacy of the conventional Nehruvian foreign policy. P.R. Kumaraswamy, 'Modi Redefines India's Palestine Policy', *IDSA Brief*, May 18, 2017, at http://www.idsa.in/issuebrief/modi-redefines-india-palestine-policy_prkumaraswamy_180517 (Accessed July 24, 2017); P.R. Kumaraswamy, 'What Does Modi's Israel Visit Mean to the Palestinians', *IDSA Brief*, July 03, 2017, at http://www.idsa.in/idsacomments/what-does-modi-israel-visit-mean-to-the-palestinians_prkumaraswamy_030717 (Accessed July 24, 207).

64. Indrani Bagchi, 'Modi Govt Shows Pakistan Its Tough Side, Calls Off Foreign Secretary-Level Talks', *The Times of India*, August 19, 2014, at http://timesofindia.indiatimes.com/india/Modi-govt-shows-Pakistan-its-tough-side-calls-off-foreign-secretary-level-talks/articleshow/40382419.cms (Accessed April 21, 2017).

65. '4 Hours, Choppers and 38 Kills: How India Avenged the Uri Attack', *The Economic Times*, September 29, 2016, at http://economictimes.indiatimes.com/news/defence/army-conducted-surgical-strikes-on-terror-launch-pads-on-loc-significant-casualties-caused-dgmo/articleshow/54579855.cms (Accessed April 21, 2017).

66. For a historical perspective on the *Hindutvite* foreign policy views on Nehru's China policy with reference to Tibet and Formosa, please see Nancy Jetly, *India-China Relations, 1944-77: A Study of Parliament's Role in the Making of Foreign Policy*, New Delhi, Radiant Publishers, 1979; Mohammed Ali Kishore, *Jan Sangh and India's Foreign Policy*, New Delhi, Associated Publishing House, 1969.

67. To be fair, Xi Jinping too, made friendly overtures, notably relating to the boundary dispute. He was reported to have remarked that the two countries should "arrive at a mutually acceptable solution to the border dispute "as soon as possible". Ananth Krishnan, 'India, China should Deepen Military ties: Xi Jinping', *The Hindu*, March 28, 2013, at http://www.thehindu.com/news/national/india-china-should-deepen-military-ties-xi-jinping/article4555334.ece (Accessed April 22, 2017). In March 2015, Foreign Minister Wang Yi said: "After many years of hard efforts, the border talks continue to make progress, and the dispute has been brought under control...at the moment, the boundary negotiation is in the process of building up small and positive developments... it's like climbing a mountain: the going is tough, and that is only because we are on the way up." 'China Says Progress Being Made on India Border Talks', *Reuters*, March 08, 2015, at http://www.reuters.com/article/us-china-india-idUSKBN0M404S20150308 (Accessed April 22, 2017). Similarly, China's decision to issue stapled visas to the Indian residents of Arunachal Pradesh was also a welcome development as previously visas had been refused in many instances on grounds that the residents of Arunachal Pradesh do not need visas as the state and its residents are Chinese. 'Stapled Visas to People of Arunachal "Goodwill" Gesture', *The Times of India*, June 10, 2014, at http://timesofindia.indiatimes.com/india/Stapled-visas-to-people-of-Arunachal-goodwill-gesture-China/articleshow/36331913.cms (Accessed May 10, 2017). At the time of presenting credentials to President Xi Jinping, Indian ambassador Ashok Kantha, along with one other ambassador out of a total of 14, was reportedly asked to stay back for a brief chat with the President. The noted commentator Prem Shankar Jha saw

this move as a goodwill gesture towards India. Similarly, Premier Li Keqiang's visit to India was his first foreign visit after assuming office. Prem Shankar Jha, 'How the Modi Government Spurned Friendly Overtures by China to Move Closer to the US', *The Wire*, July 25, 2016, at https://thewire.in/53677/narendra-modi-government-spurning-friendly-overtures-china-move-closer-us/ (Accessed May 9, 2017).

68. Details are available at the Ministry of External Affairs (MEA) website's relevant sub-sections within the two sections on Visits and Media Center/Documents at http://mea.gov.in/
Prime Minister Modi's 2015 China visit was full of evocations of the common Buddhist heritage highlighting the ancient linkages. Modi paid a visit to the Buddhist temple Da Xingshan. The temple is known for its association with Chinese monk Xuan Zang or Hieun Tsang who travelled to India in seventh century AD. Modi also gifted a replica of the casket with Bhagwan Buddha's sacred relics, to President Xi.

69. Bharti Jain, 'Intel Agencies Object to E-tourist Visa for Chinese', *The Times of India*, May 07, 2015, at http://timesofindia.indiatimes.com/india/Intel-agencies-object-to-e-tourist-visa-for-Chinese/articleshow/47181163.cms (Accessed April 22, 2017).

70. *Mail Today* Bureau, 'Modi Puts Border before Business: Straight-talking PM Raises Simmering LAC Row in Three-Hour Meeting with China's President Xi', *Mail Today*, September 8, 2014, at http://www.dailymail.co.uk/indiahome/indianews/article-2761471/Modi-puts-border-business-Straight-talking-PM-raises-simmering-LAC-row-three-hour-meeting-China-s-President-Xi.html (Accessed May 09, 2017).

71. TNN, 'Didn't Mean to Offend Indian Sensibilities: Amazon Expresses Regret in Letter to Sushma Swaraj', *The Times of India*, June 12, 2017, at http://timesofindia.indiatimes.com/india/didnt-mean-to-offend-indian-sensibilities-amazon-expresses-regret-in-letter-to-sushma-swara/articleshow/56503451.cms (Accessed May 9, 2017). The Indian reaction to the report of Amazon Canada displaying a doormat with the design of India's flag on it does not directly refer to the One-India idea. However, it does indicate the activist mood of the government on issues of national respect and sentiments.

72. Incidentally, a recent episode involving India and Turkey might help in understanding the "One India" thought. Turkey has been Pakistan's old sympathiser on the Kashmir issue in the Organisation of Islamic Countries (OIC) and elsewhere. But, since Turkey's influence on the issue has been without any significant diplomatic consequences, not much is generally heard and written about its pro-Pakistan approach, in India. However, the then Vice-President Hamid Ansari's visit to Armenia from April 24-26, 2017 and Cypriot President Nicos Anastasiades's visit to India from April 25-29, 2017 shortly before the Turkish President Recep Tayyip Erdogan's India visit (April 30-May 01, 2017), were perceived as messages from India to Turkey about its displeasure over the latter's stand on Kashmir. The visits appeared to be a quid pro quo for Turkey's support for Pakistan, since it (Turkey) has a historical bitterness with Armenia and Cyprus. The media reported that India's displeasure against Turkey's projects in the POK was also conveyed to Erdogan. On his part, Erdogan responded by raising the Kashmir issue in an interview to a Turkish TV channel, before

embarking on his India trip. In the interview, he called for a multilateral dialogue on the Kashmir issue, much against India's stated position. He also said that both India and Pakistan should be admitted into the NSG, and asked India to give up the "attitude" of opposing Pakistan's entry on account of its proliferation record. Here, the point is to underline and recognise changes that can be seen taking place in Indian foreign policy under Modi. Only time will tell whether these changes will sustain in the long run and whether the government will succeed in implementing One-India as the universally applicable official policy on the lines of the PRC's One-China policy. Shubhajit Roy, 'Visiting Turkey President: Erdogan Calls for Multilateral Dialogue on Kashmir, Cites "Long Talks" with Pakistan', *The Indian Express*, May 01, 2017, at http://indianexpress.com/article/india/erdogan-calls-for-multilateral-talks-on-kashmir-says-has-talked-at-length-with-pakistan-4634702/ (Accessed May 10, 2017); 'Erdogan's Trip to India was Anything but a Turkish Delight', *Quartz India*, May 08, 2017, at https://qz.com/978062/erdogans-trip-to-india-was-anything-but-a-turkish-delight/ (Accessed May 11, 2017).

73. PTI, 'Dalai Lama Reaches Tawang, to Start Religious Discourses', *The Hindu*, April 7, 2017, at http://www.thehindu.com/news/national/other-states/the-dalai-lama-reaches-tawang/article17866681.ece (Accessed April 20, 2017); K.S. Venkatachalam, 'Why China is Fuming over the Dalai Lama's Visit to Tawang', *The Diplomat*, April 4, 2017, at https://thediplomat.com/2017/04/why-china-is-fuming-over-the-dalai-lamas-visit-to-tawang/ (Accessed April 20, 2017); Liu Xin, 'India Using Dalai Lama's Visit to Upset Beijing: Analyst', *Global Times*, April 4, 2017, at http://www.globaltimes.cn/content/1040773.shtml (Accessed April 20, 2017).
74. Saibal Dasgupta and Indrani Bagchi, 'China Renames Six Towns in Arunachal in Retaliation for Dalai Lama's Visit', *The Times of India*, April 20, 2017, at https://timesofindia.indiatimes.com/india/china-renames-six-towns-in-arunachal-in-retaliation-for-dalai-lamas-visit/articleshow/58270993.cms (April 22, 2017); Atul Aneja, 'China Renames Six Areas in Arunachal', *The Hindu*, April 20, 2017, at http://www.thehindu.com/news/national/china-renames-six-areas-in-arunachal/article18149761.ece (Accessed April 22, 2017).
75. ENS, 'After Heat over Dalai Lama Visit, China's Foreign Minister Likely to Come in December', *The Indian Express*, November 4, 2017, at http://indianexpress.com/article/india/after-heat-over-dalai-lama-visit-chinas-foreign-minister-likely-to-come-in-december-4921686/ (Accessed January 16, 2018); PTI, 'Dalai Lama not the Reason for Foreign Minister's Decision not to Attend RIC Meet in India: China', *The Indian Express*, May 5, 2017, at http://indianexpress.com/article/india/dalai-lama-not-the-reason-for-foreign-ministers-decision-not-to-attend-ric-meet-in-india-china-4641878/ (Accessed May 17, 2017).
76. G. Parthasarathy informs that the Dalai Lama's latest visit to Tawang in April 2017 was his sixth visit to the town. G. Parthasarathy, 'When the Dalai Lama Visited Tawang', *Business Line* (*The Hindu*), April 19, 2017, at http://www.thehindubusinessline.com/opinion/columns/g-parthasarathy/how-india-should-respond-to-chinas-response-to-dalai-lama-visit-to-tawang/article9650537.ece (Accessed April 21, 2017).
77. Rahul Karmakar, 'Arunachal Borders Tibet, not China: CM Pema on Beijing's

Protest over Dalai Lama', *Hindustan Times*, April 5, 2017, at http://www.hindustantimes.com/india-news/arunachal-borders-tibet-not-china-cm-pema-on-beijing-s-noise-over-dalai-lama-visit/story-cDE3x2Nl45uRz14YmMVQwO.html (Accessed April 21, 2017).

78. 'India Slams China for Objecting to US Envoy's Arunachal Visit', *The Indian Express*, October 24, 2016 (Accessed April 21, 2017); 'Foreign Ministry Spokesperson Lu Kang's Regular Press Conference', October 28, 2016, FMPRC, (Accessed April 21, 2017); PTI, 'China Protests Pranab's Meeting with Dalai Lama, Warns of Disturbance to Ties', *The Times of India*, December 16, 2016 (Accessed April 21, 2017.

In India, there have been sections, which include the Gandhians, socialists and the hindutvites who see a "cultural and spiritual link" between India and Tibet. They view Tibet under China as a cultural loss and consider the loss of the Tibetan buffer against India's national interest. They have held the Nehru government's Panchsheel (Five Principles of Peaceful Co-existence) agreement with China in 1954 responsible for it (see *Indian Leader on Tibet*, a compilation of the speeches and statements of Indian leaders of various ideological-political backgrounds on Tibet. It is available at http://tibet.net/wp-content/uploads/2011/12/indian-leaders-on-tibet1.pdf (Accessed May 07, 2017).

79. In an unprecedented move, China publicly reacted to a Taiwanese delegation's visit to India in February 2016. The move was unprecedented as China had hardly ever publicly reacted to any development in India-Taiwan relations since they established their non-diplomatic relations in 1995. Prashant Kumar Singh, 'When the Taiwanese Came Calling: Chinese Reaction and the Indian Response', *IDSA Issue Brief*, March 03, 2017, at http://idsa.in/issuebrief/when-the-taiwanese-came-calling_pksingh_030317 (Accessed April 21, 2017).

The media reported that Mongolia either actually received or if not, misperceived signals from India that it would support Mongolia in case China took punitive measures against it (Mongolia), if it hosted the Dalai Lama. Thus, hoping for India's support, Mongolia hosted the Dalai Lama in November 2016 despite Chinese warnings. As a consequence of this 'defiance', China made Mongolia pay a price by blockading its supplies. Eventually, it prevailed over Mongolia, extracting assurances that such an invitation would not be repeated. Wen Dao, 'New Delhi Overreaches to Meddle in China's Core Interests', *Global Times*, December 21, 2016, at http://www.globaltimes.cn/content/1025055.shtml (Accessed May 10, 2017). Indo-Asian News Service (IANS), 'Will Never Let in Dalai Lama Again: Mongolia', *The Indian Express*, December 21, 2016, at http://indianexpress.com/article/world/will-never-let-in-dalai-lama-again-mongolia-4438654/ (Accessed May 10, 2017); Shastri Ramachandran, 'China Beats Mongolia into Submission, 'Friend' India Watches', *The Citizen*, December 26, 2016, at http://www.thecitizen.in/index.php/NewsDetail/index/1/9527/China-Beats-Mongolia-into-Submission-Friend-India-Watches (Accessed May 10, 2017).

80. Ram Madhav, a general-secretary and a prominent China hand of the ruling BJP, avers that India's Finlandisation is not acceptable in bilateral relations—a reference to Finland's compliance with the foreign policy of the USSR while submitting to its power during the Cold War. This analysis highlights the attitudinal change in the ruling setup in India with regard to China, though whether 'Finlandisation' is an appropriate choice of word in the context of India-

China relations is questionable. Ram Madhav, 'New India, Different China', *The Indian Express*, April 13, 2017, at https://www.rammadhav.in/articles/oped-indianexpress-new-india-different-china/ (Accessed April 22, 2017).

81. It would be counterfactual to argue how the Manmohan Singh government (or any other government) would have handled the CPEC, the terrorists and the NSG issues, as these in their present form, are products of the Modi-Xi era in India-China relations. However, a case can be made on the basis of how the Manmohan Singh government handled the 14th Dalai Lama's visit to Tawang in 2009. It very much permitted the visit without succumbing to the Chinese pressure but kept it a low-key affair banning the international media from the town during the visit unlike the Dalai Lama's much publicised latest visit to Tawang. Also, the pushing of the One-India idea and the repeated references to the POK are new developments. These changes have originated from the leadership's style and choices and certain political-ideological positioning going beyond the regular Realist explanations.

82. PTI, '"Look East" Policy Now Turned into "Act East" Policy: Modi', *The Hindu*, November 13, 2017, at http://www.thehindu.com/news/national/look-east-policy-now-turned-into-act-east-policy-modi/article6595186.ece (Accessed July 12, 2017).

83. India began enhancing its relations with the Asia-Pacific countries under its Look East policy, initiated by Prime Minister P.V. Narasimha Rao in 1991/92. The policy entered its second phase around 2003 in which a balance of power motive to contain China in coordination with other regional countries was perceived. Eryan Ramadhani, 'Lost in Southeast Asia: India's "Look East" Policy Revisited', *Yonsei Journal of International Studies*, Vol. 6, No. 2, 2014, pp. 316-333.

84. Sachin Parashar, 'In a First, India-US Joint Statement Mentions South China Sea', *The Times of India*, October 02, 2014, at http://timesofindia.indiatimes.com/india/In-a-first-India-US-joint-statement-mentions-South-China-Sea/articleshow/44028687.cms (Accessed April 21, 2014).

85. 'Is India Heading toward Alliance with US?', *Global Times*, August 30, 2016, at http://www.globaltimes.cn/content/1003574.shtml (Accessed April 21, 2017).

86. The translation of Modi's remarks, which were in Hindi, is as follows: "We have to decide if we want to have *'vikas vaad'* (development) or *'vistar vaad'* (expansionism) which leads to disintegration. Those who follow the path of Buddha and have faith in *'vikas vaad'* (development). But we see, those with 18th century ideas, engage in encroachments and enter the seas (of others)," PTI, 'China Reacts Guardedly to Modi's Expansionist Remark', *Indian Express*, September 1, 2014, at http://indianexpress.com/article/india/india-others/china-reacts-guardedly-to-modis-expansionist-remark/ (April 20, 2017).

87. Jugal R. Purohit, 'Malabar 2016: All You Need to Know about US, Indian and Japanese Joint Naval Exercise That Begins Today', India *Today*, June 14, 2016, at http://indiatoday.intoday.in/story/malabar-2016-us-india-japan-philippine-sea/1/691264.html (April 20, 2016).

88. 'Satellite Centre in Vietnam', Press Information Bureau, Department of Space, Government of India, February 24, 2016, at http://pib.nic.in/newsite/PrintRelease.aspx?relid=136692 (Accessed April 21, 2017).

89. Vishnu Som, 'On a Move that will Anger China, Vietnam Says Yes, India Denies', *NDTV*, August 18, 2017, at https://www.ndtv.com/india-news/indias-new-

move-with-brahmos-cruise-missile-likely-to-anger-china-1739183 (Accessed November 5, 2017); Manu Pubby, 'Indian Offer to Sell BrahMos Missiles to Vietnam Stalled', *The Print*, August 30, 2017, at https://theprint.in/2017/08/30/indian-offer-sell-brahmos-missiles-vietnam-stalled/ (Accessed November 5, 2017).

90. Kallol Bhattacherjee, 'India, Japan, U.S., Australia hold first 'Quad' talks at Manila ahead of ASEAN Summit', *The Hindu*, November 12, 2017, at http://www.thehindu.com/news/national/india-highlights-indo-pacific-cooperation-at-the-first-quad-talks/article20317526.ece (Accessed December 29, 2017); Cary Huang, 'US, Japan, India, Australia ... is Quad the first step to an Asian Nato?', *South China Morning Post*, November 25, 2017, at http://www.scmp.com/week-asia/opinion/article/2121474/us-japan-india-australia-quad-first-step-asian-nato (Accessed December 29, 2017); Tanvi Madan, 'The Rise, Fall, and Rebirth of the "Quad"', *War on the Rocks*, at https://warontherocks.com/2017/11/rise-fall-rebirth-quad/ (Accessed December 29, 2017).

91. 'China's Power Dynamic Factor in Asia: Full Text of Foreign Secretary Jaishankar's Speech at Raisina Dialogue', at http://www.hindustantimes.com/india-news/china-s-power-dynamic-factor-in-asia-full-text-of-foreign-secretary-jaishankar-s-speech-at-raisina-dialogue/story-g7Fxz82vcDzRnvkqHrqemK.html (Accessed April 21, 2017).

92. P. Stobdan, "To Deal with China, India Needs to Return to Strategic Fundamentals", *IDSA Website*, March 21, 2017, at https://idsa.in/idsacomments/deal-with-china-india-needs-to-return-to-strategic-fundamentals_ pstobdan_210317 (Accessed April 20, 2017).

93. P. Stobdan, 'New Gambles in Ladakh', *IDSA Website*, September 25, 2014, at http://www.idsa.in/idsacomments/NewGamblesinLadakh_pstobdan_250914 (Accessed April 20, 2014); Dinkar Peri, 'India Ramps Up its Military Presence in Eastern Ladakh', *The Hindu*, July 18, 2016, at http://www.thehindu.com/news/national/India-ramps-up-its-military-presence-in-Eastern-Ladakh/article14497721.ece (Accessed April 20, 2017).

94. Chinese Ambassador Luo Zhaohui's four-point initiative, proposed in his lecture at the United Services Institution of India (USI), a New Delhi-based think tank, came as an encouraging sign. He proposed "aligning its [China's] 'One Belt One Road' (OBOR) project with India's 'Act East Policy', restarting negotiations on a free trade pact, a China-India Treaty of Good Neighbourliness and Friendly Cooperation and prioritising early resolution of the border dispute between the two countries." He also thought aloud in his speech whether the renaming of CPEC by including India in the nomenclature would elicit India's support for the BRI. However, in an intriguing development, the phrase in this regard was later deleted from the script of his speech available on the website. The media reported that it was done following Pakistan's complaint at the direction of the Chinese foreign ministry. This development reveals the intractability involved in the issue of CPEC. It should be noted that the speech was part of China's public diplomacy exercise to convince India to participate in China's multinational Belt and Road Forum for International Cooperation organised from May 13 to May 17, 2017. PTI, 'Chinese Ambassador Moots 4-point Initiative to Improve Ties with India', *The Hindu*, May 08, 2017, at http://www.thehindu.com/news/international/china-moots-4-point-initiative-to-improve-sino-india-ties/

article18407696.ece (Accessed May 10, 2017); PTI, 'China Removes Envoy's Offer of Renaming CPEC from Speech Transcript', *The Times of India*, May 09, 2017, at http://timesofindia.indiatimes.com/world/china/china-removes-envoys-offer-of-renaming-cpec-from-speech-transcript/articleshow/58595231.cms (Accessed May 10, 2017).

95. PTI, 'India to China: Our Rise not Harmful to Your Ascent, Sovereignty', *NDTV*, January 18, 2017, at http://indiatoday.intoday.in/story/china-india-rise-foreign-secretary-s-jaishankar-raisina-dialogue-cpec-united-nations-pakistan/1/860220.html (Accessed April 21, 2017).

4

The One Belt One Road as a Chinese Vision of Regional Economic Order

Saheli Chattaraj

ABSTRACT

Since the Chinese government has proposed the 'One belt One Road' initiative, there have been several domestic and international debates that arose in the academia regarding the origin, inspiration and the construction of the initiative. The Chinese economy developed very rapidly in the past thirty years which has further increased the demands for energy, raw materials and markets for the manufacturing sector in China. Therefore the 'One Belt One Road' initiative as a connectivity project could help link China's neighbourhood and promote cooperation and support for China to fill in this gap of markets, raw materials and also energy supplies for its future and ongoing development. In this background this paper analyses Chinese sources to conceptualise the 'One Belt One Road' initiative, the domestic debates and challenges for the initiative and its significance to the Chinese leadership. It also looks into the origin of the 'One Belt One Road' initiative and how China has linked its western and central provinces to the 'Belt and Road' so as to reduce the disparity and the uneven development between the western and the eastern provinces of China. The paper has also looked into the guidelines and the guiding principles of the 'One Belt One Road' initiative as outlined by the Chinese government and the challenges that the initiative may face in lieu of implementation of the initiative.

Key words: *One Belt One Road; 18 Pivot Cities; Five Connectivities; Major Routes*

Introduction

China has used the title "One Belt One Road" or the recent "Belt and Road Initiative" (BRI) (一带一路) for its twin grand economic strategies, namely the "Silk Road Economic Belt (丝绸之路经济带)" and the "21st Century Maritime Silk Road (21世纪海上丝绸之路). On the land route, it plans to connect Asia, Europe and Africa. However, China primarily focuses on connecting China to Europe through Central Asia and Russia. Other routes are also part of this land route. For instance, it also intends to connect China to West Asia through Central Asia. These routes are to enable the passage of Chinese goods. For instance, China wants access to the Indian Ocean Region through land routes, whereby they can transport oil and gas resources to China and in return gain access to markets for Chinese goods. On the other hand, the sea route is supposed to connect the coastal regions of China to the Indian Ocean through the South China Sea. This route further aims to extend into Europe and connect China with the South Pacific Ocean. Overall, these routes would be used to link all the Chinese coastal ports together.

The BRI is the Chinese President Xi Jinping's grand geo-economic plan to unite the countries in China's neighbourhood and those along its periphery into a common economic region. It believes that it could strengthen China's economic ties with these countries and spearhead the development space in the region. President Xi first announced his intention to launch BRI when he attended the G-20 and SCO Summit in September 2013 on a 10 day visit to the Central Asian countries, namely Kazakhstan, Uzbekistan, and Tajikistan. During his tour, from 3 to September 13th, he first coined the term, "One Belt One Road (OBOR)".[1] While in Kazakhstan, on September 7, President Xi delivered a speech in Nazarbayev University entitled, "Promote People-to-People Friendship and Create a Better Future" in which he comprehensively elaborated on China's strategic initiative to build a Silk Road Economic Belt. In this speech, he spoke about adopting a common approach towards development in the region, by linking the region through a common route, which would ease the flow of intra-regional goods and resources. The OBOR is supposed to be built as individual projects and industrial sectors in respective countries which would then in the future be linked together to each other and cover the entire region.[2] Xi in his state visit to Indonesia on October 3, 2014 for the 21st APEC economic leaders' meeting propounded on OBOR.[3] In his speech at the Indonesian Parliament, on "Join Hands to Build China-ASEAN Community of Common Destiny",[4] President Xi brought historic precedence such as Southeast Asia's regional connectivity in ancient times to emphasise its relevance in the current Maritime Silk Road project. China believed that by attuning ASEAN's sensibility towards historic connectivity, then its present proposal for cooperation with ASEAN countries will bear fruit and would enhance maritime cooperation. Xi believed that then the

Chinese-established China-ASEAN Maritime Cooperation Fund that was originally envisaged for the development of partnerships for maritime cooperation, could be utilised for the implementation of the 21st Century Maritime Silk Road.[5]

After espousing the plan, China expedited the political process to implement the BRI. On November 27, 2013, the Third Plenum of the Eighteenth Party Congress approved the proposal titled, "Major Issues Concerning Comprehensively Deepening Reforms".[6] The Plenum carried out decisions, where China would institute a new and open economic system in the country that would encourage domestic enterprises to venture outside China for business collaborations with foreign enterprises. Similarly foreign enterprises would also be welcome to invest in China and set up their manufacturing bases in the country. The Plenum decided to adopt a new trend of economic globalisation, where China wants the State-Owned Enterprises (SOEs) to invest in foreign countries and learn best management practices, and also for the domestic Chinese market to attract more foreign direct investment in high-technology sectors. For China, this meant projecting an image of 'domestic openness' and its readiness to be more open to the outside world, thus integrating China's "go global" strategy and policy of attracting foreign direct investment (FDI) into China. The plenum decided to further economic reforms to more efficiently allocate the resources and integrate the market.

Significance of the Concept of the One Belt One Road

In 1978, when the Chinese economy was in a state of turmoil,, the then Chinese leader Deng Xiaoping initiated the "Reform and Opening Up Policy" for China, which broadly aimed to make Chinese markets accessible to the outside world. Initially the reform consisted of a "Bringing-In" strategy, which implied that China would open its doors to the outside world and foreign countries could invest in China. This also had the provision for China to attract technology and support from foreign investors to push its own economic and technological development. In the later phase of the economic reforms, the Chinese enterprises were also encouraged to invest in the other countries, which in turn led to substantial technological and economic advancements in China. After three decades of the opening-up policy, the Chinese economy grew at an average rate of 10 per cent in GDP and 18 per cent annually in international trade, respectively. Thus, the Chinese economy was strengthened by adopting and adapting new and advanced technologies, both from the foreign enterprises that invested in China to access the Chinese markets and also from the Chinese companies that invested in other countries. This advanced the scope, scale and the momentum of China's economic development. Keeping this reality in mind, Xi's BRI concept builds on the foundational "bringing-in" and "going out" strategy. However, the BRI expands and merges these two strategies and provides a broader and conceptual significance to the initiative.

The success of the reform process also led to overwhelming importance being accorded to the development of the eastern coastal regions and the Special Economic Zones owing to their geographic locations and proximity to ports. The national investment and manufacturing policy of China focused primarily on the eastern coastal regions of China as it also offered a more favourable investment environment compared to the provinces in the interior and the western parts of China. As a result, China witnessed a surplus production especially of consumer goods and other heavy and light industrial products in the eastern coastal provinces. Hence, China face challenges in finding new markets and destinations for these surplus goods amidst a downward trend in the global demand for the Chinese products. In addition, the Chinese economy was facing pressures from a volatile property market, the "new normal"[7] for economic growth. Thus, the Chinese economy was facing an uphill battle. Therefore, China's economic policies had to shift from reliance on an exports-based economic policy to a policy based on regional integration and inter-connectivity. To ameliorate the situation, the BRI envisages an economic policy that will integrate China's southern and western regions, promote inter-connectivity and assist Chinese enterprises to explore newer markets in its periphery and address the issue of the over capacity at home. It is imperative for China to make this strategy successful because if it is not able to create or provide new markets in the neighbourhood for its manufacturers, its domestic industry is likely to suffer immensely with lack of profits and unable to sustain its production.

Apart from overcapacity, China's over-emphasis on the eastern coastal regions has created an immense economic disparity between the eastern and the western provinces. The BRI seeks to resolve this disparity by putting 18 pivot cities, provinces and autonomous regions on the connectivity map, which would connect these regions on the western sector of China to the countries on the periphery in China's neighbourhood. This policy of the BRI aims to bring in inclusive growth and would also help bridge the increasing disparity in the economic development of the east and the west and allow the western sector the space for development. Since the western region in China would need raw materials for its manufacturing industries and enterprises, the connectivity with the neighbourhood provided by the BRI would also give China access to the region from Central Asia and Afghanistan. It also helps that these regions have a lot of untapped natural resources. However, China is faced with the problem of poor infrastructure and road and railway connectivity in these regions, to successfully access raw materials. Therefore, to access the markets or the natural resources from these regions, the connectivity network need to be consolidated and developed for the benefit of both sides. Thus, China believes that BRI offers the best solution by simultaneously providing access to China on the one hand, and building infrastructure in the region on the other.

The BRI further divides the 18 pivot cities, provinces and autonomous regions in the BRI into five major clusters. These are: Shanghai, Zhejiang, Fujian, Guangdong and Hainan on the east and south eastern sector; Heilongjiang, Jilin and Liaoning in the northeast; Xizang or Tibet, Yunnan and Guangxi in the south west; Xinjiang, Gansu, Inner Mongolia, Qinghai, Ningxia and Shaanxi in the northwest; and Chongqing in the central sector. The classification of these major clusters, including the prominent cities, is also indicative of an attempt by the Chinese leadership to maintain the inclusive nature of the OBOR, unlike the Reform and Opening Up process, which primarily focused on a particular region within China. It also indicates that through these major clusters China can also be connected with its neighbourhood across all sections of its border regions.

The cities and the provincial departments from these clusters are also actively making plans for their own respective regions. For example, Heilongjiang Province has already submitted its plan for the "Eastern Land and Sea Silk Road Economic Belt". Similarly, Xinjiang is also planning an international financial centre in the Silk Road Economic Belt region. The China Railway Corporation has proposed that it would accelerate connectivity of transport facilities, based on the mapping of the Silk Road Economic Belt Initiative from the different regions and build a China-Europe International Passageway in the three sectors i.e. the west, middle and the east.[8] Several initiatives associated with the BRI for construction of trade facilitation junctions are currently underway. Yiwu city in the eastern part of China in Zhejiang province, has been designated the pilot economic zone for international trade comprehensive reform. The Yiwu Bonded Logistics Centre has been formally operationalised to facilitate trade exchanges with foreign enterprises. Chongqing has also promoted and approved inland railway ports and has been approved for car imports and a bonded logistics centre. The Chongqing-Xinjiang-Europe (渝—新—欧) railway has already started its operation of freight transport reducing the cost of transportation to one fifth of that of transportation of cargo by air and the time required to 14 days instead of the earlier 49 days transportation time required by sea. The goods transported through this zone primarily include electronics, cars and medical equipments.[9]

Thus, the BRI follows an innovative concept that allows China to cater specifically to the needs underperforming regions as well as allow it to situate it among the overall economic reforms and opening-up policy. Moreover, it is also gives China opportunities to interact with countries on its periphery on issues of development and economic policy, increasing its regional presence. Similarly, while the bordering countries can also benefit from China's infrastructure development projects in their country, China can negotiate access to their markets and natural resources and raw materials to boost its own domestic development. This is the important shift in China's international policy under the One Belt One Road scheme.

Apart from the integration aspect of the BRI, China has been careful in projecting the BRI as an economic initiative. President Xi has also been selling the initiative as a mutually beneficial and win-win cooperation. The Chinese leadership has also often reiterated that the BRI would adhere to the "Three Nos" and the guiding principles of the Panchsheel. These principles are: non-interference in the internal affairs of the other countries; no striving for hegemony or dominance in the region; and the non-expansion of one's sphere of influence. By eschewing language that would feed geo-political rivalry and create mistrust in its dealing with BRI countries, China is determined to use the resulting positive image in other countries to gain access to infrastructure, road and connectivity projects, within their borders. Also, for the BRI to work, the BRI countries also have to recalibrate their strategies to be supportive of Chinese policies and other facilitation mechanisms of the BRI. Therefore, the Chinese leadership has factored these into the new the guidelines of BRI.

Guidelines and the Basic Principles of the BRI

In official Chinese documents, the BRI has been referred to, and represented as the modern reinvention of the ancient Silk Road that emphasised the values of, "mutual trust, equality, inclusiveness, mutual learning and win-win cooperation". It was a network of trade routes, originating from Chang'an (present-day Xian), originally built during the Han Dynasty. This network of routes was also linked to the Mediterranean in the Western sector, thus also linking China with the Roman Empire. It consisted of a series of major trade roads and since silk was one of the major products that was traded along these roads, it was named the Silk Road by the

German geographer, Ferdinand Von Richthofen, in 1877. The Chinese official sources also posit that if the BRI vision is realised, it could also create a promising economic corridor connecting most of the regions and directly benefitting 4.4 billion people, i.e. 63 per cent of the world's population, with a collective annual GDP of $2.1 billion that accounts for 29 per cent of the world's wealth.[10]

The Guiding Principles of the BRI are therefore the "five factors of connectivity or the five connectivities (五通)" and the "three commonalities (三同)". The Five Connectivities are: Policy Coordination (政策沟通); Facilities Connectivity (设施联通); Unimpeded Trade (贸易畅通); Financial Integration (资金融通); and People-to-People bonds (民心相同). The "Three Commonalities" are: "common interest (利益共同体)"; "common destiny (命运共同体);" and "common responsibility (责任共同体)". Ideally, the guidelines of the OBOR expects the BRI countries are supposed to innovate ways to increase foreign investment and enhance domestic support to their policies. China believes that this would then help build a stakeholders in the BRI countries, who will be a part of a community of 'shared interests, destiny and responsibility'. They would build an open economic system that in Chinese view would stand for principles such as mutual benefit, win-win cooperation, pluralism, balance, security and effectiveness. In other words, by developing a new language and narrative in the reforms and opening-up, China and the BRI countries will develop a new pattern of interaction and understanding that is distinct of the Western countries.

Thus, these afore-mentioned basic principles of the BRI means that both countries would develop policies on joint construction, market operation and the role of enterprises. While they would have to abide by commercial principles, China believes that the government would have to provide policy support and guidance service. As a result, China has to develop a policy-making process that has to combine the sectors China wants to cooperate with the commercial and economic policies of the countries along the routes. The integration of these approaches mean that China wishes to decentralise policy and create customised and tailored policies relevant and feasible for easy economic cooperation with individual BRI countries. People-to-people bonds have also been outlined as one of the key features of the BRI, which lays emphasis on both official and civil efforts for the realisation and the proper functioning of the BRI. Thus, the participation, coordination and collaboration of both the people and the governments would be crucial for promoting investment, trade and markets, along with sustainable growth.

While the 'Belt' component in BRI focuses on a fast and progressively developing western sector, the 'Road' component focuses on expanding maritime cooperation. The BRI aims to achieve a new model of all-round development that is not just limited to economic development but also includes: infrastructure, telecommunications; finance; energy; investment and services; cross-border trade procedural simplification and trade liberalisation; capacity-building projects; along with education, tourism and cultural exchanges. China still has a conflict situation prevailing in the South China Sea region. To gain further support on the seas and access to the Indian Ocean region for the safe and free passage for the Chinese goods, it aims to secure its maritime routes by forming allies with the countries in the neighbourhood.

Overall, BRI has outlined its goals and objectives for three different phases. In the first phase, it has immediate development goals with a time frame of two to three years, whereby it seeks to expand opportunities for development and reach a consensus with the countries along its periphery and the borders and implement schemes relating to the construction of infrastructure and connectivity projects. In this phase, industrial investment, economic and trade cooperation, facilitation of trade, investment and personnel exchanges, cooperation on customs, investment protection and immigration management would be the key areas of cooperation. Deng Xiaoping, in the early 1980s, said that China needs to learn from the experience and expertise of foreign personnel and experts and the lessons they have learned from their successes, failures in their path of development. Therefore, he advocated that the foreign experts be welcomed into China for their suggestions and expertise. A State Administration of Foreign Experts Affairs (SAFEA) was established within the apparatus of the State Council to for this purpose. Deng strongly believed that the expenditure on such advice and expertise would support and increase the efficiency of the Chinese policies, especially with respect to the reform process, as China was a novice in this respect. Similarly, before embarking on the OBOR initiative, various state departments, academic bodies, think tanks and SAFEA held various exchanges with foreign experts, including policy makers, academicians and also government officials from the countries along the 'Belt' and the 'Road' with two primary motives: the first one being to educate the outside world about the concept of BRI and also to arrive at an understanding of the public and the government opinion as well as their expectations from OBOR. This initiative to a certain extent was also expected to guarantee domestic policy support for the BRI in the countries along the Belt and the Road.

The second phase of the BRI, which extends over ten years, is slated to achieve breakthroughs in regional economic integration. Lastly, the long term goal of the BRI is to be a functional land, maritime and air transport system. The entire implementation time span of BRI is tentatively expected to cover a time period of, as much as, 35 years and is estimated to be completed in time for the 100th anniversary of the People's Republic of China in 2049.[11] The BRI project has also been incorporated in the constitution of the Chinese Communist Party, which gives it greater policy heft and impetus.[12] This ensures that the BRI project will continue even after Xi's tenure as the general secretary of the CCP Central Committee.

Major Routes of BRI

The BRI covers an area with 55 per cent of the world GNP, 70 per cent of the global population and 75 per cent of the known available energy reserves. Supported by more than 60 countries and international organisations, the route design of the BRI covers five major directions and encompasses six major economic corridors across Asia, Europe and Africa. The first route proposes to connect China with Europe till the Baltic Sea, covering the regions of Central Asia and Russia. The main corridor through this region is the "China-Mongolia-Russia Economic Corridor" and the "New Eurasia Land Bridge Corridor". The second route connects China to the Persian Gulf and the Mediterranean Sea through Central Asia and West Asia via the "China-Central Asia-West Asia Economic Corridor". The route stretches from China to South East Asia, South Asia and into the Indian Ocean region. The main corridors passing through this region are the "China-Pakistan Economic Corridor", the "Bangladesh-China-India-Myanmar Economic Corridor" and the "China-Indo-China Peninsula Economic Corridor". The Maritime Silk Route covers two major directions. It includes: the route through the coastal ports of China into the Indian Ocean through the South China Sea; and the second route stretches from the coastal ports of China to the Southern Pacific Ocean through the South China Sea. The United States has not entirely endorsed the BRI because of the 21st century Maritime Silk Route which maps through the Indian Ocean Region. The US could be considered the predominant power in the Indian Ocean Region with expectations that India would partner with the US to be the security provider for the region. Therefore, the US is not willing to give China advantage in this region.

Projects of the OBOR

China has already undertaken the planning and the construction of the Asian road and network and the trans-Asian railway network by means of 13 roads and 8 railways to be built jointly with countries in Central Asia, South East Asian and South Asia. Currently, some sections of the Trans-Asian Railway have already been completed in parts of China, Laos, Thailand and Malaysia. The Chongqing-Xinjiang-Europe Railway and the China-Kazakhstan Khorgos-Altynkol Railway are already operational. The construction of the "three vertical lines and two horizontal lines" in the Great Mekong Sub-regions are also nearing completion. Roads connecting the ports in Yunnan and Guangxi to those in South East Asia and South Asia are also under construction. The China-Kyrgyzstan-Uzbekistan Highway, Syabrubensi-Rasuwagadi Highway, Gwadar Port-Kashgar Highway and Railway are all under active construction. China has also built 18 international electric transmission channels.

Several gas pipelines like the China-Central Asia Natural Gas Pipeline, China-Russia Crude Oil Pipeline, China-Myanmar Oil and Gas Pipeline have also been constructed and have already started operating. Liberalisation and facilitation of trade investment and connectivity are important aspects of the OBOR. But although the OBOR is primarily an economic initiative, it still has several security aspects, which are raising ambiguities and skepticism in the minds of other countries.

Challenges of the OBOR

Though the background of the BRI is the spirit of the ancient Silk Road, yet it is different in several aspects. The ancient Silk Road was an initiative, whereby business communities along the silk route joint undertook trade and exchanges. On the other hand, the BRI is primarily a Chinese proposal and is China-centric because it is the primary driving force for the bilateral and multilateral projects. The BRI has also not yet come up with specific guidelines or any public document, with specific provisions, terms and conditions for the countries participating in the initiative. Most of the documents or MOUs signed under the initiative are bilateral and not multilateral. As a result, several countries have to factor that there are no reliable policy information while deliberating their policy on joining the BRI. This is also true for India, as policy makers are assessing the advantages of joining the BRI. Moreover, for India, the China-Pakistan Economic Corridor (CPEC) is being constructed on territory that is a matter of dispute between India and Pakistan.

The BRI has a broad vision, which can prove beneficial for all participating countries if carefully scrutinised and analysed. It can prove to be most powerful yet complex international phenomenon of the 21st century. For example, even for India, the BRI could prove beneficial for poverty alleviation through creation of jobs and infrastructure build-up. The New Development Bank has promised to give loans to India for building roads in Madhya Pradesh at its Second Annual Meeting held in New Delhi on April 1,2, 2017. India could also attain better environmental standards in its major cities by sharing China's green and clean technology for environmental protection.

However, pitfall remains in the BRI because large Chinese SoEs, which are overburdened with debt are gaining fresh access to capital from the banks because of BRI and they are continuing to invest these funds without regard, which would not have been possible without BRI. In addition, the less-developed provinces in China are now given animpetus to compete against each other and strive to come up with new projects. But these provinces instead have taken the BRI as a reason to rebrand few existing projects under the tag of BRI to attract central resources rather than follow the central government guidelines to develop specific BRI-related projects catering to local needs and the resources of the neighbouring countries.

Major Debates on the OBOR

The BRI encompasses both a domestic and a development strategy for China. While China wants to develop its western region, it also aims the BRI could create a benign neighbourhood. It believes that if China could manage an environment by cooperating and collaborating constructively with the neighbours, then it can focus on its domestic affairs. For instance, China's Defence White Paper of 2013 also uses the term "period of strategic opportunity," which implies that China has been a beneficiary of the benign external security environment, which has allowed it to focus more on its domestic and economic development. By focusing on economic development, it was able to achieve global economic prominence and avoid an arms race or military interventionism. In this context, the BRI is a new plan to provide another comprehensive action plan to continue this policy. Though scholars have pointed out that BRI has several strategic and security aspects, which may raise suspicions and awe amongst China's neighbours, but for China, it is more of an economic and domestic policy initiative rather than a security or a strategic mission.

Significantly, the BRI is Xi's unique contribution to the Chinese foreign policy canon and is meant to be the hallmark of his tenure as the President of the People's Republic of China (PRC). Every Chinese leader's tenure is marked by a unique political and ideological underpinning, which marks the changes and the continuities in his leadership term.[13] Under the leadership of President Hu Jintao from 2003-2013, the foreign policy canon of China focused on peaceful development (和平崛起) and the creation of a well-off society (谢康社会) by the year 2020. 'Peaceful Development' and a 'well off society' have been the mainstay of Chinese policy for more than a decade and are expected to be achieved by the year 2020. This is a very significant goal as the year 2021 also marks the 100th anniversary of the establishment of the Chinese Communist Party 共产党 (CCP). Similarly, Xi Jinping's conceptualisation of the "Chinese Dream" and the BRI as a vehicle to achieve this goal is supposed to fructify on the hundredth anniversary of the birth of the People's Republic of China in 2049. The 2049 is when China has declared that it would build a modern socialist country that would be strong and prosperous and regain the international standing that it had lost during imperialism.

Professor Justin Yifu Lin from the National School of Development at Peking University who is also a former Senior Vice President of the World Bank, speaking at the Boao Forum for Asia in July, 2015 pointed out that the BRI would be the new driver for continuous productivity enhancement and economic growth in Asia. The economic status of Asian countries will grow and continue to drive prosperity and poverty reduction in the region. The forum also discussed the inclusive form of growth through planned investment that the region aims to achieve and attain in the coming years. It was pointed out by Hu Jiaming, the Vice chairman of the Investment Strategy Group at the Goldman Sachs, China that Asia at present already accounts for 20 per cent of the world GDP and with the connectivity projects, this share would further increase, which in turn could contribute to global economic growth. There are countries in China's neighbourhood, like the Central Asian countries, most of which do not have high speed railways or even subways in their major cities and are quite enthusiastic about joining China's OBOR initiative as they can gain from China's expertise. In the last 30 years, China has greatly developed its infrastructure and achieved urban modernisation, therefore, these countries could also develop their major cities with Chinese help. But on the other hand, there are also some other countries who have joined the initiative at a later stage. According to Hu Jiaming, this is because they realised that the OBOR is also a trend and it is like a train which one needs to catch or else get left behind at the station forever. What he implied was that regional integration and interconnectivity provides a major solution to many of the global economic issues. Therefore, from a purely economic point of view, there is a need to connect the regions as one had in the past, through the ancient silk road to facilitate the movement of products from country to country.

Conclusion

The BRI is one of Asia's first infrastructure and connectivity initiatives which will have many potential beneficiaries, since the Asian region still lacks substantial roads, railways, telecommunications and other basic infrastructure essential for growth. Therefore, even though the outcome and the real consequences of the OBOR initiative remain unknown, the initiative is bound to lead to coordinated infrastructure development resulting in economic transformation. The BRI has also been documented into the constitution of the Chinese Communist Party along with 'Xi Jinping's Thought on Socialism with Chinese Characteristics for a New Era' during the 19th National Congress of the Chinese Communist Party in October 2017, which makes the BRI a significant foreign policy initiative of the People's Republic of China. The BRI initiative has been interpreted from several angles as an opening up policy for China's southern and western provinces -an attempt to cooperate with newly developing countries and also as an economic initiative to sell China's manufactured goods to the foreign markets. However, the BRI still faces several political risks as well when it comes to the security and threat concerns of the bordering and the participatory states as there are credit risks present in the new markets of the participating countries. Risks also involve political instability in the business regions, labour market risks, legal and regulatory issues of the foreign governments and also operational challenges in these countries. Despite these risks and challenges, the BRI remains a comprehensive blueprint designed by China to minimise divergence and friction among states in the region and maximise cooperation between both big and small powers.

NOTES

1. Hou, Qiang "Chinese President Delivers Speech at Nazabayev University", 2013. http://news.xinhuanet.com/english/photo/2013-09/08/c_132701546.htm Accessed January 1, 2017
2. Clover, Charles, "China's Great Game: Road to a New Empire", 2015, https://www.ft.com/content/6e098274-587a-11e5-a28b-50226830d644 Accessed on January 1, 2017
3. "President Xi Jinping Pays State Visits to Indonesia, Malaysia and Attends the 21st APEC Economic Leaders' Meeting", Ministry of Foreign Affairs of the People's Republic of China, http://www.fmprc.gov.cn/mfa_eng/topics_665678/xjpfwynmlxycx21apec_665682/ Accessed on December 26, 2017
4. Xu, Rui "Speech by Chinese President Xi Jinping to Indonesian Parliament", 2013 http://www.asean-china-center.org/english/2013-10/03/c_133062675. Accessed on January 1, 2017
5. Centre on International Cooperation, *The New Silk Roads: China, the U.S. and Central Asia*, New York, New York University 2015

6. Lan, Hongguang, "CPC announces decision on Comprehensive Reform", 2013, http://news.xinhuanet.com/english/china/2013-11/12/c_132882325.htm Accessed on February 12, 2017
7. The term "new normal" for denoting China's economic development was a phrase quoted by President Xi Jinping in May 2014 to denote the phenomenon of China's shift in economic goal from the previous high speed growth of the economy to a medium paced economic growth focussing more on innovation in economic growth rather than high volume of input and investment.
8. Li, Zhihui, *The Belt and Road Win-Win Cooperation*, Beijing: Beijing Language and Culture University Press, 2016
9. Zhou, Wa, "Rail Route to Europe improves freight transport", http://usa.chinadaily.com.cn/epaper/2013-09/13/content_16968074.htm Accessed on May 15, 2017
10. Li, Zhihui, *The Belt and Road Win-Win Cooperation*, Beijing: Beijing Language and Culture University Press, 2016
11. Bondaz, Antoine et al., "One Belt One Road: China's Great Leap Outward", *China Analysis*, European Council on Foreign Relations and Asia Centre, 2015
12. Goh, Brenda and Ruwitch, John, "Pressure on as Xi's 'Belt and Road' enshrined in Chinese party Charter", https://www.reuters.com/article/us-china-congress-silkroad/pressure-on-as-xis-belt-and-road-enshrined-in-chinese-party-charter-idUSKBN1CT1IW. Accessed on December 26, 2017
13. Johnson, Christopher K. (2016), "President Xi Jinping's Belt and Road Initiative A Practical Assessment of the Chinese Communist Party's Roadmap for Global Resurgence", A Report of the CSIS Freeman Chair in China Studies, Centre for Strategic and International Studies.

5

South China Sea Conundrum - *plus ça change*

Abhay Kumar Singh

> *Plus ça change, plus c'est la même chose*
> (the more things change, the more they stay the same)
> Jean-Baptiste Alphonse Karr, *Les Guêpes*, January 1849

One of the key sources of the fragile strategic environment are the unresolved maritime disputes in the South China Sea. Due to longstanding complex legal disputes with overlapping claims and counter claims for jurisdictions, the South China Sea dispute is an intractable issue or 'wicked problem'[1] and has remained a simmering flashpoint for conflict since the seventies. A year ago, there was genuine apprehension that the South China Sea dispute could inflame a war in Southeast Asia. Prior to the decision by special tribunal convened in The Hague under the Law of the Sea ruled in July 2016, the region witnessed dangerous brinkmanship through the use of rhetoric and sabre-rattling. The prevailing strategic tension was further exacerbated since the tribunal concluded that the Chinese territorial claim in the South China Sea had no legal basis. China swiftly rejected the tribunal decision and maintained its assertive stance. The US, through sortie by ships and aircraft, renewed its freedom of navigation operations.

Notwithstanding a short period of heightened tension in the immediate aftermath, South China Sea has been relatively calm since The Hague Tribunal ruling in July 2016. Philippines followed by other ASEAN countries decided to tone down the rhetoric and commenced rapprochement with China which reciprocated through its charm offensive. China has avoided antagonising its neighbours and initiated process for a legally binding Code of Conduct (CoC) with the ASEAN. The primary driver of current entente is the discernible behavioural change of China and South China Sea claimants. However, whether these apparent behavioural modifications are strategic or tactical, remain an open question.

The paper assesses the strategic development in the South China Sea after the landmark decision by The Hague Tribunal. The paper outlines the arguments in three parts. The first part of the paper analyses some key events post The Hague Tribunal decision. The second part charts emerging geopolitical contours in the South China Sea through analysis of current end emerging geopolitical postures of ASEAN, claimants' states and the USA. The third part analyses the change and continuity in the South China Sea conundrum. This paper argues that notwithstanding efforts towards rapprochement South China is destined to remain a regional flashpoint and existing détente in the South China Sea may turn out proverbial calm before storm.

Key Events Post The Hague Tribunal Award

China's assertive approach in the South China Sea through the proclamation of its historical claims through nine-dash line and subsequent standoff at Scarborough Shoal compelled the Philippines to approach the Permanent Court of Arbitration at The Hague against China. China refused to participate in the arbitral proceeding. Much anticipated award of the tribunal was released on July 12, 2016. Even though it was expected that the tribunal award would be against China, in its 479 page ruling of the tribunal was extraordinarily in favour of Philippines position and had considered several elements of the Chinese claim in violation of the United Nations Convention on the Law of the Sea (UNCLOS). The key findings of the arbitration award have included:

- China's expansive claims through the nine-dash line and its claims of historic rights over waters in the South China Sea has no legal basis.
- None of the land features none of the Spratly Islands is capable of generating extended maritime zones of 200 nm.
- China violated the Philippines' sovereign rights by interfering with Philippines' legitimate activities in its EEZ.
- China caused "severe harm to the coral reef environment" with its land reclamation activities and harvesting of endangered species.[2]

During the tribunal proceedings, China had consistently questioned the legality and jurisdiction of the Tribunal. Exactly one week before the ruling,

Dai Bingguo, a noted Chinese diplomat, had remarked that "the arbitration case is political intrigue, whereby *certain countries have been deliberately provoking problems and stirring uptensions*, eager to see turbulence in the South China Sea". He added that "the final award of the arbitration amounts to *nothing more than a piece of paper*" and China "will never accept any solution imposed by a third party".[3]

Chinese response after the tribunal award was on expected lines. China's response to the tribunal decision was through a government statement which reaffirmed its 'territorial sovereignty and maritime rights' in the South China Sea and expressed its desire to "resolve the relevant disputes peacefully" without making explicit reference to either the Philippines or the arbitration proceedings.[4] The Chinese Ministry of Foreign Affairs declared that the ruling is "null and void and has no binding force."[5] China's also released a white paper terming the Philippines unilateral initiation of arbitration through The Hague Tribunal as an act of bad faith.

While Chinese response about The Hague Tribunal decision was as anticipated earlier, Philippines response, in contrast, was subdued. Shortly after the verdict was announced, the Philippines Foreign Secretary simply announced that government experts "are studying the Award with the care and thoroughness that this significant arbitral outcome deserves."[6] The key driver for change in the Philippines stance was the change of guard at Manila with the newly-inaugurated Rodrigo Duterte administration at the helm, which called for "restraint and sobriety" on the tribunal decision in its favour. The Duterte administration reverted back to a rapprochement policy towards Beijing akin to President Arroyo and set aside confrontational approach of the Aquino administration.

China Island Building—Strengthening Defences

According to a Taipei-based newspaper reported in March 2017, the Chinese experts in an internal PLA Journal has claimed that China's massive land reclamation projects have helped it to acquire the PLA's strategic advantage in military security in the South China Sea to a certain extent.[7] This report confirmed earlier assessments by the Center for Strategic and International Studies' Asia Maritime Transparency Initiative (AMTI) that construction of military and dual-use infrastructure on the so-called Big three islands in the contested Spratly chain—Subi, Mischief, and Fiery Cross reefs—is in the final stages, with the naval, air, radar and defensive facilities largely complete.[8] The satellite images offered some of the most conclusive evidence that China has continued to militarise the waters.[9] The Chinese Ministry of Defence also confirmed this through a statement in December

2016, "As for necessary military facilities, they are primarily for defence and self-protection, and this is proper and legitimate. For instance, if someone was at the door of your home, cocky and swaggering, how could it be that you wouldn't prepare a slingshot?"[10]

Although land reclamation through dredging and landfill has been undertaken since the late 1970s by Philippines and Malaysia in a limited manner. Later, Vietnam and Taiwan also initiated similar efforts.[11] However, the scale and speed of Chinese reclamation efforts have been astounding.[12] Reclamation efforts were accelerated post the commencement of arbitral proceedings by the Philippines in January 2013. Till late 2015, China added over 3,200 acres of land to the seven features (Mischief Reef, Cuarteron Reef, Fiery Cross Reef, Gaven Reef [North], Johnson Reef, Hughes Reef, and Subi Reef) it occupies; other claimants reclaimed approximately 50 acres of land over the same period.[13] China in effect built large artificial islands with airstrips, port facilities, buildings, and other installations including military equipment. China has plans for the establishment of underwater observation system in the South China Sea which in addition to its stated role for exploration of hydrocarbon can be used as anti-submarine surveillance system.[14] During his first state visit to the US in September 2015, Chinese President Xi Jinping had assured that "China does not intend to pursue militarization in the Nansha/Spratly Islands".[15] Military installations on the South China Sea reclaimed islands seem to be an abrogation of the assurance provided.

Seizure of US Navy UUV

On December 15, 2016, a PLA Navy ship captured an unmanned underwater vehicle (UUV) of the US Navy Ship Bowditch from international waters about 50 nautical miles (NM) north-west of Subic Bay in an area even outside the controversial nine-dash line proclaimed by China.[16] The Chinese official responses expressed routine dismay at continued military surveillance by the US with the retrieval being explained as removal of navigational hazards along with casual assertion about the incident occurrence in the Chinese waters with no further details or possessive implications.[17] The Chinese Foreign Ministry spokesperson told that "the Chinese side is firmly opposed to the frequent appearance of US military aircraft and vessels *in waters facing China* for close-in reconnaissance and military surveys [Emphasis added]".[18] Some Chinese commentators asserted Chinese maritime rights or claims over the area in which the UUV was seized.[19] This assertion was confirmed by the Chinese Ministry of Defence spokesperson in his statement on December 20, 2016, which noted that the UUV was captured in *"its water"*.[20]

Despite repeated assertions of its sovereignty and historic rights over water claimed within the controversial nine-dash line, China has neither clearly defined nature of its jurisdictional of control nor has promulgated the geographical coordinates of the nine-dash line which remains approximated to the drawing on maps submitted to the UN.[21] Since the location of the incident was even beyond the controversial nine-dash line, the incident has prompted broad speculation about the Chinese intent, including whether China was signalling even more expansive claims over the South China Sea (SCS).[22] The incident has also revived questions about Chinese strategic ambiguity regarding its nature of jurisdiction over waters enclosed within the nine-dash line which has since been nullified by The Hague Arbitration Tribunal judgement.[23]

Chinese White Paper on Asia-Pacific Security Cooperation

On January 11, 2017, China elucidated its position on Asia-Pacific security through its first white paper on its positions and policies on Asia-Pacific security cooperation.[24] One of the key operative dictums included in the white paper- which was immediately flagged by news agencies[25]—was an advice or warning to small and medium countries in the region that they "need not and should not take sides among big countries".[26] China's jurisdictional claims in the South China Sea and maritime security in the Asia-Pacific region was a key focus area of the white paper as a regional security concern.

The white paper noted misunderstandings and lack of mutual trust among some countries about traditional security as a concern for regional peace. A key concern of China is a provocation of regional disputes by "certain countries for their selfish interest", which it "resolutely opposes" and whose action compels China's retaliatory response. This seems to be an indirect reference to the Freedom of Navigation Patrols by the US. In a clear caution against external mediation efforts, the white paper asserts that "no effort to internationalise and judicialize the South China Sea issue will be of any avail for its resolution; it will only make it harder to resolve the issue and endanger regional peace and stability."[27]

For the settlement of disputes over territories and maritime rights, China asks the parties concerned to "respect historical facts" and seek a solution through negotiations under procedures of "universally recognised international law" and UNCLOS. In the Chinese view these "rules should not be dictated by any particular country", rather "regional and international rules should be discussed, formulated and observed by all concerned."[28]

The white paper highlighted that at present certain rules and their interpretations are being imposed in the regional context unilaterally by some countries in an apparent reference to prevailing interpretations about UNCLOS. While there was no reference to the 9-dash line in the white paper, the document did not indicate any softening on the jurisdictional claims in the South China Sea.

Revision on China's Maritime Safety Law

In February 2017, the Legislative Affairs Office of the Chinese State Council announced that it is soliciting public opinions on revisions to the 1984 Maritime Traffic Safety Law.[29] This revision would make foreign submersibles travel on the surface and report their movements to authorities when in China's waters. It has been reported that draft provisions would allow maritime authorities "to stop foreign ships entering Chinese waters if the ships are judged to be a possible cause of harm to navigational safety and order."[30] Generally, such a revision would be within the rights of a coastal state as enshrined within the UN Convention on the Law of the Sea (UNCLOS) since these apply within jurisdictional waters of the state viz internal water, territorial waters and Exclusive Economic Zone. However, China's Supreme People's Court has defined jurisdictional waters as including internal waters, territorial sea, contiguous zone, EEZ, continental shelf and "any other maritime areas under the People's Republic of China's jurisdiction."[31] Applying this definition to China's proposed rules could allow Beijing to extend its articulation of hot pursuit and a variety of criminal penalties to vast maritime areas—including waters within the 9-dash line.[32] Enforcement of these jurisdictional rights within the South China Sea will certainly heighten the existing strategic tension and would increase potential of conflict which in turn jeopardise the safety of SLOC within the South China Sea.

Code of Conduct—Progress or Lack of it?

ASEAN made its first effort to create a positive atmosphere for eventual Pacific settlement by adopting the 1992 ASEAN Declaration on the South China Sea which urged all parties to exercise self-restraint. In 2002, ASEAN and China agreed to sign a non-binding political statement on Declaration of Conduct (DOC) that promised to enhance favourable conditions for peace and find a durable solution to the differences and disputes among the countries concerned.[33] The efforts to evolve an acceptable Code of Conduct for parties has not made progress due to lack of support from China. In 2012, ASEAN failed to reach common ground on the South China

Sea issue, ending a regional conference without a joint statement—the first in its 45-year history.[34] One of the key expectation of The Hague Tribunal decision was that it would provide impetus in formulating a Code of Conduct (CoC) in the South China Sea which would commit all parties to the binding norms of behaviour, reducing the risk of clashes and restoring South East Asia's faith in China's pledge for peace and cooperation.[35] During a meeting of the Foreign Ministers of ASEAN and China in Vientiane in July 2016, commitment towards the full and effective implementation of the DoC was reaffirmed along with efforts progress towards early adoption of a CoC in the South China Sea.[36]

Negotiations on CoC, since then, has been pursued through various ASEAN-China forums. Suddenly, on March 8, 2017, on the sidelines of China's parliamentary session, Foreign Minister Wang Yi announced that the first draft of a framework for the code had been reached and "China and ASEAN countries feel satisfied with this."[37] In May 2017, Senior Officers Meeting on DoC indicated completion of the negotiation on a draft framework for CoC. This draft CoC framework will be considered during ASEAN-China Ministerial Conference in Manila in August 2017.[38] The draft framework has not yet been made public. One of the main priorities of the ASEAN was to finish the CoC, 15 years after the finalisation of the DoC and on the occasion of the Association's 50th anniversary. The CoC will help the ASEAN to reaffirm its central role in maintaining peace and stability in the region.

This progress on CoC is certainly a positive indicator, however, scepticism remains.[39] Beijing has certainly turned on its charm offensive and is trying to avoid further alienating its neighbours in the block. It also wants to reduce the scope of outsiders (viz the United States and Japan) to take political or military advantage of the disputes. ASEAN core motivation is to reaffirm its relevance in the regional security paradigm. Even so, given the numerous complexities entailed in the dispute, and also considering that Beijing will probably never give up its maritime assertiveness, the latest efforts to forge a binding agreement are bound to face the same problems that nearly derailed ASEAN process in 2012 in Phnom Penh.

Revival of Joint Development Proposal

Potential hydrocarbon resources in the South China Sea is one of the key drivers of South China's disputes. The area has not yet been adequately explored due to disputes, therefore it is difficult to accurately estimate the quantum of oil and gas in the South China Sea. The Chinese National Offshore Oil Company (CNOOC) had estimated in November 2012 that the South China Sea contains around 125 billion barrels of oil and 500 trillion cubic feet of natural gas.[40] The EIA estimates the South China Sea contains approximately 11 billion barrels of oil and 190 trillion cubic feet of natural gas in proved and probable reserves.[41] A much lower estimate of about 2.5 billion barrels of oil equivalent in the South China Sea has been provided by Wood Mackenzie, an energy consultancy firm.[42] Oil and gas exploration has occasionally provoked militarised confrontation and remain a source of constant tension. However, some commentators have argued that collaborative management of oil and gas resources could encourage cooperation on other contentious issues in the South China Sea dispute, including claimant countries' broader disagreement over political sovereignty.[43]

During the recent Belt and Road Forum, Philippine's Special Envoy for Intercultural Dialogue Jose de Venecia Jr proposed the joint development of hydrocarbon resources by China and South East Asian nations in the disputed territory of South China Sea.[44] Philippine President Rodrigo Duterte also endorsed joint exploration proposal with rival claimants China and Vietnam.[45]

Joint development of disputed territory in South China Sea pending decision on the vexing issue of sovereignty was first proposed by Chinese Premier Li Peng in August 1990.[46] This offer of joint development by China remained ignored by claimants till 2003. However, Philippines, under then-president Gloria Arroyo, did a volte face and forged a radically different course in its relation with China. Along with growing economic trade and developmental assistance from China, in November 2003 the Philippine National Oil Company (PNOC) and the China National Offshore Oil Company (CNOOC) signed a letter of intent to determine the oil and gas potential in the disputed areas of the South China Sea. On September 1 2004, the PNOC and the CNOOC signed a Joint Marine Seismic Undertaking (JMSU) for hydrocarbon prospecting in an area of 143,000 square kilometres.[47] Vietnam, initially unhappy with the Sino-Philippines arrangement, later joined the JMSU through an expanded agreement in March 2005.

Joint prospecting through the JMSU yielded some positive results by January 2007 and Phase 2 which was approved in June 2007. By this time political winds in the Philippines had started changing due to corruption allegation against President Arroyo due to deals funded by China.[48] An article in Far Eastern Review highlighted the secret terms and condition of JMSU and accused President Arroyo of making "breadth taking concession".[49] The expose led to an investigation by the Philippine Congress into the JMSU. Due to these controversies, JMSU agreement lapsed on July 1, 2008.[50] The Philippines Congress subsequently formulated the Archipelago Baseline Act in February 2010 in order to prevent future occurrence of JMSU-like agreements without due process and transparency.[51] Even though the JMSU agreement has lapsed, a case about the legality of the JMSU agreement is still pending the Philippines Supreme Court.[52]

It is pertinent to highlight that JMSU was the brainchild of current Special Envoy of Philippines Mr Jose De Venecia Jr, then Speaker of House of Representative. Sino-Philippines rapprochement of Arroyo regime was reversed during the tenure of President Aquino who adopted an aggressive approach on the South China Sea including the decision to pursue international arbitration over the Scarborough Shoal an exclusive economic zone. While the assertive action assuaged domestic nationalist constituency, relation with China touched nadir in bilateral relation. President Duterte has moved the clock back towards rapprochement with China.

Joint development for exploration of oil and gas in the South China Sea has obvious benefits as it can reduce strategic tension and unlock vital energy resource for economic benefit for the claimant states. However, the approach for revival the JMSU or similar agreement will have to surmount serious hurdles. For joint exploration to return as a viable alternative for conflict management in the South China Sea, China would have to rescind its assertiveness in South China Sea which includes unilateral explorations in South China and avoid harassment Filipino fishermen within the Philippine EEZ.[53] Domestic opposition within the Philippines is another issue which continues to oppose rapprochement and joint agreement. More serious issue however, is the pending decision in the Supreme Court which is yet to decide on the legality of the JMSU or similar agreement. Vietnam is another relevant stakeholder in joint exploration proposal and it has not indicated its position as yet on the issue.

Charting Emerging Geopolitical Contours in the South China Sea

ASEAN Fragility—A (dis)United Approach

Nothing has tested ASEAN members' institutional loyalty towards ASEAN's coveted motto of "One Vision-One Identity-One Community" more than the South China Sea. China's size, proximity, and power ensure it a dominant place in the ASEAN states' strategic perceptions. ASEAN members have been a major beneficiary of China's economic rise and remain greatly dependent on China for trade and assistance. While the murmur about the lack of cohesiveness of ASEAN about the South China Sea was present even earlier, this disunity became public in June 2012, when ASEAN summit ended without a joint statement.[54] During diplomatic negotiations with China on the South China Sea, members of ASEAN has not been able to display a cohesive and collective approach. The disunity was on full display when ASEAN failed to issue a communiqué after The Hague Tribunal Decision.[55] It is a fact that even now ASEAN member-states have differing views on the issues associated with the South China Sea.[56] The recent summit in Manila witnessed similar wrangling and the Chairman's statement was delayed for 12 hours and the final statement even omitted the concerns expressed of earlier years in order to avoid antagonising China.[57] This turnaround was even more perplexing since the Philippines had displayed considerable tenacity in its insistence about similar formulations earlier.[58]

Philippines' Flip Flop

President Duterte during his address to the customs officials in Manila on February 8 said in jest that "in every five statement I make, only two are true while three are just jokes".[59] Having achieved an overwhelming legal victory at The Hague Tribunal, it was expected that one of the approaches available with the Philippines was not to overplay its legal triumph. However, in a surprising move, Duterte administration decided to set aside the verdict and sided with China by announcing an intention to distance from its close ally the United States. The Entente was duly responded by China through economic and trade assistance. However, in an apparent change of stance in December 2016, Manila filed a protest with the Chinese Embassy over Beijing's reported military buildup on the islands and reefs in the contested Spratly Islands in the South China Sea.[60] In the interim in October 2016, Duterte promised to respect defence treaties with the United States, despite Duterte's publicised embrace of Beijing and divorce from Washington.[61] The Philippines Foreign Minister during a meeting of ASEAN Foreign Ministers, in February 2017 expressed "grave concerns" about China putting weapon installations on its man-made islands in the Spratlys. This led to the cancellation of planned visit of Chinese Commerce Minister to Manila. In an apparent turnaround, Duterte claimed that remarks of the Foreign Minister were misunderstood.[62] Another turn was evident on April 17, the Philippines ordered its military to occupy uninhabited islands and shoals it claims in the disputed the South China Sea, asserting Philippine sovereignty.[63] However, Philippines reverted to rapprochement during ASEAN summit on May 17 by omitting references on the South China Sea and raised prospects of joint exploration in the South China Sea during Belt and Road Forum. With so many flip flops, it is difficult to assess which part of Philippines approach towards China is true and which one is a joke.

Vietnam—A Contingent Approach

In the South China Sea dispute, Vietnam is a major claimant which has a largest overlapping claim against expansive jurisdictional assertions by China. Contrary to the expectation of proactive approach post-arbitral ruling by The Hague Tribunal, Vietnam's response has been somewhat muted. In its official response, Vietnam Foreign Ministry simply welcomed the decision along with reassertion of its stated claims in the South China Sea and assured more detailed response at a later date which did not materialise.[64] After the tribunal ruling, there have been several high-level visits to Beijing by Vietnamese officials which included Vietnamese Prime Minister Nguyen Xuan Phuc in September 2017 and Vietnamese Communist Party General Secretary Nguyen Phu Trong in January 2017. Vietnamese President Tran Dai Quang made a state visit to Belt and Road Forum in May 2017. Three high-level visits in less than a year to Beijing is an indication of progressive improvement in bilateral ties. However, it is pertinent to note that there has not been any substantive moderation of stance by Vietnam on the core issue of South China Sea dispute notwithstanding strengthening of economic cooperation between the two countries.[65] Vietnam has undertaken construction activities on Spratly Island which included extending its runway and added a new hanger.[66] During this period, Vietnam has also increased its interaction with Japan, India and the USA through similar high-level exchanges which have included visit of Prime Minister Modi to Vietnam in September 2016, visit of Japanese Prime Minister Abe to Hanoi in January 17, and visit of the Vietnamese Prime Minister Nguyen Xuan Phuc to the USA in May 2017. Vietnam has also strengthened its defence cooperation with India, Japan and USA. Vietnam's current apparent tilt towards China seems to be contingent on the expectation of moderation in China's approach towards contentious maritime dispute. However, as a hedging strategy, it is also strengthening its relation with major power in the region.[67] Vietnam certainly understands diversification of ties ¯ it is one of the tenets of the nation's foreign policy and it has greatly increased the number of its strategic partnerships.[68]

Indonesia—A Deft Balance

Indonesia had traditionally maintained a position of neutrality in South China Sea dispute as a non-claimant state, despite overlapping EEZ of its Natuna Island with China's nine-dash line. There have been repeated instances of incursion by Chinese fishing boat in the Indonesian EEZ around Natuna, which has resulted in firing by Indonesian Navy and seizure of Chinese fishing boat in June 2016. After the incident, Indonesian Foreign Minister Marsudi reiterated Indonesian non-claimant status in the SCS dispute and Indonesian legitimate EEZ around Natuna Island as per UNCLOS.[69] Chinese foreign ministry in response maintained that China and Indonesia have overlapping claims in the area and place of incident was traditional fishing ground for Chinese fishermen.[70]

Indonesia's relation with China is essentially driven by the regime and leadership changes in Jakarta, and in certain cases, the Indonesian state and society's treatment of its ethnic Chinese minority. Simply put, Indonesian domestic politics is a key driver in Jakarta's relations with Beijing rather than the economic rise of China per se or the allure of its soft power.[71] The Sino-Indonesia relationship has improved in recent times. China has provided Indonesia with a large export market for its trade commodities, especially in raw materials. There is a significant rise in the Chinese investment.[72] However in addition to simmering dispute at sea, blasphemy trial of Jakarta's governor Purnama, a Christian of Chinese origin and his subsequent defeat has again indicated the simmering racial fault line.[73] The spurt in the Chinese investment has spurred the fear about Chinese labour flooding Indonesia. In addition, Chinese infrastructure projects in Indonesia have acquired a reputation for low quality and late completion.[74]

On the South China Sea, Indonesia has been pushing for early completion of the code of conduct and respect for the international law. Ahead of the ASEAN Summit in Manila, President Jokowi proposed that States involved in the South China Sea dispute should engage in "concrete cooperation" well before any code of conduct is developed. The area of cooperation could include joint research in maritime resources, also working together to improve the maritime infrastructure in the area, and then developing the fishing industry.[75]

Indonesia under President Jokowi can be expected to continue to take unilateral action to reinforce the Indonesian position in the Natunas, both through military deployments and an increase in state-directed economic activity.[76] The expectation of economic assistance from China is constraining Indonesia to take a stronger position against China. As a hedging strategy,

Indonesia is also continuing its effort to build up close relation with Australia, US, India and Japan.

Malaysia and Brunei—Dilemma of Small Powers

Malaysia as a claimant state in the South China Sea has maintained an unreasonably passive stance on the issue despite the potential of undiscovered oil and gas are considerably high in the areas claimed by Malaysia. Malaysia's tempered approach to China has been attributed to, among other things, the burgeoning flow of trade and investment in recent years, which among others include the Malacca Gateway Project worth 10 billion dollars as the Belt and Road initiative[77] and the 395 million invested in the Kuantan Industrial Park.[78] Defence cooperation between the two countries has progressively strengthened since the conclusion of a formal defence pact in 2005 and has increased in last two years with inclusion of bilateral exercises and port visits by ships and submarine.[79]

China's assertive behaviour in the South China Sea has been causing some concerns in Malaysia. A report by the Malaysian Institute of Maritime Affairs (MIMA) highlights that "China is not perceived as a threat by Malaysia which practices a 'soft approach' towards China. However, this perception no longer can be sustained, and Malaysia (has) began to realise that such an approach provides no benefit in the long term because of the territorial disputes in the South China Sea."[80] This duality was evident on March 16, when Malaysia's National Security Minister revealed that about 100 Chinese vessels were found within the Malaysian EEZ in the South China Sea. Malaysian Defence Minister denied this encroachment by the Chinese vessels. However, Malaysia conveyed its concerns regarding the incursions by Chinese ships to the Chinese Ambassador. This episode alludes to the fact that Malaysia is not a unitary state actor in its approach to the South China Sea issue. Instead, various actors within Malaysia have sent different signals which are contrary to Malaysia's moderate posture towards the disputes.[81] Some analysts have sought to reconcile Malaysia's increasingly vocal stance over perceived Chinese assertiveness with its moderate and flexible approach. Given their close bilateral relations, particularly in the economic sphere, it would be counterproductive to strain bilateral ties.[82] Despite growing apprehension both internally and externally, the Malaysian Government will continue to rely on diplomacy and restraint for its policy in the South China Sea.

In the South China Sea, Brunei has the smallest claim and it is also the smallest claimant state. Brunei is the only claimant state that does not occupy any maritime features or maintain a military presence in the region.[83] Brunei is economically dependent on China also which is not only a major customer of Brunei hydrocarbon resources and also helping it to diversify its hydrocarbon-based economy. Since 2014, the Brunei-Guangxi Economic Corridor has led to over $500 million in joint investment commitments to develop strategic industries,[84] and more has been promised as a part of the Belt and Road initiatives.[85] Given its economic dependence on China and also its small size, Brunei maintains a low-key approach on the South China Sea and favours resolution through ASEAN-China dialogue process.

The Non-Claimant States

At the core of ASEAN's lack of consensus on the South China Sea is ambivalence of non-claimant members which include Laos, Cambodia, Thailand, Myanmar and Singapore. Cambodia and Laos during their chairmanship, in 2012 and 2016 respectively, of ASEAN had avoided adversarial references against China in the ASEAN joint statement due to intense lobbying by China. Both the countries were critically depended on economic and trade assistance from China and were the beneficiaries of Chinese largesse due to their efforts in toning down ASEAN rhetoric on the South China Sea.

China has claimed to have achieved a four-point consensus in April 2016 on the South China Sea with Laos, Cambodia and Brunei which reiterates resolution through dialogue among claimants.[86] Despite criticism, these countries have not denied the extant consensus. In aftermath of The Hague Tribunal decision, Laos openly sided with China in its refusal to the arbitral award.[87] Cambodia blocked references to the Arbitral proceeding during the ASEAN summit at Vientiane which also had the tacit support of Laos.[88]

Thailand had traditionally maintained a neutral position but seems to be tilting towards China due to growing military and economic assistance is progressively evident.[89] Thailand official statement on arbitral proceeding merely emphasised the need for joint effort in resolution for mutual benefit. In August 2016, when the Philippines raised the issue of Chinese attempt for construction at Scarborough Shoal, Thailand issued a statement in support of China's effort towards maintaining peace in the South China Sea dispute.[90] Myanmar relation with China has been tumultuous in recent times, though it has improved since last year.[91]

On the South China Sea issue, Myanmar has traditionally maintained a neutral stand. After the Tribunal decision, Myanmar statement indicated a balancing approach and urged all parties to exercise restraint and to refrain from threats or use of force. It added that despite China's refuting of the verdict, Myanmar is committed to the principle of rule of law.[92]

Even though Singapore has officially insisted that it takes no position on an Individual claim on the South China Sea, it has been advocating compliance with International Law in dispute settlement.[93] However, Singapore's approach on the South China Sea has invited harsh criticism from China.[94] Chinese Foreign Ministry indirectly accused Singapore that it had insisted on including South China Sea issues in the final document of Non-Aligned Movement (NAM) Summit held in Venezuela in September 2016.[95] China seized Singapore's armoured troop carrier in Hong Kong when it was returning after an exercise in Taiwan.[96] China did not invite Singapore in the Belt and Road Forum, despite it being one of the biggest advocates of the Belt and Road Initiative (BRI), in an apparent display of its displeasure.[97]

Extra-Regional Players

One of the key uncertainties in the South China Sea conundrum, post The Hague Tribunal decision has been ambivalence of the USA. During the UUV seizure incident, Trump displayed its strong views terming the UUV seizure by China as 'theft'. His rhetoric during the presidential campaign and early statements from his Cabinet nominees indicated a muscular approach towards China's growing assertiveness.[98] However, Trump administration policy on the South China Sea has been termed as directionless and adrift and mixed signals has added anxiety among US allies.[99] The US credibility in the region has also been hurt by Trump's decision to abandon the Trans-Pacific Partnership (TPP), a trade pact that was expected to have significant benefits for Southeast Asia and China has moved in the vacuum. Trump administration with its unidirectional focus on North Korea seems to have allowed China a free hand in the South China Sea.[100] After a long hiatus and significant pressure from Congress, the US Navy has begun its Freedom of Navigation exercise. During the recent Shangri-La Dialogue; General Mattis, Secretary of Defence, provided reassurances to the region about continued US commitments for regional security.[101] However, a cogent US policy of Trump administration on the South China Sea is yet to emerge.

Japan, on the other hand, has displayed its proactive approach through its sustained diplomacy and military presence notwithstanding Chinese opposition towards its regional engagement.[102] Japan's Prime Minister and Emperor visited Vietnam in the beginning of 2017 in an interval of six weeks to enhance its strategic partnership with Hanoi.[103] Japan has enhanced its maritime presence in the South China Sea through regular deployments[104] and naval exercises.[105] Japan has also loaned surveillance aircraft to the Philippines in its efforts to enhance its security engagement with the Philippines.[106] Apart from adopting more substantive defence cooperation initiatives in the South East Asia, Japan is also enhancing its defence cooperation with the US, India and Australia.

South China Sea Conundrum—Changes and Continuity

Prior to The Hague Tribunal decision, there existed ambiguity about the legal status of China's historic rights based nine-dash line and island features. Even though China has repudiated its award, the Tribunal has laid down a fundamental legal benchmark for future negotiation on this issue. Notwithstanding reclamation effort, none of the land features in the Spratly Island can claim EEZ. Similarly, China's nine-dash line claims will not have a legal basis notwithstanding its unilateral proclamation, unless UNCLOS itself gets reviewed on a future date which seems unlikely in near to mid-term. The tribunal decision, though at present has been set aside by the Philippines, will certainly feature prominently in the negotiated settlement process among claimant in future. In addition, options to seek enforcement of this award through international judicial process remain open to any of the claimants in the dispute in case of deadlock on the issue.

China has certainly managed to strengthen its military capabilities in the South China Sea through its reclamation efforts. A network of surveillance systems (Radar and Underwater) sensors and airfield on reclaimed islands has strengthened China's ability to monitor air, surface and subsurface activities. Available evidence thus far only indicate placement of defensive weapon system but this could change in short time during the crisis. Other claimants viz Vietnam and Philippines are also following Chinese footsteps and strengthening their military capability on land features under their control. The militarization of South China Sea enhances instability in the region.

Along with its diplomatic charm offensive, China has maintained its approach of creeping maritime assertiveness in the South China Sea. Status of the nine-dash line remains ambiguous and its response in the UUV seizure incidents has further compounded the ambiguity about geographical limits of its jurisdiction claims. While China has displayed overt support for the CoC process, it has not given any indication thus far about expectations of moderation of its jurisdictional claims.

Concerted efforts towards the formulation of CoC and joint development proposals in the South China Sea are a positive indication towards stabilising the strategic environment. It is pertinent to mention that CoC has been under discussion for more than two decades. The CoC formulation process got a fillip after The Hague Tribunal award. Thus far, there has only been an indication about agreement on a framework for CoC and the agreed framework itself has not been made public. Whether the current initiative will be able to surmount the past impasse remains an unanswered question. Joint development proposal is a revisit of the earlier unsuccessful experiment with JMSU and bitterness about its failure still lingers. At present, there exist a legal logjam in the Philippines on joint development and Vietnam remains sceptical.

Among the claimant states of the dispute, drastic change in Philippines' stance in its tilt towards China has certainly been most noticeable. At the same time, Philippines has shown willingness for hedging through enhancing its relation with Japan and has not divorced its relation with the US. Vietnam continues to maintain its balancing posture through its relation with the US, Japan and India along with its effort to enhance its economic engagement with China. Indonesia's current approach to the South China Sea and interest in better relations with China remains conditional on the delivery of investment pledges and its behaviour around the Natuna Islands. While Malaysia has been extremely proactive in seeking Chinese investment, its position on the South China Sea is nuanced and remains pragmatic in protecting its sovereignty. Brunei maintains its low-key approach.

On the issue, the South China Sea, there exist serious divergence among the ASEAN members. The non-claimant state does not wish to jeopardise their engagement with China. Cambodia and Laos have definitely made a political choice in favour of China. Thailand seems to be tilting towards China. Myanmar and Singapore maintain their balancing posture.

One of the key uncertainty in the region remains about the future outlook of the US towards western Pacific. The US allies in the region particularly Japan and Singapore—remain worried about the US pivoting back from the region and the resultant vacuum being occupied by the China. While the US retreat from the western Pacific in near term does not seem to be within the realm possibility, a range of mixed signals from Trump administration could be expected and long-term strategic implication of the US ambivalence on the South China Sea will emerge progressively.

Conclusion

In summary, there is certainly a visible softening of stance from claimant states on the South China Sea and China has similarly has changed its stance from aggressive rhetoric to passive assertiveness. Given this shift in the claimants' narrative, the non-claimant state has adopted an even milder approach. However, this does not indicate any fundamental change in the stated position of any of the actors. It appears that claimant States and China are deliberately playing down the issue for the time being. Relevant actors have shown willingness to engage on CoC through ASEAN though there exists scepticism about a definite outcome. Simultaneously, there is also a constant exploration of a hedging strategy and enhancing their defensive postures through military preparedness.

While ongoing big power rivalry between China and the United States remains a factor in the regional security environment, territorial disputes in the South China Sea are intractable due to their resonance in the respective national sentiments and due to their perceived importance in terms of potential resources and symbolic value to the national pride. While political expediency and economic benefit may induce pragmatism in short term, as evident in current scenario due to China's economic and diplomatic outreach to the countries in the region, it will still be difficult to surmount national emotion in absence of evidence of substantial give and take. China does not, yet, seems to be ready for required compromises.

Post-Hague Tribunal Award, China has certainly shown deft diplomacy in enhancing its economic and strategic influence in the region. Other than, minor players it has not managed to win over major regional player other than the Philippines, which had flipped toward China, is capable of flopping again. The "wicked problem" of South China Sea conundrum seems destined to exemplify epigram of French novelist Alphonso Karr stated at the beginning of the paper—*'Plus ça change, plus chest la même chose'* (the more things change, the more they stay the same).

NOTES

1. A wicked problem has innumerable causes, is tough to describe, and doesn't have a right answer, as we will see in the next section. Environmental degradation, terrorism, and poverty—these are classic examples of wicked problems. They're the opposite of hard but ordinary problems, which people can solve in a finite time period by applying standard techniques. Not only do conventional processes fail to tackle wicked problems, but they may exacerbate situations by generating undesirable consequences. See Rittel, Horst (1973), "Dilemmas in a General Theory of Planning," *Policy Sciences*, pp. 155-169
2. Permanent Court of Arbitration, Hague (July 12, 2016), "Press Release- The South China Sea Arbitration," Permanent Court of Arbitration, Hague, https://pca-cpa.org/wp-content/uploads/sites/175/2016/07/PH-CN-20160712-Press-Release-No-11-English.pdf.

3. "Speech by Dai Bingguo at China-US Dialogue on "South China Sea Between Chinese and US Think Tanks," http://www.fmprc.gov.cn/mfa_eng/zxxx_662805/t1377747.shtml, accessed May 25, 2017
4. "Statement of the Government of the People's Republic of China on China's Territorial Sovereignty and Maritime Rights and Interests in the South China Sea," http://www.fmprc.gov.cn/mfa_eng/zxxx_662805/t1379493.shtml, accessed May 25, 2017.
5. "Statement of the Ministry of Foreign Affairs of the People's Republic of China on the Award of July 12, 2016 of the Arbitral Tribunal in the South China Sea Arbitration Established at the Request of the Republic of the Philippines," http://www.fmprc.gov.cn/mfa_eng/zxxx_662805/t1379492.shtml, accessed May 25, 2017.
6. Jane Perlez, "Tribunal Rejects Beijing's Claims in South China Sea," *The New York Times*, July 12, 2016, sec. Asia Pacific, https://www.nytimes.com/2016/07/13/world/asia/south-china-sea-hague-ruling-philippines.html.
7. Kyodo News, "Chinese's Military Dominance in S. China Sea Complete: Report," *ABS-CBN News*, accessed May 29, 2017, http://news.abs-cbn.com/overseas/03/20/17/chineses-military-dominance-in-s-china-sea-complete-report.
8. Gregory B. Poling (January 12, 2017), "Prepare for a Stormy 2017 in the South China Sea," *Asia Maritime Transparency Initiative*, https://amti.csis.org/prepare-stormy-2017-south-china-sea/.
9. "China Archives," *Asia Maritime Transparency Initiative*, https://amti.csis.org/island-tracker/chinese-occupied-features/, accessed May 29, 2017.
10. Ministry of Defence, People Republic of China, "Ministry of Defense: China in Nansha Deployment of Necessary Defense Facilities Legitimate—the People's Republic of China Ministry of Defense," http://www.mod.gov.cn/shouye/2016-12/15/content_4766849.htm, accessed May 29, 2017.
11. US Department of Defense, "The Asia Pacific Maritime Strategy: Achieving US National Security Objectives in a Changing Environment," Washington DC: US Department of Defense, p. 13, https://www.defense.gov/Portals/1/Documents/pubs/NDAA%20A-P_Maritime_SecuritY_Strategy-08142015-1300-FINALFORMAT.PDF, accessed May 29, 2017.
12. Bill Hayton (2014), *The South China Sea: The Struggle for Power in Asia*, New Haven: Yale University Press, p. 82.
13. Office of the Secretary of Defense, "Annual Report to Congress: Military and Security Developments Involving the People's Republic of China 2016," A Report to Congress Pursuant to the National Defense Authorization Act for Fiscal Year 2000, Washington DC: US Department of Defense, p.13, https://www.defense.gov/Portals/1/Documents/pubs/2016%20China%20Military%20Power%20Report.pdf, accessed May 29, 2017.
14. James Griffiths CNN, "Beijing Plans Underwater Observation System in South China Sea," *CNN*, http://www.cnn.com/2017/05/29/asia/south-china-sea-underwater-observation-system/index.html, accessed May 30, 2017.
15. Jeremy Au Yong (September 27, 2015), "Tensions Remain as Xi's US Visit Ends," Text, *The Straits Times*, http://www.straitstimes.com/world/united-states/tensions-remain-as-xis-us-visit-ends.
16. Missy Rayan and Dan Lamothe, "Pentagon: Chinese Naval Ship Seized an

Unmanned U.S. Underwater Vehicle in South China Sea," *Washington Post*, https://www.washingtonpost.com/news/checkpoint/wp/2016/12/16/defense-official-chinese-naval-ship-seized-an-unmanned-u-s-ocean-glider/ accessed December 21, 2016.

17. People's Republic of China, Ministry of Defence Press Statement (December 18, 2016), "China to Hand Over Underwater Drone to US in Appropriate Manner", http://eng.mod.gov.cn/DefenseNews/2016-12/18/content_4767100.htm accessed December 21, 2016.
18. People Republic of China, Ministry of Foreign Affairs (December 19, 2016), "Foreign Ministry Spokesperson Hua Chunying's Regular Press Conference", http://www.fmprc.gov.cn/mfa_eng/xwfw_665399/s2510_665401/2511_665403/t1425479.shtml accessed December 28, 2016
19. Hua Yiwen (December 19, 2016), "Op-Ed: Underwater Drone Just a Sample of US Military Action against China" *People's Daily Online*, http://en.people.cn/n3/2016/1219/c98649-9156644.html. accessed December 21, 2017
20. People's Republic of China, Ministry of Defence Press Statement "China Hands over Underwater Drone to U.S.," http://eng.mod.gov.cn/DefenseNews/2016-12/20/content_4767308.htm, accessed December 28, 2016.
21. Zhiguo Gao and Bing Bing Jia (2013), "The Nine-Dash Line in the South China Sea: History, Status, and Implications", *The American Journal of International Law* 107 (1), pp. 98–124, doi:10.5305/amerjintelaw.107.1.0098. See also Chun Han Wong, "Nine-Dash Line's Ambiguity a Good Thing, Argues Chinese Military Academic", *WSJ*, June 5, 2016, at http://blogs.wsj.com/chinarealtime/2016/06/05/nine-dash-lines-ambiguity-a-good-thing-argues-chinese-military-academic/
22. Abhay Kumar Singh, "China's Creeping Maritime Assertiveness | Institute for Defence Studies and Analyses," *Institute for Defence Studies and Analyses*, accessed May 29, 2017, http://www.idsa.in/issuebrief/china-creeping-maritime-assertiveness_aksingh_030117.
23. Jeff M. Smith, "China's Drone Grab and the Dangers of "Strategic Ambiguity"' *The Diplomat*, http://thediplomat.com/2016/12/chinas-drone-grab-and-the-dangers-of-strategic-ambiguity/ accessed December 28, 2016.
24. "China Issues White Paper on Asia-Pacific Security Cooperation," *Xinhua News*, January 11, 2017, http://news.xinhuanet.com/english/2017-01/11/c_135973890.htm, accessed January 17, 2017.
25. "China Issues White Paper, Warns Small- and Medium-Sized Countries Not to Take Sides," *Channel NewsAsia*, January 12,2017 , http://www.channelnewsasia.com/news/asiapacific/china-issues-white-paper-warns-small-and-medium-sized-countries/3430786.html, accessed January 17, 2017.
26. "In Releasing Asia-Pacific Security White Paper, Beijing Sounds Warning to Small Countries to Avoid Taking Sides," *TODAYonline*, January 11, 2017, http://www.todayonline.com/world/releasing-asia-pacific-security-white-paper-beijing-sounds-warning-small-countries-avoid, accessed January 17, 2017.
27. "Full Text: China's Policies on Asia-Pacific Security Cooperation - Xinhua | English.news.cn," January 11, 2017, http://news.xinhuanet.com/english/china/2017-01/11/c_135973695.htm, Section IV (5), Paras 3-4.
28. Ibid, Section I, Para 9.
29. "China Mulls Revision of Maritime Safety Law - Xinhua | English.news.cn,"

http://news.xinhuanet.com/english/2017-02/14/c_136056397.htm, accessed May 30, 2017.

30. Ling Shumei, "Draft Maritime Law Revisions Say China May Bar Foreign Ships from Passing through Its Waters - Global Times," *Global Times*, February 15, 2016, http://www.globaltimes.cn/content/1033094.shtml.

31. "Supreme Court Promulgates the Judicial Interpretation of Relevant Cases in China 'S Jurisdiction - China's Court Network," http://www.chinacourt.org/article/detail/2016/08/id/2047233.shtml, accessed February 26, 2017.

32. Chris Mirasola (February 21, 2017), "Proposed Changes to China's Maritime Safety Law and Compliance with UNCLOS," *Lawfare*, https://www.lawfareblog.com/proposed-changes-chinas-maritime-safety-law-and-compliance-unclos.

33. Commodore AgusRustandi (2016), "The South China Sea Dispute: Opportunities for ASEAN to Enhance Its Policies in Order to Achieve Resolution," http://www.defence.gov.au/ADC/Publications/IndoPac/Rustandi_IPSP.pdf.

34. David Tweed and David Roman, "Chinese-ASEAN Meeting on South China Sea Ends in Confusion," *The Japan Times Online*, June 15, 2016, http://www.japantimes.co.jp/news/2016/06/15/asia-pacific/chinese-asean-meeting-south-china-sea-ends-confusion/.

35. Yanmei Xie, "Landmark South China Sea Ruling Could Revive Negotiations," *Crisis Group*, July 12, 2016, https://www.crisisgroup.org/asia/north-east-asia/china/landmark-south-china-sea-ruling-could-revive-negotiations.

36. "Joint Statement of the Foreign Ministers of ASEAN Member States and China on the Full and Effective Implementation of the Declaration on the Conduct of Parties in the South China Sea," http://asean.org/storage/2016/07/Joint-Statement-on-the-full-and-effective-implementation-of-the-DOC-FINAL.pdf, accessed February 25, 2017.

37. Hong Thao Nguyen (March 28, 2017), "A Code of Conduct for the South China Sea: Effective Tool or Temporary Solution? – Maritime Awareness Project," Seattle, WA: Maritime Awareness Project, The National Bureau of Asian Research, http://maritimeawarenessproject.org/2017/03/28/a-code-of-conduct-for-the-south-china-sea-effective-tool-or-temporary-solution/.

38. "Joint Press Briefing on the 14th ASEAN-China Senior Officials' Meeting on the Implementation of the Declaration on the Conduct of Parties in the South China Sea (SOM-DOC) | ONE VISION ONE IDENTITY ONE COMMUNITY," *ASEAN | ONE VISION ONE IDENTITY ONE COMMUNITY*, May 18, 2017, http://asean.org/joint-press-briefing-on-the-14th-asean-china-senior-officials-meeting-on-the-implementation-of-the-declaration-on-the-conduct-of-parties-in-the-south-china-sea-som-doc/.

39. Mark J. Valencia (May 4, 2017), "Why Great Expectations for Code of Conduct Will Be Dashed," *The Straits Times*, http://www.straitstimes.com/opinion/why-great-expectations-for-code-of-conduct-will-be-dashed.

40. Mikkal E Herberg (June 28, 2016), "The Role of Energy in Disputes over the South China Sea – Maritime Awareness Project," http://maritimeawarenessproject.org/2016/06/28/the-role-of-energy-in-disputes-over-the-south-china-sea/.

41. US Energy Information Administration (February 7, 2013), "South China Sea," Washington DC: US Energy Information Administration (EIA), https://www.eia.gov/beta/international/analysis_includes/regions_of_interest/

South_China_Sea/south_china_sea.pdf.

42. Jeremy Maxie, "The South China Sea Dispute Isn't About Oil, At Least Not How You Think," *Forbes*, http://www.forbes.com/sites/jeremymaxie/2016/04/25/the-south-china-sea-dispute-isnt-about-oil-at-least-not-how-you-think/, accessed May 24, 2017.
43. Shicun Wu, ed. (2014), *Recent Developments in the South China Sea Dispute: The Prospect of a Joint Development Regime*, London: Routledge, pp XV-XVI. See also Vanarith Chheang, "Joint Development Prospects in the South China Sea: Divergent and Convergent Forces", in Wu Shicun, Nong Hong (Eds.), *Recent Developments in the South China Sea Dispute: The Prospect of a Joint Development Regime*, Routledge, New York, 2014, pp. 172–180.
44. Ranada Pia (May 14, 2017), "Duterte Envoy De Venecia Proposes Joint Development with China," *Rappler*, http://www.rappler.com/nation/169801-jose-de-venecia-joint-oil-gas-development-south-china-sea.
45. Agence France-Presse (AFP), "Duterte Ponders Resources Deals with China, Vietnam in South China Sea," *South China Morning Post*, May 16, 2017, http://www.scmp.com/news/asia/diplomacy/article/2094488/philippine-president-rodrigo-duterte-open-south-china-sea.
46. Nayan Chanda and Tai Ming Cheung (August 1990), "Reef Knots: China Seeks ASEAN Support for Spratly Plan", *Far Eastern Economic Review*, p. 11.
47. Bill Hayton (2014), *The South China Sea: The Struggle for Power in Asia*, New Haven: Yale University Press, pp 130-134.
48. Ellen T. Tordesillas, "OPINION: Recalling JMSU," *ABS-CBN News*, http://news.abs-cbn.com/blogs/opinions/04/25/17/opinion-recalling-jmsu, accessed May 24, 2017.
49. Ibid , p 135.
50. Donnabelle Gatdula, "Joint Exploration Pact Lapses," *Philstar.com*, http://www.philstar.com/headlines/72480/joint-exploration-pact-lapses, accessed May 24, 2017.
51. Ernest J Bower (July 27, 2010), "The JMSU: A Tale of Bilateralism and Secrecy in the South China Sea'" *Center for Strategic and International Studies*, https://www.csis.org/analysis/jmsu-tale-bilateralism-and-secrecy-south-china-sea.
52. Tordesillas, "OPINION," n. 48
53. Carlos Santamaria, "Time to Revive the Joint Marine Seismic Undertaking in the South China Sea?," Issue Briefings (Taipei, Taiwan: South China Sea Think Tank, Asia-Pacific Policy Research Association), https://storage.googleapis.com/scstt/publications/Issue-Briefings-2016-15-Santamaria.pdf, accessed May 24, 2017.
54. Tweed and Roman, "Chinese-ASEAN Meeting on South China Sea Ends in Confusion."
55. Manuel Mogato, Michael Martina, and Ben Blanchard (July 26, 2017), "ASEAN Deadlocked on South China Sea, Cambodia Blocks Statement," *Reuters*, http://www.reuters.com/article/us-southchinasea-ruling-asean-idUSKCN1050F6.
56. Liu Zhen and Catherine Wong (July 28, 2016), "Most Asean Countries 'want to Stay out of Beijing's South China Sea Dispute with the Philippines'," *South China Morning Post*, http://www.scmp.com/news/china/diplomacy-defence/article/1995991/most-asean-countries-want-stay-out-beijings-south-china.
57. Manuel Mogato (April 30, 2017), "ASEAN Gives Beijing a Pass on South China

Sea Dispute, Cites 'Improving Cooperation,'" *Reuters*, http://www.reuters.com/article/us-asean-summit-idUSKBN17W02E.

58. Prashanth Parameswaran (May 4, 2017), "The Truth About Duterte's ASEAN South China Sea Blow | The Diplomat," *Diplomat*, http://thediplomat.com/2017/05/the-truth-about-dutertes-asean-south-china-sea-blow/.
59. Alexis Romero, "Duterte Admits Only 2 out of 5 of His Statements Are True," *Philstar.com*, http://www.philstar.com/headlines/2017/02/08/1670526/duterte-admits-only-2-out-5-his-statements-are-true, accessed June 4, 2017.
60. Lindsay Murdoch (April 8, 2017), "South China Sea Dispute: Can Rodrigo Duterte Be Taken Seriously?," *The Sydney Morning Herald*, http://www.smh.com.au/world/south-china-sea-dispute-can-rodrigo-duterte-be-taken-seriously-20170407-gvfu3i.html.
61. Martin Petty Reuters, "Duterte Says Honoring Defense Pacts with 'Friends' US," *ABS-CBN News*, http://news.abs-cbn.com/news/11/11/16/duterte-says-honoring-defense-pacts-with-friends-us, accessed June 4, 2017.
62. "Duterte Says China Misunderstood Philippine Minister's South China Sea Remarks," *Reuters*, February 24, 2017, http://www.reuters.com/article/us-philippines-china-idUSKBN1630X6.
63. Manuel Mogato, "Philippines' Duterte Orders Occupation of Isles in Disputed South China Sea," *Reuters*, April 6, 2017, http://www.reuters.com/article/us-southchinasea-philippines-idUSKBN1780NR.
64. The Ministry of Foreign Affairs of Vietnam, "Remarks of the Spokesperson of the Ministry of Foreign Affairs of Viet Nam on Viet Nam's Reaction to the Issuance of the Award by the Tribunal Constituted under Annex VII to the United Nations Convention on the Law of the Sea in the Arbitration between the Philippines and China," The Ministry of Foreign Affairs of Vietnam, Hanoi, http://www.mofa.gov.vn/en/tt_baochi/pbnfn/ns160712211059/view, accessed June 4, 2017.
65. Xuan Loc Doan (January 19, 2017), "Is Vietnam Tilting toward China?," *Asia Times*, accessed June 4, 2017, http://www.atimes.com/vietnam-tilting-toward-china/
66. Derek Grossman (March 2, 2017), "China Tolerating Vietnam's South China Sea Activities, For Now," *China Brief, Jamestown Foundation* 17, no. 3, https://jamestown.org/program/china-tolerating-vietnams-south-china-sea-activities-now/
67. Andrew Chubb (February 2, 2017), "Vietnam and China: Contingent Cooperation, Not Capitulation," *East Asia Forum*, http://www.eastasiaforum.org/2017/02/02/vietnam-and-china-contingent-cooperation-not-capitulation/
68. Helen Clark (November 28, 2016), "Between an Uncertain Duterte and Trump and a Powerful China, Vietnam Sees Stability in ASEAN," *Huffington Post*, http://www.huffingtonpost.com/entry/duterte-trump-china-vietnam-asean_us_58361b9ee4b09b6056002121.
69. Liza Yosephine, "Minister Echoes Indonesia's Stance on South China Sea," *The Jakarta Post*, http://www.thejakartapost.com/news/2016/06/21/minister-echoes-indonesias-stance-on-south-china-sea.html, accessed June 6, 2017.
70. "Foreign Ministry Spokesperson Hua Chunying's Remarks on Indonesian Navy Vessels Harassing and Shooting Chinese Fishing Boats and Fishermen," http://www.fmprc.gov.cn/mfa_eng/xwfw_665399/s2510_665401/t1373402.shtml,

accessed June 6, 2017.

71. Chin, Christine. S. (2007), "The Chinese Indonesian's Role in Substantiating Sino-Indonesian Strategic Partnership", *Indonesian Quarterly, 35*(4), 333-347
72. "Why Indonesia Is Chasing China's Billions," *Bloomberg.com*, October 31, 2016, https://www.bloomberg.com/news/articles/2016-10-31/china-deepens-economic-ties-with-indonesia-as-investment-doubles.
73. Oliver Holmes (November 25, 2016), "Jakarta's Violent Identity Crisis: Behind the Vilification of Chinese-Indonesians," *The Guardian*, https://www.theguardian.com/cities/2016/nov/25/jakarta-chinese-indonesians-governor-ahok.
74. John Mcbeth, "In Indonesia, Chinese Appeal Undimmed by Power Failures," *South China Morning Post*, http://www.scmp.com/week-asia/geopolitics/article/2053395/why-does-indonesia-cling-its-plagued-chinese-infrastructure, accessed June 8, 2017.
75. Zuraidah Ibrahim (April 29, 2017), "Exclusive: Widodo's Peace Formula for South China Sea," *South China Morning Post*, http://www.scmp.com/week-asia/geopolitics/article/2091549/exclusive-widodos-peace-formula-south-china-sea.
76. Aaron L. Connelly (December 2016), "Indonesia in the South China Sea: Going It Alone" Lowy Institute for International Policy, https://www.lowyinstitute.org/sites/default/files/documents/Connelly%2C%20Indonesia%20in%20 the%20South%20China%20Sea.pdf.
77. RSN Murali (November 8, 2015), "RM43bil Investment in Malacca Gateway a Boost to Malaysia, Says Liow - Nation | The Star Online," *The Star*, http://www.thestar.com.my/news/nation/2015/11/08/china-to-spur-growth-of-ports-rm43bil-investment-in-malacca-gateway-a-boost-to-malaysia-says-liow/.
78. Melisa Goh, "Malaysia-China Kuantan Industrial Park Seals US$395m Worth of Deals," *Channel NewsAsia*, http://www.channelnewsasia.com/news/business/malaysia-china-kuantan-industrial-park-seals-us-395m-worth-of-de-8017736, accessed June 7, 2017.
79. Prashanth Parameswaran (February 2015), "Playing It Safe: Malaysia's Approach to the South China Sea and Implications for the United States," *Maritime Strategy Series*, Washington DC: Center for a New American Studies, https://www.files.ethz.ch/isn/189746/CNAS%20Maritime%206_Parameswaran_Final.pdf.
80. Sumathi Permal and Martin A. Sebastian, "Strategic Management for South China Sea: Defence and Security Options for Malaysia," Kuala Lumpur: Centre for Maritime Security & Diplomacy, Maritime Institute of Malaysia, accessed June 6, 2017, http://www.mima.gov.my/images/page/research/Strategic_managment_in_the_South_China_Sea.pdf.
81. David Han (May 5, 2016), "Why Malaysia's South China Sea Policy Seems Confused," *The Straits Times*, http://www.straitstimes.com/opinion/why-malaysias-south-china-sea-policy-seems-confused.
82. Elina Noor (January 8, 2016), "Malaysia: Recalibrating Its South China Sea Policy?," *Asia Maritime Transparency Initiative*, https://amti.csis.org/malaysia-recalibrating-its-south-china-sea-policy/.
83. Pete Cobus, "South China Sea: Conflict and Diplomacy on the High Seas," //projects.voanews.com/south-china-sea/recent/, accessed June 7, 2017.
84. Gary Sands (April 28, 2016), "Brunei, Silent Claimant in the South China Sea,"

Foreign Policy Blogs, https://foreignpolicyblogs.com/2016/04/28/brunei-silent-claimant-south-china-sea/.

85. *Xinhua* (May 12, 2017), "China, Brunei to Further Cooperation under B&R Initiative," http://english.gov.cn/news/international_exchanges/2017/05/12/content_281475653339956.htm.
86. "Wang Yi Talks about China's Four-Point Consensus on South China Sea Issue with Brunei, Cambodia and Laos," http://www.fmprc.gov.cn/mfa_eng/zxxx_662805/t1358478.shtml, accessed June 7, 2017.
87. Nandini Krishnamoorthy (July 15, 2017), "Laos Backs China over South China Sea Dispute, Rejects Hague Ruling," *International Business Times UK*, http://www.ibtimes.co.uk/laos-backs-china-over-south-china-sea-dispute-rejects-hague-ruling-1570737.
88. Mogato, Martina, and Blanchard, "ASEAN Deadlocked on South China Sea, Cambodia Blocks Statement."
89. Zhang Zhihao, "China Hopes to Boost Military Ties with Thailand, Defense Minister Says - China," *Chinadaily.com.cn*, http://www.chinadaily.com.cn/china/2016-12/13/content_27653884.htm, accessed June 7, 2017.
90. "Thailand 'Supports' China's Efforts to Maintain Maritime Peace," *Reuters*, September 7, 2016, http://www.reuters.com/article/asean-summit-southchinasea-thailand-idUSL3N1BJ27A.
91. Kavi Chongkittavorn (April 22, 2016), "Myanmar and Major Powers: Shifts in Ties with China, Russia and the US," *The Straits Times*, http://www.straitstimes.com/opinion/policy-shifts-in-myanmars-ties-with-major-powers.
92. Nyan Lynn Aung (July 19, 2016), "Myanmar Wades in to South China Sea Ruling with a Balancing Act," *The Myanmar Times*, http://www.mmtimes.com/index.php/national-news/21447-myanmar-wades-in-to-south-china-sea-ruling-with-a-balancing-act.html.
93. Charissa Yang (July 12, 2016), "Singapore Takes No Position on South China Sea Claims, Calls for Restraints," *The Straits Times*, http://www.straitstimes.com/asia/se-asia/spore-takes-no-position-on-s-china-sea-disputes.
94. "China Should Make Singapore Pay over South China Sea Dispute, Says PLA Adviser," *The Straits Times*, October 1, 2016, http://www.straitstimes.com/asia/east-asia/china-should-make-singapore-pay-over-south-china-sea-dispute-says-pla-defence-adviser.
95. Laura Zhou (September 27, 2016), "Why Singapore's Caught between China, ASEAN in New South China Sea Row," *CNBC*, http://www.cnbc.com/2016/09/27/singapore-caught-between-asean-china-on-south-china-sea.html.
96. Katie Hunt (November 30, 2016), "Troop Carriers Seized: Is China Sending Singapore a Message? - CNN.com,"http://edition.cnn.com/2016/11/29/asia/china-singapore-taiwan-troop-carriers/index.html.
97. Angela Han, "How China Snubbed Singapore at the Belt and Road Summit," https://www.lowyinstitute.org/the-interpreter/how-china-snubbed-singapore-belt-and-road-summit, accessed June 7, 2017.
98. Mark J. Valencia (May 14, 2017), "Trump's Troubling South China Sea Policy," *The Japan Times*, http://www.japantimes.co.jp/opinion/2017/05/14/commentary/world-commentary/trumps-troubling-south-china-sea-policy/.

99. Mira Rapp-Hooper, Mira Rapp-Hooper, and Charles Edel (May 18, 2017), "Adrift in the South China Sea," *Foreign Affairs*, https://www.foreignaffairs.com/articles/asia/2017-05-18/adrift-south-china-sea.
100. Javier C. Hernández (May 10, 2017), "Trump's Mixed Signals on South China Sea Worry Asian Allies," *The New York Times*, https://www.nytimes.com/2017/05/10/world/asia/trump-south-china-sea-allies.html.
101. "Remarks by Secretary Mattis at Shangri-La Dialogue," *U.S. Department of Defense*, https://www.defense.gov/News/Transcripts/Transcript-View/Article/1201780/remarks-by-secretary-mattis-at-shangri-la-dialogue/, accessed June 7, 2017.
102. "China Pledges Firm Response If Japan Interferes in South China Sea," *Reuters*, March 16, 2017, http://www.reuters.com/article/us-japan-navy-southchinasea-china-idUSKBN16N167.
103. Le Hong Hiep (April 11, 2017), "The Strategic Significance of Vietnam-Japan Ties," *Perspective*, Singapore: ISEAS-YusofIshak Institute, https://www.iseas.edu.sg/images/pdf/ISEAS_Perspective_2017_23.pdf.
104. Emiko Jozuka CNN, "Japan to Join US in South China Sea Patrols," *CNN*, http://www.cnn.com/2016/09/15/asia/japan-south-china-sea-patrols/index.html, accessed June 7, 2017.
105. CNBC (March 13, 2017), "Japan Plans to Send Largest Warship to South China Sea, Sources Say," *CNBC*, http://www.cnbc.com/2017/03/13/japan-plans-to-send-largest-warship-to-south-china-sea-sources-say.html.
106. Agence France-Presse, "Japan Loans Manila Military Planes for South China Sea," *ABS-CBN News*, http://news.abs-cbn.com/news/03/28/17/japan-loans-manila-military-planes-for-south-china-sea, accessed June 7, 2017.

6

Chinese Ambitions in the Indian Ocean Region

Adarsha Verma

ABSTRACT

China's recent and increasing forays in the Indian Ocean Region (IOR) through its maritime assets, have added a new dimension to the security dynamic of the region. The lack of an articulated Chinese maritime policy for the Indian Ocean, further accentuates the uncertainty of intent. Based on recent developments, this paper analyses Chinese ambitions in the IOR and the likely future maritime prospects. In view of China's proposed logistical infrastructure in key locations in the IOR, its naval ships could maintain a prolonged presence in the Indian Ocean. However, an understanding of its intentions is paramount. The conversion of a logistics facility into a military base is not very effort intensive. Weaker economies with large debts, may find it difficult to deny Chinese naval ships the use of their ports, in conflict like situations. Viewing the possible India-Japan-US quasi-alliance as an obstacle to achieving its ambitions in the IOR, China is preparing itself for any competition that will arise, by a deliberate attempt at strategic vagueness, thereby gaining the opportunity to escalate naval activity, at a time of their choosing.

The rise of China is accompanied by increasing maritime activity that stretches from the nearby seas into the Indian Ocean Region (IOR). It has the potential to change the status quo in the Indo-Pacific region. Moreover, it ushers in the Chinese navy as the new dominant player in the security dynamic of this region. The lack of an articulated Chinese maritime policy for the Indian Ocean further accentuates the uncertainty of the intent, behind this activity overdrive. This article attempts to track developments in the IOR, explore Chinese ambitions in the Indian Ocean and the likely future maritime implications for this region.

The Indian Ocean Region is diverse with resource-rich emerging markets, trading hubs and varied geo-political entities. It has the world's largest concentration of hydrocarbon reserves on its west and an industrial powerhouse on its east, thereby becoming a maritime highway which converges at the Malacca Straits, resulting in a confluence of the Indian and Pacific Oceans. Geographically, the Indian Ocean is connected to other oceans through constricted water passages or 'choke points' which also act as the gateways to the outside world. Afonso De Albuquerque, the legendary Portuguese sailor and a military genius of the 16th century had attempted to close all the Indian Ocean naval passages to the Atlantic, Red Sea, Persian Gulf and to the Pacific, transforming it into a Portuguese *mare clausum*, in spite of the opposition of the Ottoman Empire and its allies.[1] Though a similar closing of the Indian Ocean may seem far-fetched, but the wresting of control of the Sea Lines of Communications (SLOCs) by a few select countries will cause consternation in the rest of the world. The increasing Chinese naval presence in the Indian Ocean region in the Chinese view, would protect their energy supply against any undue disruption, during any potential conflict situation. As the Chinese global presence is expanding, the criticality of securing its energy supplies seems to be driving the Chinese maritime strategy in the Indian Ocean region.

Global Expansion of the Middle Kingdom

China's global presence is not an anomaly. Since the Zhou dynasty (1122-256 B.C.), China has considered itself to be the Middle Kingdom and the epitome of civilisation, with power flowing from this Middle Kingdom outwards to the world. The king, with a mandate from heaven, was considered to be the mediator between heaven and earth.[2] This narrative still runs strong and China harbours the ultimate ambition of establishing itself as a global power. There is a strong connection between its vision of being a great power and the resurgence of the Chinese nation. As the Chinese scholar Ye Zicheng said: "If China does not become a world power, the rejuvenation of the Chinese nation will be incomplete. Only when it becomes a world power can we say that the total rejuvenation of the Chinese nation has been achieved."[3]

These themes are a common feature of Chinese political discourse. The Chinese President Xi Jinping, in one of his keynote speeches, spoke about the China Dream and said; "In my view, to realise the great renewal of the Chinese nation is the greatest dream for the Chinese nation in modern history". Similar views have been articulated in greater detail in the book, *The China Dream: Great Power Thinking and Strategic Posture in the Post-American Era*, by Colonel Liu Mingfu, where the author argues that China should challenge the dominant position of the US and try to replace the US as the number one power. Liu apparently believes that the era of US dominance is over, and as such, China should stand up and seek global leadership. The phrase 'China Dream' is prominent in the references by government officials and has become a sort of national slogan, repeated widely in the social media and newspapers and celebrated in schools and universities.[4] The central authorities have promulgated several new concepts, on the road to rejuvenation including the two Centennial Goals, which embody the grand vision and ambitious ideals of the China Dream.[5]

Right from the Third Plenary Session of the 11th Central Committee in December 1978, Chinese firms and organisations have been urged to focus on "reform and opening", thus paving the way for China's global expansion. Throughout the 1980s and 1990s, Chinese firms and organisations were urged to 'go global' by means of various policies and incentives. This globalisation mission was holistic and comprehensive as the Chinese realised that this was an imperative for 'power,' which needs to be multifarious and multi-dimensional.[6] Having been a territorial power throughout history, maritime power had been neglected and was under developed. Consequently, Chinese leaders commenced upon a naval modernisation drive and China embarked upon building a strong naval arm. Then in November 2012, President Hu Jintao in his work report to the Chinese Communist Party's 18th Party Congress declared that China's objective is to be a *haiyang qiangguo*—that is a strong or great maritime power.[7] President Xi on the other hand took a leaf out of the Mahanian concept of power, which was evident in an internal speech that he gave to the Central Military Commission. He stated that:

> In the 21st century, mankind has entered the age of the large-scale exploitation of the sea.... History and experience tell us that a country will rise if it commands the oceans well and will fall if it surrenders them.... We must adhere to a development path of becoming a rich and powerful state by making use of the sea.[8]

Also, Chinese official documents have been stressing the importance of enhancing China's maritime presence. For example, China's Defence White paper of 2015 states, "the traditional mentality that land outweighs the sea must be abandoned" and greater attention has to be paid to "managing the seas and oceans and protecting maritime rights and interests". Simultaneously, the readership for the works of naval strategists like Mahan and Corbett has also been growing rapidly and strategic naval discourse has slowly started embedding itself in Chinese strategic thinking. Liu Cigui, director of State Oceanic Administration (SOA), explains it thus: "Building China into a maritime power is an essential path on the way to the sustained development of the Chinese nation and [achievement of the status of a] global power. A 'maritime power' is a country that has great comprehensive strength in terms of the development, use, protection, management, and control of the seas."[9]

Whereas Chinese activities in the near seas (Pacific Ocean) point towards maritime consolidation with security and economic overtones, their activities in the far seas, especially the Indian Ocean, indicate their strategic ambitions that also have a economic, military and political dimension, because of their overarching desire to attain global power status. These economic, military and political dimensions are deeply intertwined, complementary and reveal the likely Chinese intentions in the IOR.

Economic Imperatives

China has strong economic imperatives for its growing maritime presence in the IOR. According to scholars like Chen Shaofeng of Peking University, oceans have been important sources of economic wealth, commercial growth and national security since historic times. In other words, he re-iterates the primacy of oceans in present day Chinese thought. This is, particularly, true for Asian countries like China that are dependent on the sea for their commercial life and economic health.[10] In fact, the US Energy Information Administration (EIA) data has revealed that China has been the world's largest energy consumer since 2010[11] and projects that by 2040, China will consume more than twice as much energy as the United States.[12] This would result in China being increasingly reliant on imported oil and gas with the import dependence increasing to almost 60 percent by 2020.[13] A major share of its energy requirements (approximately 68 percent) are being met from sources in the IOR (Refer figure on the distribution of Chinese energy imports given on next page.)

Therefore, the primary concern for China is ensuring the security of its shipping assets in the IOR from the Persian Gulf to the West Pacific that are carrying these much-needed hydrocarbons. This is in keeping with its ambition to dominate the SLOCs. Its sense of vulnerability must also be seen in conjunction with the non-conventional maritime threats of piracy and terrorism. It is symptomatic that SLOC protection thus calls for capabilities that can maintain a maritime presence under hostile conditions for prolonged periods, even under unfavourable maritime conditions.

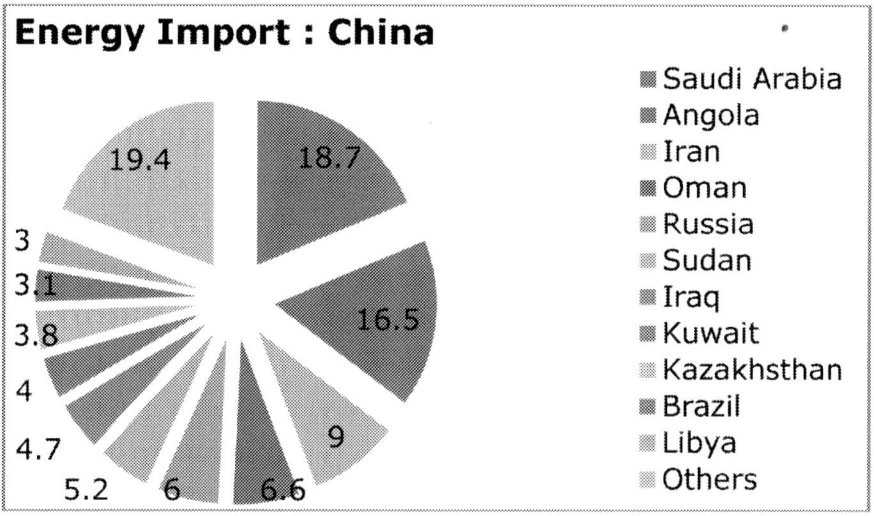

Source: EIA and FACTS Global Energy 2015.

China requires unhindered access for Chinese ships that carry 60 per cent of its domestic energy requirements across the IOR expanse.

The Malacca Strait which is 2.8 kms (1.5 nautical miles) at its narrowest is a bottleneck, in this thriving supply chain in the IOR and thus is often referred to as the 'Malacca Dilemma' in Chinese security circles. James Holmes and Toshi Yoshihara writing on 'China's Naval Ambitions in the Indian Ocean' have quoted Shi Hongtao as saying that, "it is no exaggeration to say that whoever controls the Strait of Malacca will also have a stranglehold on the energy route of China. Thus, excessive reliance on this Strait poses an important potential threat to China's energy security".[14] The phrase the, "Malacca Dilemma" (*Maliujia kunju*) is not new in Chinese thinking. It was first coined by President Hu Jintao, at the closing of a Chinese Communist Party (CCP) economic work conference in November 2003, when he publicly commented on the increasingly complex problem of energy security in the light of China's increasing dependence upon oil imports, especially those from the Middle East. Hu noted that, "certain powers have all along encroached on and tried to control navigation through the strait,"[15] This is a direct reference to the US, which has been exerting significant influence on navigation through the Strait. An attempt to *mare clausum*[16] the Indian Ocean by China's adversaries would significantly hamper the economic rise of China and this in turn, will negatively affect the economic well-being of the people of China—a core interest of the CPC. The economic dimension thus is an important security imperative for controlling the entire energy route from the source up to the Chinese shores. Though this is also true for other East Asian countries like Japan and South Korea, the level of mistrust between China and dominant powers in the IOR like the US and India, spurs China to strengthen its own security arrangements in this region.

The security arrangements that China would like to develop in the future form part of its Belt and Road Initiative (BRI). The IOR because of its enhanced significance for China features prominently in the Maritime Silk Route (MSR) (part of the BRI). In China's view, the 21st Century Maritime Silk Route is consistent with the rising status of China. Given that the Chinese government, from Xi downward, has committed vast diplomatic and financial resources, as well as personal prestige to take the BRI forward,[17] the ambition to execute it, is evident. In particular, the MSR entails making the Indian Ocean the maritime bridge that connects China with South Asia, Africa and Europe. As part of its vision for common development and a "community of shared future", the MSR will encompass a number of ports and bases along the old Silk Route, followed by Zheng He, in the 16th century during the rule of the Ming dynasty. Incidentally, the littorals in the IOR are all developing and infrastructure hungry nations that are seeking avenues for mitigating poverty and going up the development ladder. These ports and bases will be developed with Chinese assistance (financial and infrastructure) and would greatly enhance trade prospects of China, especially at a time when it is facing declining domestic growth rates.

Currently, Chinese firms are vigorously investing outside China, more so in the littorals of the IOR. China's foreign direct investment (FDI) outside China exceeded $ 220 billion in 2016 surging 246 per cent from 2015, a major part of which went to the 'Belt and Road' countries.[18] Chinese loans to many IOR littorals in Asia and Africa far outstrip the loans that these countries receive from IMF or other developed countries. FDIs tend to monopolise resources and favour the investor while supplanting domestic enterprises and creating a balance of payment problem, for recipient countries. Political and diplomatic dependence follows shortly, if the countries are unable to pay the loans.

In addition to the outside investment, China is also looking at the IOR sea-bed for resource extraction for continued economic growth. Currently, the China Ocean Mineral Resources Research and Development Association (COMRA) has been granted exploration rights over an area of 10000 sq. kms in the South West Indian Ocean Ridge (SWIR) till November 17, 2026, for exploration of polymetallic sulphides.[19] The SWIR is a divergent tectonic plate boundary between the African and Antarctic plates, in the Indian Ocean, south of Madagascar. A similar exploration is also underway in the Clarion-Clipperton Fracture Zone (Pacific Ocean), for exploration of polymetallic nodules. India believes that this could impact its security, as it requires the extended presence of Chinese ships in the Indian Ocean.[20] Also, China would be able to map the ocean floor and have the opportunity to intercept undersea communication links. Understanding India's concerns, China has invited India to participate in the joint seabed mining of the ocean to blunt India's resistance to the Chinese presence.

Arguably, natural resources are of prime strategic importance for China. Overall, China's cultivated acreage per person is only 40 per cent of the world average and its supply of fresh water per person, is just a quarter of the global level. Because of impending serious shortages of food and water resources, China is turning more and more towards the seas. In fact, Chinese experts believe that the increased demand for more protein in the Chinese diet means that the fishing industry—in particular, the distant water fishing (DWF) component—must be expanded and play a growing role in assuring China's food security.[21] Since the IOR is rich in fishery resources, aquaculture, minerals and rare earth metals, it has become a preferred destination. The new trend therefore, is towards an omnidirectional maritime strategy, including the development of new fields like renewable maritime energy sources and deep-seabed mineral resources, prevention and mitigation of marine disasters and the expansion of Arctic and Antarctic observation activities.[22]

Military Imperatives

Apart from the economic dimension, China's security concerns dominate its maritime strategy in the IOR. The Chinese Defence White Paper 2015 explains the Chinese dream and lays down certain new tasks for the Chinese military, in addition to its previously defined tasks. These are: 'to safeguard China's security and interests in new domains; and to safeguard the security of China's overseas interests.[23] This indicates that the Chinese military would be looking at theatres across the globe, building strategic power projection capabilities and its Navy will shift from 'offshore waters defence' to a combination of 'offshore waters defence' with 'open seas protection' and build a combined, multi-functional and efficient marine combat force structure".[24] The ambition to attain great power status is therefore the prime driver of Chinese activities and interests in the Indian Ocean.

In order to address the Malacca dilemma, Chinese are seeking land connectivity through different ports to transport oil and cargo, through pipelines and roads. They are exploring different routes like the Lombok and the Sunda Straits; or new openings through the Isthmus of Kra in Thailand. The 'String of Pearls' theory propounded in a report titled *Energy Futures in Asia,* by US defence contractor Booz Allen Hamilton in 2005, suggested that China is building strategic relationships along the sea lanes from the Middle East to the South China Sea in ways that suggest defensive and offensive positioning at ports of China's choosing to protect its energy interests, as also to serve broad security objectives," According to Mahanian logic, this string of pearls would permit larger-scale military deployments in the future to protect Chinese interests.[25] Port development and related activity in the IOR is currently in progress at Sri Lanka (Hambantota and Colombo), Bangladesh (Payra), Myanmar (Kyaukpyu), Pakistan (Gwadar), Djibouti (Obock Harbour), Kenya (Lamu) and Mozambique (Beira and Maputo) (Refer figure below).

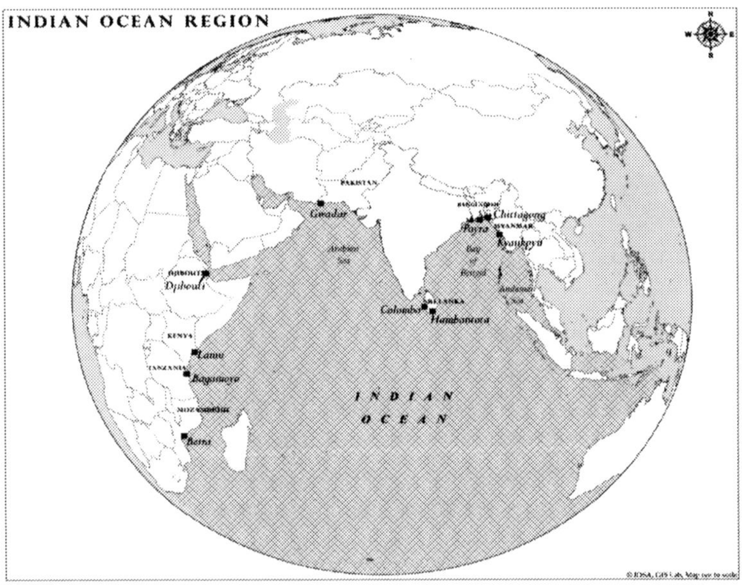

However, the String of Pearls theory has been rubbished by the Chinese. Most Chinese political leaders and intelligentsia articulate similar views as Zhou Bo of the Chinese Academy of Military Science, who said that China has only two objectives in the Indian Ocean: economic benefit and the security of shipping lines.[26] According to this view, these will be supply, berth and maintenance bases and will be built in the relevant countries for "mutual benefit and through friendly consultations". Chinese media stresses that these bases will be different from American type of bases.[27]

Moreover, the Chinese media reports also indicate that official Chinese publications including *Xinhua* advocate that the PLA Navy should build as many as 18 overseas naval military bases in the greater Indian Ocean area, possibly including: Chongjin port (North Korea), Moresby port (Papua New Guinea), Sihanoukville port (Cambodia), Koh Lanta port (Thailand), Sittwe port (Myanmar), Dhaka port (Bangladesh), Maldives, Seychelles, Lagos port (Nigeria), Mombasa port (Kenya), Dar-es-Salaam port (Tanzania), Luanda port (Angola) and the Walvis Bay port (Namibia).[28]

However, the strategic implications of the bases in the IOR cannot be ignored. Historically, trade has always been followed by military domination, be it in the case of the Portuguese, the Dutch or the British. The adage that the 'flag will always follow trade', holds true even now. China is already indicating the initial signs of such neo-colonialism in its negotiations with Pakistan and Sri Lanka. For instance, the Gwadar port is on lease to the Chinese company, COPHC, for 40 years at 9 percent revenue. A Pakistan navy official has already confirmed that ships of the Chinese navy will deploy alongside the Pakistan Navy for the security of the Gwadar port.[29] China will also have an 80 percent stake in the Hambantota port of Sri Lanka under a proposed lease of 99 years. The Chinese government has also signed a 10 year agreement with Djibouti, to set up a navy base that will serve as a logistics hub for the People's Liberation Army-Navy (PLA-N) ships engaged in anti-piracy operations off the coast of Yemen. The Djibouti port can accommodate vessels drawing up to 18 metres of water, including China's aircraft carrier, or its largest forward-deploying warship, the *Type 071 LPD*. On August 01, 2017, a flag raising ceremony and military parade marked the stationing of Chinese troops in Djibouti, with an understanding to station 10,000 troops up to 2026.[30] The periodic sighting of submarines in the waters of the Indian Ocean and in the ports of Colombo, Gwadar and Djibouti belie the projected peaceful and commercial nature of the bases. With its increasing economic clout and large-scale investments in the Indian Ocean littorals, more such bases are likely to come up over time, given the propensity of China to trade the waiving of heavy debts in lieu of berthing spaces for Chinese PLAN ships.[31]

Interestingly, the military strain in the proposed 21 century Maritime Silk Route (MSR) are also very evident. Cloaked in the soft approach of Zheng He, that ancient Chinese always came with gifts and for trade, China seems to have repackaged the String of Pearls Theory into the 21st century MSR. As Brahma Chellaney in *China's Indian Ocean Strategy* states:

> By presenting commercial penetration as benevolent investment and credit as aid, Beijing is winning lucrative overseas contracts for its

> state-run companies, with the aim of turning economic weight into 'strategic clout' (own emphasis). Through its Maritime Silk Road—a catchy new name for its "String of Pearls" strategy—China is already challenging the existing balance of power in the Indian Ocean.[32]

To fulfil its ambitions of being a maritime power, China has embarked upon a massive maritime modernisation programme that includes submarines, surface combatants, naval aviation and sealift assets. China's two largest state-owned shipbuilders—the China State Shipbuilding Corporation and Shipbuilding Industry Corporation—collaborate for ship designs and construction information to increase shipbuilding efficiency. China continues to procure propulsion units from foreign suppliers but is gradually building up indigenous production capability. China is the top ship-producing nation in the world and the commissioning into service, of the first aircraft carrier *Liaoning* has been a crucial step in advancing China's ability to project naval power. The *Liaoning* was declared combat ready in December 2016. The second aircraft carrier will be operational by 2020 and the third is also under construction. China is outfitting its latest classes of surface combatants with increasingly sophisticated anti-surface, anti-air, and anti-subsurface defensive and offensive capabilities. China's ambitious naval modernisation programme has resulted in a more technologically advanced and flexible force and the PLAN now possesses the largest number of vessels in Asia, with more than 300 surface ships, submarines, amphibious ships, and patrol craft.[33]

Following the implementation of the new guidelines the 'Technical Standards for New Civilian Ships to Implement National Defense Requirements'[34] by the Chinese government in June 2015, the PLA Navy's own increasing sea-based logistics capability can be supplemented by the capacity of state-owned commercial ships. The guidelines lay down not only the provisions for requisitioning civilian ships for naval missions, but also how future construction of Chinese merchant vessels would need to adhere to naval specifications.[35] A new 98,000-ton heavy lift mega-ship, *Guang Hua Kou,* built for Cosco Heavy Transport in April 2016, is one example of the growing fleet of support ships that China has been building in recent years, to operate alongside their fleet of powerful modern warships," According to Eric Wertheim, the author of the *Naval Institute Guide to Combat Fleets of the World,* "the massive ship is part of China's efforts to establish a world class navy and maritime force that is capable of operating worldwide". The *Guang Hua Kou* will be on call as part of PLAN's fleet of military heavy support ships that will facilitate broader PLAN naval and amphibious assault operations around the world.

Unconfirmed reports gleaned from Chinese-language articles and Western defence industry reports suggest that China will be building fleet command headquarters at Sanya on Hainan Island. James Holmes, co-author of the book, *Red Star Over the Pacific* and a US Naval War College professor, suggests that the Chinese Navy may be creating the organisation for an Indian Ocean fleet without assigning many, or any, assets to that fleet permanently, like the US Navy's 6th Fleet, which has only a command ship and shore facilities. China may be thinking about a similar arrangement for now, and perhaps permanently."[36]

Though reports of an additional fleet may be unconfirmed, Beijing is wary of the actions and perceived efforts, by the maritime nations in the IOR, to contain it. In order to ensure pre-eminence, it has enhanced the presence of its ships and submarines. At least three Chinese submarines are sighted every four months in the IOR.[37] Defending the recent deployment of Chinese submarines in the Indian Ocean, a Chinese military strategist at the People's Liberation Army's official think-tank said that the Chinese navy was right "to protect its interests" in the region, which India should be "broad minded" enough to accommodate.

Political Imperatives

In addition to the imperatives of energy, trade security and resources, the security and well-being of the vast Chinese Diaspora is also a concern for the Chinese leadership. People of Chinese origin currently constitute the fourth largest overseas population[38] and China devotes considerable attention to this diaspora and considers them an important link in the growth of Chinese influence worldwide. Thus, the protection of the diaspora and the desire to retain the capability to provide security to them, is foremost in the minds of the Chinese leaders. The evacuation of 613 Chinese nationals and 279 foreign nationals, mostly oil exploration workers from Yemen's southern port of Aden, amid fierce fighting in 2015 and the evacuation of more than 35000 Chinese nationals, over a 12-day period in February-March 2011, from civil war-torn Libya[39] was appreciated by the international community as well as the Chinese people. One commentator on *Sina Weibo*, the Chinese microblogging platform, wrote: "The strength of the motherland is not about the visa-free agreements with other countries, but that it could bring you home from danger."[40] The Chinese naval base at Djibouti is strategically located to ensure the security of Chinese nationals in Africa and the Middle-east.

In addition, the economic aid provided by China to IOR littorals, irrespective of their internal political dispensation, presents many political opportunities such as support for China in international forums and an increase in its overseas influence. The voting alignments of aid dependent countries will facilitate the moulding of global and regional opinion in its favour.[41]

Evolving Maritime Environment in the IOR

Globally, China is attempting to create the narrative of the inevitability of a Chinese hegemonic order, supplanting the US-led order. The OBOR is an important instrument for building that narrative. Regionally, it is no longer willing to accept Indian primacy in the sub-continent or in the Indian Ocean. It is determined to build its own primacy.

Some Chinese experts have predicted that the real push by China into the Indian Ocean will come after the resolution of the Taiwan issue, when China has adequate forces to spare from its eastern front for force projection in the IOR.[42] However, given the imperative of the timelines of the Two Centennials, and the leadership's need to ensure that the China Dream is realised, it is unlikely that China will opt for sequential force projection in these two regions. The operationalisation of the oil pipeline from Myanmar to Kunming; the construction of a naval base at Djibouti; investments in Hambantota Colombo and Gwadar; the interest shown for port development in other littorals; massive ship building efforts; emphasis on the 21st MSR; and likely raising of new fleet headquarters, all point towards a greater future Chinese involvement in the IOR, irrespective of the status of issues with respect to Taiwan and South China Sea in East Asia.

Ports and bases being developed by the Chinese are gradually becoming operational. Chinese cargo ships have been docking at Gwadar port since October 2016 and goods will now be transported to Central Asia and the Middle East from there, across land routes. Post completion of the CPEC, Gwadar is likely to become a hub for transshipment and transportation of Chinese goods. The Chinese have already indicated their intention to deploy navy ships in conjunction with the Pakistan Navy for the protection of the Gwadar port.[43] Gwadar has the potential to transform China as an IOR littoral. Once the logistical infrastructure is established in key locations in the IOR, Chinese naval ships can mark an enhanced and prolonged presence in the Indian Ocean. The real question thereafter, will relate to the intent. Conversion of a logistics facility into a military base is not very conspicuous, time consuming or effort intensive. Weaker economies with large debts may find it difficult to deny the use of their ports for Chinese naval ships, in conflict like situations. The congruence of economic influence and military muscle is bound to overshadow the national interests of other powers like India in the IOR. In addition, China also stands to gain economically and politically, when many of its trade partners would willingly side with it, on international issues at various international forums.

In the strong presence of maritime powers like the US, India, UK and France, China feels the need to add more weight to its presence and influence. China views the possible US-India-Japan quasi-alliance as standing in the way of its ambitions in the IOR and is therefore readying itself for any competition that could arise. China refutes the narrative that the Indian Ocean is India's Ocean. Senior Captain Zhao Yi, associate professor at the Institute of Strategy in China's National Defence University, during a candid interaction with resident Indian journalists in Beijing on this issue said, "The word backyard is not very appropriate to use for an open sea and international areas of sea."[44]

Overall, China with its enhanced outreach into the IOR has shown its willingness to project power far from its shores and also its capability to protect its interests worldwide. Its activities will be viewed with suspicion, and will trigger counter measures by maritime nations like India, US, Japan thereby increasing competition and confrontation. Whatever be its future intent, the Chinese have been less than transparent while laying out their plans and strategies for the Indian Ocean. There seems to be a deliberate attempt at strategic vagueness that will give them the opportunity to test the waters and escalate naval activity at a time of their own choosing. The imperative of fulfilling its above mentioned ambitions, is prompting China to enhance its influence in the IOR.

Evolving out of Mao Tse Tung's approach of *"tao guang yang hui"*—a Chinese idiom that literally translates as "to hide one's talents, and bide one's time for the right opportunity," an enhanced Chinese presence in the IOR, is inevitable. The strategic intentions of the Chinese and the response of the US, India and other navies will dictate whether this zone of peace will transform into a region of confrontation, conflict or cooperation.

NOTES

1. David Brewster, *India's Ocean: The Story of India's Bid for Regional Leadership*, London and New York Routledge, 2014, Chapter 1, Shifting Balance of Power in the Indian Ocean, page 5.
2. June Teufel Dreyer, *Middle Kingdom and Empire of the Rising Sun-Sino-Japanese Relations, Past and Present*, New York, Oxford University Press, 2016, Part One, page 4.
3. Leon Whyte, 'China's Elegant, Flawed, Grand Strategy', *The Diplomat*, July 25,

2015 at http://thediplomat.com/2015/07/chinas-elegant-flawed-grand-strategy/ accessed May 19, 2017

4. *BBC News*, 'What does Xi Jinping's China Dream mean?', June 06, 2013, at http://www.bbc.com/news/world-asia-china-22726375, accessed July 27, 2017.
5. *The Two Centennial Goals*, Updated November 18, 2014, China.org.cn at http://www.china.org.cn/english/china_key_words/2014-11/18/content_34158771.htm, accessed July 12, 2017.
6. David Shambaugh, *China goes Global—The Partial Power*, Oxford University Press, page 7.
7. Rear Admiral Michael McDevitt, 'Becoming a Great Maritime Power: A Chinese Dream', Smith Richardson Foundation Report, June 2016, at https://www.cna.org/cna_files/pdf/IRM-2016-U-013646.pdf, accessed July 28, 2017.
8. John H. Maurer, 'The Influence of Thinkers and Ideas on History: The Case of Alfred Thayer Mahan', *Foreign Policy Research Institute,* August 11, 2016 at http://www.fpri.org/article /2016/08/influence-thinkers-ideas-history-case-alfred-thayer-mahan/, accessed July 28, 2017.
9. Liu Cigui, 'The First-Ever Reference to 'Maritime Power' in the Political Report to the 18th Party Congress has important Practical and Strategic Significance' [十八大報告首提"海洋强国"具有重要的現実和戦略意義], *China Oceanology Review* [中国海洋报], November 12, 2012. [↵].
10. Chen Shaofeng, *China's Self-Extrication from the "Malacca Dilemma" and Implications*, Peking University, at https://ics.um.edu.my/images/ics/IJCSV1N1/chen.pdf, accessed June 10, 2017.
11. US Energy Information Administration data available at https://www.eia.gov/outlooks/aeo/data/browser/#/?id=1-IEO2016&sourcekey=0, accessed June 10, 2017
12. DC Andrew, China's Growing Energy Demand: Implications for the United States', *Working Paper Series* Congressional Budget Office Washington, June 2015, at https://www.cbo.gov/sites/default /files/114th-congress-2015-2016/workingpaper/50216-China_1.pdf, accessed June 11, 2017.
13. Erica Strecker Downs, China's Quest for Energy Security, Chapter 2: Energy Demand and Supply in China, RAND Report MR-1244-AF at https://www.rand.org/content/dam/rand/pubs/monograph_reports/MR1244/MR1244.ch2.pdf, accessed June 14, 2017.
14. James R. Holmes & Toshi Yoshihara, 'China's Naval Ambitions in the Indian Ocean', *Journal of Strategic Studies* Vol. 31, Iss. 3,2008, pp. 371, at http://www.tandfonline.com/doi/full/10.1080/01402390802024700?scroll=top&needAccess=true, accessed July 28, 2017.
15. Marc Lanteigne, 'China's Maritime Security and the "Malacca Dilemma"', *Asian Security,* 4:2, 143-161, DOI: 10.1080/14799850802006555 at http://www.tandfonline.com/doi/pdf/10.1080/ 14799850802006555accessed July 28, 2017
16. In 1609, the Dutch jurist Hugo Grotius published "Mare Liberum" (Freedom of the Seas), asserting that the seas were incapable of domination and thus available for use by all seafarers. In 1635, the book *Mare Clausum* was published by the English jurist John Selden. He argued that the sea was virtually as capable of appropriation as the land.

17. L K Cheng, 'Three questions on China's "Belt and Road Initiative', *China Economic Review*, 40 (2016) 309-313.
18. Y. Huang, 'Understanding China's Belt and Road Initiative: Motivation, framework and assessment, *China Economic Review* 40 (2016) pp 314-321.
19. 'International Seabed Authority, What areas are being explored', at https://www.isa.org.jm/faq/what-areas-are-being-explored, accessed on January 04, 2017
20. Ajoy K Das, 'India identifies first-generation mining site in Indian Ocean basin', *Creamer Media Mining Weekly*, December 13, 2012 at http://www.miningweekly.com/article/india-identifies-first-generation-mining-site-in-indian-ocean-basin-2012-12-13, accessed December 31, 2016.
21. Rear Admiral Michael McDevitt, Becoming a Great Maritime Power: A Chinese Dream, Smith Richardson Foundation Report, June 2016, at https://www.cna.org/cna_files/pdf/IRM-2016-U-013646.pdf, accessed July 28, 2017.
22. Takeda Jun'ichi, 'China's Rise as a Maritime Power: Ocean Policy from Mao Zedong to Xi Jinping', at https://www.spf.org/islandstudies/research/a00011/, accessed July 28, 2017.
23. Full text of Chinese Defence White Paper 2015 available at http://news.xinhuanet.com/english/china/2015-05/26/c_134271001_2.htm, accessed June 20, 2017.
24. Ibid.
25. Alexandre Sheldon-Duplaix, 'Beyond the China Seas-Will China become a Global "Sea Power"', *China Perspective* No. 2016/3
26. Ibid.
27. Chan Kai Yee, 'China to build 18 naval bases in Indian Ocean', November 22, 2014, at https://chinadailymail.com/2014/11/22/china-to-build-18-naval-bases-in-indian-ocean/, accessed July 28, 2017.
28. Ibid.
29. *Times of India*, 'Pak navy official: Chinese navy ships to be deployed at Gwadar', PTI dated November 25, 2016 at http://timesofindia.indiatimes.com/world/pakistan/Chinese-navy-ships-to-be-deployed-at-Gwadar-Pak-navy-official/articleshow/55622674.cms, accessed June 28, 2017.
30. François Dubé, 'China's Experiment in Djibouti,' *The Diplomat*, October 5, 2016, at http://thediplomat.com/2016/10/chinas-experiment-in-djibouti/, accessed October 4, 2017.
31. PK Balachandran, 'China agrees to convert Sri Lanka's *project debt into equity*', October 22, 2016, *Indian Express*, at http://www.newindianexpress.com/world/2016/oct/22/china-agrees-to-convert-sri-lankas-project-debt-into-equity-1530526.html, accessed July 28, 2017.
32. Brahma Chellaney, 'China's Indian Ocean strategy' at http://www.japantimes.co.jp/opinion /2015/06/23/commentary/world-commentary/chinas-indian-ocean-strategy/#.WGNGCtR97Gg, accessed December 28, 2016
33. Annual Report to Congress: Military and Security Developments Involving the People's Republic of China 2016 at http://www.defense.gov/Portals/1/Documents/pubs /2016%20China% 20Military% 20Power%20Report.pdf accessed December 13, 2016

34. Yao Jianing, 'New rules mean ships can be used by military', *China Military Online,* June 18, 2015, at http://english.chinamil.com.cn/news-channels/china-military-news/2015-6/18/content_6546905.htm, accessed December 28, 2016.
35. Gurpreet Singh Khurana, 'Sea-based' PLA Navy may not need 'string of pearls' August 12, 2015 at http://cimsec.org/sea-based-pla-navy-may-not-need-string-pearls/18053, accessed December 26, 2016
36. Wendell Minnick, 'Experts: Chinese '4th Fleet' Appears Unlikely' Defence News, February 6, 2015 accessed through http://www.defensenews.com/story/defense/naval/navy/2015/02/06/taiwan/22913337/ on 06 January 2017.
37. Sanjeev Miglani and Greg Torode, '*Wary of China's Indian Ocean activities, U.S., India discuss anti-submarine warfare*', *Reuters* May 02, 2016 at http://www.reuters.com/article/us-india-usa-submarines-idUSKCN0XS1NS, accessed January 09, 2016.
38. Data provided by United Nations Department of Economic and Social Affairs, Population Division, at http://www.un.org/en/development/desa/population/migration/data/estimates2/estimatesgraphs.shtml?4g4accessed July 28, 2017.
39. *China Daily,* 'Ministry of National Defence the People's Republic of China, Opinion: Birth of truly Global Chinese Navy', April 10, 2015 at http://eng.mod.gov.cn/Opinion/2015-04/10/content_4579364.htm, accessed July 27, 2017.
40. Jane Perlez and Yufan Huang, 'Yemen Evacuation Shows Chinese Navy's Growing Role' March 31, 2015 at http://sinosphere.blogs.nytimes.com/2015/03/31/yemen-evacuation-shows-chinese-navys-growing-role/?_r=0, accessed June 28, 2017
41. Research by Rayna Martinez (Portland State University, 2011) with 13 years data from 1999-2011 on correlation between Chinese aid to 23 African countries and their voting behavior and alignment in the UN General Assembly has concluded an average of 85.7% voting affinity with China. The research is constrained due to lack of transparency of Chinese FDI, constraints of quantitatively measuring effects of aid, debt forgiveness, loans as well as the context of the resolutions put to vote.
42. Prof John Garver, Talk on India, Indian Ocean and the PLA Navy, United Service Institution, New Delhi, November 28, 2016
43. NDTV *Report,* 'Chinese Navy Ships To Be Deployed At Gwadar Port: Pak Official, November 26, 2016 accessed through http://www.ndtv.com/world-news/chinese-navy-ships-to-be-deployed-at-pakistans-gwadar-port-1630354 dated 02 January 2017
44. The *Economic Times,* Indian Ocean cannot be backyard of India: China, July 01, 2015, at http://economictimes.indiatimes.com/news/defence/indian-ocean-cannot-be-backyard-of-india-china/articleshow/47891860.cms, accessed July 28, 2017

7

Response of India's Neighbours to China's South Asia Policy

Smruti S Pattanaik

ABSTRACT

"In the recent years China has made deeper forays into the south Asian region. From being the largest supplier of weapons to many of the Indian neighbours, it has now engaged in building large infrastructures, ports and airports and have a dominant economic presence. China's massive loans to build infrastructure has generated a debate on what is known as 'debt diplomacy' that many fear would cripple the fledging economies of the South Asian countries. It is true that China's has banked on the fear of India that most of the India's neighbours nurse to make a strategic presence, the injection of huge loans also serve China's strategic interests. In this context the paper examine China's South Asia policy and analyses how India's neighbours perceive China's presence, role and investment and finally to study to what extent China fits into the larger strategy of India's neighbours in relations with their approach to India. This paper is limited to examining the responses of Pakistan, Nepal, Sri Lanka, Maldives, and Bangladesh where the Chinese investment have generated a larger debate on financial sustainability of the projects and the likely implications of the huge loan on the strategic and foreign policy matters of these countries."

Key words: *India-China; South Asia; Debt Trap, Sri Lanka.*

China's South Asia policy has two important parameters. First, the development and stability of its periphery, and embedded in this is the second, that is, the state of its relations with India and their rivalry in Asia. So, China's South Asia policy has both economic and strategic content in which however, the latter plays an important role. While elaborating China's periphery strategy at the Peripheral Diplomacy Conference, President Xi Jinping said:

> We should sincerely treat peripheral countries to obtain more friends and partners. We should insist the principle of mutually beneficial when cooperating with peripheral countries to weave a closer network bearing common benefits, enhance fusion of two-party benefits to a higher level, make peripheral countries benefit from China's development, and enable China to obtain interests and help from the development of peripheral countries.[1]

Prima facie it appears that most of India's neighbours are keen to have a no-strings-attached Chinese investment in infrastructure and other areas, which would boost their economic growth. And, China actively fulfils this consideration. Besides, except for India and Bhutan, it does not have any territorial dispute with India's immediate neighbours. Moreover, many of India's neighbours—except for Pakistan and now Maldives—are conscious of the strategic consequences of their relationship with China and the likely Indian response. Yet, they have deftly played the China card to pressurise and send a message to New Delhi. Realising that India's security would be imperilled by the Chinese presence, almost all the countries of South Asia at some point of time, have played the China card to pressurise New Delhi and extract concessions, and at times, to reduce Delhi's pressure on the regimes. New Delhi has been concerned about the larger Chinese presence in the region that is aimed at creating an anti-India strategic periphery, which would box India into a South Asia geo-strategic complex.

Of late, especially since 2000, China has increased its footprint in the region, and largely engaged in infrastructure development that would give Beijing strategic foothold in the region. Its trade with the countries of South Asia has increased manifold (see Tables 1 and 2). China's engagement with India's neighbours is not new. It has forged close military ties and has supplied weapons to them in the past; however, it appears that its present policy is aimed at maintaining a robust strategic presence in the region in general, and the Indian Ocean region in particular. China's unprecedented investment in the neighbourhood in the recent past to the tune of $62 billion in Pakistan and $24 billion in Bangladesh has raised eyebrows in India. Can it be that China has billions of spare money in its coffers and wants to invest it to get economic returns as some would believe; or is it that China wants to achieve its strategic intentions, through such an economic presence as others would argue? The chapter focuses on China's relationship with four important South Asian countries Nepal, Bangladesh, Sri Lanka and

Maldives, which is analysed within the larger framework of Chinese investment and defence cooperation with these countries in South Asia. The chapter analyses these four countries' responses to China's engagement.

Chinese investment in South Asia and the interest levied on the loans that China has extended to South Asian countries, has generated the larger debate about the economic vulnerability of the South Asian countries and their propensity to fall into debt traps. Most of the countries' ability to repay the loan is questionable especially in cases where the projects have not been able to earn profit. Therefore, the recent debt equity swap agreement between Sri Lanka and China whereby the Hambanttota port was handed over to China on a 99-year lease, only confirmed what India had always feared. This chapter will look at three important factors. First, where do the countries of South Asia fit within larger Chinese strategy? Second, how do the neighbours perceive China's presence, role and investment and finally where does China fit into the broader strategies of India's neighbours, with regard to their approach to India. This chapter is

Table 1: China and India's Import from Select South Asian countries

	2007	*2009*	*2011*	*2013*	*2015*	*2016*
China's Import from Bangladesh	114.2	140.7	449.0	602.4	803.7	861.9
India's Import from Bangladesh	233.3	234.4	579.1	530.8	639.9	677.0
China's Import from Nepal	0.0	5.3	13.9	43.3	23.0	19.4
India's Import from Nepal	469.8	416.3	508.2	376.7	489.6	385.3
China's Import from Sri Lanka	48.0	70.1	152.9	182.6	259.2	273.0
India's Import from Sri Lanka	441.4	328.8	718.0	515.3	848.8	631.9
China's Import from Maldives	0.3	0.1	0.1	0.4	0.2	0.2
India's Import from Maldives	3.6	2.4	18.0	4.1	5.1	6.3

Source: http://www.trademap.org/Bilateral

Table 2: China and India's Export to Select South Asian Countries

	2007	*2009*	*2011*	*2013*	*2015*	*2016*
China's Export to Bangladesh	3349.8	4441.1	7810.7	9705.1	13101.0	13611.2
India's export to Bangladesh	2063.8	2177.4	3405.5	5994.0	5521.5	5667.6
China's export to Nepal	386.4	408.9	1181.2	2210.9	830.0	870.5
India's Export to Nepal	1237.1	1327.4	2559.9	3176.2	3195.1	4525.4
China's Export to Sri Lanka	1389.8	1569.5	2988.7	3436.5	4308.1	4331.2
India's export to Sri Lanka	2594.2	1724.6	4452.0	4754.0	5501.0	4116.1
China's Export to Maldives	24.9	40.7	97.1	97.4	172.6	333.2
India's export to Maldives	79.7	108.4	118.3	124.2	166.9	180.2

Source: http://www.trademap.org/Bilateral

limited to examining the responses of Pakistan, Bangladesh, Nepal, Sri Lanka, and Maldives where the Chinese investments have generated a debate on the likely implications of the huge loans on the strategic and foreign policies of these countries. Moreover, in these countries China is seen as a strategic competitor to India.

China's South Asia Policy

China's South Asia policy has revolved around Beijing's relations with India. Throughout the Cold War period, Beijing encouraged India's neighbours to challenge India's perceived dominance. It consciously challenged India's position as a successor state of the British regime especially in the context of India's treaty relations with Nepal and Bhutan. China's relationship with Pakistan is fundamentally geared towards establishing a rival power in South Asia who can question the legitimacy of India's 'hegemony' and challenge its pre-eminent position in the region. China's bilateral relations is often couched in terms of 'five principles' with an emphasis on 'non-interference' and 'sovereign equality' to juxtapose what is seen as Indian 'interference' in the internal affairs of its neighbours. India's policy is largely guided by a security linkage with its neighbours, as it is perceived that instability in the neighbourhood would directly impinge on its stability, which is heightened by the various insurgencies that afflicted its borderlands and the fear of external power using India's neighbours to balance India. India's policies during the cold war were geared towards denying strategic space to external powers in the region which India thought would affect its security. The flow of refugees from the turbulent neighbourhood to the border states that are witnessing an assertion of ethno-nationalism is also an area of major concern.

China's South Asia policy is very much linked to its relations with India. The relations between India and China improved significantly after 1988 with the visit of the then, prime minister, Rajiv Gandhi to Beijing. The thaw between the two rivals had an impact on China's South Asia policy. As a result, in 1989, it advised Nepal to resolve its problems with India bilaterally; it also advised Pakistan to improve its relations with India and largely discouraged South Asian countries from seeking its help in resolving their bilateral conflicts/disputes with India.[2] However, it continued to cultivate a strong relationship with Pakistan, which remained special compared to other countries of South Asia. The China-Pakistan axis is aimed at limiting India's sphere of influence in South Asia and also diluting its dominant presence in the Indian Ocean Region.[3] China assured that the improvement of bilateral ties does not undermine the importance of its relations with other South Asian countries and China remains relevant for their 'balance India' policy if need arise. For example: Chinese Foreign Minister Qian Qichen who visited India in 1990—nine years after his first visit in 1981—while speaking at a banquet held by the then Prime Minister Gujral, said:

> As there exists a time honoured friendship between the Chinese people and the peoples in South Asia, the improvement and development of Sino-Indian relations will by no means adversely affect existing friendly relations between China and other South Asian countries. Rather, it will be conducive to the maintenance of peace in the region and in Asia as a whole.

He further added that, "China never interferes in the internal affairs of other countries and is firmly opposed to any *outside interference in its internal affairs*."[4] China's allusion to 'outside interference' meant 'interference' by India. However, China's policy demonstrates a 'balance of power' approach to South Asia where India remains a main contender for influence.

Nonetheless, throughout the Cold War period China had questioned the 'unequal' Indo-Nepal Treaty of 1950 and the Indo-Bhutan Treaty of 1949 questioning the sovereignty of these two countries. It subtly encouraged both Nepal and Bhutan challenge and dilute their treaties with India. Though Nepal under the Monarchy substantially undermined the treaty with the support of India, Bhutan periodically asked for the revision of 1949 treaty. China was the first country to accept Kathmandu's 1972 proposal for designating Nepal as a zone of peace which was aimed at ending its special relationship with India. It refused to recognise India's role in Bhutan's external relations by refusing to hold boundary talks on behalf of Bhutan while constantly pressuring Bhutan by showing large chunk of Bhutan's territory as part of China. China's political recognition of Bangladesh came only after the assassination of its founding father Mujibur Rahman who was seen as being friendlier to India. The military regime that succeeded Mujib's government, cultivated close relations with China, and India's 1972 Treaty of Peace and Friendship with Bangladesh was informally put into cold storage. Therefore, China played a significant role to undermine India's pre-eminence in the region by co-opting regimes and undermining bilateral treaties 'of those countries with India.

At the same time a dominant narrative is subtly engineered that consciously frames India as a 'hegemon' and China as a 'benign' neighbour. The author of this propagation are authoritarian and unelected governments in the neighbourhood, who continue to see Indian democracy as a primary threat to their regimes' interests. The intellectual elites that benefit from such regimes are at the forefront of constructing this narrative, citing some real and imagined grievances against India and projecting China as countervailing force. This narrative helps them in creating a public opinion in support for a close relationship with China as a security guarantor. Moreover, the disputed and porous borders were often a matter for contestation with neighbours—a British legacy that India inherited. The large size of India, its burgeoning economy, central geographical location in South Asia and its capacity to influence and effect a regime change in the neighbourhood, if it so wished, also contributed to this narrative. Therefore, China, which defeated India in the 1962 war, is seen as a major balancing force. It is also apparent India will not accept a "Sino-centric regional order" and China will look at India, a challenger to China's primacy in Asia as a "potential peer competitor that must be contained".[5] This provides space for the countries of the region to play the China card effectively.

India's redemption of its strategic image or regional pre-eminence and China's inability to help Pakistan during the 1971 war notwithstanding, the India-China relationship shaped the South Asian countries' policies towards both. Unlike the past, developments in Tibet and its decision to develop its periphery, its BRI initiative transcended its engagement with India's neighbours. China's rise and its economic and military might made it to reassert its relationship with South Asia. For example: The increasing protests and self-immolations in Tibet since 2000, made China to pressurise Nepal to curb anti-China activities in Kathmandu. Also, China decided to increase aid and soft loans to Nepal to wean Kathmandu away from India. It decided to sell weapons to Nepal to fight Maoist insurgency, even as India decided to discontinue the supply of weapons; it came to the rescue of Sri Lanka in its fight against Tamil separatists, taking advantage of India's inability to supply weapons, given the political repercussion it may have for the government in Tamil Nadu. All these helped China to convert the goodwill it had in South Asia to strategic space at the cost of India. Though some analysts have attributed this reaction to the Indo-US nuclear deal and their subsequent strategic partnership, nevertheless China's approach to South Asia predates the nuclear deal.[6] The larger convergence of India and US in their approach to South Asia, their approach to Indo-Pacific and the tension between Washington and Beijing and Beijing and India significantly contributes to the dynamics of China's relations with India and their approach to South Asia. Therefore, it was not surprising that Prime Minister Modi who was keen to improve ties with China, during his first visit to China in 2015 underlining the South Asia regional dynamics, emphasised that "We must ensure that our relationships with other countries do not become a source of concern for each other."[7]

India's relationship with South Asian countries faced several political and security hurdles. New Delhi got drawn into the ethnic conflict in Sri Lanka in the early eighties; with Nepal, the Maoist insurgency emerged as a major challenge, coupled with the assassination of King Birendra who was succeeded by King Gyanendra who took over direct control of power creating a political crisis; in Bangladesh it was dragged into the bitter political contest of the two dominant political parties. One of the parties, the Bangladesh Nationalist Party (BNP) that perceives India as its ideological other, in its political prudence decided to shelter Indian insurgents and adopt a belligerent approach towards India—a country considered as close to its bitter political rival, the Awami League (AL). On the other hand, Maldives courted China to keep India out as New Delhi was seen as being too sympathetic to former President Nashid while Pakistan, eagerly seeking opportunities to beat India, remained China's all-weather friend. Thus, China's role as a countervailing force in South Asia coupled with its relationship with the military forces in the region that nurtures a strategic doctrine of Indian threat all contributed to China's pre-eminence in the region that consequently heightened India's security concerns.

In contrast, China was able to strengthen its economic ties in a relationship that was built on strategic cooperation. Therefore, Chinese investment needs to be seen in the larger strategic context and as part of its larger objectives in South Asia, i.e. to effectively curb India's influence, and limit its strategic relevance. There are several articles in the state funded *Global Times* that have underlined the importance of South Asia for China. Ai Jun writing in the context of Chinese defence minister's visit to Sri Lanka and Nepal said, "When an increasing number of Chinese companies get established in these countries, it is inevitable that Beijing will boost defence collaboration with them to protect not only China's, but also the region's interest."[8] The same article accuses India of being responsible for the absence of diplomatic relations between China and Bhutan. In this context it would be important to discuss individual South Asian countries and how Beijing stepped up its cooperation with particular regimes to address their concerns regarding India.

India's Neighbours' Response to China's Engagement: Analysing Issues, Discourses and Narratives

The role of China in South Asia has become an intensely debated topic among the strategic community in South Asia, especially in the context of India's role in the neighbourhood. Although in the post-Cold War period,

China distanced itself from India's conflictual relations or bilateral disagreements with its neighbours and encouraged India's neighbours to settle their problems with India bilaterally since it was facing internal challenges beginning with the June 1989 Tianmain Square massacre.[9] China's policy underwent change in the 2000s as China emerged as a major Global player. It was not hesitant to make statements on domestic politics of the south Asian countries as its economic profile and influence grew.[10] It openly warned Nepal against ethnic based federalism.[11] In Sri Lanka during the 2015 election, China advertised how its investment had helped generate employment in Sri Lanka. The role of China has now become part of domestic discourse in the neighbouring countries, with some of them seeking to benefit from China's growing economy; and others expressing their apprehensions regarding the impact of large Chinese investments in South Asia and the political implications of such investments.[12]

China's proposed maritime silk route and One Belt One Road (OBOR) or Belt and Road Initiative was eagerly accepted by the leaders of the South Asian countries for two reasons. First, it promised investment and much needed infrastructure that will boost economy, create employment and help them to win elections despite the high rates of interest. Second, it would help balance India's influence, and blunt its ability to pressurise them in domestic politics order to protect India's national interest. While Sri Lanka emerged as a classic case of how a regime can engage the Chinese to invest in economically unviable infrastructural projects. China's $62 billion investment in Pakistan under the CPEC was an attractive proposition for the countries of South Asia. Investments in infrastructure were low. Apart from the Asian Development Bank (ADB), most of the projects were funded bilaterally by India or Japan through a line of credit. However, the debates on Chinese investment are diverse.

Pakistan and China: India Factor in the All Weather Friendship

No other countries in India's neighbourhood enjoys as close relationship as China enjoys with Pakistan. This is a relationship that has been described as "all weather", "sweeter than honey, deeper than ocean". Pakistan's relationship with India and deep sense of threat perception coupled with partition narrative and the Kashmir issue have all contributed to the construction of a narrative that China remains an insurance against India. The relationship deepened especially after the 1963 Sino-Pakistan boundary agreement and its diplomatic support to Pakistan. Both the country collaborated on nuclear and missile development. To China, Pakistan remained the only country that can thwart India's emergence as a regional power and bound India to the region by getting it tied down to bilateral conflicts with Pakistan and thereby impeding its emergence as a major rival Asian power that can play a global role. China has emerged as a major weapon supplier to Pakistan since 1965 when US sanctioned Pakistan and India over the 1965 war. Though it has played a significant role in strengthening Pakistan's offensive capability, it has advised Pakistan to resolve its disputes with India through bilateral dialogue in 1995 when Jiang Zemin visited Islamabad and also during the Kargil conflict.

Over the period of time China has helped Pakistan in developing its nuclear arsenal and in fact have argued strongly for Islamabad's membership of the Nuclear Supplier Group (NSG).[13] China has also blocked US proposal to put Masood Azhar, chief of militant outfit Jaish e Mohammad and the person believed to be behind Mumbai attack, in the United Nations Security Council Sanctions list. These are two of the recent Chinese positions that is seen as protecting Pakistan. Moreover, China has always endorsed Pakistan's credential as a country that is fighting terrorism especially after US exhorted Pakistan to deliver more on the issue of terrorism.

Pakistan's relationship with China is seen as an insurance against any aggressive action by India and the US. As a veto wielding power in the Security Council who is also a member of various international regimes, China has helped Pakistan in ensuring that Pakistan does not become a victim of Global power politics. It is the only country that has defended Pakistani track record on terror cooperation in the face of intense US pressure. All these have contributed to a narrative of a relationship that is deeper than the Ocean.

Interestingly, the $62 billion Chinese investment in Pakistan on China-Pakistan economic Corridor is creating some apprehensions in the minds of both policy makers as well as the strategic community in Pakistan about the strategic consequence of huge debt. As retired Col Syed Tahir Hussain Mashhadi, Chairman of Senate Standing Committee on Planning and Development said, "China is our brother, but business is business."[14] In the same meeting apprehensions were expressed about the employment of Pakistanis in the projects, the maintenance costs of the road infrastructure and the clash of cultures, as they fear that a China town will come up in the area.

The lack of transparency in the CPEC projects has only added to the economic viability of the projects and its benefit to Pakistan. In June last year, the Dawn revealed that CPEC proposal not just include energy and infrastructure but would include agriculture where China plans to make large investment.[15] According to a news report, "Pakistan's total debt has surged to Rs 22.8 trillion as of December 2017, owing to loans under the China-Pakistan Economic Corridor (CPEC), borrowings to maintain foreign reserves and infrastructure, and floating Euro and Sukuk bonds".[16] Because many of the early harvest projects are being built on loan on commercial interest rate.[17] There is a strong perception that the CPEC will benefit China and serves its geo-political interest and some members of National Assembly likened it to "East India Company."[18] This perception was not out of place as Federal Minister for Ports and Shipping Mir Hasil Bizenjo said to the Senators that 91 per cent of the revenues that would be generated from the Gwadar port as part of the China-Pakistan Economic Corridor (CPEC) would go to China, while the Gwadar Port Authority would get 9pc share in the income for the next 40 years.[19]

Bangladesh and China: Constructing the Narrative

Over a period of time China has managed to persuade Bangladesh to overcome its reservations about China's role during the liberation war, when it vetoed Bangladesh's admission to the UN as an independent country. In the larger context Bangladesh's relations with India and its perception of India have largely coloured Bangladesh's policy towards China—as that of a countervailing force. China is seen as a militarily and economically powerful country that can be courted to keep India at a distance and can challenge the US hegemony. In this context, it is significant to understand Bangladesh's security concerns and how India and China fit into its strategic calculation. Many in Bangladesh portray India as a threat.[20] China's relationship with Bangladesh has been part of China's larger strategy which has bipartisan support in Bangladesh. However, its relations with India, have more or less, followed a regime centric approach. During the rule of the Awami League, Bangladesh tried to ensure that its relations with China were not at the cost of India. Therefore, any analysis of China's relations with Bangladesh or Bangladesh's approach to China has to factor in India, and the dynamics of their relations with Delhi. According to an analyst, in many ways the Sino-Bangladesh, "relationship helped close, to a degree, the enormous power-gap that existed between Bangladesh and India...".[21] However, a balance India policy has been a major pillar of the South Asian countries' approach towards China. A former diplomat of Bangladesh opines, "China's foreign policy eschews coercive diplomacy and emphasises win-win economic cooperation."[22] And unlike India, China "attaches great importance to its relations with regional neighbours."[23] In the past, China supported Bangladesh's position on

Ganges water as it tried to mend its ties post 1971. For example, explaining significance of China's support, former President of Bangladesh and founder of BNP, General Zia ur Rahman not only appreciated China's support on the issue of sharing Ganges water but its effort to: "safeguard its *national independence*".[24] Similar sentiments were expressed by former military ruler General Ershad when he said during of his visits to China, "relations between China and Bangladesh had most solid foundation since both countries enjoyed common targets and interests."[25]

Bangladesh has been an enthusiastic backer of China's South Asia policy, whether in recommending China's membership to the South Association for Regional Cooperation (SAARC) or its keenness to operationalise Bangladesh-China-India-Myanmar (BCIM) Forum for Regional Cooperation. There are academics, policymakers and retired bureaucrats and armed force official who support a close Bangladesh-China relations. For example, Ruksana Kibria, Professor in the Department of International Relations at the University of Dhaka argued that "It would be in the interest of Bangladesh to promote China's geo-political goals in South Asia, since a convergence of their strategic interests would augur well for the regional balance of power."[26] Therefore, strategic aspects of China-Bangladesh relations cannot be completely ignored. Military to military ties between them remains the cornerstone of their bilateral relations and clearly indicate the India factor in this relationship.

Xi Jinping's visit to Dhaka, a visit by a Chinese President after 30 years, was regarded as a new era in China-Bangladesh relations. As a commentator argued, "China invested about USD128 billion in 2015. Beijing showed huge interest to invest in Bangladesh's port, railway, highway, energy sector and other key infrastructure. President Xi's visit could be a game changer as far as China-Bangladesh investment relation is concerned."[27] President Xi, in a joint statement emphasised, "I hope to use this visit to chart the course for future growth of China-Bangladesh relations from a strategic and long-term prospective together with the leaders of Bangladesh... To some extent, the South Asian region is also one of China's backyards."[28]

Perhaps, Dhaka's eagerness to sign Strategic Partnership Agreement and its ready acceptance of the $24 billion dollar loan was in a way to compensate Beijing for Bangladesh's decision to shelve the construction of the Sonadia port, in a last minute decision, ostensibly under external pressure. Bangladesh also realises that massive investment by China would oil its economy and accelerate its growth. Unlike Pakistan, interestingly there is no debate in Bangladesh on how to repay the debt. But many perceive the loan as major investment opportunity. According to a media report "Since independence, China has provided Bangladesh $1,519 million in soft loans and grants. Of the sum, $916 million came in the last seven years from FY10 to FY16 alone. It was $303 million in the preceding seven years from FY02 to FY09."[29] Yet, after promising a $24 billion investment; China last year proposed to convert part of this investment into commercial loans.[30] Dhaka resisted it strongly.[31]

Though there is always an emphasis on Bangladesh maintaining close ties with China, Dhaka at times has tried to balance the relationship between India and China and has played the China card, especially during the BNP regime.[32] Political parties in Bangladesh also maintain close ties with China and many in the strategic community nurture a belief that China is an insurance against possible belligerent behaviour by India in the future. Interestingly, the Chinese veto against Bangladesh at the UN is rationalised as a compulsion of the then prevailing circumstances, but similar expressions of sympathy regarding any omissions by India is rare. It needs to be mentioned that the trade imbalance with China does not have domestic political currency; it is hardly raised in public unlike the imbalance with India. Therefore, there exists an opinion that China is a friend of Bangladesh therefore its proposal for investment and the rate of interest is rarely debated as Bangladesh remains investment hungry. Engaging China to some extent dispels any notion of Awami League being close to India and gives the government a strategic breather.

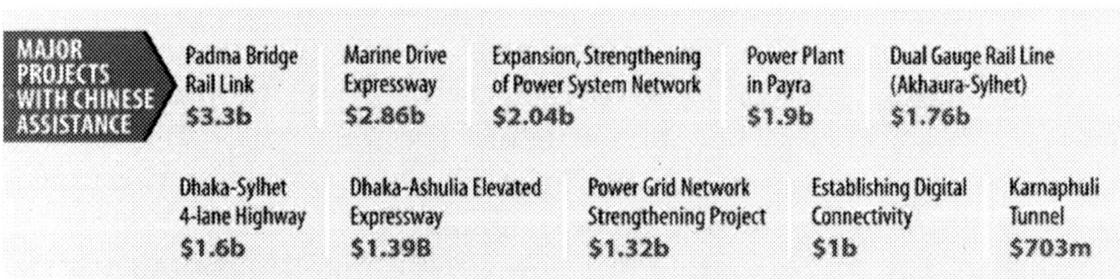

Source: *The Daily Star*, October 15, 2016.

Bangladesh forms a vital part of Belt and Road initiative. As Xi Jinping wrote in an article in the *Daily Star*, "Bangladesh, with its favourable geographic location and huge population, market potential and cooperation space, is an indispensable partner for China to advance the Belt and Road initiative and production capacity cooperation in South Asia and the Indian Ocean region."[33]

Chinese investment is perceived as major booster of Bangladesh economy. But, some have advised caution. For example, Mahfuz Anam while praising Hasina's diplomatic skill in terms of engaging both India and China and emphasing the importance of both, wrote, "Bangladesh needs all the assistance it can get and India cannot for the moment match China in terms of the funds that Bangladesh needs. Bangladesh's one and only goal is development and it needs both India and China."[34]

China has close defence ties with the Bangladesh military to which it has recently supplied two submarines. Many in Bangladesh look at China from two perspectives: a supplier of weapons and therefore a partner in Bangladesh's security; and second as a trade and investment partner therefore inalienable partner of its prosperity. The Bangladesh Foreign Secretary speaking at the World Economic Forum in New Delhi said:

> We can't forget what the people want and before joining BRI we had several discussions with civil society, and it was clear, what we need is connectivity. For us as a country, what we need is quick upgradation of our infrastructure and our generation wants much more interaction and connectivity...." Economic issues now dictate how much sovereignty one should exert.[35]

In the context of the Rohingya crisis, while Bangladesh expressed its utmost unhappiness with India's position on the issue, its reaction to China's stance was muted. There was public anger against India's position. Whereas many in the civil society and also the general public did not have any expectations from China. The narrative that Bangladesh is a benign strategic friend prevailed and the refugee crisis did little to dispel the relevance of China in Bangladesh's external relations.

Sri Lanka: From Balancing Game to Debt Trap

Sri Lanka's relations with China date back to the days of Rubber-Rice Pact of 1952, and were subsequently strengthened by various regimes in response to India's increasing role in island's ethnic conflict. China provided the Sri Lankan army with weapons, and training. However, the India factor in Sri Lanka's China policy became more visible after 2009. The China card was deftly played by President Rajapakse post-2009 to renege on his promises to India—to deliver on the political resolution of the Tamil issue.[36] China, which had been looking for an opportunity to expand its presence in Sri Lanka, moved into a role of security provider and created a commercial space for itself during the fourth Eelam War. However, China's presence and investment came into the limelight post-2009, even though, according to a report, the terms and conditions of the loans were negotiated in 2007.[37] Sri Lanka's close military cooperation with China started in 2007, when it supplied arms and ammunition, after US suspended the supply of arms to Sri Lanka and India abhorred defence ties due to domestic pressure. It is not surprising that China reaped the benefits in the post war politics.

In 2013, Sri Lanka and China concluded a Strategic cooperative Partnership Agreement. China, at present is engaged in commercial projects including the Hambanttota Port, Matala airport, the Colombo Port south container terminal where two submarines docked in 2014, and the Colombo city project. Most projects were awarded without proper evaluation and tender as Colombo was eager to court China for strategic purpose to balance India and the US and other Western countries due to the pressure they exerted in the United Nations Human Rights Commission (UNHRC). Sri Lanka looks at China from three broad perspectives. First, to ease pressure of India on the issue of political settlement of the Tamil issue and the pressure built by UNHRC resolutions that asked for investigation into the last phase of war for alleged human rights violation. China's veto would help to avoid international intervention; second, China is the only country with large capital that is willing to invest in Sri Lanka especially in projects that serve the interest of the then ruling regime; and third, China's loans do not have political strings attached. Chinese presence and investment in Sri Lanka is perceived from strategic perspective. There are also three narratives that have emerged in Sri Lanka. First, the political parties that look at China from the prism of oppositional politics, second, the strategic community as well as the well-entrenched perception of China as a balancer in ethnic politics and third, the value of China as a strategic partner in a dynamic geopolitical game.

Chinese debt was hotly debated topic in the last general election held in 2015 as opposition perceived that the then ruling party received a huge kickback and pushed the country into a debt trap. For instance, in 2014, the manifesto of a faction of the Sri Lanka Freedom Party under President Sirisena read, "Sri Lanka is a country with excessive state debt and a dangerous ratio with regard to loan payment and state revenue".[38] After the election, the then Finance Minister, Ravi Karunanayake who belonged to the United National Party in an interview with CNN Money said, "The Chinese companies used the opportunity of a corrupt regime to crowd out other companies coming in.... There was no even playing field. It was basically anybody who achieved their objective, to get money in their pockets".[39] Allegation of massive corruption and kickback and rising debt fuelled anti-China sentiment. In spite of the fact that the election was bitterly contested with dramatic loss of power of Rajapakse regime, the government handed over the controlling stake in Hambanttota and handed back the Colombo port city project to China in 2017, which were suspended for some time, finding no alternative to the debt that the country had already incurred.

The debt payment for Hambanttota port alone stood at $147 million a year when China took over the port in a debt-equity swap for 99 years, and agreed to write off a $1.2 billion loan. However massive protest broke out against China's investment in Hambattota and its plan to develop exclusive economic zone interestingly spearheaded by the former President Mahinda Rajapakse who was instrumental in pushing Sri Lanka into a debt trap. According to the Annual report of the Central Bank, the total outstanding external debt of Sri Lanka as a percentage of GDP increased to 59.5 per cent by end-2017 from 56.8 per cent at end-2016. The long-term portion of the total external debt increased, albeit marginally, to 85.2 per cent by end-2017, compared to 84.2 per cent at end-2016.[40] Some Sri Lankans view Chinese investment as "Eastern colonisation," which is being projected as better than "western colonisation".[41] Sri Lankan political scientist, Laksiri Fernando however cautioned the Sinhalese of severe repercussion if Sri Lanka does not play along with China.[42] Others view Chinese investment as an opportunity and some even argue that if China is ready to invest there is no harm in accepting the loan as there is no alternative to this huge investment.[43] There are others who have accused the government of non-transparency in the taking of Chinese loans, the rates of interest and the massive corruption involved in granting the projects to China.[44] The opposition, especially the Tamil National Alliance (TNA) saw this engagement with China as a means of keeping India at bay.[45] Other Sri Lankan analysts contend that the projects undertaken by China are a Chinese priority and not a Lankan priority.[46] Many in Sri Lanka give the example of the Norochcholai power plant, built with the help of China, which shut down frequently and as a result, the Ceylon Electricity Board incurred more than Rs 60 billion in debt in 2014. Therefore, there are a lot of concerns regarding the repayment of the huge loans taken by China. Sri Lanka took a loan of $6 billion from China Development Bank to repay its loan maturing in 2018. In 2019, Sri Lanka's debt repayment will stand at US$4.2 billion and from 2020 to 2022 it is going to be 3.6 billion annually which is going to place enormous stress on the economy.[47] According to the Finance Minister Mangala Samaraweera, 77 percent of the next year repayments are for debts obtained by the previous government.[48] Government is also preparing to refinance big debts that is due up to 2022 further pushing the country to a debt trap.

Nepal: The Balancing Game

Since the abolition of monarchy in Nepal in 2006, China has tried to build relations with various political parties to protect its interests. This is an attempt to ensure that the ethnic fault lines that was deepened during people's war, do not extend into the restive Tibetan region, as did the Tibetan activities in Nepal, especially after the April and May 2008 protests by Tibetan refugees in Kathmandu, on the eve of Beijing Olympics. Unlike Mao Zedong era, China's effort to reduce tension with India led it to keep a low profile during the early 1990s and for the time being was reluctant to be drawn into India-Nepal bilateral conflicts, is now eager to emerge as a major player in Nepal. Moreover, in the past Beijing has tried to raise questions about Nepal's sovereignty, 'unequal treaty', due to India's overwhelming influence. Kathmandu has always insisted on an equidistance between India and China. China however, has always emphasised on a 'mutually beneficial cooperation' with Nepal while India sees it as a 'special relationship' with a country with which it shares 1751 kilometres of open border and whose citizens enjoy resident status in each other's country. From Nepal's perspective, a close relationship with China will free it from its overwhelming dependence on India. It will also help Nepal build its infrastructure as the Chinese are willing to invest in it. Most importantly, it will end India's 'hegemony' and its ability to influence Nepal's internal politics which can be curtailed through the presence of China. This is basically the perspective of the left political parties that have traditionally framed their debate on Nepal's relations with India from a class perspective.

China's influence in Nepal has grown in proportion to the unpopularity of India. China's sale of weapons to Nepal Army was a major bone of contention that led to the 1988 crisis when India decided to close all the border points, except two, for Nepal's trade entrenching an anti-India sentiment and fear of repercussion of its overwhelming dependence of India. Maoist insurgency also build up on anti-India constituency and other domestic grievances that were not fulfilled by political parties. However, the palace massacre and later King Gyanendra's decision to directly takeover power in 2005, prompted India, the UK and the US to suspend the sale of weapons to the Nepal Army. China moved in to supply weapons and was able to endear itself to the ruling elites. China, which had supplied weapons to the Nepal army to fight against the Maoists, soon had to confront the Maoists who came to power in 2008. However, China changed its position and took steps to cultivate the Maoists. Although India played a crucial role in negotiating an end to the civil war through a 12-point agreement, it could not politically reconcile to the emergence of Maoists, about whom it still nurtured suspicion, as the ruling elites in Kathmandu.

India's position in fact helped the Chinese to step in and forge close ties with the Maoists. India's suspicions about the Maoists were confirmed when the Maoist prime minister, Prachanda, chose to visit China first. The party continued its anti-India rhetoric, which contributed to the tension between India and Nepal, especially the sacking of Army Chief General Rookmangud Katawal, that was perceived in India as an effort to establish one party rule at a time when the Maoists were demanding the integration of their cadres into the Nepal Army. Though Prachanda visited India subsequently, several issues remained sore points between the two countries. During the Madhav Kumar government, India and China jostled for influence through political leaders who were perceived to be closer to them. For example, the United Marxist-Leninist (UML) position on India was balanced by Jhala Nath Khanal who was seen as being close to China. When the Maoists and the CPN-(UML) joined hands to pass the first republican Constitution in 2014, India's concerns that the denial of rights to the marginalised community would exacerbate internal divisions and lead to instability, only deepened. The Madheshi agitation against the new Constitution and India's unofficial support for them only heightened the tensions between the two countries and, more specifically with the Hill elites, who perceived India's position as a threat to their power. In the aftermath of the Madheshi blockade, the Kathmandu based hill political elites successfully projected it as an issue of sovereignty. The Nepali media also plays up India's interference, as much of it is owned by Nepali hill businessmen, and argued that the relationship with China would put the Indian 'hegemony' to rest. Wang Yi, the Chinese foreign minister in December 2015, without referring to the Madheshi protest, said "China has all along believed that countries irrespective of their size are equal. China and Nepal have always treated each other sincerely and as equals. We hope that the same policy and practices will also be adopted by India."[49]

The then Nepal prime minister K.P. Oli's visit to China in early 2016 brought temporary relief as China supplied the oil required to meet Nepal's emergency needs. To reduce its dependence on India, Nepal and China signed an Agreement on Transit Transport between China and Nepal and a concessional loan for Pokhara Regional International Airport Project etc. In the joint communique issued after the visit, the Chinese side "welcomed" the promulgation of the Constitution, unlike India, which in a statement said that it had taken 'note' of promulgation of a Constitution. In contrast to India's position on the Constitution, the China-Nepal joint statement further read, "Chinese side firmly supports and respects Nepal's own choice of social system and development path, and effort made by Nepalese side in upholding its sovereignty, independence, territorial integrity, national unity and stability."[50] Though the trade and transit agreement was projected as a major victory for Nepal over India; the distance between Nepal and ports in China will not make business lucrative at least for the moment.[51] However, the agreement was considered as a major leverage over India in the context of Madheshi blockade and Nepal's quest and its hope to break free of its dependence over India.

China's *Global Times*, in an article said, that because of Prachanda's "pro-India" policy "the Sino-Nepalese relationship has fallen into low ebb"[52] more so since Prachanda withdrew support to Oli in July 2016, resulting in the fall of the government. The capacity of the Kathmandu elite to play the two countries against each other is not lost on the Chinese. For example, an article in the *Global Times*, points out:

> When Kathmandu needed Beijing to relieve pressure from New Delhi, it got close to China and signed a series of crucial agreements with Beijing which would help Nepal get rid of its reliance on India. But once India's attitude toward Kathmandu relaxed a bit and the former made some promises to the latter, Nepalese politicians immediately put the nation's ties with China on the back burner.[53]

Accusing India of spoiling China-Nepal relations, a Chinese scholar wrote, "China has never disturbed India-Nepal relations, but New Delhi has been interfering Sino-Nepalese ties every once in a while. Hence, from whatever perspective, Beijing is more deserving of Nepal's trust."[54]

In the past few years, Kathmandu has awarded several projects to Chinese companies. These include the: CAMC Engineering Company for carrying out a feasibility study for construction of the Kathmandu-Pokhara electric railway; Zhong Xing Telecommunication Equipment Company Ltd (ZTE) for building four high-technology data centres for Ncell Pvt Ltd; a telecom company in Nepal for earthquake-resistant data centres at the cost of $43.75 million in Biratnagar, Kathmandu, Hetauda and Pokhara.[55] It has also provided $ 32.3 million to the Nepal Army (NA) for capacity building. In 2015-16, while China topped the list with a commitment of $57 million as FDI, India stood third with $18 million investment. The total FDI pledged to Nepal in 2015-16 was roughly $140 million.[56] Over 59 per cent of Nepal's trade is with India, which is its largest trading partner and around 14.9 per cent of its total trade is with China.[57] India also accounts for nearly 40 per cent of total FDI flow to Nepal.[58]

In spite of the Nepali narrative that portrays China as a friend and India as the 'hegemonic' other, India has invested in 629 projects with an amount of Rs 80657 million, i.e. an average investment of Rs 128 million per industry; whereas China has invested in 29 projects costing Rs 25131 million, with average investment of Rs 867 million per industry.[59] India remains the fifth top donor to Nepal and the largest foreign investor in Nepal industries according to Ministry of industry of Nepal.[60] Though President Xi Jinping cancelled his visit to Nepal last year, Defence Minister Chang Wanquan visited Kathmandu to strengthen defence ties between the two countries. Nepal has now cancelled the Western Seti hydel project which was proposed to be built by Chinese Three Gorges Corporation and declared that Nepal will build the hydel project after mobilising Nepal's internal resources. Nepal's decision to cancel the Budi Gandak project awarded to Gezhouba Group, to build a 1,200 MW hydroelectric plant as per the Parliamentary committee recommendation, following irregularities by the Chinese company, has raised the old debate of China vs India with the UML, publicly declaring that if voted to power, it will renew the contract with China. However, after coming to power Nepal is planning to invite fresh bidding for the project. In the meanwhile India's guidelines for cross border electricity trade makes it difficult for foreign entities with 100 per cent ownership to export electricity to India.[61]

Nepal is part of the BRI which it signed in 2017. On this occasion the then Foreign Minister of Nepal Foreign Minister Prakash Sharan Mahat said, "Nepal needs the maximum investment and we want Chinese investment channelled in Nepal through this new project," The BRI is seen as an instrument for reducing Nepal's dependency on India.[62] However, some analysts think this playing of one country against the other is not a viable option for Nepal. It will make Nepal feel "stifled rather than liberated."[63] However, with the re-election of KP Oli in 2017 and visit of Mr Modi, though the bilateral relations appear to be back in track,[64] it is likely that Nepal will continue to play the balancing game to secure its interest. This is a narrative that has the backing of the elite.

Maldives: Engaging China, the Domestic Political Dimension

Maldives in 2013, was one of the first countries to welcome OBOR even though the initial statement said its endorsement has the approval of India as India had welcomed the maritime silk route,[65] which was officially denied by India. China opened its Embassy in Male in 2011. Since then it has established significant commercial interests in the island. China's Maldives policy is part of its larger strategy in the Indian Ocean. In 2014, during the visit of Chinese President to Maldives, both countries signed nine agreements to deepen their relationship very significantly, at a time when Maldives relationship with India had suffered a downward slide.[66] However, for India, the Chinese presence has been a major concern. The India-Maldives Framework Agreement for Cooperation and Development signed in 2011, which promised that, "Neither Party shall allow the use of its territory for activities harmful to the national security and interest of the other", faced a serious political challenge after the ouster of democratically elected President Nasheed, in a military coup. The cancellation of the GMR contract for building the Ibrahim Nasir International Airport (INIA) in Male, put serious strains on bilateral relations. This contract was subsequently awarded to China. The act was seen as an attempt by Maldives to endear itself to China which was supportive of the Yameen governments that succeeded Nasheed. The cancellation of the GMR contract was soon followed by Nasheed's decision to take refuge in the Indian High Commission to escape arrest, which dragged India into the domestic politics of Maldives. As the relations between the two neighbours deteriorated, and Maldives faced international isolation over how it treated its political opposition, China emerged as the main beneficiary.

Xi Jinping visited Maldives in 2014, and was the first Chinese President to do so, especially when Maldives was facing international isolation. President Yameen characterised Xi Jinping's South Asia policy as, "friendship, sincerity, reciprocity and inclusiveness". According to the joint statement the two countries issued after the Chinese President's visit, both countries decided to establish a "Future-Oriented All-round Friendly and Cooperative Partnership" and committed to support each other "on issues of core interests that bear on sovereignty, territorial integrity, stability and development. The Chinese side adheres to the principle of non-interference in internal affairs, and supports Maldives independent choice of development path." Interestingly Maldives also stated that it would support China's effort to upgrade its relationship with SAARC.[67]

In May 2015, public finance regulations were changed by the ministry of finance, to bypass the previously mandatory bidding and evaluation processes for projects worth more than MVR 1.5 million ($97,276). In July 2015, the government allowed foreigners, who could invest more than a billion dollars, to purchase land in the project site provided 70 per cent of the land was reclaimed from the sea. Many in Maldives thought that this change was being made to accommodate China.

To ensure that the crucial island nation does not come under Chinese security umbrella, India was cautious not to antagonise the regime while remaining neutral in the Commonwealth Forum which deliberated on Maldives turn to authoritarianism and contemplated its exclusion from the forum. India has boosted the security of the island country by setting up a network of 26 radars across the 26 Maldives atolls and has provided offshore patrol vehicles. India signed an "Action Plan for Defence Cooperation" that seeks to "institutionalise" the cooperation with meetings at the level of defence secretaries with Maldives in 2017 and the Maldivian President said that the security of Maldives is intimately linked to security of India.[68] The Chinese had shown an interest in the Ihavandhippolhu Integrated Development Project (iHavan), as they wanted it to be part of Maritime Silk Route, However, Abdullah Yameen in 2015 asked India to develop iHavan, which is under the active consideration of India. Yameen moved to placate Delhi's interest in signing the agreement on 'action plan on defence cooperation' as he was facing increasing domestic pressure from the main opposition party in Maldives, whose leader and former president Nasheed is seen as being close to India. While the main opposition party in Maldives is against the selling of the island and accuses the government of corruption; it was not critical of the Maldives growing relationship with China. Some opposition members unofficially assure India that once they are elected they will not take any steps that could compromise India's security—an assurance the present President has already given New Delhi. President Yameen though reiterated his 'India first' policy, he did everything to undermine India's interest. For example: Maldives signed an FTA with China, without any debate. It also ensured that opposition was not present in Parliament when the FTA was passed. It also suspended three local councillors who met the Indian High Commissioner, while he was touring some islands.

However, as the domestic political situation deteriorated with the arrest of the Supreme Court Chief Justice, India expressed its concern about the imposition of state of emergence. Special envoy was sent to China to appraise about the domestic political situation as China warned of any external interference in Maldives following a tweet by the opposition leader Nasheed asking India to intervene. As India is seen as a stakeholder in Maldives democratic transition, the Yameen government is keen to play the China card to blunt India's ability to interfere. In a sign of deteriorating relationship, Maldives did not participate in the trilateral exercise this year and return the two Dhruv Light Helicopter that was gifted as a part of the bilateral Defence agreement saying that it needs Dornier maritime surveillance aircraft. Maldives has been playing the China card effectively with close cooperation on security issues signalling India not to get involved in its domestic politics.

Conclusion

The reaction of South Asian countries to China's investment has been positive as most countries are looking for large scale investment without pre-conditions. Countries like Nepal and Bangladesh have struck a balance between India and China, and have engaged with them for stimulating growth through infrastructure projects, trade and for promoting their own security interests. China has extensive defence relations with all the countries of the South Asian region and supplies military hardware to them as well. India's domestic politics has prevented New Delhi to effectively leverage its relations through defence cooperation. For example: though India provided non-lethal weapons to Sri Lanka during the last Eelam war, which contributed substantially and decisively to Sri Lanka's victory; it could not supply defence hardware during the war and Beijing moved in. Therefore, in the domestic political narrative the Chinese contribution is portrayed as the game changer. Similarly, India's decision to suspend sale of weapons to Nepal after the monarchy decided to assume power by dismissing the elected government in 2005, endeared China to the ruling regime. China was portrayed as a country that does not interfere in the domestic politics of the country especially during the Madhesi blockade. Similarly, the ruling party in Maldives have withstood the pressure exerted by India and the Western countries on democracy due to support of China. The advantage the China enjoys is that it does not have border disputes with most countries, except India and Bhutan. The domestic politics of South Asian countries, the ethno-cultural linkages, the baggage of partition, the identity politics and porous border—all have contributed to India becoming a factor in their internal politics. A security narrative that nurtures the threat of India can only be balanced by a close defence engagement with China—India's rival and a country that defeated India. Hence, all these works in favour of China.

Second, unlike China, India's economic engagement with its South Asian neighbours is miniscule. Most Indian projects are not completed in time due to the joint venture method adopted by India, and its decision to employ local entrepreneurs and labourers through a lengthy tendering process. China does not face such problems. It has taken up mega projects and completed them in time. Chinese projects are visible, thus its contribution is acknowledged by the people. Infrastructure projects are very new to India's economic engagement. However, India is now engaged in infrastructure projects that project India's soft power. For example, the buildings such as: the Afghan Parliament; hospitals in Afghanistan and Nepal; the restoring of the Jaffna library, railways and the building of 50,000 houses for war victims in Sri Lanka; providing electricity to Bangladesh, etc. are some of the efforts that are likely to create a positive perception of India.

Third, it is only in Sri Lanka, that Chinese investment has evoked negative public opinion, as many see these projects as benefitting China and imposing a massive debt burden on Sri Lanka. Some also perceive massive corruption in the allocation of these projects to China, which benefitted the then ruling Rajapakse family. However, in Bangladesh the offer of a $ 24 billion investment is seen as a game changer. Many in Bangladesh compare the Chinese investment with its $ 62 billion investment in Pakistan's CPEC. In Nepal, Chinese investment is seen from the perspective of negating Indian domination and providing alternative transit to Nepal. Similarly, Chinese investment and the establishment of Confucian study centres are not seen as economic and cultural intrusion. Indian projects are over scrutinised and always viewed from the 'sovereignty' perspective. China does not have to deal with the 'sovereignty' narrative. Rather, it is seen as a country that believes in sovereign equality.

Fourth, the perception of China among India's neighbours is conditioned by their relations with India. There is a strong narrative created by powerful vested interests, which portrays India as a 'hegemon' and China as a 'benign' neighbour. China has always portrayed itself as a country that respects the sovereignty of smaller countries. In the joint statements made by China and each of India's neighbours, words like sovereignty and non-interference find special mention. India is seen as a country that is unfair to its neighbours in terms of a massive trade imbalance. China also has a massive trade imbalance with these countries but that hardly finds a mention in the popular narrative.

Fifth, the military continues to play a significant role in most neighbouring countries. China has close military relationships with all these countries and thus, has powerful supporters to whom it continues to sell military hardware. Though India is now involved in capacity building and training, it has yet to make a mark as a supplier of weapons. Regime centric elite narrative would see India as a threat as opposition to the regime would like to cultivate India's support in political transition. Therefore China would remain as a guarantor to autocratic regimes in South Asia in the name of 'non-interference' and 'sovereignty' while in return trying to expand its strategic footprint. At the popular level, issues like granting of visa, experience of border crossing, its ethno-cultural linkages that portrays India as close to one ethnic group or the other and India's cultural domination through Bollywood will shape the perception of common people about India. What is most important is: unlike China, India has a stake in the ethnic accommodation in Sri Lanka, the political accommodation of Madhesis in Nepal, electoral fair play in Maldives as well as a stake in the non-fundamentalist polity in Bangladesh. China has no such stakes and it protects its interest by aligning itself with regime interest. Therefore, while China would remain an important factor in the economies of South Asian countries; India on its part, would be a major political factor and its close cultural relationship would stand it in good stead.

NOTES

1. China Council for International Cooperation on Environment and Development", Important Speech of Xi Jinping at Peripheral Diplomacy Work Conference", October 30, 2013, at http://www.cciced.net/encciced/newscenter/latestnews/201310/t20131030_262608.html, January 16, 2015.
2. John Garver, Protracted Contest: Sino-Indian Rivalry in the Twentieth Century", Oxford University Press, Delhi, 2001, p.73, Andrew small, "The China-Pakistan Axis: Asia's New Geopolitics", Hurst, London, 2015, p.29, Sturat Harris, "China's Foreign Policy", Polity Press, Cambridge, 2014, p. 160.
3. John Garver, n. 2, pp. 81 and 83.
4. *Asian Recorder*, April 30-May 6, 1990, p. 21126.
5. Mohan Mallik, "Balancing Act: The China-India-U.S. Triangle" World affairs, Spring 2016, http://www.worldaffairsjournal.org/article/balancing-act-china-india-us-triangle, accessed 27th May 2016.
6. To balance India after the Indo-US nuclear deal, China significantly stepped up its nuclear cooperation with Pakistan agreeing to expand Chashma to match a 2008 nuclear energy deal between India and the United States citing bilateral deal sealed before China joined the NSG in 2004. Fredrick Dahl, "West worried by China-Pakistan atomic ties: sources", *Reuters*, June 27, 2012, https://www.reuters.com/article/us-nuclear-china-pakistan/west-worried-by-china-pakistan-atomic-ties-sources-idUSBRE85Q0YL20120627, accessed on May 27, 2018.
7. Address by Prime Minister at the Tsinghua University Beijing (May 15, 2015), http://www.mea.gov.in/Speeches-Statements.htm?dtl/25242/Address_by_Prime_ Minister_at_the_Tsinghua_University_Beijing_May_15_2015. Accessed on March 5, 2017
8. Ai Jun "India over-sensitive on China's engagement in South Asia", *Global Times*, March 21, 2017, http://www.globaltimes.cn/content/1038736.shtml
9. Garver, n.2, p. 165.
10. China pays 'close attention' to Bangladesh's political situation, *bdnews24.com*, March 21, 2018, https://bdnews24.com/world/2018/03/21/china-pays-close-attention-to-bangladeshs-political-situation. Accessed 27 May 2018.
11. Yubaraj Ghimire, "China tells Nepal what to do", *Indian Express*, October 27, 2014, http://indianexpress.com/article/opinion/columns/china-tells-nepal-what-to-

do/, *The Economist* "Ad hoc country", June 22, 2013, http://www.economist.com/news/asia/21579882-election-called-political-stability-remains-distant-dream-ad-hoc-country

12. Li Ruogu former President of Export Import Bank of China, the main financer of Belt and Road Initiative warning on the increasing debt burden on the recipient countries. He said, "countries' average liability and debt ratios had reached 35 and 126 per cent, respectively, far above the globally recognised warning lines of 20 and 100 per cent." See "Is China's belt and road infrastructure development plan about to run out of money?" *South China Morning Post*, April 14, 2018, http://www.scmp.com/news/china/economy/article/2141739/chinas-belt-and-road-infrastructure-development-plan-about-run, accessed on May 27, 2018.
13. "China helped Pakistan block India's NSG membership bid: Aziz", *The Hindu*, March 9, 2016, http://www.thehindu.com/news/national/China-helped-Pakistan-block-India%E2%80%99s-NSG-membership-bid-Aziz/article14145539.ece
14. Syed Irfan Raza, "Senate panel wants Pakistan's interests fully protected under CPEC", *Dawn*, March 1, 2017, https://www.dawn.com/news/1317736/senate-panel-wants-pakistans-interests-fully-protected-under-cpec
15. Khurram Hussain, Exclusive: CPEC master plan revealed", *Dawn*, June 21, 2017, https://www.dawn.com/news/1333101
16. Maidah Haris, "Pakistan needs to watch out as CPEC-related debt soars", *Express Tribune*, May 5, 2018, https://tribune.com.pk/story/1702654/2-pakistan-needs-watch-cpec-related-debt-soars/
17. Khurram Hussain, "CPEC cost build-up", *Dawn*, December 15, 2017, http://www.dawn.com/news/1302328/cpec-cost-build-up
18. Syed Irfan Raza, "'CPEC could become another East India Company", *Dawn*, October 16, 2016, https://www.dawn.com/news/1290677. Also see Danish Hyder and Mushtaq Khan "CPEC: The devil is not in the details", *Dawn*, September 29, 2016, http://herald.dawn.com/news/1153597
19. Iftikhar A Khan, China to get 91pc Gwadar income, minister tells Senate", *Dawn*, November 25, 2017, https://www.dawn.com/news/1372695. Also see, Nadir Hussain "Let's not romanticise CPEC" News International, May 19, 2017.https://www.thenews.com.pk/print/205277-Lets-not-romanticise-CPEC
20. M. Jashim Uddin and Mahbubur Rashid Bhuiyan, "Sino-Bangladesh relations: An Appraisal", *BIISS Journal*, Vol. 32, No. 1, January 2011, pp. 18 and 22.
21. Iftikhar Chowdhury, in Muni and Yong ed., A Resurgent China: South Asian Perspectives, Routledge, Delhi, 2012, p. 44.
22. C.M. Shafi Shami, Ibid., p. 36.
23. M. Jashim Uddin, n. 20,. p. 7
24. Emphasis is that of the author's. http://bd2.mofcom.gov.cn/aarticle/bilateralcooperation/inbrief/200411/20041100003924.html, accessed on September 26, 2006.
25. http://bd2.mofcom.gov.cn/aarticle/bilateralcooperation/inbrief/200411/20041100003924.html, accessed on September 26, 2006.
26. Ruksana Kibria, "Strategic Implications of Bangladesh-China Relations", Bangladesh and the World, 15th Anniversary Special, *Daily Star*, February 19, 2006 at http://www.thedailystar.net/suppliments/2006/15thanniv/bangladesh&theworld/bd_world12.htm

27. *The Daily Star* "Xi Jinping's visit: Implications for Bangladesh-China relations", October 14, 2016, http://www.thedailystar.net/op-ed/economics/implications-bangladesh-china-relations-1298533
28. Rezaul Karim and Shakhawat Liton, "Strategic Partners", October 15, 2016, *The Daily Star*, http://www.thedailystar.net/frontpage/strategic-partners-1298923
29. Rejaul Karim Byron, "China likely to pledge big", *The Daily Star*, September 26, 2016, http://www.thedailystar.net/frontpage/china-likely-pledge-big-1289737
30. Zafar Ahmed, "China seeks to convert part of soft loans into commercial credit for Bangladesh", *bdnews24*, June 13, 2017, https://bdnews24.com/economy/2017/06/13/china-seeks-to-convert-part-of-soft-loans-into-commercial-credit-for-bangladesh. China provides development assistance to Bangladesh in the form of grant, interest free loan, Chinese Government Concessional Loan, and Preferential Buyer's Credit. See Economic Relations Division, Government of Bangladesh, http://www.erd.gov.bd/site/page/e0ed373a-4243-4dd4-aa10-f402dea4a3cf/Wing-8:Asia-&-JEC, accessed on January 8, 2018.
31. The *Global Times* wrote, "Charging an appropriate level of interest may impose pressure on the borrower, which should be helpful to enhance its productivity and stimulate the vitality of the local economy. That's what the B&R is really for, rather than offering a free lunch." Wang Jiamei, "China should not try to compete for projects by offering low interest rates on loans", June 18, 2017, http://www.globaltimes.cn/content/1052266.shtml. Accessed on June 20, 2017. Also see Jagaran Chakma, "China policy change may throw projects off track", *The Independent*, December 7, 2017, http://www.theindependentbd.com/post/126951, accessed on January 8, 2018.
32. China card implies emphasise on a strong and strategic relationship with China and projecting China as a friend while projecting India's role in a negative light and using China as a balancer in future conflict with India.
33. *The Daily Star*, "China-Bangladesh cooperation will bear golden fruits", October 14, 2016, http://www.thedailystar.net/frontpage/china-bangladesh-cooperation-will-bear-golden-fruits-1298536 accessed on January 9, 2018.
34. Mahfuz Anam, "Will Xi Jinping's visit to Bangladesh be a regional game changer?", *The Daily* Star, November 14, 2016, http://www.thedailystar.net/opinion/asian-editors-circle/will-xi-jinpings-visit-bangladesh-be-regional-game-changer-1314082.accessed on February 18, 2018.
35. *Dhaka Tribune*, Foreign secretary in Delhi: Bangladesh supports China's One-Belt-One Road, October 7, 2017, http://www.dhakatribune.com/bangladesh/foreign-affairs/2017/10/07/foreign-secretary-bangladesh-supports-chinas-one-belt-one-road/ accessed on January 8, 2018.
36. Nirupama Subhramanium, '13th Amendment Plus': India sceptical of Sri Lankan promise", *The Hindu*, March 26, 2011, http://www.thehindu.com/news/the-india-cables/lsquo13th-Amendment-Plusrsquo-India-sceptical-of-Sri-Lankan-promise/article14962436 accessed on March 26, 2012.
37. "Sri Lankan expert says interest rate of Chinese loan for port project appropriate", According to Sri Lankan experts as quoted in *Xinhua*, "Some 77 percent of the loans are preferential loans, of which the interest rate is 2 percent per year. The remaining fund gap has been covered by commercial loans." Article republished in *Lanka WeB*, January 17, 2017, http://www.lankaweb.com/news/items/2017/

01/12/sri-lankan-expert-says-interest-rate-of-chinese-loan-for-port-project-appropriate/, accessed on January 8, 2018.

38. http://www.asianmirror.lk/news/item/5782-full-text-of-maithripala-sirisena-s-election-manifesto, accessed on January 8, 2018.
39. http://money.cnn.com/2015/04/02/news/sri-lanka-china-corruption/, accessed on January 8, 2018.
40. Central Bank of Sri Lanka, *Annual Report 2017*, p. 176.
41. Laksiri Fernando, "Too Much China Connection", *Colombo Telegraph*, December 19, 2014, https://www.colombotelegraph.com/index.php/too-much-china-connection/, accessed June 14, 2015.
42. Ibid, According to Fernando, "Alakeshvara, who was first a military commander/minister and then the real Kotte ruler broke his promises to the Chinese, he and his entourage/family were taken as prisoners to Nanjing in 1411.... It is unclear how the colonial ambitions of the Ming Dynasty died down in Greater and South Asia thereafter. If not, Ceylon could have been a colony of the Chinese even before the Portuguese."
43. Sanja De Silva Jayatilleka, "Is China A Threat To Our Island & The Indian Ocean Region?", *Colombo Telegraph*, February 25, 2017, https://www.colombotelegraph.com/index.php/is-china-a-threat-to-our-island-the-indian-ocean-region/
44. Editorial, "Enter the dragon", *Sunday Times*, November 2, 2014,, http://www.sundaytimes.lk/141102/editorial/enter-the-dragon-125695.html, Tisaranee Gunasekara, Abracadabra In China", September 18, 2014, *Sri Lanka Guardian*, http://www.srilankaguardian.org/2014/09/abracadabra-in-china.html, accessed January 17, 2016.
45. R. Sampathan, "China Should Use Its Goodwill Over Sri Lanka In A More Reasonable Way", *Colombo Telegraph*, November 14, 2014, (adapted from his speech in the Sri Lankan Parliament), https://www.colombotelegraph.com/index.php/china-should-use-its-goodwill-over-sri-lanka-in-a-more-reasonable-way/, accessed January 11, 2016.
46. Charitha Ratwatte, China, A Reality Check", *Colombo Telegraph*, February 24, 2015, https://www.colombotelegraph.com/index.php/china-a-reality-check/ accessed January 19, 2016.
47. 2018 crucial for strengthening foreign reserves to meet massive debt repayment in 2019, *Sunday Times*, January 21, 2018, http://www.sundaytimes.lk/180121/columns/2018-crucial-for-strengthening-foreign-reserves-to-meet-massive-debt-repayment-in-2019-278032.html, accessed on May 28, 2018.
48. Shihar Aneez, " Sri Lanka accepts $1 billion, eight-year syndicated loan from China Development Bank", May 25, 2018, https://in.reuters.com/article/sri-lanka-china-loan/sri-lanka-accepts-1-billion-eight-year-syndicated-loan-from-china-development-bank-idINKCN1IQ2FT, accessed May 28, 2018.
49. PTI, "Nepal should not become 'boxing arena' for India, China: Wang Yi", *Indian Express*, December 25, 2015, http://indianexpress.com/article/world/world-news/nepal-should-not-become-boxing-arena-for-india-china-wang-yi/ accessed on March 5, 2018.
50. Ministry of Foreign Affairs, Joint Press Statement between the People's Republic of China and Nepal", https://www.mofa.gov.np/joint-press-statement/ May 23,

2016, http://kathmandupost.ekantipur.com/news/2016-03-24/oli-ends-beijing-business-with-joint-communiqu.htmlaccessed on January 8, 2018.

51. *Kathmandu Post*, "Nearest port in China—Tianjin—is almost four times far from the Nepal border than the port in Kolkata. Movement of trucks in the north is virtually impossible; train is the only viable means of transportation. The station closest from Nepal where Chinese trains arrive is in Shigatse, which is almost 540km away from the Nepal-China border in Rasuwagadi. So due to these problems, it is very difficult to implement the Transit Transport Agreement with China." See interview with Purushottam Ojha, former secretary at the Ministry of Commerce and Supplies. "Transit accord with China marks an important milestone for Nepal" March 28, 2016, http://kathmandupost.ekantipur.com/news/2016-03-28/transit-accord-with-china-marks-an-important-milestone-for-nepal.html, accessed on January 8, 2018.
52. Shubin, "Will Nepal's PM repair ties with China?" *Global Times*, March 20, 2017. http://www.globaltimes.cn/content/1038667.shtml, accessed on January 8, 2018
53. Xu Liang, "Nepal risks missing chance with China", *Global Times*, September 19, 2016, http://www.globaltimes.cn/content/1007091.shtml, accessed on January 8, 2018.
54. Ibid.
55. Thomas K Thomas, "Security agencies take guard as China invests in Nepal telecom", *Business Line*, October 19, 2012, http://www.thehindubusinessline.com/info-tech/security-agencies-take-guard-as-china-invests-in-nepal-telecom/article4013647.ece, accessed on April 20, 2018.
56. Sachin Parashari, India watches warily as China further ramps up FDI into Nepal", *Times of India*, February 7, 2017, http://timesofindia.indiatimes.com/india/india-watches-warily-as-china-further-ramps-up-fdi-into-nepal/articleshow/57008982.cms
57. Nepal Economic Survey, http://www.mof.gov.np/uploads/document/file/Economic%20Survey%202015-16%20-%20English_20160812062624.pdf
58. PTI, "Nepal needs more conducive framework for higher Indian FDI: Jaitley", *Hindustan Times*, March 3, 2017, http://www.hindustantimes.com/business-news/nepal-needs-more-conducive-framework-for-higher-indian-fdi-jaitley/story-SrKkMjzSYiEG6jU1EIgIsJ.html. According to the *Economic Times*, "India's actual disbursement of aid to Nepal in the financial year 2010-11 was USD 50,728,502. In 2011-12, it was USD 50,620,749 and in 2012-13 it rose to USD 63,813,269. In 2013-14, the Indian aid, however, fell to USD 47,796,349 and it dwindled to USD 22,227,306 in 2014-15. On the other hand, China's aid to Nepal has been steadily growing from USD 18,843,988 in 2010-11 to USD 28,344,923 in 2011-12 and USD 34,120,033 in 2012-13. The financial help again grew to USD 41,381,522 in 2013-14 and stood at USD 37,948,75 in 2014-15. *Economic Times*, "India's aid to Nepal dwindles, China now among major donors", April 25, 2016, https://economictimes.indiatimes.com/news/politics-and-nation/indias-aid-to-nepal-dwindles-china-now-among-major-donors/articleshow/51984004.cms, accessed on January 8, 2018.
59. *Economic Survey*, Fiscal Year 2015-16, p. 150.
60. Ministry of industry, Government of Nepal, Industrial Statistics, Fiscal Year 2072/073 (2015/2016), p.111, http://www.doind.gov.np/images/industrial-static/Industrial_statistics_7273.pdf, accessed on January 8, 2018.

61. Government of India Ministry of Power, "Guidelines on Cross Border Trade of Electricity", December 5, 2018, No. 14/1/2016-Trans, p.3, https://powermin.nic.in/sites/default/files/webform/notices/Guidelines%20for%20Cross%20Boarder%20Trade.pdf, accessed on January 8, 2018.
62. Editorial, "Endorse OBOR", *Rising Nepal*, http://therisingnepal.org.np/news/17949, accessed on January 31, 2018.
63. Subhas Ghimire Editor in Chief of *Republica* quoted in Rishi Iyengar, "What the Nepalese Prime Minister's Visit to China Says About the Wider Politics of Asia", *Time*, March 24, 2016, http://time.com/4270239/nepal-prime-minister-oli-visit-china-beijing-india/, accessed on April 7, 2018.
64. The two countries this month laid the foundation stone of the foundation stone of Arun-III hydro power project and agreed to construct Kathmandu with Raxaul rail project.
65. Foreign Minister Dunya Mamoon said "Indian government also welcomed the Silk Route initiative during Chinese President Xi's visit to New Delhi in September" see, "Maldives not obliged to consult neighbours before joining China's Silk Route, says foreign minister", https://minivannewsarchive.com/politics/maldives-not-obliged-to-consult-neighbours-before-joining-chinas-silk-route-says-foreign-minister-90814, accessed June 7, 2018.
66. http://www.presidencymaldives.gov.mv/Index.aspx?lid=11&dcid= 14808
67. Joint press communique between the Republic of Maldives and the People's Republic of China, September 15, 2014, Male' http://www.presidencymaldives.gov.mv/Index.aspx?lid=12&dcid=14810
68. https://eoi.gov.in/male/?4918, accessed on January 8, 2018.

8

Southeast Asian Views on China: Paradoxes and Prospects

Sampa Kundu

ABSTRACT

China's rise as an influential factor in Asia-Pacific has led countries in the neighbourhood to intensify debates and attempt to comprehend the implications for their security. Therefore, an analysis of the responses of China's immediate neighbours could help understand the complexity of China's rise in the region. In this regard, Southeast Asia's responses to China's rise are relevant and contemporary. In recent times, many have perceived that the Chinese influence in the Southeast Asian region is increasing exponentially. For instance, the Association of Southeast Asian Nations' (ASEAN) inability to condemn China for its assertiveness on South China Sea is often cited as an example of this influence. In the given background, this study will take into account three inter-linked questions. First, how individual Southeast Asian countries view the rise of China or, in other words, what are their perceptions towards China's leadership role in the region? Second, how they are responding to the regional complications emerging out of China's multidimensional relations with Southeast Asian countries? Third, what are the drivers or factors that are shaping individual Southeast Asian countries' responses to China? In order to understand these aspects, this chapter will analyse the individual responses of some of the ASEAN countries towards China on a case-by-case basis. These country-specific responses will show that Southeast Asia is never united as far as China is concerned. For instance, Cambodia and Vietnam have differing perceptions towards China. While Cambodia may be classified as a close aide of China, Vietnam contrarily, has always been resistant to Chinese assertiveness. However, there are some countries who are ambivalent towards China. Some ASEAN economies like Thailand, Indonesia, Singapore, Malaysia and Brunei can be clubbed together in this group. Myanmar, on the other hand has diversified its economic and foreign relations to reduce its over-reliance on Chinese economic cooperation. Philippines too, under President Rodrigo Duterte, has indicated its willingness to cooperate with China, and maintain less dependence on the US. Hence, the paper argues that by studying individual Southeast Asian countries' assessments of China, the country's position and role in the region could be understood.

Introduction

China's influence in the global order has been steadily increasing. This is especially evident as the Chinese President Xi Jinping has expressed his desire to pursue grand strategic ambitions across the world. Several countries view China as a significant power in the region. In East Asia, the Asian Barometer Survey Wave 4 (2014-2016) found that most of the East Asian countries with the exception of Philippines perceived China as the most influential country in the region.[1] In a Pew Research Center survey, (April 6 to May 27, 2015) conducted on 15,313 respondents in 10 Asia-Pacific countries and the US, around 47 per cent people praised President Xi, compared to other Asian leaders including Japanese Prime Minister Shinzo Abe and Indian Prime Minister Narendra Modi.[2] On the question of China replacing the US as the super power, the survey found a mixed result, where 41 per cent respondents voted in favour of China and 38 per cent against China.[3] Countries that share major territorial disputes namely Japan, Vietnam and Philippines were particularly vocal against China's rise as 77 per cent, 67 per cent and 65 per cent respondents from these three countries respectively mentioned that China will never replace US as the super power.[4]

In Southeast Asia, the differing perceptions towards China are caused by the role of its economic and security interests in the region. Few factors can briefly explain the beginning of Chinese influence in the region in the post-Cold War era. On the one hand, the US failed to provide necessary security partnership to its allies in the region and on the other hand, post the 1997-98 Financial Crisis, China showed readiness in helping the Southeast Asian economies. However, China was also expanding its naval modernisation programmes. As a result, the People's Liberation Army Navy (PLAN) started deployments in the adjacent waters off the Chinese coasts. Thus, by the early 2000s, Southeast Asian countries believed that neither they are in a position to compete with China (both militarily and economically) nor there is any alternative power, which can support the smaller Southeast Asian economies in the time of any crisis. Hence, for them (as will be argued in this chapter), it only became pragmatic to accommodate China's interests and search for own benefits within China's global ambitions and agenda.[5] This chapter will further argue that the degrees of accommodation of China's interests by individual Southeast Asian countries are certainly different from each other, depending on various factors, especially domestic political system, the level of economic cooperation with China and involvement in territorial disputes with China (for instance South China Sea issues). While it is certain that there is no uniformity in perceptions and responses towards China amongst the Southeast Asian states and many of them actually follow ambivalence towards China, few scholars believe that historically, anti-establishment and anti-great power sentiments are nothing new for Southeast Asia.[6] For the most parts of nineteenth and twentieth centuries, the region showed hostility towards imperial powers including US and European colonisers (to regain independence and sovereignty) and hence, it may be argued that some Southeast Asian countries' animosity towards China is not a new feature for the region, especially when seen in the light of protecting national interests and prestige or image in the international community.[7] To understand all these aspects, this chapter will briefly discuss the trajectory of China-Southeast Asia relations as it has been unfolding in the recent past; a brief conceptual inquiry into Southeast Asia's responses to China through a combination of balancing, hedging and engaging China policy; rest of it will offer individual country analyses to comprehend the implications of China's rise for Southeast Asia.

Historical Interfaces with China: From Anti-Imperialism to Anti-Communism to Softer Attitude towards China

Southeast Asia's anti-imperial attitude faded away (with a few exceptions) with the wave of independence gained by many of the countries in the region. Rather, in general, the post Second World War (WWII) period saw the emergence of anti-communist (and to some extent anti-Chinese) rhetoric in many parts of Southeast Asia. The rise of anti-Chinese sentiments could be attributed to several factors including the Sino-Vietnamese War, fear of spread of communism, trade imbalances, domestic regime changes and the force of democratization.[8] In many cases, Southeast Asian countries purposefully instigated anti-Chinese sentiments among the population to facilitate the process of building ethnocentric nation-states. For instance, as Indonesia was grappling with the fear of growing Chinese population and spread of Communism, President Suharto used the anti-Chinese sentiments for his political aspirations. In Thailand, Prime Minister Phibum Songkhramdrew closer to the US and participated in the Southeast Asia

Treaty Organisation (SEATO) in 1954 to counter the expansion of Communism in the region. Malaysia and Myanmar too saw strong anti-Chinese sentiments as the Chinese were instrumental in providing support to the Communist parties/leaders in those countries. However, in the latter part of the Cold War, China started supporting existing regimes and curtailed its support to the communist activities across Southeast Asia. Therefore, from the mid-1990s, China's relations with many Southeast Asian countries received major breakthroughs. In this regard, improved economic relations between China and Southeast Asia became a driver in augmenting relations. China's foreign policy also sought to cultivate relations with Southeast Asia as a part of its larger foreign policy decision-making to enhance relations with all its neighbours. China's contributions to the domestic political and economic stability in Southeast Asia in the years followed by the 1997-98 financial crisis were recognised and reciprocated well. China acceded to ASEAN's Treaty of Amity and Cooperation (TAC), supported ASEAN to fight the SARS epidemic and signed the Declaration of Conduct on South China Sea (DoC). These achievements characterised China-Southeast Asia relations till the early half of the 2000s.

The Contemporary Era: Neither a Modern-day 'Tributary' System nor Bandwagoning; But a Multifaceted Combination of Balancing, Hedging and Engaging China Policy

Martin Stuart Fox (2003)[9] has noted that a large part of Southeast Asia followed the tributary system with China and in return of their obedience to China, they expected security and independence. Based on this precedent, some argue that the Southeast Asian countries might be forced to rely on China's benevolence again. For instance, Fox (2003) has argued that a modern-day tributary system might develop because of China's insistence that it follows a policy of non-interference in the internal affairs of other countries and the lack of credibility in the resilience of US leadership in the region. He believes that the smaller neighbours of China may accept security and independence in return of their acknowledgement of China's great power status. Through their support to the Asian Infrastructure Investment Bank (AIIB) and One Belt One Road (OBOR) these countries may cooperate in China's global interests. Consecutively, they may not resist China's assertiveness in the South China Sea. However, these arguments fail to justify why Southeast Asian countries, who are nation-states, would perceive themselves as tributaries of China, especially when several of them have significant territorial and sovereignty disputes with it. Therefore, while an evolution of a modern-day tributary system is not a realistic option for the Southeast Asian countries, do they consider bandwagoning with China to escape being attacked by China and to get some economic benefits?[10] The answer is perhaps a no. Roy (2005)[11] has indicated that key documents of the Association of Southeast Asian Nations (ASEAN) including the Bangkok Declaration 1967, the Zone of Peace, Freedom and Neutrality Declaration (ZOPFAN) 1971, and the TAC 1976 uphold sovereignty and independence as the principal foreign policy. Hence, bandwagoning with China, which often shows disrespect for the sovereignty and independence of the neighbours who share territorial disputes with China, does not seem to be an option for Southeast Asian countries. Bandwagoning for gaining economic opportunities is again not applicable to understand China-Southeast Asia relations as trade and investment have really not been able to reduce political and strategic tensions in the region. For instance, despite having robust economic relations, countries like Vietnam have often opposed China's position on South China Sea and have not shied away from being vocal against it.

Conversely, individual Southeast Asian nations have found it convenient to follow a combination of balancing, hedging and/or engaging China.[12] While many Southeast Asian countries take efforts not to displease China, they also demonstrate enthusiasm to harness defence and security partnerships with extra-territorial powers. For instance, the Five Power Defence Arrangement (FPDA) (though it is defunct now) was perceived as an instrument to involve outside powers in the region. The actions of the various Filipino administrations, prior to President Duterte, too, showed a clear balancing strategy against China. For instance, the US-Philippines defence relationships was strengthened in the last two decades and that resulted in the Mutual Logistics Support Agreement between the two countries and the Philippines' recognition as a non-NATO ally in 2003. Thailand, on the other hand, followed a hedging policy as it neither wanted to displease China nor isolate itself from the US. As Thailand shares no major or minor territorial disputes with China, it has avoided any confrontation with China over its sovereignty. But, as a non-NATO ally of the US, Thailand has allowed US forces to use its bases during its War on Terror, followed by the September 11 Attacks in the US. Besides balancing and hedging, the ASEAN members also often practice the policy of engaging China. The ASEAN Regional Forum (ARF), ASEAN Plus China, ASEAN Plus Three are few examples which, at many levels, demonstrate Southeast Asia's efforts to accommodate and engage China.[13] In brief, the Southeast Asian countries share multifaceted interpretations about China and a closer look at the bilateral relations between China and some of the Southeast Asian countries would elaborate that.

Philippines

Before President Rodrigo Duterte, Philippines was widely considered to be a close ally of the United States and Manila appeared to have embraced a strong balancing approach against China by letting the US use its territory. As the previous administration under the leadership of Benigno Aquino III had approached the arbitral tribunal at The Hague against Chinese historical claims on parts of South China Sea, strong signals were sent about Manila's resentment towards China. After President Duterte assumed office, he brought out few changes in Manila's China policy. In his October 2016 visit to China, Duterte had 'declared' that his country would break all ties with the United States. Later, though, Duterte withdrew his comments about US-Philippines relations, the sudden shift in Philippines' foreign policy is still unfolding. One reason behind such shift may be attributed to Manila's fear of receiving 'punishment' by China.[14] For instance, in 2013, Philippines reportedly could not attend a trade expo in China as the condition of withdrawing the arbitration process was allegedly placed on Manila if Philippines needed to be there.[15] In addition, China has also alleged that Philippines violated the DoC by calling a third party for resolving the South China Sea territorial disputes. There were hardly any ASEAN member, who had expressed support towards Philippines and issued any joint statement in Manila's favour. Clearly, ASEAN does not see itself opposing China dominantly and this might explain President Duterte's accommodative approach towards China given the tough external situation. During President Duterte's China visit in 2016, Manila and Beijing issued a joint statement, where both the countries had mentioned the tensions in South China Sea and both reaffirmed that "contentious issues are not the sum total of the Philippines-China bilateral relationship".[16] Additionally, unlike the US which has been critical of Duterte for his headstrong attitude to fight the drug menace in Philippines, China has always shown its support towards the new administration and its way of handling domestic issues by requesting the international community to respect the country's choice to fight the threat. This happened in May 2017 as the United Nations Human Rights Council (UNHCR) had urged Manila to withdraw its plan of bringing back the death penalty if found guilty in having connections with drugs. However, regardless of Philippines's closeness with China, its ties with the US too will be sustained. President Duterte and President Donald Trump are unlikely to abandon existing military-defence partnerships between Manila and Washington. Philippines has to apply pragmatic decisions if it wants to maintain cordial partnership with China and the US simultaneously.[17]

Vietnam

The territorial conflict between Vietnam and China on South China Sea is another challenge the region has been facing for the last several decades. Vietnam was not always hostile to China, especially in the first phase of Cold War. Communist Party of Vietnam (CPV) considered the Communist Party of China (CPC) as its ideological master. In fact, CPC provided financial, moral and material support to the CPV during its war against South Vietnam and the US. However, the war between Cambodia and Vietnam caused tensions in Sino-Vietnam relations.[18] In the recent past, as CPV undertook few political reforms to partially democratise the party structure, the solidarity between the two parties faced a new challenge. As China increased its maritime assertiveness, the ideological differences between Vietnam and China have been increasing and Vietnam has resorted to adopting a balancing approach against China by nurturing close defence and security partnerships with an array of strategic partners including the US. Recently, Hanoi welcomed the US decision of withdrawing the small arms embargo on Vietnam. Besides, Vietnam is considering regular naval exercises with countries like Japan, Singapore, India, Philippines and even with the US.[19] Vietnam is also strategizing its defence ties with neighbours like Philippines and Indonesia and all these efforts indicate that Vietnam is far from complying with the Chinese pressure. Rather, Vietnamese leaders have been seen holding press conferences to denounce Chinese actions on the South China Sea issues and Vietnamese commoners launched protests against a Chinese oil rig deployment in 2014 in Hanoi and Ho Chi Minh City in front of the Chinese envoy offices. Despite all these developments, Hanoi has preferred to keep the diplomatic channels open for China. The joint statement during the visit of Chinese Defence Minister Chang Wanquan in March 2016 demonstrated that diplomacy has not failed to mention about restraint use of force as a key to the regional stability.[20]

Indonesia

By virtue of its sheer size, democratic institutions, geographic location and a sizable population, Indonesia is often regarded as the de facto leader of ASEAN. However, the third largest democracy in the world too has an uncertain stand, often termed as 'see no China policy' towards its giant neighbour.[21] This uncertainty stems from the fact that China is one of the largest foreign investors in Indonesia and Indonesia's foreign policy priorities do not oblige the archipelagic country to see China as an immediate security threat. Last year, Indonesia's bilateral trade with China stood at around US$ 44 billion. The Investment Coordinating Board (BKPM) of Indonesia confirms that China is one of the top ten foreign investors in the country.[22] Additionally, Indonesia's own Maritime Fulcrum Initiative appears to have synergies with China's Maritime Silk Road (MSR). In fact, China's first announcement about its grand MSR strategy was held in Indonesia in October 2013. Indonesia's foreign policy principles mention the importance of economic diplomacy and economic self-reliance for improving relations with great powers that can bring the country economic opportunities, adherence to multilateralism and maintaining an independent and active foreign policy. In every aspect of these principles, China has been a much closer ally of Indonesia than any other country including the US. China's AIIB and OBOR and Regional Comprehensive Economic Cooperation (RCEP—an initiative where both China and ASEAN are major stakeholders along with some other countries) are believed to be beneficial for Indonesia's participation in the economy of the region, multilateral initiatives and to enhance the country's overall economic capacities. On the other hand, former US President Barack Obama's Pivot to Asia policy and Trans Pacific Partnership are no longer part of US's Indo-Pacific policy. Hence, it is only obvious for Indonesia to accommodate Chinese interests and engage with China in a more robust way. However, like most other countries, Indonesia's desire to maintain independent foreign policy explains that it will definitely maintain required closeness with the US and other major powers to sustain a low-level of hedging against China. Indonesia believes, it helps in preserving the regional security and stability too. This was evident, in late 2015, when during his trip to the US, President Joko 'Jokowi' Widodo mentioned about the importance of Trans-Pacific Partnership (TPP) and his interests in the project. Indonesian expert, Shankaran Nambiar (2016) mentioned it as a 'friendly yet firm' attitude towards China.[23] In fact, the anti-Chinese sentiments are very strong in the minds of some of the Indonesians. Since October 2016, thousands of *Pribumi* elites of Indonesia have started marching against the Governor of Jakarta, Basuki "Ahok" Tjahaja Purnama for alleged displacement policies from some slums in the capital city of Indonesia. Ahok is an ethnic Chinese and there were fears about spreading anti-Chinese rhetoric at the end of 2016 and beginning of 2017.[24] Same anti-Chinese feelings were expressed by the government representatives of Indonesia several times. One such incident happened in June 2016 when some Chinese vessels were confiscated from Natuna islands. Indonesia's Maritime Affairs and Fisheries Minister Susi Pudjiastuti firmly mentioned that she 'will not consider relations between countries in this matter'.[25] She also noted that such intrusions are 'a serious offense'.[26] These incidents partially explain that Indonesia will not become a Chinese satellite in near future; however, it will continue to practise the engaging China policy.

Singapore

The majority Chinese population in Singapore, the country's participation in the Chinese economy and vice-versa as well as Singapore's non-claimant status in the South China Sea disputes are some positive forces in China-Singapore relations. In fact, Singapore is often considered to be a distant relative of China.[27] While Singapore prefers not to take any side in the South China Sea territorial disputes, it has always maintained the balance of power concept while dealing with the great powers. Singapore and the US had signed a Memorandum of Understanding for US's use of facilities in Singapore in November 1990 and it was October 1990 when Singapore became the last of all five ASEAN countries to have restored diplomatic relations with China.[28] Lee Kuan Yew, the founding father and first Prime Minister of Singapore, was architectural in designing Singapore's strategy of balancing the great powers to ensure a smooth journey for the island-state by pleasing every great powers. Singapore continues to follow that legacy. In November 2015, Singapore hosted a historic meeting between President Xi Jinping and Taiwanese President Ma Ying-Jeou. Then, in December 2015, Singapore concluded an enhanced defence cooperation agreement with the US.[29] The most recent incident to endorse this argument happened in 2016. In September, PM Lee Hsien Loong visited Beijing to attend the G20 Summit and mentioned,

> "But when we have different perspectives, I think we have to manage them and accept them, and we should not allow them to affect the overall relationship because we have many cooperation areas going with China, they are basically win-win cooperation."[30]

One month after this visit, Singapore joined the hands with other ASEAN states to update the Non-Alignment Summit (NAM) partners about the Permanent Court of Arbitration (PCA) ruling against China. Thus, it may be argued that the 'little red dot' of Southeast Asia is, in many ways, better positioned than any of the ASEAN members, to play the balance of power game with China, primarily due to its economic strength and vigorous military and defence ties with the US. While Singapore is China's largest foreign investor, it has been consistently a key security partner of the US in the Asia-Pacific region.[31] Singapore is well aware that China's MSR would enhance the connectivity infrastructure in the region and like many other Southeast Asian countries, Singapore wants to play a safe game by recognising it as an 'economic opportunity', not as a 'strategic or security threat'.[32] In August 2016, the Chinese Construction Bank (CCB) and Singapore's International Enterprise (IE) signed an MoU to offer €20 billion to the Chinese and Singaporean firms who will be investing in the MSR project.[33] The list of such cooperation is countless. Hence, it can be argued that Singapore has benefitted from Chinese investments while maintaining balanced relations with the US and China simultaneously.

Malaysia

Malaysia's reserve of crude oil and natural gas (5 billion barrel and 80 trillion cubic feet respectively) in South China Sea makes it the strongest claimant state in the region. Thus, Malaysia is often expected to object vociferously to China's assertiveness in the seas. However, it is not so. China's status of the largest foreign investor in Malaysia critically shapes Malaysia's responses towards China.[34]

Despite Malaysia's non-opposition to some of the Chinese activities, tensions between the two countries have occurred at times. For instance, in March 2016, the Malaysian Maritime Enforcement Agency (MMEA) reported that around 100 Chinese vessels came near the Luconia Shoals, which Malaysia claims as its territory. However, later, the Malaysian Defence Minister Hishammuddin Hussein mentioned that the Royal Malaysian Navy (RMN) had confirmed that there were no encroachments by the Chinese vessels in Malaysian water. After this incident, Prime Minister Najib Razak mentioned that South China Sea issues are to be resolved through ASEAN and Malaysian sovereignty is not at stake because of such incursions.[35] Malaysia responded by only summoning the Chinese Ambassador after the March incident. Such remarks and responses show the traditional moderate way which includes handling the contentious issues at the bilateral level and through diplomatic channels. This moderate approach was adopted by Malaysia in dealing with territorial disputes with China. Malaysia too, like other all ASEAN members, is dependent on China economically. Thus, it receives little support from the ASEAN members for creating a robust response to Chinese assertiveness as most members follow an ambivalent policy towards China. In the recent years, as the Malaysian Prime Minister Najib Razak has been accused, both domestically and internationally, for his alleged involvement in the scandalous 1MDB case,[36] the Malaysian Prime Minister's dependency on China has grown rapidly. While the western countries blamed the Malaysian Prime Minister for his involvement with the corruption and his alleged role in influencing the Malaysian judiciary in the same case, China promptly acted by offering 60 per cent stake in Bandar Malaysia, a 1MDB company, through China Railway Construction Corporations and another help of $2.3 billion in cash to another power plant, owned by the debt-ridden 1MDB.[37] China's efforts to cooperate with Malaysia through these agreements could be viewed as the rewards for maintaining silence to activities of Chinese vessels in the disputed waters near Malaysia. Prime Minister Najib Razak echoed his inclination towards China again in November 2016 when he alarmed the western countries for 'lecturing the countries, once exploited by them in the colonial era, on how to manage their own internal affairs'.[38]

However, there are certain domestic factors in Malaysia, which sometimes show apathy towards China, much in the line with Indonesia, Vietnam and Myanmar. This nationalistic discourse reflects on the Malaysia-China spat on South China Sea as a sovereignty issue for Kuala Lumpur and rejects Malaysia's 'China dependency' syndrome. For instance, the Deputy Prime Minister Zahid Hamidi in his speech in November 2015 at Borneo, mentioned that "if our country is threatened or being encroached, we Malaysians should rise to defend our country".[39]

Cambodia

Cambodia, being one of the poorest countries in the region, faces the dilemma of handling the super powers in a most challenging way. For Cambodia, the challenge is to continue getting benefits from its international donors including the US and China. However, the difference in the approaches of US and its allies and China is the decisive factor behind Cambodia's inclination towards China. While the US has always been critical of Prime Minister Hun Sen's three-decade long authoritarian regime, human rights abuses in the kingdom and lack of democratisation, China has never put any conditions or asked any questions before giving aid and financial assistance to Cambodia. China's insistence on building infrastructure including roads, bridges and public buildings comes without any requirement for any changes in the existing political structures, institutions and government policies. By 2014, China became the largest foreign investor in Cambodia with collective commercial investments worth of $10 billion and development assistance of around $3 billion.[40] Additionally, Beijing also provides military assistance and equipment including trucks and aircrafts to the Cambodian forces. China is also involved in assisting Cambodia in military training. As China provides unconditional aid and developmental assistance to Phnom Penh, Cambodia has become the most compliant and trustworthy friend of it in the region. This was evident as Cambodia blocked ASEAN's efforts to issue a joint communique to condemn China's actions in the ASEAN meetings twice-once in 2012 and then again in 2016.[41] Cambodia has also joined the hands of China along with Brunei and Lao PDR in making a four-point consensus few days before the PCA verdict speaking about peaceful resolution of the territorial disputes without involving any outside powers or third parties other than the concerned stakeholders.

Myanmar

Traditionally, Myanmar has always shared a very warm relation with China, often described as *'baobo'* (brothers and relatives). Similar to Cambodia, Myanmar's relations with China have been characterised by aid and developmental assistance, bilateral trade and investment, infrastructure building as well as defence and security partnerships. Myanmar-China kinship was developed at a time when the military-ruled country was at the receiving end of criticism by the international community for not allowing the democratic forces to take control of the government and maintaining rule based law. China's 'non-interference' in the domestic affairs of other countries was appreciated in Myanmar for almost two decades. However, with President Thein Sein's nominally civilian government, as Myanmar started experiencing lifting of economic sanctions steadily and receiving foreign direct investments from all possible corners of the world, Nay Pyi Taw was quick to revisit its China dependency policy. Myanmar's geographic location and its resource-richness give it confidence to make a suitable position for itself in the region vis-à-vis the world. This explains President Thein Sein's suspension of the Chinese sponsored Myitsone Dam and another copper mine project. The year 2016 was a landmark year for Myanmar as for the first time, a democratic government, led by National League for Democracy (NLD) and its founder Daw Aung San Suu Kyi came to power. Under her leadership also, Myanmar is playing the balancing game very well. Suu Kyi chose to visit China before her visit to Washington DC and was assured by Chinese President Xi Jinping of his support to curb ethnic insurgency along the China-Myanmar border. In order to appease the Chinese investors, she appointed a review committee to introspect various aspects of the hydropower projects on River Irrawaddy including the Myitsone dam. On the other hand, during her visit to the US, she received assurance from the former President Obama on lifting of all the remaining sanctions on Myanmar. Definitely, Myanmar, despite being a weak country in the region, is following an independent foreign policy and is trying to gain benefits from both China and the US and this helps Myanmar in keeping national interests in the front row other than anything else.

Conclusion

This chapter has tried to answer some questions. First, what has been the nature of Southeast Asia's interactions with China in the past couple of years? Second, what are the factors that are shaping individual Southeast Asian countries' responses to China? Are they influenced by domestic factors or the external ones or a combination of both? Third, what are the inconsistencies in Southeast Asian countries' stand towards China? Fourth, how divided are ASEAN members in their dealings with China? David Shambaugh (2016) remarked that China is now an international power and this reality has complicated China's relations with the world in general and with its neighbours, in particular.[42] The complications emerge from the combination of fear of China's muscle power on the one hand and prospects offered by China on the other. The fear emanates from China's troublesome relations with some of the countries in the neighbourhood (here concerned Southeast Asian countries), China's naval deployments in the strategic locations, its modernisation of the People's Liberation Army Navy (PLAN) which has no match in the region and finally China's demonstration of power by building habitation and accumulating military equipment in the disputed waters. On the other hand, China is considered to be an opportunity primarily because of its bilateral and multilateral economic engagements with the concerned countries. Hence, it can be argued that China is viewed through the prism of threats and opportunities by the Southeast Asian countries simultaneously. At times, their relations with China are shaped by history, sometimes by anti-China sentiments, often by domestic political concerns and economic parameters and sometimes by national interests and sovereignty issues. For few of them (like Cambodia), Chinese assistance is a big saviour; for some (for instance, Singapore), it's a two way process; but for all them China seems to be unavoidable and thus, a blend of nominal balancing and hedging as well as accommodating Chinese interests is regarded to be the best possible way to survive.

NOTES

1. Yun-han Chu, Min-hua Huang and Jie Lu (2015), "Enter the Dragon: How East Asians View a Rising China", *Global Asia*, Vol. 10, No. 3, at http://www.asianbarometer.org/publications//e1098f2f4f411eb17e100ea7f 91a0a9e.pdf. Accessed December 19, 2016.
2. Bruce Stokes (2015), "How Asia-Pacific Publics See Each Other and Their National Leaders", *Pew Global Research*, September 2, 2015 at http://www.pewglobal.org/2015/09/02/how-asia-pacific-publics-see-each-other-and-their-national-leaders/. Accessed December 19, 2016.
3. Richard Wike, Bruce Stokes and Jacob Poushter (2015), "Views of China and the Global Balance of Power", *Pew Global Research*, June 23, 2015 athttp://www.pewglobal.org/2015/06/23/2-views-of-china-and-the-global-balance-of-

power/. Accessed December 15, 2016.
4. Ibid.
5. Derek Da Cunha (1998), "Southeast Asian Perceptions of China's Future Security Role in its 'Backyard'", In Jonathan D. Pollack, Richard H. Yang Eds. *Regional Perspectives On Chinese Foreign Policy And Military Development*, at http://www.Rand.Org/Content/Dam/Rand/Pubs/Conf_Proceedings/CF137/CF137.Chap6.Pdf. Accessed December 13, 2016.
6. *Il Hyun Cho and Seo-Hyun Park (2013),* "The Rise of China and Varying Sentiments in Southeast Asia toward Great Powers", *Strategic Studies Quarterly*, Summer 2013, at https://dspace.lafayette.edu/bitstream/handle/10385/1461/Cho-StrategicStudiesQuarterly-vol7-2013.pdf?sequence=1. Accessed December 13, 2016
7. Ibid
8. *Il Hyun Cho and Seo-Hyun Park (2013),* See No 6.
9. Martin Stuart Fox (2003), *A Short History of China and Southeast Asia*, Australia: Allen and Unwin, pp. 224-245.
10. Randall L. Schweller (1994), "Bandwagoning for Profit: Bringing the Revisionist State Back In", *International Security*, Vol. 19, No. 1 (1994): 72–107 as quoted in Denny Roy (2005), "Southeast Asia and China: Balancing or Bandwagoning?" *Contemporary Southeast Asia*, Vol. 27, No. 2, pp. 305-322.
11. Denny Roy (2005), "Southeast Asia and China: Balancing or Bandwagoning?" *Contemporary Southeast Asia Vol.* 27, No. 2, pp. 305-322.
12. Ibid
13. Denny Roy (2005), See Note 11
14. Munir Majid (2014), "Southeast Asian View of China's 'Not So Neighbourly' Rise", *International Politics*, Vol. 51, No. 3, pp. 398-403
15. Ibid
16. *The Phil Star* (2016), "Joint Statement of the Philippines and China", October 21, at http://www.philstar.com/headlines/2016/10/21/1635919/full-text-joint-statement-philippines-and-china. Accessed December 13, 2016.
17. The Forbes (2016), "Will Duterte's 'Springtime' in China-Philippines Relations Prove Short-Lived?" November 3, at http://www.forbes.com/sites/riskmap/2016/11/03/will-durtertes-springtime-in-china-philippines-relations-prove-short-lived/#1c9175cc64ef. Accessed December 13, 2016.
18. Yun Sun (2016), "The Undercurrent of Sino-Vietnamese Relations", *The Asan Forum*, August 24, at http://www.theasanforum.org/the-undercurrent-of-sino-vietnamese-relations/ Accessed December 16, 2016
19. Joshua Kurlantzick (2015), "A China-Vietnam Military Clash Contingency Planning Memorandum", *Council for Foreign Relations*, September, No. 26, at http://www.cfr.org/china/china-vietnam-military-clash/p37029. Accessed December 19, 2016
20. Mimi Lau (2016), "China, Vietnam vow to boost military ties amid strained relations over South China Sea", *South China Morning Post*, March28, at http://www.scmp.com/news/china/diplomacy-defence/article/1931295/china-vietnam-vow-boost-military-ties-amid-strained. Accessed on December 5, 2016.
21. Pierre Marthinus (2016), "See No China: Indonesia's South China Sea Policy", *The Jakarta Post*, June 17, at http://www.thejakartapost.com/academia/2016/

06/17/see-no-china-indonesias-south-china-sea-policy.html. Accessed December 5, 2016.

22. Shankaran Nambiar (2016), "Will Indonesia Succumb to China?", *The Forbes*, October 19, at http://www.forbes.com/sites/realspin/2016/10/19/will-indonesia-succumb-to-china/#276275a54eda. Accessed December 20, 2016.
23. Ibid.
24. Johanes Herlijanto (2016), "How Indonesia's Pribumi Elite View the Ethnic Chinese Today", *Today Online*, August 6, at http://www.todayonline.com/world/asia/how-indonesias-pribumi-elite-view-ethnic-chinese-today. Accessed December 20, 2016.
25. Amelia Long (2016), "Indonesia's South China Sea Dilemma", *Nationalinterest.org*, June 24, at http://nationalinterest.org/blog/the-buzz/indonesias-south-china-sea-dilemma-16707. Accessed December 20, 2016.
26. Ibid.
27. Sun Xi (2015), "China and Singapore are Distant Relatives at Best", *The Globalist*, December 20, at http://www.theglobalist.com/china-and-singapore-are-distant-relatives-at-best/. Accessed December 24, 2016.
28. At that time, ASEAN only had five members.
29. Sun Xi, See Note No. 27.
30. Today Online (2016), "S'pore, China should build on strong bilateral ties, says PM Lee", September 5, at http://www.todayonline.com/singapore/different-views-should-not-affect-singapore-china-ties-pm-lee. Accessed December 28, 2016.
31. Eva Pejsova (2016), "China's Rise: The View from Singapore", *European Union Institute for Security Studies*, May 2016, Paper 18 at http://www.iss.europa.eu/publications/detail/article/chinas-rise-the-view-from-singapore/. Accessed December 23, 2016.
32. Ibid.
33. Eva Pejsova (2016), See Note No. 31.
34. Ralph Jennings (2016), "Why Malaysia Stays Quiet about its Claims in the South China Sea", *The Forbes*, June 2, at http://www.forbes.com/sites/ralphjennings/2016/06/02/why-malaysia-stays-quiet-about-its-claims-in-the-disputed-south-china-sea/#2124c5851beb. Accessed December 28, 2016.
35. David Han (2016), "Why Malaysia's South China Sea Policy Seems Confused", *The Straits Times*, May 5, at http://www.straitstimes.com/opinion/why-malaysias-south-china-sea-policy-seems-confused. Accessed December 27, 2016.
36. 1MDB (1Malaysia Development Berhad) is an investment fund, founded by the Finance Ministry of Malaysia in 2009. Prime Minister Najib Razak led its advisory board till early 2016. In 2015, it was alleged that the prime minister had transferred USD 700 million into his personal account from the funds channelled through 1MDB. The company had taken money from several stakeholders (including international companies) and it now has nearly USD 11 billion in debt to repay.
37. Nyshka Chandran (2016), "Malaysia's Najib Razak in China, As 1MDB Scandal, South China Sea Dispute Loom Over Talks", *CNBC*, October 30, at http://www.cnbc.com/2016/10/30/malaysias-najib-razak-in-china-as-1mdb-scandal-south-china-sea-dispute-loom-over-talks.html. Accessed December 28, 2016.
38. The Guardian (2016),"China and Malaysia Agree on Military Cooperation in the

South China Sea", November 2, at https://www.theguardian.com/world/2016/nov/02/china-and-malaysia-agree-on-military-cooperation-in-the-south-china-sea. Accessed December 28, 2016.

39. David Han (2016), See Note No. 35.
40. Cheunboran Chanborey (2015), "As Cambodia Approaches China Over the US, It Should Remember Machiavelli's Lessons", *The Diplomat*, August 11, at http://thediplomat.com/2015/08/as-cambodia-approaches-china-over-the-us-it-should-remember-machiavellis-lessons/. Accessed December 30, 2016.
41. Ananth Baliga and Vong Sokheng (2016), "Cambodia Again Blocks ASEAN Statement on South China Sea", *The Phnom Penh Post*, July 25, at http://www.phnompenhpost.com/national/cambodia-again-blocks-asean-statement-south-china-sea. Accessed December 28, 2016.
42. David Shambaugh (2016), *China's Future*, Polity Press: Cambridge, 137-172.

9

West Asia in China's Energy Policy

Vrushal T. Ghoble

ABSTRACT

Energy is vital for the overall growth and development, and therefore, it affects both the West and the rising Asian economies equally. The changing dynamics have reconfigured the energy geopolitics today, as new facets have come into the picture. The 2011 Arab Uprisings may not have had a significant impact over trade, but, the unrest did stir the market. Following which, the Shale Revolution began, clashing with the OPEC producers; with the prices crumbling down. The oil glut that was created, resulted in lower oil prices, which was not good for the producers; while the growth in the demand side was skeptical. Apart from this, the renewable energy phenomenon also added to the changing configuration. Looking at these developments, it will be topical to probe how major consumers like China are pursuing their energy interests in the Middle East. The chapter will also look into, what extent has been China's policy in the region has been driven by its appetite for energy?

Although, the stakes of renewables are rising in the energy segment, oil and gas will continue to be the core agents of growth. As the enhanced gap between the available reserves and demand that has to be met, Chinese oil companies have been acquiring energy assets overseas. Consequently, China has been successful to a large extent. Also a pointer that, President Xi made more than 10 foreign visits in 2015 alone, emphasizes China's mounting international profile and appeal towards the region. Its participation in the Middle East, especially the Syrian crisis also marks a new era for the Chinese policy. This chapter intends to address the leading trends of last few years and the changing China-Middle East relations in the emerging energy paradigm.

The chapter is divided into four sections. It begins by highlighting the changing energy dynamics and identifying China's growing appetite for energy. It then talks about China's energy interests in the Middle East; followed by a brief subtopic of other alternatives available vis-a-vis the Middle East; finally, summing up.

Energy has been an integral element, for bringing economic prosperity to the West. As a result, several countries of rising Asia have also joined this race of economic boom. Energy security is essential for economic development. Therefore, securing adequate, affordable and reliable supplies of energy has become a necessity for the growth and development of a nation. The global energy security today includes a number of issues, most importantly, to meet the needs of large mass of population that lives in poverty. Thus, "...the promises of new sources of supplies specially from the Caspian, the entry of Russian oil in international market, the dramatic gains of technology in enhancing oil recovery and reducing the cost have changed the dimensions of energy security."[1]

The Middle East continues to be the most reliable energy source, where energy sales are their major source of income. As Hazem Beblawi puts it, a rentier economy is thus an economy where the creation of wealth is centered around a small fraction of the society; the rest of the society is only engaged in the distribution and utilization of this wealth.[2] According to Gregory Gause, as rentier states do not have to tax their citizens, they do not have to deal with serious demands for participation.[3] Conversely, in the past few years, there has been a subtle move for demands. The 2011 Arab Uprisings are well stated, illustrate the same. Gause further states that, "these demands are the in intentional, but in many ways inevitable,... It is a mistake to assume that oil wealth has once and for all 'depoliticized' the citizenry in these states."[4] Also, the fact that the production costs in the Middle East is the lowest as compared to any other region, attracting major players. For example, "...Saudi Arabia and Kuwait have the lowest total production cost at $10 per barrel and $8.50 per barrel, respectively."[5]

The new set of consumers has not just enhanced competition for these resources, but also increased the competitive advantage of the producers. Since, the discovery of oil as a resource, the consumers have brought in huge investment as well as technology. The 21st century sees the addition of new consumers joining the energy market, significantly Asia and China to be precise. There is competition for these resources, however, consumers are gradually moulding into a collaborative approach. Transportation through pipelines and sea routes also represents a different security challenge.

Positioning China in the Global Energy Market: Demand and Supply Scenario

Energy security had been defined on different scales. The simplest approach to define it is through its sufficiency for the population; the reliability of sources; and lastly, its affordability by the population. The joining of new actors as consumers has further taken the geopolitics to another level. New consumers like China are prominent in this context. Beijing's rise was a head turner, which not just changed the geopolitics, but also made energy security, its national agenda. Apparently, by the beginning of the 21st Century witnessed the scramble for energy had begun that was surprisingly motivated by China's growing potential. China does have its own oil and gas reserves. "CNPC's Daqing field, ...is one of China's oldest and most prolific fields, constituting 19 per cent of China's overall crude oil production. CNOOC's production in the Bohai Bay was 404,000 bbl/d in 2014, ...the South China Sea (SCS) is known to be gas rich, ...In 2014, CNOOC's total oil production in the SCS was 222,000 bbl/d, a majority coming from the Pearl River Mouth Basin in the eastern SCS. In 2014, CNOOC commenced production from oil fields in the Panyu 10, Enping 24, and Lufeng 7 blocks of the eastern SCS and added 115,000 bbl/d of peak production in the next few years."[6] However, these fields are maturing and prone to decline.

During the height of the Cultural Revolution in 1969, China ranked 25th in world oil demand.[7] In the Tenth Five Year Plan, the Chinese Government hammered out an energy strategy composed of four items: (i) to diversify the energy supply and demand structure; (ii) to achieve energy security; (iii) to improve the energy utilization efficiency; and (iv) to promote environmental protection.[8] Post 1970s, the economic development that was pursued by China marked an era of growth and development where these programmes expanded throughout years. The Twelfth Five Year Plan (2011-15) also focused on energy security and emphasized on developing the country's indigenous energy resources.

The relations between China and the Middle East carry civilizational linkages and historical baggage, marked by well known trade routes, popularly known as the Silk Route. "The founding of the People's Republic of China and the independence of Arab countries created a new era for China Arab friendly exchanges. From 1956 to 1990, China established diplomatic relations with all 22 Arab countries. Arab countries have given China strong support in restoring its lawful seat at the United Nations and on issues like the Taiwan question. In 2004, China Arab States Cooperation Forum was set up. Since then, it has developed into a collective cooperation platform covering many fields and with more than ten mechanisms. In 2010, China and Arab countries established the strategic cooperative relations of comprehensive cooperation and common development...."[9] China's growing populace and its expectations made the country a powerhouse, leading basically to the policy of 'made in China' for which industrialization process was initiated, and for which oil became an essential factor. This position of China made it a net importer of crude oil, where it used economic and political clout to acquire oil concessions from several Middle Eastern countries.

Second, only to the US, China's appetite for energy (second for oil & third for natural gas) grew over time (in 2015).[10] "In 2002, China transcended Japan and emerged as the second largest energy consumer, following the United States. As China's demand for energy continues to grow, its domestic oil yield is failing to keep pace."[11] The main reason for this growth is principally due to the better living standards and attained self sufficiency that has enhanced the spending capacity of the people. Through 1950s and 70s, China had adequate energy supplies from its own fields. However, its expanding industrial structure compelled it to become an exporter of coal and oil in exchange of industrial goods, which saw the decline of its oil and gas production as its indigenous demand grew. Looking at China historically, "in 1959 China's crude oil production stood at 3.73 million tones,... In that year, the Daqing oil field in northeast China produced 4.3m tones of crude, making up the bulk of the 6.48m tones of nationally produced oil."[12] China's crude oil exports reached a peak of 30 million tons by 1985, but declined afterward due to growing domestic consumption and slower growth in production,[13] finally making China an importer of oil from Oman. This demand continued to increase, "from 2002 to 2011, China's oil consumption increased from 223.9 million tons to 458 million tons. From 2002 to 2011, China's oil consumption rate rose from 31 per cent to 56 per cent."[14] By 2012, around 66 per cent of China's energy demand was met by coal that was followed by petroleum. This need domestically compelled the People's Republic to go overseas and become a net importer of crude oil in 1993.

China's oil consumption growth accounted for about 43 per cent of the world's oil consumption growth in 2014.[16] Some percentage of this exponential demand is expected to be met by oil, but more by gas. "The US Department of Energy expects that China's imported oil will climb to 9.4 million bpd by 2025...."[17] As a source of cleaner form of energy, "China became a net natural gas importer for the first time in 2007."[18] Natural gas demand is further expected to grow to ~eight per cent (222 mt or ~300

Graph 1:[15] China Energy Consumption by Fuel (2012)

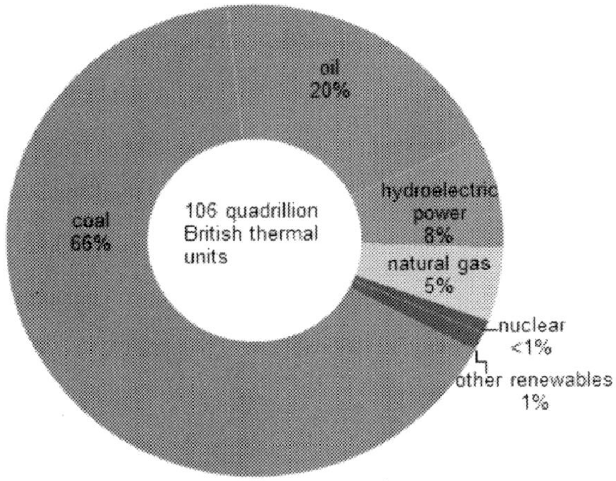

Source: EIA (14th May 2015), *China: Overview,* p. 3. Accessed May 8, 2017. See, https://energy.gov/sites/prod/files/2016/04/f30/China_International_Analysis_US.pdf

bcm) by 2020.[19] "...per capita energy consumption in China will increase by about 2.7 times from 0.73 toe in 2000 to 2.0 toe in 2030."[20] The People's Republic has been importing natural gas but is slowly moving towards LNG. "...in 2012 gas consumption in China was 147.1 billion cubic meters, 13 per cent more than in 2011, with imports making up 42.5 billion cubic meters, an increase of 31.1 per cent, denoting 29 per cent external dependency."[21] "In 2014, China imported 20 mt (27 bcm) of LNG, (where) natural gas demand was 5.5 per cent of primary energy mix (148 mt or ~200 bcm), ~70 per cent domestic, 16 per cent pipeline imports, 14 per cent LNG imports."[22]

Tones of Gulf energy exports head not just to the west, but also towards Asia. As oil is acting as a major pollutant, new forms of sustainable energies are to be invented and brought in use at the commercial level. As the alternative and renewable energies are being experimented and produced on a mass scale for commercial usage, Natural gas serves as a bright fuel, which is eco-friendly and an available alternative to oil. "Compared to the 2000 level, ...Natural gas consumption will increase from the 2000 level by 250 million toe by 2030."[23] China's move towards clean energy is quiet vigorous and exciting to the onlookers. China is looking at nuclear, wind and solar to move away from its dependence on fossil fuels, especially the transportation sector is shifting towards hybrid or fuel cells at a faster pace.

The country has made an effort to diversify its energy supplies, hydroelectric sources (8 per cent), ...nuclear power (nearly 1 per cent), and other renewables (more than 1 per cent) accounted for relatively small shares of China's energy consumption.[24]

Locating Middle East in China's Energy Mix

Given the vigorous industrial expansion, the energy demand is also expected to rise in the coming years. The estimated projections have pushed China's dependence on overseas oil, making it a net importer since 1993. Ever since, securing overseas oil and gas resources have been a significant policy for the People's Republic. "China's oil consumption growth is forecast in IEO 2014 to rise by about 2.6 per cent annually through 2040, reaching 13.1 million bbl/d in 2020, 16.9 million bbl/d in 2030 and 20.0 million bbl/d in 2040. EIA forecasts that China's oil consumption will exceed that of the United States by 2034."[25] To acquire these resources, China has been competing tooth-and-nail with other consumer countries. Building strategic petroleum reserve (SPR) has been a high priority for China in reducing its vulnerability to imports. "The SPR is supposed to eventually hold 500 million barrels, although some are now estimating that figure is meant to rise to 600 million by 2020, based on new demand assumptions and added facilities...."[26] From Middle East to Central Asia, Africa and Russia; China has been tapping energy from across the globe and consequently, it has also signed many energy accords with the producing states. For instance, in February 2009, China and Russia entered an oil for loans agreement. "The China Development Bank is lending $ 25 billion at 6 per cent annual interest to Russia's state owned oil company Rosneft and oil pipeline monopoly Transneft. In return, they will deliver some 20 million tons of oil annually, or an average of 300,000 barrels per day, to China during the agreement's 20 year lifetime starting in 2011."[27] In 2014, Saudi Arabia, Angola and Russia were the top three largest sources of oil imports (see graph 2).

Saudi Arabia

The bilateral ties between the two countries have not remained limited to trade and investments, but have further ventured into areas like culture and education. While, Beijing supports Riyadh's Vision 2030 and its move for diversification; the latter welcomes the investment and the former's 'New Silk Route' Vision, which would be flourishing for both. Like any other country, China has also diversified its source of hydrocarbons. The uncertainties that prevail due to occurrence of an accident in the maritime straits or a war like situation, leading to supply disruptions have brought

Graph 2[28]: China's crude oil imports by source (2014)

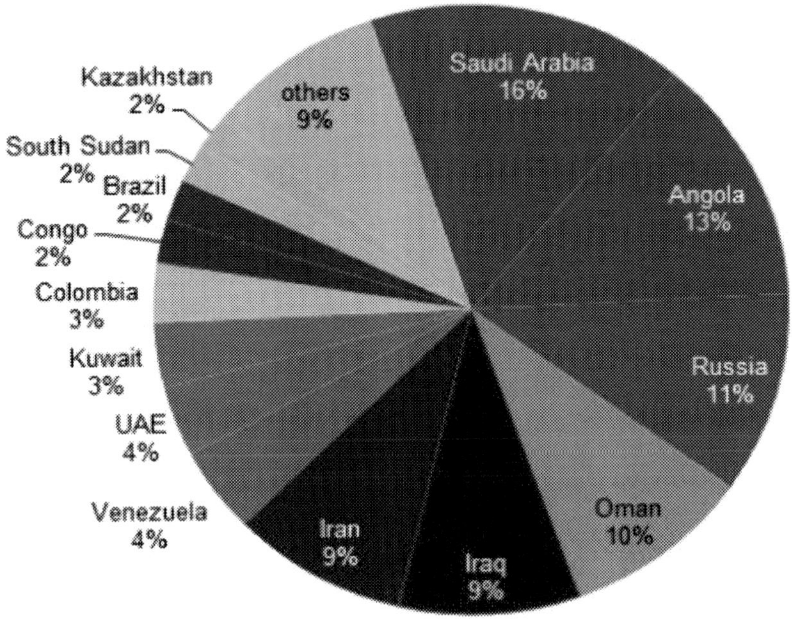

Source: Energy Information Administration (EIA) (May 14, 2015), " China: International energy data and analysis", p. 11. Accessed April 30, 2017. See, https://www.eia.gov/beta/international/analysis_includes/countries_long/China/china.pdf

many of these countries under scrutiny. Hence, the more diversified are the sources, the better it is for the sustenance of the consumers. Between 1993 and 1998, a few countries like Oman, Saudi Arabia, Russia, Angola, etc. have been major exporters to China. It is expected that in a decade's time, Chinese economy will showcase huge change with an expected growth in the market and thereby, energy consumption. "...in November 1999 President Jiang Zemin made the first-ever visit by a Chinese head of state to Saudi Arabia, heading to Dammam, the heart of Saudi oil country, after a stop in Riyadh. He has characterised China's evolving relationship with Saudi Arabia as a 'strategic oil partnership'."[29] "Though Chinese refining capability was not well suited to heavier Saudi crudes, the Saudis shifted some of their lighter crudes to the Chinese market from other customers with more developed refining infrastructures."[30] Soon after, a series of agreements were signed. In "March 2004: Sinopec signed a $300 million gas exploration license for nearly 40,000 square km in the Empty Quarter deserts of Saudi Arabia's Rub al-Khali Basin; (and in), January 2004: China's Sinopec signed an agreement with its Saudi counterpart,

Saudi Aramco, to develop natural gas resources near the Ghawar field in the country's east over 10 years. (Also, in) March 2007: Aramco inked an agreement with Sinopec and Exxon Mobil Corp. to upgrade a refinery at Quanzhou, in the southeastern Chinese province of Fujian to 240,000 bpd and to operate around 750 filling stations locally. (And, in) June 2007: China Petroleum Pipeline Bureau and China Petroleum Engineering and Construction (Group) Co. Ltd signed an agreement to jointly lay a crude oil pipeline for Saudi Arabia."[31] In 1999, the partnership between Saudi Arabia and China became significantly oil centric. This partnership primarily focused on the Chinese desire to diversify its source of imports and the Saudi intension to have diverse oil export options.

The recent visit (May 2017) of the US President Trump to Saudi Arabia, has been referred as historic, that revives the old ties between the two allies. This move is specifically mentioned as an important event due to the awkward relationship of the earlier US administration with Riyadh, as human rights aspect of the Sunni monarchy has been questioned, while the Iranian nuclear deal was a precursor. With President Trump's visit, there has been an attempt to solidify the US-Saudi ties and further corner Iran. The post 9/11 scenario, implicated in the hostile behaviour of the US towards the Middle East, especially Saudi Arabia, which brought the Asian counterparts closer to the region. Since, then China has formed a close linkage with the Middle Eastern countries, soon to surpass US as a major oil importer; much of which came from the region itself. Once diplomatic and military in nature, China's goals have become more strategic and focused. One of the first levels of China's engagement was with the Kingdom of Saudi Arabia. Having a threat perception from the Iranian revolution, the Saudi-Chinese relationship saw a growing military angle with sale of the Intermediate-Range Ballistic Missiles (IRBMs) from China. "Saudi Arabia, the United Arab Emirates, Iraq, and Egypt have all purchased the (Chinese manufactured,) CH-4. Saudi Arabia and the UAE are using them in their campaign against Yemen's Houthi rebels, while Iraq has used them in action against ISIS forces operating in the country."[32] This bond grew further as, "Saudi Arabia's King Salman met with China's premier on Friday (March 2017), day after the two nations signed a memorandum of understanding on investment cooperation valued at $ 65 billion. The landmark agreement aims to boost joint efforts in fields including energy, investment, finance, culture and aerospace, part of Saudi Arabia's drive to develop a growth strategy less dependent on oil."[33]

Iran

The traditional and historical ties between China and Iran assisted the two in carving cordial ties, which prospered in due course of time. The emergence of Mao's leadership and the coup d'etat, that overthrew the then Iranian Prime Minister Mohammad Mosaddegh in 1953, nearly happened during the same period. This not only gave the Shah immense access to the country making him influential, but also restored his trust; consolidating the friendship between Iran and the West, US in particular. The time passed and the alliance between Shah and US also developed into vital bilateral ties, enhancing trade. "...by the mid 1960s the US Iranian military relationship evolved from one based upon US aid to Tehran to a credit partnership. He (Shah) played upon US fears of Soviet advances in the Middle East and the dangers of radical Arab nationalism to the region, and after threatening to acquire arms from the Soviet Union he convinced the Johnson administration to conclude three military credit agreements with his government between 1964 and 1968."[34] China-Iran relations has been quiet evident and historic in nature. These ties date back to the Iran-Iraq war, where Chinese weaponry entered Iran.

The Iran-Iraq war in the 80s was a precarious situation for China, as both Iran and Iraq were its allies, and, therefore, it was more of a balancing act. As the Chinese oil imports from Middle East grew, it became much more involved in the regional politics creating an environment and taking a stand towards stability, so that Middle Eastern oil keeps flowing. The China US competition in the Middle East can be seen by the latter's policy of providing nuclear technology to Iran. Hence, the US containment policy towards China in the Middle East and keeping Iran away from the Asian power has been one of its intentions. July 2015, marked a new era for the Iranian economy as the Joint Comprehensive Plan of Action (JCPOA) between Iran and P5+1 was signed. This gave Iran an access to market, which it was deprived of. However, "...Iran would be facing constraints due to emerging global energy dynamics where the supply side of the equation is determined by larger flow of hydrocarbon coming from outside the region and the demand side is influenced by de-carbonization of the economies."[35] The Syrian crisis further made this fracture among these powers more visible. On January 23, 2016 Iranian President Hassan Rouhani and Chinese leader Xi Jinping reached a pact, as part of the 17 agreements that were signed, to have China build two nuclear power plants in southern Iran and for Iran to provide long term supplies of oil to China.[36]

"...Russia's increasing military ties with Iran, especially in the area of weapons proliferation, have grown since 1994...."[37] The post-sanctioned

Iran will be ideal player and will be supported by China and Russia (possibly). Chinese officials worry that alleged Saudi funding of Islamic schools or madrasahs in Xinjiang (an autonomous region, populated by Uighur Muslims) may be encouraging Uighur militants who have staged several attacks in a low intensity campaign for equal rights and autonomy, if not independence.[38] This factor may have pushed Beijing towards Moscow, as "Russia beat Saudi Arabia to become the biggest seller of crude to China (in 2015)... Asia's largest economy bought a record 4.04 million metric tons of crude from Russia, or about 988,000 barrels a day, in September. That's 42 per cent more than a year earlier and 31 per cent higher than in August...."[39] The armed crackdown on the Uighur's was largely condemned by Tehran.

The new Suez Canal officially opened in 2015, bringing more revenues to the Egyptian economy. This will also add to China's One Belt One Road (OBOR) policy, which comprises of the Silk Road Economic Belt (SREB) and the Maritime Silk Road (MSR). In 2016, the Asian Infrastructure Investment Bank (AIIB) provided $1.7 billion in loans, including $300 million of financing to expand Oman's Duqm Port and to lay the groundwork for the country's first railway system.[40] "....Piraeus (port city in Greece) is emerging as Europe's fastest-growing and most dynamic port. With China's securing Pireaus as its western maritime outlet for the OBOR, Israel and its neighbors, from Egypt to Iran, are now situated in the middle of Beijing's ambitious project to create a combined land-sea commercial superhighway...."[41] China's financial support for Iran, might be perceived as a threat factor by Saudi Arabia. For China, Iran has a great potential specifically it falls in the former's OBOR policy; while, Saudi Arabia's nature is quiet unpredictable when it comes to China, as compared to strong Riyadh-Washington relations.

Qatar

It is China's wish to reduce its dependency on coal, and shift to a more eco-friendly fuel natural gas. Thus, the relations between China and Qatar underlines the potential consumer-producer dialogue. The China-Saudi Arabia relations or the former's ties with Iran dominate, if compared with other countries like Qatar; as, the two Middle Eastern countries have had closer military/trading ties. Apparently, two facts that Qatar has the third largest natural gas reserves in the world; and, the Emirate being the largest producer and exporter of LNG makes it a significant energy player internationally, underpinning the China-Qatar relations. The dramatic political and economic conditions in Middle East have also put uncertainties and apprehensions regarding the stable future of the region. As projected, sectarianism has been in the forefront of this divergence of approach, where Saudi Arabia and Iran are at the centre of this conflict. Hence, it also sounds wise to look elsewhere for energy requirements, inevitably making Doha a favorite destination. "Since 2013, China has been the world's largest consumer of oil from the Middle East. Qatar ...in 2014 was China's largest supplier of LNG...."[42] Wood says, that the shift in Chinese imports could have consequences for its relations with the Gulf states.[43]

Starting from relations that were modest, there was a steady rise in the trade between the two which grew during 1996 and thereafter. It was post Arab Uprising, that the relations became strategic in nature. According to Reuters, the total two way trade between China and Qatar tripled between 2008 and 2013 to about US$ 11.5 billion, (while), according to the World Bank, in 2015, Qatar imported US$ 3.77 billion in goods from China, much of it consumer, machinery or electrical goods.[44] Along with the growth in the percentage of Qatari LNG, it is observed that Beijing is successfully navigating through Riyadh and Tehran; and striking strategic deals, particularly in the energy sector with Doha. As this happens, a chunk of Qatari gas will flow away from West to East (China), giving Qatar a chance to expand its consumer base. "Qatar, ...has seen its market share in China reduce from 34 per cent in 2014, to 19 per cent in 2016."[45] However, distance and flow consistency wise, Qatar stays a more reliable market.

Alternative Energy Sources for China vis-a-vis Middle East

Beijing has become a significant player in the Central Asian energy market. The visit of President Xi Jinping to the region in 2013 is called as a historic event which resulted in energy trade worth billions. Since, there is a land border between the two, tapping the Central Asian reserves is quiet easy and economically feasible. China controls approximately 20 per cent of Kazakhstan's oil production and has constructed one of the world's longest oil pipelines, running 2,300 km from the Caspian Sea to Xinjiang province.[46] Kazakhstan also transits gas through the Central Asia-China Gas Pipeline (CACGP) from Turkmenistan and Uzbekistan and exports oil via the Kazakhstan-China oil pipeline.[47] The refineries are supplied by the CNPC-run oil fields in neighboring Kazakhstan, and produce 1.35 million tonnes of refined product annually.[48] "Turkmenistan is the region's main gas exporter, and exports its reserves directly to China. Uzbekistan also supplies gas through the upgraded pipeline network and has attracted Chinese investment in recent years, typified by a $15 billion bilateral energy deal concluded in 2013."[49] "Turkmenistan plans to increase its natural gas exports to China to 38bn cubic metres (bcm) in 2017. (And) ...planned to export 65bn cm by 2021, with the CACGP pipeline supplying 55bn cm of gas...."[50]

Russia has the largest reserves of natural gas in the world and a bulk of its gas flowing to Europe, has given it an edge over other producers. The geopolitical risks that are involved for China when it imports energy from other countries have pushed it to move to alternative sources like Russia. China has become a significant trading partner of Russia. The "... potential Chinese investment in upstream assets in Russia, Chinese financing for Russian projects, ..."[51] has made the relations even more healthier. "China and Russia have signed deals for Russia to send China up to 800,000 bbl/d of crude oil by 2018, mostly by pipeline. Currently, Russia sends oil to China via pipeline, ship, and rail, primarily from Russia's fields in East Siberia."[52] However, "Russia is likely to scale back volumes of gas it plans to ship to China later this decade,... due to the dive in global energy prices and uncertainty hanging over the Chinese economy. ...sales to China will initially be lower than envisaged when Moscow reached the $400 billion deal with Beijing in May 2014. Flows (oil and gas) through the Power of Siberia pipeline, which starts in East Siberia...."[53] The deal is "...supply CNPC with up to 38 bn cubic meters of gas for 30 years."[54] Apparently, there are many LNG options available today; and, with the Russian gas flow is lesser, a more reliable source, the Middle East is at disposal.

Summing Up

The Chinese outlook is to build a society which is self sufficient, embarking the socio-economic development. "The Chinese leadership proposed the win-win dialogue for the US and the People's Republic by building a new model of major country relationship."[55] which is meant to foster friendly ties between the two powers. The long standing energy ties between China and the Middle East, where energy trade holds a central position, also facilitated to some extent to keep the western interference at bay.

The US imposed Iran Libya Sanctions Act (ILSA) put Iran in the most disadvantageous position, as strict punishment was adhered to companies investing more than $ 20 million in the country. Now, with sanctions being withdrawn, Iran can trade hydrocarbons with many countries that would pave its development. The LNG demand and sources like Qatar willing to expand production and are looking for growing markets, will be the defining factor in the future China-Middle East energy ties.

China is quiet similar to India, as it follows the principles of peaceful coexistence. It appears that the former is not having any specific policy or plan towards Middle East, unlike the West. However, Beijing respects autonomy of the individual state and does not believe in interference in the domestic affairs of any country. The method of engagement between China and the Middle Eastern countries are on a one to one basis, principally centered around energy. Having principle stakes in the Middle Eastern energy prospects, Beijing has also invested in the regional infrastructure projects; especially the New Silk Route projects, which are well received by the countries in the region. While, the US Middle East (especially the GCC) ties are based on the security arrangement, Beijing's policy of land and maritime corridors through the OBOR, emphasize on promoting its economic interests which broadly illustrates its foreign policy dimension. The New Silk Route projects also refer to investment worth "...$ 333 m for an airport in Gwadar, the site of a deepwater port that is to provide an outlet to the Arabian Sea from the far western Chinese province of Xinjiang, establishment of the Havelian dry port in Pakistan, agreement on economic and technical cooperation ($ 160 m) for the East Bay Expressway linking Gwadar to Pakistan's highway network."[56] It appears at the moment, that the Chinese investment in the Gwadar port will be more prolific, as "Chinese investment in Pakistan is... aimed at boosting trade with the rest of Asia, and Pakistan won't become a hurdle in China's quest to reach the Middle East... That's because Pakistan is currently on the receiving end of a huge Chinese investment, which will revamp Pakistan's feeble economic structure."[57]

Beijing support of Damascus against the West's opposition of President Assad on one side; and, the Uyghur retaliation on the other, has placed the former in situation where it has to steer clear, with caution. Under the given circumstances, the Middle East will continue to be a key ingredient in China's future growth; moreover, the latter's presence in the region has contributed immensely; thus, cannot be taken lightly. The Chinese oil companies particularly, are welcome due to their policy of non interference in the political matters and for articulating development. The nuts and bolts of China's relations with the Middle Eastern countries have become stronger with years of reliance and dependence, that have far reaching effects, significant for geoeconomic concerns. Besides energy imports, Middle East is also a huge market for the Chinese goods. Thus, the development that is pursued is a win-win situation, that will bring the two at par with time and new age technology in the coming years. In the mean while, it appears that, China and Asia at large, is anticipated to shoulder a bigger responsibility in the region, as it can give a fair chance to the Middle East; give means and ways to resolve issues; and, ensure co-prosperity.

NOTES

1. Pant, Girijesh (2002/2), India's Energy Security: The Gulf Factor (paper 2), *Gulf Studies Programme (GSP), Occasional Paper Series (Energy Issues in the Persian Gulf Region)*, Centre for West Asian and African Studies (CWAAS), School of International Studies, New Delhi: Jawaharlal Nehru University (JNU), p. 4.
2. Beblawi, Hazem (Fall 1987), "The Rentier State in the Arab World", *Arab Studies Quarterly*, 9(4): 385.
3. Gause, Gregory F. III (1994), "Oil Monarchies: Domestic and Security Challenges in the Arab Gulf States", New York: Council on Foreign Relations Press, p. 80.
4. Ibid, p. 84.
5. Kristopher, Gordon (Jan 13, 2016), "Crude Oil's Total Cost of Production Impacts Major Oil Producers", *Market Realist*, Accessed May 11 2017, See, http://marketrealist.com/2016/01/crude-oils-total-cost-production-impacts-major-oil-producers/
6. Energy Information Administration (EIA) (May 14, 2015), " China: International Energy Data and Analysis", p. 6, 7, Accessed April 30 2017, See, https://www.eia.gov/beta/international/analysis_includes/countries_long/China/china.pdf.
7. Gordon, Deborah, Yevgen Sautin and Wang Tao (May 6, 2014), "China's Oil Future", *Carneigie Endowment for International Peace*, Accessed April 28 2017. See, http://carnegieendowment.org/2014/05/06/china-s-oil-future-pub-55437
8. Li, Zhidong, Kokichi Ito and Ryoichi Komiyama, "Energy Demand and Supply Outlook in China for 2030 and A Northeast Asian Energy Community—The Automobile Strategy and Nuclear Power Strategy of China", p. 25. Accessed April 29 2017. See, http://eneken.ieej.or.jp/en/data/pdf/300.pdf.
9. The Ministry of Foreign Affairs of the People's Republic of China, (January 13, 2016), "China's Arab Policy Paper". Accessed September 2, 2017. See, http://www.fmprc.gov.cn/mfa_eng/zxxx_662805/t1331683.shtml
10. Eni (2016), "World Oil and Gas Review 2016", p. 20, 52. Accessed September 2 2017. See, https://www.eni.com/docs/it_IT/eni-com/azienda/fuel-cafe/WOGR-2016.pdf
11. Li, Lifan, "Energy Security And Energy Risk Management", *Journal of International Affairs*, Accessed April 28 2017. See, https://jia.sipa.columbia.edu/energy-security-energy-risk-management.
12. Daojiong, Zha (2006), "China's Energy Security: Domestic and International Issues", *Survival*, 48:1, p. 179.
13. Ghafouri, Mahmoud, "China's Policy in the Persian Gulf" Accessed on April 28 2017. See, http://www.mepc.org/journal/chinas-policy-persian-gulf
14. Li, *op. cit.*
15. Energy Information Administration (May 14, 2015), China: Overview, p. 3, Accessed May 8 2017, See, https://energy.gov/sites/prod/files/2016/04/f30/China_International_Analysis_US.pdf
16. Energy Information Administration (EIA), *op. cit.*, p. 1.

17. Liu, Xuecheng (September 2006), "China's Energy Security and Its Grand Strategy", The Stanley Foundation, *Policy Analysis Brief*, p. 3, Accessed April 30 2017, See, http://www.stanleyfoundation.org/publications/pab/pab06chinas energy.pdf
18. Peng, Zhou, "China's Energy Import Dependency: Status and Strategies", *College of Economics and Management & Research Center for Soft Energy Science*, Nanjing University of Aeronautics and Astronautics, China, p. 19, Accessed May 1 2017, See, http://esi.nus.edu.sg/docs/event/zhou-peng.pdf
19. Accenture, "Gas Grows Up Part 1: Developing New Sources of LNG Demand", p. 14, Accessed April 29 2017. See, https://www.accenture.com/t20160309 T024135__w__/us-en/_acnmedia/PDF-7/Accenture-Gas-Grows-up.pdf
20. Li, Zhidong, Kokichi Ito and Ryoichi Komiyama, "Energy Demand and Supply Outlook in China for 2030 and A Northeast Asian Energy Community—The Automobile Strategy and Nuclear Power Strategy of China", p. 8, Accessed April 29 2017, See, http://eneken.ieej.or.jp/en/data/pdf/300.pdf
21. Zhu, Qing, Quan-Ying Lu, Xiao-Yang Zhou and Kin Keung Lai (2014), "A Driving Force Analysis and Forecast for Gas Consumption Demand in China", Mathematical Problems in Engineering, Volume 2014 Accessed April 29 2017. See, https://www.hindawi.com/journals/mpe/2014/980410/
22. Accenture, *op. cit.*, p. 14.
23. Li, "Energy Demand and Supply Outlook in China for 2030 and A Northeast Asian Energy Community—The Automobile Strategy and Nuclear Power Strategy of China", *op. cit.*, p. 12.
24. Energy Information Administration (EIA), (May 14, 2015), "China: International Energy Data and Analysis", p. 2, Accessed April 30, 2017, See, https://www.eia.gov/beta/international/analysis_includes/countries_long/China/china.pdf
25. Energy Information Administration (EIA), *op. cit.*, p. 3.
26. Opsal, Ryan (October 3, 2015), "What will Happen to Oil Prices When China Fills its SPR?", *OilPrice.com*. Accessed September 2 2017. See, http://oilprice.com/Energy/Crude-Oil/What-Will-Happen-To-Oil-Prices-When-China-Fills-Its-SPR.html
27. Socor, Vladimir (February 20, 2009), "Oil-for-Loans Deal will Increase Russian Oil Deliveries to China", *Eurasia Daily Monitor*, The Jamestown Foundation, Volume: 6 Issue: 34, Accessed April 30 2017, See, https://jamestown.org/program/oil-for-loans-deal-will-increase-russian-oil-deliveries-to-china/
28. Energy Information Administration (EIA), *op. cit.*, p. 11.
29. Manning, Robert A. (Spring 2000), "The Asian Energy Predicament", *Survival*, The International Institute for Strategic Studies, 42(3): 79 & 81 Accessed September 3 2017. See, http://www.encarnation.com/site/HARVARD_LECTURES/Entries/2009/2/18_Energy_Demand_files/Manning%20-%20Asian%20 Energy%20Predicament%20-%20Spring%202000.pdf
30. Leverett, Flynt and Jeffrey Bader (Winter 2005-06), "Managing China-US Energy Competition in the Middle East", The Center for Strategic and International Studies and the Massachusetts Institute of Technology, *The Washington Quarterly*, 29:1, p. 191 Accessed September 3, 2017. See, https://www.brookings.edu/wp-content/uploads/2016/06/20051216_leverett_bader.pdf

31. Jiang, Wenran (July 12. 2007) "China's Growing Energy Relations with the Middle East", *China Brief*, The Jamestown Foundation, 7(14). Accessed September 3, 2017. See, https://jamestown.org/program/chinas-growing-energy-relations-with-the-middle-east/
32. Mizokami, Kyle (December 22, 2015), "For the First Time, Chinese UAVs Are Flying and Fighting in the Middle East", *Popular Mechanics*, Accessed May 9 2017, See, http://www.popularmechanics.com/military/weapons/news/a18677/chinese-drones-are-flying-and-fighting-in-the-middle-east/
33. "China, Saudi Arabia Sign $65 Billion in Cooperation Deals" (March 17, 2017), *USA Today*, Accessed May 27 2017, See, https://www.usatoday.com/story/money/2017/03/17/china-saudi-arabia-sign-65-billion-cooperation-deals/99295228/
34. Fain, Taylor (January 3, 2015), "Review—US Arms Policies Towards the Shah's Iran", *E-International Relations*,. Accessed September 2 2017,. See, http://www.e-ir.info/2015/01/03/review-us-arms-policies-towards-the-shahs-iran/
35. Pant, Girijesh (2016), "Iran Returns to Global Energy Market: Issues and Prospects", *Contemporary Review of the Middle East*, 3(1): 24.
36. Olga Samofalova, Vzglyad (January 28, 2016), "A New Era in Iranian-Chinese relations threatens Russian interests", Russia Beyond the Headlines, Accessed May 6 2017, See, https://rbth.com/international/2016/01/28/a-new-era-in-iranian-chinese-relations-threatens-russian-interests_563003
37. Cohen, Ariel (5th April 2001), "Countering Russian-Iranian Military Cooperation", *The Heritage Foundation*, Accessed 6th May 2017, See, http://www.heritage.org/europe/report/countering-russian-iranian-military-cooperation
38. Dorsey, James M. (January 28 2016), "China and the Middle East: Tilting Towards Iran?" *RSIS Commentary*, No. 20, pp. 1, 2. Accessed May 6 2017 see http://www.rsis.edu.sg/wp-content/uploads/2016/01/CO16020.pdf
39. "Russia Races Past Saudi Arabia in Tussle for Chinese Oil Market" (October 21 2015) Accessed May 6 2017 see http://www.bloomberg.com/news/articles/2015-10-21/russia-races-past-saudi-arabia-in-tussle-for-chinese-oil-market
40. Dusek, Mirek and Maroun Kairouz (April 4, 2017), "Is China Pivoting towards the Middle East?" *World Economic Forum*, Accessed May 9 2017, See, https://www.weforum.org/agenda/2017/04/is-china-pivoting-towards-the-middle-east/
41. Tanchum, Michael (January 24 2017), "China's One Belt, One Road Reshapes Mid-East", *The Jerusalem Post*, Accessed May 9 2017, See, http://www.jpost.com/Opinion/Chinas-One-Belt-One-Road-reshapes-Mideast-479492
42. Wood, Peter (July 7, 2017), "China-Qatar Relations in Perspective", *The Jamestown Foundation* Accessed September 3, 2017. See, https://jamestown.org/program/china-qatar-relations-perspective/
43. Ibid.
44. Hollingsworth, Julia (June 12, 2017), "Why Qatar Matters to China, in spite of Gulf Isolation", *South China Morning Post* Accessed September 3 2017 See, http://www.scmp.com/news/china/diplomacy-defence/article/2097206/why-qatar-matters-china-spite-gulf-isolation
45. Zeng, Xiaolin (May 3 2017), "Resurgence in China's LNG Imports Seen", *Fairplay*

Accessed September 3, 2017 See, https://fairplay.ihs.com/commerce/article/4285561/resurgence-in-china-s-lng-imports-seen

46. Hart, Michael (August 18, 2016), "Central Asia's Oil and Gas Now Flows to the East", *The Diplomat,* Accessed May 1 2017, See, http://thediplomat.com/2016/08/central-asias-oil-and-gas-now-flows-to-the-east/
47. Shaku, Kanat (July 11, 2017), "China Rising: Beijing's Insatiable Appetite Transforms Central Asian Oil and Gas Flows", *Intellinews*. Accessed September 2, 2017. See, http://www.intellinews.com/china-rising-beijing-s-insatiable-appetite-transforms-central-asian-oil-and-gas-flows-125124/
48. Hart, *op. cit.*
49. Ibid.
50. Shaku, Kanat (July 11, 2017), "China Rising: Beijing's Insatiable Appetite Transforms Central Asian Oil and Gas Flows", *Intellinews*. Accessed September 2, 2017. See, http://www.intellinews.com/china-rising-beijing-s-insatiable-appetite-transforms-central-asian-oil-and-gas-flows-125124/
51. Henderson, James and Tatiana Mitrova (August 2016), "Energy Relations between Russia and China: Playing Chess with the Dragon", *Executive Summary,* The Oxford Institute for Energy Studies, University of Oxford, p. 1, Accessed May 2, 2017, See, https://www.oxfordenergy.org/wpcms/wp-content/uploads/2014/07/Executive-Summary-Energy-Relations-between-Russia-and-China-Playing-Chess-with-the-Dragon.pdf
52. Energy Information Administration (EIA), *op. cit.*, p.11.
53. Astakhova, Olesya and Chen Aizhu (January 15, 2016), "Exclusive: Russia Likely to Scale down China Gas Supply Plans", *Reuters* Accessed September 2, 2017. See, http://www.reuters.com/article/us-russia-china-gas-exclusive/exclusive-russia-likely-to-scale-down-china-gas-supply-plans-idUSKCN0UT1LG
54. Buckley, Neil (May 11, 2016), "Sino-Russian Gas Deal: Smoke without Fire", *Financial Times*. Accessed September 2 2017 See, https://www.ft.com/content/eea4f2ec-16c0-11e6-b197-a4af20d5575e
55. "Xi Offers Ways to Build New Model of Major-Country Relationship with US" (September 23, 2015), Accessed May 21, 2017, See, http://www.chinadaily.com.cn/world/2015xivisitus/2015-09/23/content_21963566.htm
56. Abbasi, Athar Z. (May 20, 2017), "OBOR Summit and Pakistan", *The Nation*, Accessed May 27, 2017, See, http://nation.com.pk/columns/20-May-2017/obor-summit-and-pakistan
57. Fazil, Muhammad Daim (June 9, 2016), "5 Reasons Gwadar Port Trumps Chabahar", *The Diplomat*, Accessed May 21, 2017, See, http://thediplomat.com/2016/06/5-reasons-gwadar-port-trumps-chabahar/

10

China-Central Asia Relations: Centrality of the Shanghai Cooperation Organisation

Sana Hashmi

ABSTRACT

China's economic and military capabilities have grown at an unprecedented scale in the past few decades, making it one of the principal actors in the international system. From the 1980s, as China moved forward on the path of economic reforms and opening-up to the international community, its profile at the international stage started rising to match up to its power projection. The advent of the twenty-first century saw a major shift in China's regional approach. Encouraged by its phenomenal economic capabilities, China has pursued a pragmatic and proactive diplomatic strategy designed to convince its neighbours, particularly the Central Asian Republics, of its 'peaceful rise', now known as 'peaceful development' as also the consolidation of its role as a key international actor. This chapter argues that establishment and gradual expansion of Shanghai Five to SCO has helped China with the avenues to strengthen its position in the region and also reinforce ties with the countries of the Central Asian region.

Key words: *China, China-Central Asia, Shanghai Cooperation Organisation, China's regional standing, China's neighbourhood.*

Introduction

Since the 1990s, China has been focusing on improving relations with its neighbours. These efforts began to take shape after the Tiananmen Square incident in 1989 when China was pushed towards the margins due to human rights issues. Since then, Chinese leaders have made deliberate efforts to formulate an integrated peripheral policy (*zhoubian zhengce*) also known as 'good neighbourly policy' (*mulin zhengce*), aimed at exploring common grounds with neighbouring countries in economic and security domains and conveying the image of China as a responsible international actor willing to contribute towards greater stability and cooperation in its neighbourhood.[1] While 14 countries share their boundaries with China, the Central Asian Republics form an integral part of China's peripheral as well as neighbourhood policy. The Central Asian Republics, since their emergence as independent sovereign states in the 1990s, has been an area of special interest to China. The actions of the Chinese leadership have been indicative of this policy. To cite examples, China decided to resolve the boundary disputes by compromising on its stand on the disputed territories in the 1990s and much later in 2013, the Chinese President Xi Jinping chose Kazakhstan to announce the revival of the Ancient Silk Road.

Clearly, over the years, China has been able to conceptualise and gradually implement its multifaceted Central Asia policy, both at bilateral as well as multilateral levels, which has yielded numerous benefits for it.

China's Central Asia Policy

China's Central Asia policy can be broadly categorised into three phases: The first phase runs from the year 1991 till 2000 i.e., broadly from the time of the dissolution of the Union of Soviet Socialist Republics (USSR) till the expansion of the Shanghai Five grouping. During this period, the focus was mostly on resolving the issues relating to the border and strengthening border security. Much of the attention was given to addressing unrest in Xinjiang, ensuring border stability, and focusing on border demilitarisation. The second phase started from 2001 when the Shanghai Five was expanded to become what is now called as the Shanghai Cooperation Organisation (SCO). One of the prime outcomes of this phase was the evolution and steady consolidation of China's Central Asia policy, as other factors too were included in China's engagement with the countries of the region. The third phase began in 2013 when the Chinese President Xi Jinping invited Kazakhstan and other Central Asian countries to be a part of Beijing's much-ambitious Silk Road Economic Belt (SREB), the land component of the One Belt, One Road (OBOR). This phase is also marked by the efforts for expansion of the SCO.

First Phase (1991-2000): The collapse of the USSR and the subsequent establishment of the Central Asian Republics provided China with an opportunity to resolve the outstanding issues with the countries of the region. Given that China was militarily as well as economically stronger than Russia and the Central Asian Republics, it was easier for Beijing to engage them in constructive negotiations. The main tasks for China, during this period, were to resolve the boundary dispute, have a secure border, and ensure stability in Xinjiang by controlling any cross-border support for the Uyghur separatists. At the same time, establishing foothold in the Central Asian region was vital to China's long-term interests, in both regional as well as global terms.

Second Phase (2001-2012): China increased its presence in the region by strengthening diplomatic and economic ties with the Central Asian Republics. During this period, China introduced the 'Western Development Programme'. The main objective of China's 'Western Development Programme' has been to develop its western and northwestern provinces, where the five Central Asian Republics had a great role to play due to contiguous boundaries. Secondly, Shanghai Five was expanded to become the SCO and began to gain prominence with the expansion of membership to Uzbekistan as well as goals such as countering terrorism, separatism and extremism. China effectively used the SCO to increase its influence in the region. At the same time, it restricted the growth of the organisation in such a way that it remained a tool to ensure that China remains at the centre. In other words, China made attempts to keep it an exclusively Eurasian organisation to achieve its regional consolidation and, thus benefiting the most out of it.

Third Phase (2013-Present): China's relations with Central Asian countries were further strengthened and institutionalised in the third phase through the SCO. China has been paying increasing attention to the SCO, where it has played a role of a facilitator of integration and peace and stability. Focusing on issues of regional growth, stability, development as well as other concerns is the primary focus of the SCO. President Xi Jinping visited four of the five Central Asian Republics namely Kazakhstan, Kyrgyzstan, Turkmenistan, and Uzbekistan in September 2013; thus, making it clear that Central Asia is significant for the Xi government as well. President Xi proposed the establishment of SREB between China and the Central Asian region and beyond as a joint construction initiative and a 'trans-Eurasian project spanning from the Pacific Ocean to the Baltic Sea' that would benefit about three billion people in the region.[2] In addition, China and other members accepted India and Pakistan's request to grant them full membership of the organisation.

China's Central Asia policy has been largely shaped by the China-Russia rapprochement. The rapprochement which did not just began with the end of the Cold War but the seeds of which were sown by the Mikhail Gorbachev in his famous 1986 Vladivostok Speech. The speech was aimed at improving the relations with China. Gorbachev showed eagerness to remove what China termed as three obstacles: "withdrawing Soviet troops from Afghanistan, withdrawing troops from Mongolia and stop providing support to Vietnam". These efforts continued to shape China's moves in the region even after the collapse of the USSR. Therefore, it was relatively easier for China to forge closer ties with Russia and simultaneously with Central Asia.

Since the collapse of the USSR, Central Asia has been regarded as Russia's backyard and it would have been difficult for China to maintain close relationship with Central Asian Republics without Russia's consent to allow China into the region. While China was not on good terms with the USSR, it made efforts to improve relations with post-Soviet states mainly Russia. With the declaration of a new strategic partnership in 1996, the strategic aspect of Beijing's relations with Moscow attained a prominence not seen since the Sino-Soviet alliance of the 1950s.[3] Alteration in China's Russia policy has been attributed to three factors. First, Taiwan and the support of the United States to Taiwan in the 1990s were bigger challenges than maintaining enmity towards Russia. China found it convenient to cooperate with Russia to keep the United States out of the region. It was important for China to demilitarise the China-Russia/Central Asia border so that it could focus more on Taiwan. China was well aware of the fact that it could not face threats from several sides. Joining hands with Russia was the most viable option. Second, when the independent Central Asian Republics came into being, there were trust issues between China and the newly independent countries. Countries of the Central Asian region were obviously tilted towards Russia than China. Beijing knew that without Russia's support, it would not be able to win over the trust of the Central Asian Republics. Russia realised that Central Asian countries were striving for growth and development. Under such circumstances, it had no option but to let the Chinese companies in Central Asia. Third, it was mutually beneficial for both China and Russia to work jointly in Central Asia. United States' sudden interest in Central Asia in the 1990s alarmed both China and Russia that did not want the United States to enter the region. Subsequently, in 1999, China and Russia considered the war in Kosovo as an aggressive war against Yugoslavia, a sovereign state which is out of North Atlantic Treaty Organization's (NATO) area, perpetrated by NATO under the leadership of the United States. This aggression was also perceived by the two countries as the reinforcement of the unipolar world order with only superpower United States. The political and military leaderships of the two countries started to review their defence policies because they recognised the United States' policy of pursuing its global supremacy as an increasing military threat to them.[4] Through NATO's air campaign against Yugoslavia, Russia realised NATO's offensive nature and concluded that NATO had become a serious military threat to Russia.[5] China also realised a serious threat from NATO because of the mistaken missile attack on the Chinese Embassy in Belgrade by a US fighter at the time of the air campaign against Yugoslavia.[6] Both China and Russia found convergent interests and this also played as a contributory factor for China-Russia cooperation in Central Asia and subsequently, for the evolution of the SCO.

China's Interests in Central Asia

The last two decades have been particularly interesting for China's relations with the Central Asian Republics. Since the independence of the Central Asian States, China has been one of the most important players in this strategically-located and resource-rich region. Central Asia has attained a significant position in Beijing's strategic and economic calculus. Its geographical proximity for instance is one of the reasons for continuity in the cordial relations with China. Through Xinjiang, China shares a long border of 3,700 km with three Central Asian countries namely: Kazakhstan, Kyrgyzstan, and Tajikistan. Second, resolving major outstanding issues with the countries of the region in a timely manner helped China to convince its neighbouring countries of its benign image. China's willingness to address the issue of the boundary disputes at the earliest on mutually convenient terms worked in China's favour. Newly established Central Asian countries did not have resources and manpower to fight against China on the boundary issue. Therefore, Central Asian countries appreciated China's gesture of resolving the border disputes. Even after the resolution of border disputes, the common pursuit of border security keeps joining China and Central Asia together.[7] Third, China has been actively interacting with the countries of the region. Regular summit-level meetings and exchange of high-level visits have helped them in maintaining political trust. In this context, leaders' meeting in the SCO have proved instrumental. Contrary to the other member countries that have not been able to make full use of the SCO's potential, China's initiatives were driven by its objective to make the most of the institutional framework in the region.

China has emerged as one of the largest economic as well as security partners for the countries of the region. The idea of win-win cooperation has been at the core of China's policy formulation towards the Central Asian region. China has several important broader considerations including countering insurgency and separatism that also motivated China to take substantial steps. Disturbances in Xinjiang have been the primary reason in that regard. Developments in the recent years also suggest that China's interests in Central Asia now include securing its future energy supplies and increasing its influence in the region through the SCO.

Border Stability and Xinjiang

Border stability was at the core of China's Central Asia policy in the 1990s. In the aftermath of the collapse of the USSR, China had to deal with a daunting task of safeguarding its border by putting an end to its long-standing border disputes with the Central Asian Republics and Russia. Given that Xinjiang, China's western-most and the most restive province, shares a long border with post-Soviet states, China was uneasy about Uyghurs getting support from the other side of the border. The issue of Uyghur-Xinjiang made the Central Asian Republics more important factor than anything else in comparison, at least in the 1990s. Thus, good neighbourly relations with the Central Asian Republics formed a core component of China's Central Asia strategy in dealing with the Xinjiang challenge. Clearly, Uyghur separatism has been a major concern for China, a reason most of the scholars find convincing enough. For instance, Loro Horta opines: "China's new focus in the region has been on cultivating good relations with the newly independent Republics that bordered its restive western province of Xinjiang, home to several Turkic groups such as the Uyghur, Uzbeks and Kazaks. Uyghur nationalists and separatists, or "splittists" as Beijing calls them, have on occasion used the neighbouring countries to organise anti-China activity."[8] Therefore, the resolution of boundary issues and border security had been a prerequisite for China's goal of a favourable environment.[9] In 1992, after the dissolution of the USSR, negotiations between China and Central Asia began, which eventually consolidated into nine panel meetings in 1993. Subsequently, on April 26, 1996, China, Russia, Kazakhstan, Kyrgyzstan, and Tajikistan signed the "Treaty on Deepening Military Trust in Border Regions" in Shanghai, China, which was lauded as a defining step in the evolution of the SCO. China, Russia, and the three Central Asian Republics agreed to participate in the annual summit, later termed as the "Shanghai Five" Summit. In April 1997, in order to take the border relations to next level, members of Shanghai Five signed the "Treaty on Reduction of Military Forces in Border Regions".[10] From then on, Shanghai Five served as a platform for China in initiating a range of dialogues with the newly founded Republics of Central Asia.

Fighting the 'Three Evils'

It is widely believed that one of the long-term goals of China in engaging the post-Soviet Central Asia is to maintain the status quo of non-Islamist and non-democratic states.[11] According to Stephen Blank:[12]

> "Growing Islamic militancy and extremism in the region emerged as a common threat for the countries of the region as well as Russia and China. Beijing opted for proceeding cautiously in dealing with Central Asia as well as Russia by laying greater emphasis on the maintenance of peace and stability in the region. At the same time, China tried to get the Central Asian regimes to commit to upholding China's unity and territorial integrity while abstaining from any assistance or encouragement to Uyghur separatism in Xinjiang".

Therefore, China's priority has been to fight three evils [described by Chinese government as terrorism, extremism and separatism] with the support of its Western neighbours. Xi Jinping echoed these sentiments in September 2014 as he urged the countries of the region to step up efforts to fight three evils and cyber terrorism. He stated, "(We) should make concerted efforts to crack down on the 'three evil forces' of terrorism, extremism and separatism."[13] One of the main features of the SCO has been to contain the three evils to spread in the Asian region. Priority for the SCO has always been maintaining and reinforcing peace, ensuring security and stability in the region, first of all, by organising joint efforts against fighting the three evils.[14] Regional Counter-Terrorism Structure (RCTS) under SCO deals with fighting three evils.

China-Central Asia Economic Relations

So far as the China-Central Asia economic relations are concerned, the trends show a great pattern. Two-way trade between China and Central Asia increased 100-fold between 1992 and 2012. Since there is a high degree of complementarity in trade between China and Central Asia, both sides have benefited enormously from the increased trade relations. By 2010, China had become the largest foreign commercial presence in Central Asia, the centre of its money markets, and the source of huge amounts of aid, trade, loans and investments in infrastructure and energy.[15] China is not only the biggest importer of Central Asia's natural gas and a range of other types of natural resources, but also the biggest commodity exporter to almost all the Central Asian Republics. Starting with a US$ 1 billion investment in the region in 2000, it has spent up to US$ 50 billion in trade and investments in the region according to the IMF; from developing its western border regions, so as to ensure its capabilities for trade, to building infrastructure like highways, pipelines, and railways throughout the region via the 2013 SREB initiative, China is determined to secure the region as its own zone of economic interest and appears to be achieving this goal.[16]

While one cannot deny the fact that compared to other countries and regions, China's commercial ties with the Central Asian Republics has not been very strong, it is equally valid that China's diplomatic endeavours have succeeded in its ability to exert influence on the Central Asian countries in a several ways positive towards China.

Energy

One of such ways is in the field of energy. Often referred to as the 'Second Persian Gulf', Central Asia is gaining traction due to abundance of untapped natural resources in the region. One of the reasons for China's sustained interests in the region is its quest for energy that has now driven it to search for energy supplies in Central Asia.[17] China's investment in Central Asia's oil and gas development broadened the prospects for bilateral economic cooperation, expanding both sides' energy channels and rejuvenating the historic Silk Road.[18]

The policymakers in China are cognisant of the fact that the rapidly rising Chinese economy needs abundant energy supplies and China's energy requirements are estimated to only get higher in future. The International Energy Outlook 2016 estimates that "China's oil imports in 2015 amounted to about 6.6 million barrels per day (b/d), representing 59 percent of the country's total oil consumption.[19] By 2035, the Energy Information Administration (EIA) projects China's oil imports to rise about 9.7 million b/d, accounting for about 62 percent of total oil consumption".[20] Furthermore, "by 2035, China's GDP (in terms of purchasing power parity) will grow to US$ 43.7 trillion, about 1.6 times larger than the US$ 26.7 trillion projected for the United States or US$ 27.8 trillion estimated for the European Union (EU). China has the economic and financial capacity to underwrite the costs of its ambitious effort to develop alternate land routes to bypass current maritime routes".[21] In this context, it looks towards Central Asia to fulfill its energy requirements. Central Asian countries, particularly Kazakhstan and Turkmenistan, could substantially contribute towards that. Therefore, since 2005, the SCO has prioritised joint energy projects including the oil and gas sector, the exploration of new hydrocarbon reserves and the joint use of water resources and within the SCO, Kazakhstan and Uzbekistan are of greatest interest to the Chinese policy-makers because of the large supplies of oil and gas these countries can have at their disposal.[22] Under such circumstances, it is self-evident that

China would keep working closely with Central Asian Republics, thereby offering an important advantage exclusively to China: proximity with Chinese borders in the context of availability of hydrocarbon resources. This makes the supplies relatively more cost effective and less time consuming, and their being relatively inaccessible to the outside world. It is much more difficult for the Central Asian Republics to export to the other countries than to China, and this gives China an upper hand in terms of negotiating hydrocarbon deals with the Central Asian Republics.

Shanghai Cooperation Organisation

The SCO, since its expansion from its predecessor- Shanghai Five, has been one of the most important mechanisms that contributed in shaping up of China's Central Asia policy. China has several reasons to engage with Central Asia, as mentioned in the previous sections of the chapter. China's multilateral equation with the countries of the region has also been remarkable. Through the effective utilisation of the SCO mechanism, it has demonstrated that it believes in the idea that one of the most efficient approaches in international relations is to engage through multilateral institutions and a regional organisation and the SCO turned out be a fitting solution to China's engagement plan with Central Asia.[23]

On the fifth anniversary of Shanghai Five in June 2001, with the inclusion of Uzbekistan, the Shanghai Five was expanded to become the SCO. Leaders of the member states signed a joint declaration admitting Uzbekistan as the sixth member of the Shanghai Five mechanism. The Declaration on the Establishment of the SCO announced that for the purpose of upgrading the level of cooperation to more effectively seize opportunities and deal with new challenges and threats, the six states had decided to establish SCO on the basis of the Shanghai Five mechanism.[24] According to the declaration, the establishment of the SCO aims at strengthening mutual trust, good-neighbourly and friendly relations among member states, encouraging their further effective cooperation in politics, economy, science and technology, culture, education, energy, transportation, environmental protection and other fields, jointly ensuring regional peace, security and stability, and creating a new international political and economic order featuring democracy, justness and rationality.[25] On the eve of the expansion of the Shanghai Five, all the members adopted Convention on Combating Terrorism, Separatism, and Extremism unanimously, which expanded the scope of the organisation. Therefore, the focus was extended from border security to combating non-traditional security threats.

Virtues of the SCO are more than one. First, this was the first ever-multilateral grouping that had China as the prime initiator and a major driving force. Second, it is one of the rare regional organisations that have been able to metamorphose itself in a short span of time, meeting the new requirements of the countries, particularly China. For instance, the first five formative years of the grouping were primarily devoted to issues concerning border security and stability. In this regard, the Shanghai Group was given a very important task, i.e., to arrive at an understanding for the terms of the settlement of outstanding border issues between China and the Central Asian Republics. With a long-term objective of strengthening mutual trust, the member countries worked on inking agreements, which would facilitate in demarcating the borders and help with the demilitarisation of the common borders. The Shanghai Five helped the member countries in resolving the border issues for good. The grouping became integral to the border negotiations as it helped to overcome apprehensions.

It has been observed that China prefers to deal with contentious issues bilaterally rather than multilaterally. This has been particularly true in case of boundary related issues. Contrary to this, however, Shanghai Five worked as a landmark forum in tackling the boundary issues. It offered a forum for negotiations between China, Russia, and the Central Asian Republics. The most important reason for China to get into such a dialogue mechanism has been that it was apprehensive of the adverse developments happening in Xinjiang. China was fully aware of the fact that resolving the boundary dispute would be a fundamental prerequisite to raise the bigger trans-national issues such as terrorism and ethnic separatism. This compelled China to come up with a comparatively more long-term plan to tie down ethnic unrest and eliminate threat on its north-western border. This led to a shift in group's focus towards combating non-traditional security threat. Visibly, over the years, the focus of the grouping has been shifted from boundary to capping and eliminating the three menaces and bringing about more stability in the region.

Situating Central Asia in China's Approach towards SCO

China has been employing both bilateral as well multilateral methods to proactively engage the countries of Central Asia. While there are several explanations of the purpose and functioning of the organisation, most notable is that it has been evolved to address internal security issues of the member states. For example, China shows interest in the SCO to keep a check on its Xinjiang problem and gain other states' support for curbing cross-border cooperation on anti-China activity in Xinjiang and Central Asian Republics by Uyghur diaspora and sympathisers. China also uses

SCO to garner support against the three evils. Another perspective is that SCO is derived from the prism of geopolitics and interstate strategic interaction.[26] China, through the SCO, attempts to reinforce its position in Central Asia.[27] Russia intends to keep a check on the increasing Chinese influence in the region from within the organisation;[28] whereas, Central Asian states are trying to mutually constrain Russia and China through an institution.[29] They are also attempting to gain maximum out of China-Russia equation through the SCO.

From China's perspective, Central Asia is the safest bet to increase its regional outreach. Over the years, one of the most fundamental shifts in the regional strategic architecture came about with the rise of China, and more importantly its willingness to take the mantle of the regional leader. While China is not generally perceived as a responsible stakeholder in Southeast Asia and East Asia due to its assertive behaviour in the maritime disputes, it has no conflict of interests with Central Asian countries. In fact, their interests converge against fighting terrorism and extremism. Therefore, the functioning of the organisation has never been halted and it is easier for the Chinese leadership to work with the Central Asian countries towards achieving mutual as well as individual interests.

Reasons for China's Success

It is beyond doubt that China has been successful in wooing the countries of the Central Asian region. Several factors have contributed in making China's diplomacy in Central Asia a success. For instance, the collapse of the USSR, tardy political and domestic transition in the countries of the Central Asian region, poor economic situations in Central Asia, and lack of foreign investments in Central Asia have been cases in point.

Arguably, however, the factor that has contributed the most in making China such a great success in shaping the region and fostering cooperation in Central Asia is that the other countries did not take much interest in the region. United States, Japan, and India, either found the region not too attractive for trade and economic reasons or did not have enough financial resources like India. The only other major power, which had the wherewithal to have the predominant position in the region, was Russia. However, in the aftermath of the dissolution of the USSR, the Russian economy was not in a position to take the lead. On the political front, Russia was still able to exert influence, as most of the leaders of the Central Asian Republics had strong linkages with the Russian leadership. As a matter of fact, Russian and the Central Asian leaders were familiar with each other in terms of working. Moreover, decades of strong linkages have made it possible for the leaders and people of the Central Asian countries to feel comfortable with the Russian presence. Still, it is true that the entry of the Chinese investments and political manoeuvring curtailed the scope for the Russian influence. The United States, on the other hand, tried to take a lead in the initial years after the end of the Cold War but could not sustain the momentum as it had several other, and arguably more important priorities to deal with: the war in Afghanistan, Iraq, and elsewhere in West Asia, difficult situations in the Asia-Pacific particularly with respect to the China and North Korea made it even more difficult for the United States to focus immensely on the Central Asian region. The other major Asian power that could have contributed significantly in the Central Asian region was Japan. However, Japan had been awfully narrow in terms of its vision for Asia. It was only after Prime Minister Shinzo Abe's coming to power that in 2015 Japan made its presence felt in the region with the first-ever visit by any Japanese Prime Minister to the region. While it is still too early to predict the role of Japan in the region, it does not seem likely that Japan would get into the SCO in the short to medium term. So far as India is concerned, while it has attempted to engage the countries of the region using historical linkages, commonality in culture, etc., it has not been able to play a leading role due to limited economic engagement and constraints on the financial front. Limited land connectivity has proved to be the major obstacle and lacking borders with the Central Asian states, India is denied land access through Pakistan's territory due to constant friction between the two countries.[30] Despite efforts, India has not been able to establish viable land routes to reach Central Asia.

Moreover, by not investing enough into the region, in both diplomatic and economic terms, the other powers gave China the opportunity to move forward with its Central Asia plan without much difficulty.[31] Needless to add that, much to its credit, China managed to live up to the expectation of the countries of the region, and to itself also, and managed to keep its position pivotal in the regional dynamics.

Major Challenges to China's SCO Strategy

From the organisational perspective, it is often argued that SCO has been a moderately successful organisation. Arguably, the progress of the organisation has been slow on several counts. For China, persuading its SCO partners, particularly Russia, to engage in functional cooperation according to the wishes of the Chinese side is no easy task and Chinese analysts consistently complain about Russia's lukewarm attitude toward strengthening substantive cooperation in the SCO and the inadequacy of the Central Asian states' contribution to functional cooperation through the SCO.[32]

However, there have been multiple challenges ahead for China on its way to making SCO a fully bloomed completely success organisation. One of the major reasons in this regard has been China's attitude towards Pakistan, terrorism, and inequitable relations regarding energy supplies. To make OBOR a success, and to get Pakistan's support on dealing with the Xinjiang separatism, China's understanding on terrorism has been blurred. It seems to be overlooking the fact that terrorism is a trans-national threat to countries across the world, and irrespective of their geographical location.

The second major criticism has been that due to its own insecurities, China has deliberately kept SCO a low-key regional grouping, which essentially means that China has deliberately made steps away from achieving its true potential as a multilateral organisation. A possible explanation on that count is that China's focus has been on making SCO an exclusive regional platform rather than a grouping with many non-regional representatives. Thus, China, for a very long time, wanted to keep the organisation confined to the region, and not involve other countries, which are not from the region. However, the situation will be changed with the full-fledged membership of India and Pakistan. It has also been striving to keep the grouping more inward looking and away from the hype that surrounds the typical organisations.

Conclusion

In summation, it may be argued that China's Central Asia policy has hinged on the effective use of the SCO. To make the optimal use of SCO to meet its foreign policy objectives, China has triggered the transformation in the overall objectives of the SCO. Over the years, SCO has undergone tremendous changes, providing the region with a common platform to deal with issues of trans-national importance. Over the years, it has emerged as an important regional organisation, which does not belong to western states. Being a multi-faceted organisation ranging from security to economic cooperation, it has projected its role.

China's emphasis on the SCO as an active regional player has yielded positive results, and yet China has kept the grouping inward looking and controlled by the two major powers i.e., Russia and China. China's growing influence in the organisation and the region signals towards China's intrinsic desire that Asian affairs are taken care of by Asian only. Clearly,

China's dynamism in the SCO is linked to its long-standing objective of building new regional security architecture. No other organisation exists to deal with security problems in Central Eurasia. Thus, SCO's development into a full-fledged security organisation would be fruitful for the member states.

Terrorism has become a menace for the entire region, affecting almost all countries of the Asian region. However, China seems to be still focusing on its own interpretations depending on its domestic experience and strategic objectives. Its excessive focus on Xinjiang, overlooking the concerns of other member countries, has not been of much support to India and other countries of the region. China's failure to work as a responsible stakeholder vis-à-vis terrorism would not lead it far in the regional dynamics. With the addition of India, the SCO has the potential to become an important player in the regional as well as global politics, and an organisation of regional decision-making, and it can achieve such goals if it applies a long-term perspective with a responsible role-playing intentions.

Disclaimer: The views expressed here are those of the author and do not represent the views of Ministry of External Affairs and the Government of India.

NOTES

1. Zhiqun Zhu (2010), *China's New Diplomacy: Rationale, Strategies and Significance*, England: Ashgate, p. 111.
2. Wu Jiao and Zhang Yunbi (2013), "Xi Proposes a 'New Silk Road' with Central Asia", *China Daily*, available at http://usa.chinadaily.com.cn/china/2013-09/08/content_16952304.htm, Accessed on December 24, 2016
3. Mark Burles (1999), *Chinese Policy toward Russia and the Central Asian Republics*, Washington, D.C.: RAND, p. ix
4. Sakaguchi Yoshiaki and Mayama Katsuhiko (2001), "Significance of the War in Kosovo for China and Russia", *National Institute for Defence Studies, Japan*, available at http://www.nids.mod.go.jp/english/publication/kiyo/pdf/bulletin_e2001_1.pdf. Accessed on June 12, 2017
5. Celeste A. Wallander (March 2000), "Wary of the West: Russian Security Policy at the Millennium," *Arms Control Today*, pp.7-10
6. Yoshiaki and Katsuhiko, n. 4.
7. Zhao Huasheng (2012), "China's Central Asia Policy", in Charles Hawkins and Robert Love (eds.) *Chinese Strategies on Central Asia: The New Great Game*, New Delhi: Manas Publications, p. 26.
8. Loro Horta, "Central Asia's New Silk Road, Paved by China", *East Asia Forum*, October 26, 2013. http://www.eastasiaforum.org/2013/10/26/central-asias-new-silk-road-paved-by-china/. Accessed on December 27, 2016
9. Zhao Huasheng (2007), "Central Asia in China's Diplomacy", in Eugene Rumer,

Dmitri Trenin and Huasheng Zhao (eds.), *Central Asia: Views from Washington, Moscow and Beijing, Armonk,* N.Y.: M.E. Sharpe, p. 140.

10. For more information on the role of Shanghai Five in China-Central Asia boundary dispute resolution, see Sana Hashmi (2016), *China's Approach towards Territorial Disputes: Lessons and Prospects,* New Delhi: Knowledge World, pp. 59-86.
11. John W. Garver quoted in Gang Lin, "China's 'Good Neighbor' Diplomacy: A Wolf in Sheep's Clothing?" *Wilson Center,* no. 126, p. 1.
12. Younkyoo Kim & Stephen Blank (2013), "Same Bed, Different Dreams: China's 'Peaceful Rise' and Sino–Russian Rivalry in Central Asia", *Journal of Contemporary China,* vol. 22, issue 83, pp. 773-790.
13. "China Urges Central Asian Neighbours to Step Up Extremism Fight", *Reuters,* September 13, 2014, https://in.reuters.com/article/china-xinjiang/china-urges-central-asian-neighbours-to-step-up-extremism-fight-idINKBN0H802J20140913. Accessed on February 2, 2017.
14. "Fighting Three Evils", February 2, 2011, http://infoshos.ru/en/?idn=7678. Accessed on February 2, 2017.
15. Kim and Blank, n. 12
16. Victoria Kelly-Clark (2016), "Why is Central Asia Dumping Russia for China", *Global Risk Insights,* May 23, http://globalriskinsights.com/2016/05/why-central-asia-is-dumping-russia-for-china/ Accessed on February 2, 2017
17. Stephen Blank (2006), "China's Emerging Energy Nexus with Central Asia", *China Brief,* vol. 6, no. 15.
18. Xu Haiyan (2015), "China-Central Asia "Twin-Track" Energy Cooperation", *China Institute of International Studies,* http://www.ciis.org.cn/english/2015-05/11/content_7894391.htm. Accessed on February 6, 2017.
19. Samir Tata (2017), "Deconstructing China's Energy Security Strategy", *The Diplomat,* http://thediplomat.com/2017/01/deconstructing-chinas-energy-security-strategy/. Accessed on February 10, 2017.
20. Ibid.
21. Ibid.
22. Cited in Ralph Wrobel (2014), "China's New Energy Geopolitics: The Shanghai Cooperation Organization and Central Asia", *ASIEN,* vol. 133, pp. 24–25.
23. Weiqing Song (2014), "Interests, Power and China's Difficult Game in the Shanghai Cooperation Organization (SCO)", *Journal of Contemporary China,* vol. 23, no. 85, p. 86
24. For more details, see "Shanghai Cooperation Organization", *Ministry of Foreign Affairs, People's Republic of China,* January 7, 2004, http://www.fmprc.gov.cn/mfa_eng/topics_665678/sco_665908/t57970.shtml. Accessed on January 2, 2017
25. For more details, see "Declaration of Shanghai Cooperation Organization", *People's Daily Online,* June 15, 2001, http://en.people.cn/200106/15/eng20010615_72738.html. Accessed on January 2, 2017
26. Song, n. 23.
27. Chien-peng Chung (2006), "China and the Institutionalization of the Shanghai Cooperation Organization: Problems of Post-Communism", vol. 53, no. 5, p. 10
28. Andrei Kazantsev (2008), "Russian Policy in Central Asia and the Caspian Sea Region", *Europe-Asia Studies,* vol. 60, no. 6, p. 1080

29. Gill Bates (2001), "Shanghai Five: An Attempt to Counter US Influence in Central Asia?", *Newsweek Korea*, http://www.brookings.edu/opinions/2001/0504china_gill.aspx. Accessed July 2, 2011. Chien-peng Chung (2004), "The Shanghai Co-operation Organization: China's Changing Influence in Central Asia", *The China Quarterly*, vol. 80, pp. 989–1009.
30. Sabena Siddiqui, "India's Connect Central Asia Policy", *china.org*, October 12, 2017, http://www.china.org.cn/opinion/2017-10/12/content_41721919.htm. Accessed on December 19, 2017.
31. Author's conversation with Dr. Rahul Mishra, Research Fellow, Indian Council of World Affairs, New Delhi.
32. Weiqing Song (2014), "Interests, Power and China's Difficult Game in the Shanghai Cooperation Organization (SCO)", *Journal of Contemporary China*, Vol. 23, No. 85, p. 93.

11

Chinese Perspectives on the US Alliances in East Asia: A New Type of Great Power Folly?

Swati Arun

ABSTRACT

The changes in China's foreign policy, from prioritising relations with the US to peripheral diplomacy, have their underpinnings in its economic stability and the availability of surplus. There is no doubt that China has yearned to return to the glorious days of its past, a desire more visible in its foreign and defence policies of the last decade. Since 2008, China has transitioned from a tier two power to a challenger of the status quo. In this context, China sees the alliance system as a threat, a bid for containment, restricting its expansion into the seas. While the Chinese approach towards the region is in keeping with the tenets of realism, the strategy in the long term could prove counter-intuitive. Chinese belligerency has pushed nations into internally balancing themselves against China. The lack of credible assurance from the US projects China, with its credible nuclear capabilities, as the next real threat.

Background

China made an official declaration in 2010 that it would walk the path of peaceful development. This concept was elaborated by State Councillor Dai Bingguo, and is deemed to be very Chinese in nature. Later a few other catch phrases also began to be used regularly in official speeches and newspapers. These included 'win-win cooperation'; 'working together toward a better future for Asia and the world'; 'promoting peace and stability'; 'peaceful development'; 'mutually beneficial strategy of opening up'; and 'pursuit of friendly cooperation with all countries'.

Also in 2010, Foreign Minister Yang Jiechi supported China's larger involvement in international affairs in his speech, 'Shape the Future of Asia Pacific with Confidence and Cooperation'. This marked a shift in Chinese foreign policy thinking, that was contrary to that of his predecessor, who had denounced all hegemonic intentions of expansion and leadership.[1] This shift indicated a China that was willing to push for a new security architecture, to ensure its economic success and influence by acquiring great power status.

In 2015, China further enunciated the tenets of this shift in its white paper on military strategy.[2] The white paper laid out plans for expanding China's naval power, stating that: "The PLA Navy (PLAN) will gradually shift its focus from 'offshore waters defence' to the combination of 'offshore waters defence' with 'open seas protection', and build a combined, multi-functional and efficient marine combat force structure."[3] The statement revealed China's intentions to expand its interests into the South China Sea and the East China Sea.

The controversial claim by China conceptualised as nine dash line, encompasses most of the South China Sea, challenging the territorial claims of other South East Asian nations and the legitimate claim over the 12 nautical miles Exclusive Economic Zone (EEZ) of nations, such as Philippines and Malaysia. In the east, China lays claims on the Diaoyu Island and has declared an Air Defence Identification Zone over a portion of the East China Sea in November 2013, that overlaps that of Japan. In the same way, China is hinting at its serious resolve to reunify Taiwan, impose its dominance over the East China Sea and claim and control the South China Sea area.

The United States is a treaty ally of Japan and Taiwan, and has strong defence ties with several South East Asian nations, with military bases and strategic assets located on their territories. This architecture compels the US to protect these nations, maintain stability in the region and ensure a favourable balance of power. Thus, the Chinese policy statement also challenges the credibility of the US alliance commitments and its principle of free and open navigation on the high seas.

While China was always wary of the close US presence, the dynamics between the two nations have drastically changed. As an after effect of its rise, it has become confident, assertive and belligerent in ignoring the international institutions and twisting the law in its favour to realise its territorial claims. The annexation of Scarborough Shoal in 2012 and the rejection of ruling in the case of the South China Sea Arbitrations exemplifies China's unilateral nature and hegemonic intentions. China's assertiveness at sea can be noted from 2010, when China expanded its 'core interests' to include the South and East China Sea. There can be two reasons for this shift: First, China is wary of US alliances in East Asia as they restrict Chinese movement, and limit its activities, to secure its own national interests in East Asia; and second, China is opening up the political space to manage sovereignty and territorial disputes through threats or by use of force.

The existing 'China threat theory', which is popular among American scholars, was compounded further by the 'Pivot to Asia' strategy, creating fertile ground for contention and conflict between the two countries. President Xi Jinping's foreign policy—'New type of Great Power Relations' and the 'Belt and Road Initiative' announced China's entry into global politics as an equal to the US, thus disturbing the status quo.

Previously, China had followed the principle of 'keeping a low profile' (KLP) since the time of Deng Xiaoping who had said: "We will only become a big political power if we keep a low profile (*Tao Guan Yang Hui*) and work hard for some years; and we will then have *more weight* in international affairs."[4] It was only in 2013, however, that Xi replaced this term at the Working Conference on Neighbourhood Diplomacy with 'strive to achieve'. The departure from KLP reflected concrete changes in the Chinese elite's thought and the role they saw China playing in the future. It is possible that China may flex its military muscle openly and declare its intentions to achieve global power status. This perceptional change implies that China believes that it does not need to maintain a low profile anymore. With a $ 11 trillion GDP and modern military, China seems confident that it can influence other countries, by economic and security means.

The Chinese strategy to create an international system more conducive to its political rise has become more visible during Xi's term. To counter the growing negative perception of the actions of the People's Liberation Army Navy (PLAN), Chinese officials continued to subdue the harsh reactions generated in the world media. The officials made statements such as guaranteed 'peace and stability', 'prosperity and mutual respect', to remake its image as a champion of world peace, in particular relation to China's territorial disputes with its neighbours. In 2014, Xi articulated the idea of 'Asia for Asians, and an 'Asian Security Concept' for a new Asia, whereby only Asians would resolve their disputes and protect themselves, thus clearly de-legitimising the US alliance system, which had been termed a 'relic from past world and Cold War mentality' in several Chinese white papers (Military doctrine[5] and Asia Pacific Cooperation[6]) and official statements. Due to the binding US promise of providing protection to East Asian nations, since the end of World War II, nations have enjoyed free and protected navigation on the high seas, resulting in the limited militarisation of the region. At present China's neighbours are starkly weak without the US presence, leaving the region at the mercy of China, which is currently the wealthiest, the most ambitious and has the most modern military. While China ignored the 'binding' alliances between Asia and the US, in its white paper on 'Asia-Pacific Security Cooperation', it also warned the region about the consequences of persisting with a 'Cold War mentality' with regard to their relations with China.

In addressing the new framework for security in Asia, China rolled out several 'new' concepts: 'Active defence' (2010); 'new type of major power relations' (2013); 'new type of Asian security concept' (2014) and 'peace through strength' (2014). But behind the plans of multilateral cooperation, China began to behave increasingly unilaterally in its decision making, from expanding 'core interests', to the Air Defence Identification Zones (ADIZ) and building artificial islands in disputed territories.

Thus, China seems to be following the dual strategy of reforming existing institutions from within to create an international environment that is conducive for its growing comprehensive national power, while on regional issues it resorts to unilateral solutions. Unilateral actions in the disputed region of East Asia have a myriad consequences for the region and China itself, but they expose its intentions of achieving a hegemonic presence in South East Asia. In this scenario, China is increasingly becoming a strategic competitor of the US.

US Alliances in East Asia

The US has been dominating maritime security in Asia for over a half a century. Beginning with the 'San Fransisco System' in 1952, the US and Japan signed a security treaty, signaling a long term American presence in East Asia, and hence expanding its idea of national interest and securing its influence, far from its territorial bounds. As per the treaty, Japan relinquished its right to an army, and accepted protection under the US nuclear umbrella. This network with the US as a sole security provider discouraged East Asian nations such as South Korea and Japan from initiating military modernisation, thus creating an imbalance of capabilities in East Asia. Consequently, a once militarily powerful and aggressive Japan accepted the role of a pacifist state. The US also signed defence treaties with South Korea (1953), Philippines (1951), Thailand (1951), Australia and New Zealand (1951) and the Republic of China or Taiwan (1954), in the backdrop of the US having emerged as a single most powerful nation in the West after the devastating World War II. The expansive matrix of alliances in the East Asia were also a part of the US stratagem during the Cold War tensions with Soviet Russia.

This reliance on the US protection, while allowing these nations to pay greater attention to economic prosperity, restricted individual action against the perceived threat from a rising China. In the years since 2008, Chinese assertiveness has been seen to be on the rise, its consistent growth rate allowed it to undertake an extensive military modernisation programme, acquiring capabilities that were greater than those of all its neighbours, combined. Such an assertiveness, rationally, should have been met with an equal (and deterrent) response from the US on behalf of its allies, to keep the favourable balance of power intact.

The lack of action encouraged Chinese belligerency and its unilateral control over disputed territory. One recent example of the lack of response to Chinese action, that marked a shift in the balance of power, was the construction of three artificial islands since 2014, in the disputed South China Sea. The islands—Subi, Mischief and Fiery Cross reefs—are part of the Spratly chain, which is claimed wholly or in part by China, the Philippines, Vietnam, Malaysia, Taiwan and Brunei. As of now, as per satellite images, the People's Liberation Army Navy (PLAN) has inducted new weapons on the island, providing a hardcore military backup to its territorial claims[7]. Subsequently China threatened the use of force against Vietnam and Philippines to prevent them from exploring for natural resources (e.g. oil and natural gas) or conducting military exercises in the area.

However, its alliances made the US a stakeholder in regional politics. Bound by treaty obligations, any assertive action by China in the region could lead to conflicts between Japan and China, testing the resilience of the Japan-US alliance. The quandary that China is not only the US' largest trading partner but also its strategic competitor could lead to security dilemmas in Sino-US relations.

Chinese apprehensions with regard to US alliances in Asia are not new. While China communicated its displeasure towards the US, with Mao Zedong calling the US the 'most dangerous imperialist power'; China's isolation from the world could not pose any challenge to American superpower status. After a period of open conflict (Korean War and Vietnam War), and before the opening up of the Chinese economy, both nations reached an understanding (the 1971 rapprochement), wherein the Soviet Russia, and not the US was seen to be the imminent threat. After this, Sino-US relations enjoyed relative stability, with only few complications, e.g. the bombing of the Chinese embassy in Belgrade and the Taiwan Strait Crisis.

Since countering the US alliance structure openly, would mean an armed conflict that China is keen on avoiding, it is actively creating friction between East Asian nations and the US. The said security network helped China prosper in a peaceful environment and since the Japanese power was entwined with the US alliance structure, Japanese concerns about China could not attract concrete action. However, now China has the capability to challenge this structure.

Both China and the US could not escape the structural impediment that exists between a rising power and an established power, and this has been particularly apparent from 2008 onwards. During the second Obama administration, given the perceived hegemonic intentions of China, the US announced its new strategy towards Asia-Pacific—'rebalance to Asia' or 'pivot to Asia'—that involved deploying about 60 per cent of its navy to the region.[8]

Currently, China's territorial disputes present a challenge for the US and its allies' interests and commitments in Asia. The US created, and continues to maintain the East Asian order, which revolves around its alliances with South Korea, Japan, Taiwan, Philippines, Thailand and Australia. Hence, China's attempts to create an 'Asia for Asians', or its policy of absolute adherence to its 'core interests' or its 'new type of great power' politics is in opposition to the US policies.

Moreover, China's belligerency in the neighbourhood, combined with its proactive attempts to create a special understanding between Sino-US, while ignoring East Asian concerns about China, did not fare well. As a result, both Philippines and Vietnam received financial assistance from the US and Japan, to upgrade their maritime capabilities. But in the subsequent months, Chinese assertion in the South China Sea had been met with inaction from the regional powers, leaving Vietnam to fend for itself. The vicious motion of military escalation has been set in East Asia, making it the most militarised region of the world. Consequently, the US lifted the four decade long embargo on transfer of arms and technology to Vietnam, while Japan amended its constitution and treaty with the US to allow arms sales, participation in military exercises, and to provide external assistance to other nations. There were also defence budget increases in Vietnam, Japan, Philippines, signalling the awakening of their collective consciousness about national security.

However, thus far, these countries cannot match China's military expenditure, which supersedes that of any nation in Asia at $ 147 billion in 2017, second only to the US.[9] The Chinese military expenditure cannot be attributed only to power maximisation, but also to core security concerns.

First, the historical evidence of Japan's aggression against China does not allow it to take a sober approach towards the US-Japan alliance and overlook the US military capability in the region. Second, US interventions in different parts of the world, make it difficult for China to forgo its military modernisation in order to allay the concerns of the 'smaller nations' around its periphery. Moreover, as China's 'core interests' diverge from that of the US, conflict becomes much more probable and preparing for conflict becomes an imperative.

New Thinking in Chinese Foreign Policy

Keeping Low Profile or Making Bold Alliances

Despite the endurance of the KLP policy, there were many who had argued in favour of an active approach. For instance, Yan Xuetong, one of the most vocal critics of the KLP and non-alignment, advocated active alliance making by China, if it wanted to create a position for itself. He viewed the international system as rapidly evolving into "two superpowers and many great powers"[10]. However, in the 1990s, Yan argued that the system was "one superpower, many great powers", China being one among many. There was near consensus in China on this position which changed structurally, post 2008. In subsequent articles, written over the years, he injected a note of pragmatism into Chinese thinking, wherein alliance-making was a prerequisite of the successful defence of "core interests".

In 2012, Yan proposed moving away from KLP and instead embracing 'act modestly and prudently'.[11] He wrote that "without reliable friends, we have no one."[12] Other scholars had also made similar arguments. Ye Zhicheng in 2002 advocated the view that China should replace KLP with a new strategy, in view of China's enhanced power.[13] One of the widely held arguments against KLP is China's rising national strength, that warrants protection from external powers fracturing economic prosperity, rendering the nation vulnerable.

In 2010, Senior Colonel (PLA National Defence University) Liu Mingfu suggested that China should challenge the dominant position of the US and try to take its place as the predominant power.[14] Luo Yuan, a retired major general, from the PLA Academy of Military Science, a strong critic of US intentions and actions in East Asia, urged China to show its strength through armed conflict when necessary. This was in direct violation of peaceful development, mutual respect, and win-win cooperation and KLP. But on matters of alliance he chooses the middle path—a quasi alliance,[15] as the preferred solution to China's dilemma, whereby a de-facto alliance with Pakistan and North Korea would be a better option. Over the years this discourse has been shaped into 'no development without security', whereby national security is paramount for the sustenance of economic security. As Xi Jinping said in his SCO speech on June 9, 2017, "Security is a prerequisite for development". Previously in 2015, while speaking on security issues at the CICA, Xi had said, "There can be no development without security".

While alliance politics is still rejected in China's official policy—as it is considered to be a relic of the Cold War era—discussions on the feasibility and necessity of a Sino-Russian alliance are gaining momentum. Dai Xu, a PLA Air Force colonel while citing his concerns about the US intention of global domination, concluded that it was necessary for China and Russia to establish a 'Euro-Asian grand alliance'.[16]. He also advocated attacking the US where it hurts—in the Eurasian heartland—to defeat its strategy of strategic encirclement. On this issue, it should be noted that arguments against the US presence in Asia, in Chinese foreign policy are strategic and take a realistic view of the world, underpinned by their desired future for China (rejuvenation of the Chinese nation), where its national interests are not threatened and it returns to its former glory.

In other words, for many political scientists in China, there are structural impediments to the Sino-US relationship and an alliance policy would help China protect its interests. In 2012, Yan said that given their common interests China should join hands with Russia in opposing American encroachment.[17] Zhang Wenmu of Beijing University proposed elevating the Sino-Russia strategic partnership to an alliance, where only *their* legitimate interests would be safeguarded vis-à-vis the US. Moreover, Zhang also criticised non-alignment as an unnatural policy for the long term, concluding that a permanent adherence to this concept is like "digging one's own grave before conflict begins".

Moreover, Chinese scholars have acknowledged that China has become more assertive in the maritime sphere. They support these actions because according to them Beijing should assert itself on issues of core interest such as the Diaoyu Islands and South China Sea, thus declaring the KLP unfit to fulfil the goals of Chinese foreign policy. There is surely a gap between China's statements on peaceful development, keeping a low profile, mutual respect and its unilateral actions against its neighbours. Thus, Wang Jianwei calls for a new phase of diplomacy combined with assertion and reducing the confusion that stems from harping on KLP while practicing something different.[18]

On the other hand, prominent scholars—Wang Jisi, Wang Zaibang, Qin Yaqing—have all argued that the KLP, is a timeless strategy which is much more appropriate at the current stage of Chinese development. According to this view, China needs a stable environment to develop, but its accelerated rise has invited scrutiny and hostility. Under such circumstances, departing from KLP will only aggravate the international community's response, making it difficult for China to maintain its current pace of development.

A call for a different approach to diplomacy in Chinese foreign policy has opened up a debate on how to secure the best interests of China without completely departing from the old principles. The concept of quasi-alliance has therefore surfaced and gained traction. This ensures defence in need without the added complications of a formal alliance.[19] In this regard, Feng Zhang argued that, "relatively cheap, flexible and convenient, quasi-alliances are seen to entail no loss of the foreign-policy independence cherished by China". A Sino-Russian quasi-alliance is seen as, "potentially developing into a new model of great-power relationship". Yu Zhengliang describes the Sino-Russia quasi alliance as a structural necessity and a strategic reaction to the developing situation. Tang Shipping (Fudan University) criticises China's reluctance to adopt a alliance strategy. He urges that China should employ all strategies necessary for safeguarding its interests in the world. While the government has not yet departed from its official policy of peaceful development, Xi's approach to seems to underlie this pattern.

An alliance is a prescription for external balancing. According to Kenneth Waltz external balancing can employ strategies to strengthen and expand one's own alliance or weaken and shrink an opposing one. While in the past, alliances have been of irreplaceable value as leverage against a common enemy, they lost their traditional importance in the post-Cold War decades. Neo-liberalism captured the intellectual market, negating the need for alliances and replacing them with the universal pursuit of economic prosperity and national development.

The multilayered concept of national development (which includes military and economic development) could be understood as an effective strategy designed and promoted by China to alter attention to its military activities in the region. But President Xi Jinping in his address warned that national development cannot be achieved without a reliable security apparatus and it would be incomplete without it. However, the rejected concepts resurfaced with the varying speculations suggesting that China's rise/development was affecting the power structure of prevailing system, thereby threatening US interests in Asia and by extension, its national security.

Chinese analysts are considering both aspects of the strategy: building up China's own alliances by working with Russia and other countries, and undermining the American alliance system by applying measured strategic pressure on America's regional allies and by raising the cost of America's commitment to them. Moreover, there is a distinctive Chinese understanding of alliance politics with respect to its neighbourhood policy. It holds, that alliances with neighbours would contribute to building strategic trust with them, thus dampening their suspicions and consolidating strategic cooperation, while at the same time reducing the attraction of the United States as a security provider.

If such ideas become policy, they may result in two opposing alliance systems in the Asia-Pacific, creating a Sino-US version of the Cold War confrontation for the 21st century. If nothing else, the region would see the revival of a realist logic. The rise of Chinese power and the country's apparent assertiveness in recent years has elicited a vigorous strategic response from Washington and its regional allies, which in turn has stimulated Chinese domestic discussion on the merits of an equally robust response centred on reclaiming alliance strategy, foregoing the historical limbo of Chinese foreign policy. One can interpret this as an example of the intensifying security dilemma that exists between China and those of its neighbours, who are strategically backed by the United States. This results in one side, seeking greater security by expanding its military capabilities, which in turn gives rise to fear in the other and hence drives it to build up its own capabilities, thus rendering neither side more secure than it was before.

Equally plausibly, one can interpret this as a strategic competition between a rising power (China) and an existing hegemon (America) over the future configuration of the regional order. Either way, if America continues its 'pivot' without reassuring China, and if China finds itself compelled to adopt an alliance strategy, the outcome may be a struggle for strategic dominance in the Asia-Pacific.

Rebalance Strategy (RS)

The China threat theory has been rampant for a long time in the Western media, much before it even became a real threat. China's apprehensions relating to US policy makers are therefore justified given their hostile representation of China's rise in several congressional reports and scholarly works that portray China as a looming threat that must be dealt with.

The Bush administration narrowed its focus to the War on Terror and pooled resources in the Middle East, effectively ignoring the other emerging issues. On the other hand, while the Obama administration appeared to be appeasing China, it was under pressure from allies in Asia and thus took steps to rectify the emerging imbalance of power through the 'pivot to Asia-Pacific' or the 'rebalance to Asia-Pacific' strategy. The strategy was meant to reassure its allies in the face of a stronger, assertive and more confident China.

But this shift divided Chinese scholars even further as to how to view the US and its alliance system, as a rising China tries to achieve its own objectives and ambitions. A few Chinese scholars have viewed the US alliance system as the stabilising factor in Asia-Pacific, in view of the demilitarisation of Japan. Another section of scholars sees the RS as hedging instead of containment, as a measure to balance China's rise through competition and maintain US primacy in Asia-Pacific. Other scholars, taking a realist perspective, view the RS as posing a challenge to China's interests in the security, diplomatic, economic and strategic domains.[20]

Fu Ying points out that the, "intentions of the US military alliances in the Asia-Pacific remain a particular source of concern for China," especially after the pivot'.[21] For the hardliners, the rebalance strategy only manifests China's apprehensions with regard to the US motive of "keeping China down", serving its own interests by adopting the "Cold War mentality", and raising tensions in the Asia-Pacific. Yuan Zheng held that the US' reasons for returning to Asia were two-fold: one, a strategic readjustment aimed at handling challenges due to rise of China, compelled by territorial disputes with allies; and two, "returning to Asia" for economic reasons. The North Korean factor is potentially a destabilising regional issue, challenging the US strategic outlook and rationalising a heavier presence in Asia-Pacific. And given that the Asia-Pacific region is the "most dynamic region in the world", the Obama administration believed that the recovery of the US economy, particularly the expansion of US exports, depended on the Asia-Pacific countries. Wang Jisi argued against China over-extending its interests and thereby stretching its capacity into strategic and competitive space to respond to rebalance.

Under Xi's presidency, China is undergoing exactly this process. China replied to rebalance in its signature style of dual strategy. On the one hand it is extending its interests beyond Asia to Europe through the Belt and Road Initiative, and maintaining a tough stance on territorial disputes by engaging with the world in a great power like manner. This, essentially conveys the message that China will engage in matters of business and trade but would not be as open when it comes to its core interests.

Fu Ying, former vice foreign minister, stated that after the 'pivot', it is US 'intentions' that remain a particular source of concern for China, fuelling the suspicions of hardliners, that the US is trying to contain China. The strategic trust between the two countries has therefore eroded, but China has not abandoned the hope for better bilateral relations, where China is not one among many, but rather one of the two super powers.

Response to Rebalance Strategy: One Chinese response to the rebalance was shifting the focus of its diplomacy from being US centric to being periphery oriented. This of course marked a crucial foreign policy change, where the importance of the smaller maritime states of Asia, with healthy economies could not be ignored. China held its first Conference on the Diplomatic Work with Neighbouring Countries on October 24-25 in 2013. Xi delivered an important speech on redirecting Chinese foreign policy towards the smaller maritime nations on the immediate periphery. The increased emphasis on peripheral relations illustrates the CCP's realisation that dominance in its own region is a prerequisite to the 'rejuvenation of the Chinese nation". Xu Jin and Du Zhenyuan wrote China "must first rise in the region to which it belongs."[22]

Xue Li, foreign policy expert CASS, while responding to Kurt Campbell's description of China's reaction as calm and moderate, said a calm reaction does not mean Chinese indifference or inaction. But while the Chinese understand that 'containing' it is not the intention of the rebalance strategy, it is motivated by heading and competition. What America characterises as 'balancing' China's rise, however, is seen by China as a hegemonic attempt to entrench the inherent imbalance of the post-Second World War regional order—that is, to maintain America's regional dominance.[23] Fu Ying, the former vice foreign minister said, "intentions of US military alliance in Asia [...Pacific] remain a particular source of concern for China", especially after the 'pivot'.[24] But he also suggested that rebalance is not the same as containment.

In his study of the debates on US rebalance strategy in China, Dr Wong Dong (Peking University) wrote:

> Nevertheless, it was not until Beijing and Washington spat with each other at the Copenhagen summit on climate change in December 2009, and then over US arms sales to Taiwan, Obama's meeting with the Dalai Lama, the Google incident, US military exercises in the Yellow Sea, etc., that the concerns of the US returning to Asia were on a rapid rise in mainland China. This trend can be discerned from the academic and public discourses in mainland China.

Major General Luo Yuan of the Academy of Military Science and Zhu Chenghu of National Defence University, argued that the US arms sales to Taiwan constituted a hostile policy that aimed at 'disturbing' and 'containing' China's rise.[25] Seeing the US move as damaging Chinese 'core interests' (*hexin liyi*), many mainland Chinese analysts called for inflicting a 'strategic combination blow' (*zhanlue zuhe quan*) as a countermeasure, which included imposing sanctions against US companies, involved in the arms sales and adopting a 'non-cooperation' approach towards regional and global challenges.

In response to the US announcement of a joint US-South Korean military exercise in July 2010 in the Yellow Sea, the MFA expressed mainland China's 'resolute opposition' and called the move "detrimental to China's security interests." Mainland Chinese strategic analysts argued that the Yellow Sea was the 'strategic passage' of China's heartland and military exercises conducted by other countries in the region would bring "pressures to China's security."

Similarly, a 2010 *Global Times* poll also found that 81.6 per cent of the mainland Chinese public believed that the United States had either the intention, or both the intention and behaviour of containment against mainland China, an increase of about 3 per cent as compared to the 2009 number.

In response to US military exercises, the People's Liberation Army (PLA) also held a series of drills. Between the June end and early August 2010, the PLA held seven military exercises, including a live fire exercise near the Yellow Sea undertaken by the artillery troops of the Nanjing Military Region, and a joint live fire exercise in which the destroyers from the East China Sea Fleet, the North China Sea Fleet, and the South China Sea Fleet participated.

Wu Xingtang (2010), former Director of the Research Institute of the International Department of the Central Committee of the Communist Party of China (CC CPC), argued that US 'returning to Asia' was aimed at "encircling and blocking" ... China while acknowledging that, "cooperation and win-win remains mainstream" in U.S.-China relations and the "areas of cooperation continue to expand and deepen."

Zhu Feng, a prominent international security expert and deputy director of the Centre for International and Strategic Studies at Peking University, argued that while the Obama administration's assertive 'returning to Asia' strategy was meant to "continue to consolidate its leadership" and essentially was a 'peaceful containment' ... strategy, the United States would continue to maintain an 'engagement policy' toward mainland China and would not "seek a direct strategic confrontation with China."

Wang Jisi, wrote that the "perception gap on important international issues between the two is increasing rather than narrowing" and predicted that "the space for future strategic cooperation between the two countries will be squeezed, and big confrontations will be difficult to avoid."

Yuan Peng, a leading US specialist at the China Institute of Contemporary International Relations affiliated with the Ministry of State Security, attributed the origins of the 'structural contradictions' to the shift in the relative power balance between mainland China and the United States caused by mainland China's "over- expectation- rise" and the serious injury inflicted on the US by the unexpected financial crisis as well as the "perceptual dislocation" of the change in each other's power position.[26]

Only one authoritative comment has been made on the US defence doctrine associated with the Pacific Pivot, particularly the Air-Sea Battle Concept (ASBC). Again, at a Ministry of National Defence (MND) press conference, the ASBC was unsurprisingly described as 'destabilising' (by advocating confrontation and stressing the security of the United States at the expense of the security of others), a manifestation of a Cold War mentality and against the dominant global trend of "peace, development, and cooperation."[27]

The cumulative response to RS remained sanguine in China. Despite the hardliners' efforts to sway the debate, the majority still believes in cooperating with the US, in view of the guarantee that keeps Japan from militarising. But the fact that the US is trying to hedge even while engaging, is also a widely accepted.

From Peaceful Development to New Type of Great Power Relations

New Type of Great Power Relations (NTGPR) (2013): The concept of 'new type of relations' had appeared earlier in Chinese discourse; it was last used by Jiang Zemin to describe relations with Russia. In 2009, President Hu Jintao and Barack Obama agreed upon "building a positive, cooperative, and comprehensive US-China relationship for the 21st century". China's state councillor Dai Bingguo, (who also wrote the white paper on Adhere to the path of peaceful development's 2010, making 'peaceful rise/ development' the official policy) was credited with articulating the concept during a Strategic and Economic Dialogue meeting in 2010.

In February 2012, during his visit to the US, Vice President Xi Jinping addressed the US-China Business Council where he called on China and the United States to work towards a "new type of relationship between major countries in the 21st century". Xi's model included: increasing mutual understanding and strategic trust; respecting core interests and major concerns; deepening mutually beneficial cooperation; enhancing cooperation and coordination in international affairs and global issues. At the same time, he highlighted China's three core interests. These were: Taiwan, Tibet and China's development path.

In keeping with its dual strategy, China attempted to engage with the US on a platform of equality. Cordial relations with the US and the lowering of threat perceptions are fundamental for China's economic growth. This was one of attempts by China, under Xi, to appease/pacify the US. Originally the strategy (or concept) was designed for the US, Russia and the EU. Following the initiation of 'Pivot to Asia' strategy, during the Sunnyland summit, Xi's proposed vision for the China-US relations—'New type of Great Power Relations'—was approved by President Obama as he spoke of the need to "forge a new model of cooperation between countries based on mutual interest and mutual respect".

However, in 2014, Douglas and Glaser wrote:

> US patience has been stretched to the breaking point by Chinese state media repeatedly spinning America's acceptance of the framework in ways it does not support... US officials privately complain about the Chinese misrepresenting Washington's position to ASEAN countries, suggesting the United States is privileging Chinese interests at their expense.[28]

The three principles proposed by China ignored US defence alliances, not promising action against the defector, in this case probably China.

The US faced several problems in adopting the NTGPR. First, as the title itself suggested, this concept was propounded to address the great power anxiety between the two systems of power, one rising and the other established. For US allies, this move was a delineating Chinese tool designed to diminish importance of the alliances and a sign of declining importance of US commitments to them regarding the rise of China. Feng Zheng in his article 'Challenge Accepted: China's Response to the US Rebalance to the Asia-Pacific' wrote: "Beijing is signalling, in effect, that the US must now respect China's interests and treat it as an equal great power." The message China is sending to the US is that it will not accede to US coercion and demands, or accommodate its interests at the cost of China's self-interest.

New Asian Security Concept[29]

The need to restructure the prevailing security system in Asia had come up earlier also, which only suggests that dissatisfaction with the current US alliances in Asia, is also not new. In 1997 a *People's Daily* editorial outlined four principles with which China disagreed—hegemonism, power politics, military alliances and arms race. Later, Foreign Minister Qi Qichen expounded the concept in his address at the 4th ASEAN Regional Forum (ARF) in 1997; and subsequently People's Liberation Army published a paper on 'New Security Concept'. Defence Minister Chi Haotian, also mentioned the concept in his speeches in Japan and Australia in 1998. In the backdrop of this bold 'shift' in outlook was the US-Japan renegotiation of their defence cooperation guidelines and the US forward deployment of forces and sales of arms to Taiwan (during Taiwan Strait Crisis in 1996, arguably leading to closer Japan-US relations). The Chinese understanding of the US alliance system also changed; the system that kept powers like Japan in check and helped maintain a certainty of peace in the region was no longer of benefit to Chinese strategy. The emergence of the US threat perception in Chinese foreign policy can also be perceived after the first Gulf Crisis in 1991.

A new wave of posturing against the US alliances in Asia came with the incumbent President Xi Jinping's address at the Fourth Summit of the Conference on Interaction and Confidence Building Measures in Asia (CICA) 2014. After the Sunnylands summit in 2013, Xi proposed a drastic shift in the prevailing security structure towards an Asia where Asians resolved their disputes and managed the affairs of Asia themselves—'Asia for Asians'. In his words, "security must be universal...equal...inclusive...."[30]

The outsider in this scenario is the US, and it is the US alliance system that China believes is not equitable and inclusive. Hence, now such a system must 'change with the changing time'. He further added that, "It is for the people of Asia to run the affairs of Asia, solve the problems of Asia and uphold the security of Asia. The people of Asia have the capability and wisdom to achieve peace and stability in the region through enhanced cooperation." He proposed a set of principles, that can be followed instead of military alliances targeted at third parties, which are not conducive to comprehensive security. He said, "We need to advance the process of common development and regional integration, foster sound interactions and synchronised progress of regional economic cooperation and security cooperation, and promote sustainable security through sustainable development."

By this logic, while China was trying to mend and improve its relations with the US, discard the 'Thucydides trap' theory and follow the principle of 'New type of great power relations', to remove structural impediments, it was persuading /warning US allies and potential partners and other smaller nations in China's backyard to reject alliance politics, zero-sum-game and work towards a more 'comprehensive security'.

Conclusion

While even today China's policy making remains a mystery, its presence in the world cannot be ignored. China is the world's second largest economy and has the largest population. To impress upon Sino-US relations, the question about intentions of both parties come to play UNCLEAR. Even though both nations continue to declare that their militarsation has nothing to with the threat posed by the other, the observers on both sides remain sceptical.

However, there are elements on both sides who are putting their faith in the economic interdependence of the two nations which would in turn diminish chances of conflict. Meanwhile, many others are positive about an impending clash—the Thucydides trap—but they also remain optimistic that peace will prevail because that is more crucial to China, for its internal reasons than an external conflict.

Now that China has reduced the gap between itself and the superpower, from eight times in 2003 to three times in 2013, for many thinkers it is just a matter of time before China establishes its hegemony, rather than how. Conscious of China's growing economic power and along with it, its rapid military modernisation, China's evident assertiveness and its willingness to employ all means of statecraft to strategically and economically shape its neighbours' behaviour suggests that its intentions are not peaceful.

For example, Philippines, won the key arbitral tribunal ruling of July 12, 2016, according to which Beijing was infringing the sovereign rights of the Philippines in its EEZ (in breach of Art. 60 & 80). Though lacking executive power, the ruling was a big win, which could have translated into collective action to signal that China's assertive moves will not be well received. But instead, Philippines prioritised its fruit exports, infrastructure investment and a prospective soft loan of $500m for buying weapons from China, over security concerns about Beijing's territorial encroachment. China proved that its charm offensive works where economic prosperity trumps territorial security.

In 2014 Xi said that China should focus on a 'Period of Strategic

Opportunity' (POSO). This encapsulates CCP primary external strategic guideline—that China is enjoying a window of opportunity in which a benign external security environment allows it to focus on its internal development, validated by three party congresses (the 16th in 2002, the 17th in 2007, and the 18th in 2012). China's external security environment is largely benign and too economically inter-dependent to venture into a military conflict anytime soon, which also makes it difficult for the Chinese government to justify any act of coercion.

NOTES

1. Deng Xiaoping's 24 character strategy-'Observe calmly; secure our position; cope with affairs calmly; hide our capacities and bide our time; be good at maintaining a low profile; and never claim leadership.' See Menon, Shivshankar, 'The China Conundrum'; *ICS Analysis*, No. 39, May 2016; ICS, New Delhi; http://www.icsin.org/uploads/2016/05/30/b535261dfb1d2bf2a6807fc581202fee.pdf
2. 'China's Military Strategy'; The State Council Information Office of the People's Republic of China; May 2015, Beijing. http://eng.mod.gov.cn/Press/2015-05/26/content_4586805.htm
3. Ibid.
4. Deng Xiaoping, *Selected Works of Deng Xiaoping, III* Beijing: People's Publishing House, 1993, p. 321.
5. Among the various Chinese White Papers that have mentioned alliances making as a "cold war mentality", are China National Defence Strategy 2015; China National Defence 2000; A list of White papers can be found on http://www.china.org.cn/e-white/
6. 'China's Policies on Asia-Pacific Security Cooperation,' China's State Council Information Office, Jan 11, 2016; http://www.scio.gov.cn/32618/Document/1539667/1539667.htm
7. "A Constructive Year for Chinese Base Building", Asia Maritime Transparency Initiative, *CSIS.* https://amti.csis.org/constructive-year-chinese-building/ Accessed 12 June 2017
8. John O'Callaghan, Manuel Mogato, 'The U.S. military pivot to Asia: when bases are not bases', *Reuters*, November 14, 2012; https://www.reuters.com/article/us-usa-asia-military/the-u-s-military-pivot-to-asia-when-bases-are-not-bases-idUSBRE8AD05Y20121114 Accessed on 12 June 2017
9. David Tweet, 'How Asia's Military growth spending is outpacing the World', *Bloomberg*, July 2016 "Military outlays in Asia and Oceania—which includes Australia and New Zealand—grew 5.4 percent in 2015, outpacing a 1 percent rise in global spending, according to the Stockholm International Peace Research Institute. Indonesia boosted spending last year by 16 percent, the Philippines by 25 percent and Vietnam by 7.6 percent." https://www.bloomberg.com/news/articles/2016-05-31/asia-military-spending-rises-in-china-s-shadow-spurring-deals Accessed 12 June 2017
10. Yan Xuetong, 'The Structure of One Superpower, Many Great Powers Begins to Evolve into 'Two Superpowers, Many Great Powers', *Global Times*, December 30,

2011, http://opinion.huanqiu.com/roll/2011-12/2313232.html.

11. Yan Xuetong, 'From the South China Sea Problem to the Adjustment of China's Foreign Policy', *World Affairs*, no. 1, 2012, p. 33.
12. Yan Xuetong, 'From Keeping a Low Profile to Striving for Achievement', *Chinese Journal of International Politics* (2014) 7 (2): 153-184; https://academic.oup.com/cjip/article-lookup/doi/10.1093/cjip/pou027
13. Ye Zicheng, 'On 'Keeping a Low Profile' and "Get Some Things Done" ', *Pacific Journal 1* (2002): 62–6. See also Xing Yue and Zhang Yibing, 'Rethinking "Keeping a Low Profile" Strategy", *International Observation* 6 (2006): 13–9.
14. Liu Mingfu, *The China Dream: Major Power Thinking and Strategic Planning in a Post-American Era,* Zhongguo meng: Hou Meiguo shidai de daguo siwei yu zhanlue dingwei, Beijing: China Friendship Publishing Company, 2010
15. *Global Times* Annual Summit: 2012, 'World Transformation and China's Strategy'
16. Feng Zhang, 'China's New Thinking on Alliances', *Survival*, Vol. 54, No. 5, pp.129-148, 2012
17. Yan Xuetong, 'Does Opposing a Sino-Russian Alliance Make Absolute Sense?', *Consensus* website, June 8, 2012, http://www.21ccom.net/articles/qqsw/zlwj/article_2012060861511.html. See also Feng Zhang, 'China's New Thinking on Alliances', *Survival*, Vol 54:5, pp.129-148, 2012. He writes, American pressures on China and Russia are frequently cited by analysts as a primary justification for a Sino-Russian alliance.
18. Wang Jianwei, 'China's Rise Calls for New Diplomatic and Strategic Concepts', *United Post*, January 21, 2011.
19. Sun Degang, 'China's Quasi-alliance Diplomacy in the New Era', *World Economics and Politics*, no. 3, 2012, pp. 57–81.
20. Zhang Feng, "Challenge Accepted: China's Response to the US Rebalance to the Asia-Pacific", *Security Challenges*, Vol 12, no. 3 (2016), p.4.
21. Fu Ying, 'How China Sees Russia', *Foreign Affairs*, Vol 95, no.1 (2016), p.104.
22. Xu Jin, Du Zheyuan; "The Dominant Thinking Sets in Chinese Foreign Policy Research: A Criticism"; *Chinese Journal of International Politics*, 2015, Oxford University Press; pp 251-279.
23. Zhang Feng, "Challenge Accepted: China's Response to the US Rebalance to the Asia-Pacific", *Security Challenges*, Vol 12, no. 3 (2016), p.5. Also, Liu Guozhu, 'Meiguo "yatai zaipingheng" zhanlu˜e mianlin de tiaozhan' [The Challenges of America's 'Asian Rebalance Strategy'], *Meiguo yanjiu* [*Chinese Journal of American Studies*], no. 3 (2014), p. 98.
24. Fu Ying, "How China Sees Russia", *Foreign Affairs*, Vol. 95, no.1 (2016), p.104
25. Dong Wang; Chengzhi Yin; "Mainland China Debates U.S. Pivot/Rebalancing to Asia"; *Issues & Studies*, September 2014, Vol. 50 Issue 3, pp. 57-101. p. 45.
26. Dong Wang, Chengzhi Yin, 'Territorial Issues in Asia, Drivers, Instruments, Ways Forward', 7th Berlin Conference on Asian Security (BCAS), July 2013, Berlin https://www.swp-berlin.org/fileadmin/contents/products/projekt_papiere/BCAS2013_Wang_Dong.pdf Accessed on 17 June 2017.
27. See "Defence Ministry's Regular Press Conference in November, 2011," Ministry of National Defence of the People's Republic of China, November 30, 2011, http://www.mod.gov.cn/affair/2011-11/30/content_4347180.htmACCESSED 17 June 2017. As one military analyst observed: "This is the first [and last] time a Chinese

government department openly criticised the 'air-sea battle' theory of the United States." See Yang Yi, "U.S. Air-Sea Battle Theory Targets China's Military Modernisation," *People's Daily Overseas Edition*, December 10, 2011, OSC CPP20111210708003.

28. Bonnie Glaser and Jake Douglas, 'The Ascent and Demise of "New Type of Great Power Relations" Between the US and China', 28-30 http://sdsc.bellschool.anu.edu.au/sites/default/files/publications/attachments/2016-12/2015_10_regional_security_outlook_2016_cscap.pdfACCESSED 18 June 2017
29. http://www.fmprc.gov.cn/ce/ceun/eng/xw/t27742.htm
30. http://www.fmprc.gov.cn/mfa_eng/zxxx_662805/t1159951.shtml

Another more explicit statement is present in the 2015 white paper, where it acknowledges Chinese apprehensions of the US presence in the Asia-Pacific region through its 'rebalancing' strategy and the role of its naval forces in the region. The paper states,

> "...the PLA Navy (PLAN) will gradually shift its focus from "offshore waters defense" to the combination of "offshore waters defense" with "open seas protection," and build a combined, multi-functional and efficient marine combat force structure."[8]

The paper thus redefined that PLA will not only be performing ground operations but also marine and aerospace military activities. It was the first official document to discuss about China's military strategy and in particular to show an openness within China of its growing presence as a maritime power. It argues, "the traditional mentality that land outweighs sea must be abandoned, and great importance has to be attached to managing the seas and oceans and protecting maritime rights and interests".[9]

The 2015 white paper also alludes to the Southeast Asian countries, such as the Philippines and Vietnam for causing concerns to China's territorial sovereignty and maritime rights.[10] It shows a China that is more open and upfront about the countries which were troublesome for its maritime interests and territorial sovereignty and unlike earlier, it directly named the United States and Japan for causing discontent.

China has moved from Deng Xiaoping's "Tao Guang Yang Hui" (hide capabilities and keep a low profile) to Fen Fa You Wei (striving for achievement). China is now more outspoken mainly about three 'Ps', which are its 'policies', 'plans' and their 'proclamations.' China also understands the importance of the Internet in the world today and through the white papers, it proclaims its policies and plans, both domestic and foreign. It no more believes in the theory of hiding capabilities and through the official white papers; inform the world about its diplomacy. The white papers in turn, help in assessing and analyzing the psychology of Chinese politics.

An analysis of the recent official white papers of China concludes that the Chinese have become more assertive of its maritime sovereignty and rights. Their position on the maritime claims is unshaken and though they believe in a peaceful rise, any discrepancies with what they consider theirs is intolerant.

Assessing the Five Year Plans on Maritime Capabilities

Apart from the White Defense Papers, the 12th and the 13th Five Year plans (FYP) also unveiled China's growing interest in becoming a maritime power. China's FYPs are an important source to assess the plans and policies that are being implemented in the country. They describe national goals and aspirations, including maritime. For instance, the 10th and the 11th FYP, the 12th and 13th FYP particularly defined China's growing interest in exploring marine resources for developing its energy sector as well as mentioned about safeguarding the maritime sovereignty and rights.

The 12th Five Year Plan for National Economic and Social Development of People's Republic of China (PRC) had a separate chapter titled, "Promoting the Development of Ocean Economy". The very first paragraph of this chapter indicates on implementing strategy for developing, controlling and managing the oceans.[11] It directly reflects the Chinese interests in dominating the surrounding waters. Apart from talking about safeguarding maritime interests and rights, it also talked about raising competence of marine development and its management and incorporated policies for perfecting the maritime development and its mechanism through exploration of oil and gas resources from these ocean beds. The chapter also reflected upon the Chinese desire of increasing the intensity of maritime law enforcement.

Similarly, the 13th Five Year Plan approved in March 2016 also labored several maritime aspirations. Chapter 41 of the 13th FYP titled, "Widen Space for the Blue Economy" which was further divided into three synonymous sections that yet again talked about strengthening, protecting and safeguarding the marine resources and the maritime rights and interests.[12] It specifically discussed about using the South China Sea resources for the national marine economic development. It also called for building "an effective system for safeguarding overseas interests",[13] apparently meaning a growth in overseas military efficiency. Though China was battling an arbitration case under UNCLOS with the Philippines regarding contested sovereignty claims in the South China Sea, it still went on to discussing business strategies, Internet networking enhancements and further developing the contested islands. Such developments echo China's inflexible attitude towards its 'historical claims' in the South China Sea.

Energy Resources and Maritime Disputes

he documents that China has released so far all point to the intention of the Chinese leadership in increasing its security by dominating the maritime space. Moreover, for continued economic growth, China has to rely on energy sources through the Sea Lanes of Communication. Thus, energy risk for China has only been increasing. For instance, the China National Petroleum Corp's (CNPC) in its annual report calculated that China's net crude oil reports would rise by 5.3 per cent to 396 million tons in 2017 with a consumption of 12 million barrels per day (bpd).[14] Thus, the grand vision is to enhance its maritime arena and progress towards building a "Smart Ocean" by placing under water high tech robots and space stations and the same is under surveillance by the Institute of Oceanology, Chinese Academy of Sciences.[15] In order to meet the over growing energy risks, China has realized the importance of becoming a maritime power and hence, has strongly inculcated maritime goals in its ongoing grand strategy.

South China Sea Resources

With an approximate annual maritime trade of $5 trillion[16] and huge mineral resources under its ocean bed, the South China Sea (SCS) has become a topic of heated debate especially in the past few years. Though the South China Sea has a long history, it came into the limelight only in 1969 when the UN's special investigation of the South China Sea found out that SCS had huge reservoirs of oil and gas.[17] Following that, in 1973, United Nation Convention on the Law of the Sea (UNCLOS) under Article 57 (Part V) stated, "The exclusive economic zone shall not extend beyond 200 nautical miles from the baselines from which the breadth of the territorial sea is measured."[18] This led to curiosities of interest in the South China Sea amongst the neighboring regional countries.

China has been trying to build islands beyond its Exclusive Economic Zone in the South China Sea. Its famous rhetoric of historical claims on the South China Sea have led them to demarcate their territorial waters through a U-shaped dotted line (which is now commonly referred to as the nine dash line) in an officially issued map called "The Location Map of the South China Sea Islands". The map was issued by the Territorial section of the Ministry of Interior Affairs in 1947. The nine dash line's legal status was challenged in the 1990s by the regional countries and until then, this geographical claim did not incur any challenge. What is to be noted is that China has only made sovereign claims on the islands within the nine-dash line and not the seawaters.[19] These South China Sea islands constitute the Dongsha Islands, Xisha Islands, Zhongsha Islands and the Nansha Islands.[20] China, through the construction of such islands which but of course are beyond its exclusive economic zone is trying to establish military bases. Such military basis will help China in risk reduction in case of a military face off. Apart from safe siding itself through establishing such pro-military islands, it will also provide China in establishing its control and dominance over the sea, which as already mentioned is one of the most significant economic passages.

Due to overlapping claims with China in the South China Sea, the Philippines had initiated an arbitral process under the International Tribunal for the Law of the Sea in January 2013[21] and on July 12, 2016, The Hague Arbitration tribunal backed the Philippines. The tribunal denied China's historical claims in SCS. China refused to recognize the arbitration award and the Foreign Ministry of China declared the tribunal as "null and void" and also said that China is open for bilateral negotiations with the Philippines but will not negotiate because of any arbitration ruling.[22]

On July 13, China released a white paper titled, "China Adheres to the Position of Settling Through Negotiation the Relevant Disputes Between China and the Philippines in the South China Sea" and asserted that China has claims and sovereignty over SCS islands for more than 2000 years. The white paper further said that the Philippines claims were 'illegal, groundless and void.'[23]

The white paper attacked the Philippines for repeatedly taking actions, which led to intensification and further complication of the conflict.[24] Chinese reiterated their firm stands on the maritime rights and sovereignty of SCS and reiterated that they were open for bilateral and peaceful negotiations with the Philippines.

On January 11, 2017, China released another white paper titled, "China's Policies on Asia-Pacific Security Cooperation" and apart from discussing about the Korean nuclearisation and other non traditional security issues, reinforced its stand on the South China Sea and rejected the July 2016 arbitration tribunal award's decision. The white paper restated that the regional countries involved in the maritime disputes should directly negotiate with China in order to conclude a peaceful settlement. The White paper asserted, "China has indisputable sovereignty over the Nansha Islands and their adjacent waters.... No effort to internationalize and judicialize the South China Sea issue will be of any avail for its resolution; it will only make it harder to resolve the issue, and endanger regional peace and stability."[25]

All these official documents and statements suggest that China is unwilling to give up its sovereignty over SCS but in order to promote stability and peace in the region, it is willing to negotiate with the concerned parties directly. China has also mentioned that it might create Air Defense Identification Zone (ADIZ) above the South China Sea if it further feels threatened.[26]

However, in October 2016, the ideologically left-leaning Philippines President, Rodrigo Duterte resumed direct talks with China over the South China Sea during his state visit to China. This hinted on de-escalation of tensions in the South China Sea. This came ahead of his announcement of "separation" with the United States over the concern of human rights violations in the Philippines. China and the Philippines also signed trade deals worth $13.5 billion. The US looked up to the Philippines in the region to curtail China's swelling ambitions but such changing dynamics prove China to be a clear winner. On the South China Sea arbitration, President Duterte stated that it would "take a back seat". Such regional ideological swings seem to be working in favor of China's expansionist and salami-slicing strategies of foreign policy.

East China Sea Claims

China is in a conflicted relationship with Japan due to the overlapped claims on the Diaoyu/Senkaku Islands in the East China Sea. The issue over the islands aggravated when Japan purchased these islands on September 11, 2012. Despite several warnings of escalated security threats from China, Japan went on to "nationalize" these islands.

Following this, China released a white paper titled, "Diaoyu Dao, an Inherent Territory of China" and stated that the "affiliated islands are an inseparable part of the Chinese territory", historically, geographically as well as legally. It also stated that the "backroom dealings" between the US and Japan have led to the "grabbing" of Diaoyu Islands from China.[27]

In November 2013, China established Air Defense Identification Zone (ADIZ) over the disputed islands and raised security threat in the region. ADIZ is a zone, which is created by a maritime nation in order to meet potential air threats. It also helps in increasing the early-warning ability of a country.[28] The established zone gets covered under that particular country's Air defense systems such as radars, surface to air missiles, interceptor aircrafts and other forms of command and control.[29] China's Defense Ministry spokesman, Yang Yujun in a press briefing said ADIZ was established in order to "protect its state sovereignty and territorial and airspace security, and maintaining flying orders" and had no particular target or did not aim at restriction of freedom of flight in relevant airspace".[30] ADIZ could also be viewed as a reaction to an increased US military presence and as a step to counteract the same. China has actively been enforcing its rights on the Senkaku Islands by regularly sending law enforcement vessels in order to ensure its overlapping control over the islands.

While China has the Locations Map and a nine-dash line as its legitimized proofs for the South China Sea, it lacks the same for the East China Sea. Another important fact is that the claimant parties around the

East China Sea are the US' close allies. In contrast, China is more dominant about its claims in the South China Sea and fortuitously the regional powers around it lack military powers as strong as that of China. The ultimate goal, though, is to attain physical power in the East China Sea.

In the recently released Asia-Pacific security cooperation white paper by the Chinese Government on January 11, 2017, Beijing reinforced its historical claims over Diaoyu Islands and said that it is an integral part of China. It stated that through continued dialogue and consultations, the issue would be managed for resolution.[31]

China is Japan's biggest regional threat and this could be viewed as a natural conduct because when two powers from the same region are aspiring for similar power, they tend to become fictitious rivals.

Chinese Ambitions and US Interests

The US interests in regard to the apparently claimed China Seas came into a clearer limelight when Hillary Clinton, the then Secretary of State mentioned the freedom of navigation in the South China Sea as U.S. "national interest" at a regional security conference in Vietnam. Later, in 2011, President Obama announced a rebalancing strategy in the Asia-pacific, especially hinting to resolutions in the East and South China Sea.

The rebalancing strategy of the US in the Asia-Pacific Region initiated a conflicted relationship between China and the U.S. China referred to such developments by the US along with Japan as a national security threat in its 10th Defense White Paper, which was released in May 2015.

The new US administration of Trump vowed to protect its interests in the South China Sea. Earlier in January, Trump's nominee for State secretary, Rex Tillerson said, "We're going to have to send China a clear signal that, first, the island-building stops and, second, your access to those islands also is not going to be allowed." On January 23rd, White House Spokesman, Sean Spicer said that the international territories would be defended and not be allowed to be taken by one country. The Chinese retaliated by stating that the so-called international territories were Chinese territories and that the outside countries should respect the common interests and wishes on the countries in the region.[32]

On being asked a clarification on the remarks by Team Trump on the SCS as international waters, Foreign Ministry Spokesperson Hua Chunying in a Regular Press conference stated that China's position remains unchanged and consistent in regard to SCS. China is committed to peaceful settlement of the disputed islands with direct negotiations with the involved parties but would want the US, which is an outside party to not interfere and avoid causing any instability in the region.[33]

The unsaid reality of the rise of China economically, militarily and now as an upcoming naval power can be predicted as a hegemonic threat to the United States and therefore, the US could be seen intruding into the Asia Pacific Region to "rebalance" the region. China has time and again been asking US to not interfere in its personal affairs as China would be a "wrong opponent" to showcase its power of deterrence.[34] Due to great power competition, the US interference has been a major reason behind China's steady maritime growth.

In the name of deterrence and "freedom of navigation", the US has conducted several military drills in the SCS, show-casing its military and naval power. The US has mirrored the growth of China with security apprehensions in regard to the stability of the region and it could easily do so because it enjoys the hegemonic power of marketing global interests. However, China has always been supportive of regional peace and stability and this has been exemplified in different official documents as well as press briefings of the People's Republic of China. It is open to engage in bilateral negotiations with the regional countries but is not in favor of any outside, third party involvement.

Nonetheless, with the passage of time, the Trump presidency does not seem to really have any vivid Asian strategy as of now, which as aforementioned, they had intended to have when they were newly elected. However, they seem to be busy developing and resolving their country's domestic issues. Trump also does not seem to be very keen on formulating new goals in order to maintain US hegemony in the Indo-Pacific or Asian region. It recently has taken actions in support of Taiwan's independence and it definitely could be one of the US' containment policy against China but this does not stop Beijing from expanding its territory as well as military and naval power. Apart from India, the neighboring states lack military capabilities and are not as mighty as China. A lacking support of the US and strained relationships for example, between the US and the Philippines could lead to a successful China Dream and a hegemonic regional power.

Conclusion

Ever since Xi Jinping has come to power, the Chinese national interests have strongly advanced from being a continental power to maritime power. The recent defense white papers as well as the five-year plans have depicted increased prioritization of the Chinese maritime interests. The East China Sea as well as the South China Sea offer Beijing a unique upshot for military and national growth and Beijing is aware of the importance, the seas offer to it.

China's maritime growth has become an ascending concern for different important external countries especially the United States and factually, all recent frictions in foreign relations that China faces have surfaced from the seas. China has realized that becoming a global maritime power is not as easy as economic development and that it requires to deal with several diplomatic challenges and hence, fundamental structural changes in China's domestic as well as foreign policies to deal with the same.

Three recent international challenges have intrigued China from a smooth maritime growth. First, the Japanese claims in the East China Sea.[35] Second, the July 12th, 2016 result of an international tribunal in favor of the Philippines over the overlapping claims in SCS and third, the increasing military presence of the United States to showcase the freedom of navigation in the aforesaid waters.

Apart from international challenges, China is weak in its domestic maritime laws and the power structure of the five main maritime law enforcement agencies overlap each other. Four of these five maritime law enforcement agencies, Border Control Maritime Police, Fisheries Law Enforcement Command, China Maritime Surveillance and Anti-Smuggling Bureau were clustered under the Chinese Coast Guard (CCG) but the Maritime Safety Administration (MSA) which is under the Ministry of Transport was not integrated under CCG. Though, CCG, PLA Navy and MSA conduct regular patrols in these seas, there is a lack of a clear operational plan.[36] The legal status of CCG whether it should be declared an armed force is yet not clear. While MSA plays the role of a 'soft power' agency, the integration of MSA with CCG, which is more of an armed police, is also highly debated in Chinese scholarship. There is a competition among these different law enforcement agencies and their duties are overlapped, causing circumvention of responsibility.[37]

Though, China has achieved significant success in unifying different maritime agencies and have achieved operational accomplishments, it needs to focus on improvising the coordination amongst these different agencies. However, it has integrated four out of five agencies under CCG, their psychologies and way of functioning still differs and hence becomes problematic. China needs to solidly work on the coordination of these law enforcements agencies as an initial step to achieve maritime success and support its national interest as well as territorial sovereignty.

There is a consequential increase in the role of PLA Navy (PLAN) as well as PLA Air Force (PLAAF) and the 2015 Defense White Paper depicts the same as well. On outlining strategy of "active defense", it states how the PLAN will not only focus on "offshore water defense" but also on "open seas protection" by building an "efficient marine combat force structure". PLAAF will build both offensive as well as defensive air-space capabilities. PLAN and PLAAF are not only conducting surveillances which are of domestic importance but are also showcasing their potential at a strategic level through different operational missions and joint naval exercises.

China ranks number two after the United States in military spending and a defence budget report stated that China's defence budget is likely to double in the next 10 years and be four times more than that of UK.[38] In no time, the PLA forces have developed advanced A2/AD (Anti-access, Area-denial) capacities along with home grown sophisticated conventional submarines, and advanced ballistic and cruise missile technologies.

China challenges the accepted norm of a fixed ideological and hegemonic system of the world and stands firm about on its position not just in regard to the maritime territories but also in regard to many other opinions, which are of political significance. China is undoubtedly a rising power but many of its ambitions are idealistic as well as contradictory. While China talks about regional peace and prosperity, on the other hand it talks about enhancing its military power, giving rise to a conflict of interests and motives. In addition, China needs to optimize its domestic political and social conditions. Along with an attention on the domestic conditions, China needs to ensure that the geopolitical security of the Asia-Pacific region is not harmed by its maritime strategy. Securing regional peace should be an important aspect of China's maritime strategy. Along with administering the external challenges, China should reconsider its domestic structural reforms, political challenges and social development.

Table 1: Five Dragons of Sea

Maritime Law Enforcement Agency	*Earlier Supervisory Body*	*Functions*
Border Control Maritime Police	Ministry of Public Security	(i) It operates speedboats and small cutters, often armed with machine guns or small cannons, (ii) It is responsible for border and coastal public security administration, and (iii) ports and border inspection and surveillance.(a)
Fisheries Law Enforcement Command	Ministry of Agriculture	Protection of the Chinese fishermen against for example pirate attacks.(b)

Maritime Law Enforcement Agency	*Earlier Supervisory Body*	*Functions*
China Maritime Surveillance	State Oceanic Administration	(i) Surveillance of disputed maritime area is a priority, and (ii) CMS is one of the Chinese agencies with the law enforcement responsibilities along the coast, (iii) It is responsible for law enforcement within the PRC's territorial waters, exclusive economic zones (EEZ) and shores and (iv) Work of maritime rights and interests maintenance, sea area utilization management, marine environmental protection, and island law enforcement in accordance with the relevant laws.(c)
Anti-Smuggling Bureau	General Administration of Customs	(i) Conducting investigations, making detentions and arrests and carrying out preliminary inquiries, (ii) Investigating the smuggling cases and administrative smuggling and law-breaking cases, and (iii) Receiving and handling the smuggling and administrative illegal cases handed over by local police station, business and financial administrative, tobacco exclusive agency and other administrative agencies. Trial and making administrative punishments of the smuggling acts.iv. In charge of the comprehensive treatment of anti-smuggling and analysis of anti-smuggling situations, contacting the anti-smuggling department of different levels, administrative management departments, industrial governing departments, economic governing department and grand groups.(d)
Maritime Safety Administration*	Ministry of Transport	(i) MSA missions include inspection and registration of Chinese vessels in Chinese ports, (ii) Investigation of maritime accidents, (iii) The training and certifying of seafarers, (iv) Supervision of maritime traffic control, (v) Maintenance of aids to navigation, (vi) Implementation of domestic and international maritime laws, and (vii) Maritime search and rescue.(b)

*not merged under CCG

{*Sources:* (a): http://www.globalsecurity.org/intell/world/china/cmpb.htm
(b): Five Dragons Stirring Up the Sea : Challenge and Opportunity in China's Improving Maritime Enforcement Capabilities; Naval War College, China Maritime Studies Institute; Number 5; Lyle J. Goldstein (c): http://www.globalsecurity.org/intell/world/china/cms.htm (d): http://service.customs.gov.cn/tabid/32508/Default.aspx (accessed on January 18, 2017) }

NOTES

1. "China's Diplomatic Power", China Goes Global-The Partial Power, David Shambaugh, Oxford University Press, 2013
2. "China Voice: Building China into maritime power essential for future development", *Xinhua News*, November 14, 2012, http://news.xinhuanet.com/english/special/18cpcnc/2012-11/14/c_131973164.htm (accessed on 10 January, 2017)
3. "Nation merging maritime patrol forces", China Daily, March 11, 2013, http://www.chinadaily.com.cn/china/2013npc/2013-03/11/content_16296448.htm (accessed on 10 January, 2017)
4. See Table 1
5. "Dangerous Waters: China-Japan relations on the rocks", International Crisis Group, April 8, 2013
6. "IV. Supporting National Economic and Social Development", The Diversified employment of China's armed Forces April 2013, http://eng.mod.gov.cn/Database/WhitePapers/2013-04/16/content_4442755.htm (Accessed on 11 January 2017)
7. " I. New Situation, New Challenges and New Missions", The Diversified employment of China's armed Forces April 2013, http://eng.mod.gov.cn/Database/WhitePapers/2013-04/16/content_4442752.htm (accessed on 11 January 2017)
8. "China's Military Strategy", May 2015, http://eng.mod.gov.cn/Database/WhitePapers/2015-05/26/content_4586713.htm (Accessed on 11 January 2017)
9. Ibid
10. Indirectly hinted to The Philippines and Vietnam by stating, "On the issues concerning China's territorial sovereignty and maritime rights and interests, some of its offshore neighbors take provocative actions and reinforce their military presence on China's reefs and islands that they have illegally occupied." In "China's Military Strategy", May 2015 http://eng.mod.gov.cn/Database/WhitePapers/2015-05/26/content_4586688.htm, (Accessed on 11 January 2017)
11. "12th Five Year Plan for National Economic and Social Development (full text)", *Xinhua News Agency*, http://www.gov.cn/2011lh/content_1825838_4.htm (Accessed on January 12, 2017)
12. "The 13th Five Year Plan for Economic and Social Development for The People's Republic of China", http://en.ndrc.gov.cn/policyrelease/201612/P020161207645766966662.pdf (Accessed on January 12, 2017)
13. Ibid
14. "Oil rises on supply cuts, record China demand forecast", *Reuters*, January 12, 2017, http://www.reuters.com/article/us-global-oil-idUSKBN14W03V (Accessed on January 14 2017)
15. "China to Build a 'Smart Ocean'- The Next Great Maritime Power", September 28, 2016, http://www.dailygalaxy.com/my_weblog/2016/09/china-to-build-a-smart-ocean-the-next-great-maritime-era.html, (Accessed on January 16, 2017)
16. "$5 Trillion Meltdown: What If China Shuts Down the South China Sea?", The National Interest, July 16, 2016, http://nationalinterest.org/blog/5-trillion-meltdown-what-if-china-shuts-down-the-south-china-16996 (Accessed on January 13, 2017)

17. "South China Sea: Disputes and Great Powers", Li Jinming, CIR, Vol. 21, No. 4, July/August 2011, p.71.
18. Part V, Exclusive Economic Zone, http://www.un.org/depts/los/convention_agreements/texts/unclos/part5.htm (Accessed on January 13, 2017)
19. "Behind the dotted line on the Chinese Map of the South China Sea", Li Jinming, CIR, November/December 2012
20. "Statement of the Government of the People's Republic of China on China's Territorial Sovereignty and Maritime Rights and Interests in the South China Sea", July 2017, http://www.fmprc.gov.cn/mfa_eng/zxxx_662805/t1379493.shtml (Accessed on January 13, 2017)
21. Spotlight: Arbitral tribunal on South China Sea illegal, ridiculous, July 2016, http://news.xinhuanet.com/english/2016-07/08/c_135499086.htm (Accessed on January 13, 2017)
22. Ibid
23. "China Adheres to the Position of Settling Through Negotiation the Relevant Disputes Between China and the Philippines in the South China Sea", July 2017, http://english.gov.cn/state_council/ministries/2016/07/13/content_281475392503075.htm (Accessed on January 14, 2017)
24. Ibid
25. China's Policies on Asia-Pacific Security Cooperation, January 2017, http://www.fmprc.gov.cn/mfa_eng/zxxx_662805/t1429771.shtml (Accessed on January 13, 2017)
26. China says ADIZ in South China Sea depends on threat, July 2016, http://news.xinhuanet.com/english/2016-07/13/c_135510516.htm (Accessed on January 13, 2017)
27. "Diaoyu Islands cannot be bought", 14 September 2012, http://www.fmprc.gov.cn/mfa_eng/topics_665678/diaodao_665718/t970602.shtml (Accessed on January 10, 2017)
28. " China Exclusive: Defense Ministry Spokesman responds to air defense identification zone questions", November 2013, *Xinhua News*, http://news.xinhuanet.com/english/china/2013-11/23/c_132912145.htm, (Accessed on January 10, 2017)
29. "Cause and Effect of the ADIZ over East China Sea", Naval Jagota, IDSA Comment, December 2013, http://www.idsa.in/idsacomments/CauseandEffect of the ADIZover_NavalJagota_061213, (Accessed on January 10, 2017)
30. "China Exclusive: Defense Ministry spokesman responds to air defense identification zone questions", November 2013, *Xinhua News*, http://news.xinhuanet.com/english/china/2013-11/23/c_132912145.htm (Accessed on January 10, 2017)
31. China's Policies on Asia-Pacific Security Cooperation, January 2017, http://www.fmprc.gov.cn/mfa_eng/zxxx_662805/t1429771.shtml (Accessed on January 13, 2017)
32. After Team Trump's strong comments regarding South China Sea, Chinese Foreign Ministry spokesman, Lu Kang in an interview with NBC News reaffirmed its position on SCS.
33. Foreign Ministry Spokesperson Hua Chunying's Regular Press Conference, January 24, 2017, Ministry of Foreign Affairs of the People's Republic of China,

http://www.fmprc.gov.cn/mfa_eng/xwfw_665399/s2510_665401/2511_665403/t1433525.shtml (Accessed on January 25, 2017)

34. U.S. display of military power act of hegemony, Zhong Sheng, People's Daily, http://en.people.cn/n3/2016/0622/c90000-9075995.html, (Accessed on January 15, 2017)
35. In 2012, Japan bought/nationalized the Senkaku/Diaoyu Islands causing an escalated conflicted relationship between Japan and China as China historically claimed those islands.
36. "China's 2013 Reform of Maritime Law Enforcement: Progress and Unsolved Issues", Mike Chia-Yu Huang, The Korean Journal of Defense Analysis, December 2016, Vol. 28, No. 4.
37. Ibid.
38. From $123 Billion in 2010, China's defence budget will be $233 Billion by 2020, IHS Markit, http://news.ihsmarkit.com/press-release/2016s-15-trillion-global-defence-spend-kick-decade-growth-ihs-markit-says (Accessed on January 15, 2017)

13

China's Military Modernisation and Consequences for Asia

M.V. Rappai

There is an old adage which states that when history repeats itself normally it is likely to manifest as farce first. This old saying can be seen in different contexts, many a time when we discuss the reality of nation states and their power position we take recourse to the historical aspects. This approach is evident in many a discussions surrounding the ongoing debates about China's ambition to emerge as a decisive player in the present day world. This ambition need to be studied in relation to its all out efforts to become an advanced power centre, especially its efforts to revamp its old military establishment also needs close attention. The ambitious military modernisation programme certainly leaves an impact on China's immediate neighbours and other powers of the present day world.

Current global position is undergoing vast changes, at one level change is a normal process, however, the unprecedented transformation taking place all around us must be taken note of. Few years back all pundits surmised that globalisation and free enterprise can cure all ills of the modern society, yet now we are seeing huge setbacks to these avowed project right from advanced nations of the world to most backward areas where people are carving out niche spaces based on narrow identity issue or locale preferences. Most observers cite Briton's exist from the European Union (Brexit) and Donald Trump's election as the President of the United States as examples of the backlash to the globalization move.

Within a week after his election, as promised he withdrew from the Trans Pacific Partnership (TPP) and warned to impose additional taxes on goods imported from China. These developments are certainly changing the way we deal with the world and its destiny. These issues will certainly complicate the relations among various nation states of the world, however, the growing military aspirations of China as largely reflected in her ambitious military reform programmes would provide some indication about its future course of progress.

Since last several months, the Central Military Commission (CMC) of China has announced a series of fundamental changes to the organisational structure of the People's Liberation Army (PLA). These reform measures are bound to radically change the way some of the major components of China's Military conducts its business. The four General departments—General Staff, General Political, General Logistics and General Armament, which used to be the basic functional formations of the PLA for a long time has been restructured into fifteen new organs directly under the CMC. These new bodies comprise of six new departments: joint staff, political work, logistical support, equipment development, training and national defence mobilization.

Further, PLA has formally established five theatre commands on 1st Feb 2016, basing on their geographical locations: Eastern theatre command, Southern theatre command, Western theatre command, Northern theatre command and Central theatre command. These five commands will be replacing the existing seven regional commands, better known as Military Regions (MRs), named after the cities where their headquarters were located—Beijing, Shenyang, Jinan, Lanzhou, Nanjing, Chengdu and Guangzhou.

This series of reforms by and large follows the programme announced by nation's President and CMC chairman Xi Jinping after the conclusion of a three day long CMC Reform work conference on 26 November 2015. The conference attended by the top brass of China's military and the all powerful Communist Party of China (CPC) agreed upon a long drawn plan to reform the traditional Maoist outfits of the People's Liberation Army (PLA) largely patterned on the conventional Soviet military apparatus. President Xi committed to a major breakthrough in the overhaul by 2020, which tallies with Party's goal of making China a well off society by 2021, the centenary year of the establishment of the CPC.

The work conference also decided to streamline and consolidate the work of the existing seven military regions. Following these decisions, at a formal ceremony on 31 December 2015, President Xi in his capacity as the Chairman of the CMC officially constituted the newly formed the PLA Army general command, the PLA Rocket Force and the PLA Strategic

Support Force. This decision by the CPC Central Committee and the Central Military Commission to realize the Chinese dream of a strong military, and a strategic step to establish a modern military system with Chinese characteristics. It will be a milestone in the modernization of the Chinese military and will be recorded in the history of the people's armed forces.

However, one should not lose sight of the significant political thought process behind these reforms. Basically, PLA still remains the fighting arm of the Party, according to the official constitution of the People's Republic of China, this proviso has necessary legal sanction under relevant Party and State rules. Many of these changes also clearly reflect China's approach towards the ongoing process of transformation happening in military technology and tactics. Over, last twenty years both the military and political leadership of China have closely followed the unprecedented changes taking place in military thinking the world over.

According to ancient Chinese tradition, the military command(er) is nation's bulwark. His proficiency in war can make the country strong, his deficiency make it weak. Sun Tzu's Art of War specifies, "three ways by which a sovereign may bring disaster to his army:

> One, he arbitrarily orders his army to advance or retreat when in fact it should not, thus hampering the initiative of the army.
>
> Two, he interferes with the administration of the army when he is ignorant of its internal affairs, thus causing confusion among the officers and men.
>
> Three, he interferes with the officers' command, unaware of the principle that an army should adopt different tactics according to different circumstances. This will create misgivings in the minds of the officers and men."

The disastrous experiment of Great Cultural Revolution under the notorious 'gang of four', played havoc with the command and control structure of China's military. After the cultural revolution and the death of former Chairman Mao Zedong, China under the charismatic leadership of Deng Xiaoping carried out a series of changes in PLA's command structure. In 1983 the military leadership convened enlarged CMC work conference and proposed a series of measures to modernise the existing military set up of China. By late 1980s China re-introduced the rank system among its services and reduced the number Military Regions from the existing eleven to seven.

Towards the end of nineties, PLA leadership took another major step in streamlining its command set up and formed the General Armament

Department in addition to the existing three key departments directly under the control of Central Military Commission. The GAD was specifically tasked to take care of large scale procurement for PLA and also for managing major space launches, especially the ones related to military applications. With this China also managed the separation of military related industries as well as other related and not related business ventures under PLA.

Under a rapidly evolving security scenario around the world, Chinese leadership has become more convinced that their old command and control mechanisms are not yielding the desired results. Another lesson they learned from the experiences of other matured armies, especially the US military system, was gaining momentum of jointness in fighting the modern wars.

Xi Jinping's own understanding of military building has certainly played a major role in this restructuring process. After graduating from the famous Tsinghua University of China as worker-peasant—soldier student in 1979, Xi Jinping was assigned to work in the Party—Government head quarters as Secretary to the then Defence Minister Geng Biao. Then Geng was also working as the Secretary General of the CMC.

His first job as a secretary in the military headquarters provided him with many opportunities to understand the original thinking of the first generation leadership including Chairman Mao and others. As a child Xi grew up at Zhongnanhai, the senior leadership residential compound, in Beijing (then Peking) and attended school with other children, many of them become key players in CPC leadership. Some of these friends/ classmates includes, current PLA Generals Zhang Youxia, Liu Yuan and others.

Prof. Cheng Li notes, "it has been widely reported that General Zhang Youxia, director of the PLA General Armaments Department, is Xi's most trusted confident in Central Military Commission, Xi once proposed (according to a Reuters source) promoting Zhang to be vice chairman of the CMC in 2012. The first instalment of this series (of articles) revealed the strong family ties between Xi Jinping and Zhang Youxia; their fathers were not only natives of Shaanxi but also "bloody fighting comrades" in the Communist Revolution in northern China. ...Zhang is currently one of very few active duty officers in the PLA who have had war experience. He participated in the two Chinese wars with Vietnam, first as a company commander in 1976, and then as a regiment commander, in 1984. Zhang is qualified to serve another five year term in the CMC after 2017, and he will be a leading contender for the post of vice chairman of China's most powerful military leadership body."

How much Xi Jinping can push this military organisation to serve his own aims has to be watched closely. Some of the results of these reforms would be more manifest in coming few years. One of the fundamental aim is to tighten the control of Party over the army. After taking over the reins of the Party in 2012, Xi paid a lot of attention on making the military stronger and cleaner. He also started the periodic visits to former revolutionary base, Gutian town in Fujian province. Before Xi kicked off the military overhaul, in October 2014, he ordered more than 400 senior military officials to gather in Gutian for a two-day conference.

Towards end 1929 the Fourth Army held its Ninth Party congress in Gutian, under the leadership of Chairman Mao Zedong, the congress reiterated the absolute leadership of Party over PLA. With this the CPC decided to keep the "gun" under its firm control. Xi Jinping is determined about absolute control over the PLA and the military serving as the vanguard of the Party. Xi also wanted to preserve the purity of the PLA, therefore, he launched the move to eradicate corruption from the Party and military. Hence, Xi wanted the "armed forces to maintain a high degree of conformity with the CPC Central Committee and the CMC, strictly obey political discipline and rules, and carry out their orders and instructions to the letter."

With these set of reforms, the Chinese leadership intends to introduce a new work culture among all services. Earlier in September 2015, Xi Jinping announced to reduce the number of troops from 2.3 million to 2 million. Reform also plans toweed out outdated armaments, developing new weapons systems and reducing the size of the militia. Overall security scenario around China is changing rapidly, the tremendous changes taking place in technology, especially in the fields of surveillance techniques and reaction timings, PLA leadership were planning to adopt more changes to make its forces to enable itself to fight a modern war under hi-tech conditions.

One has to wait still longer to understand the full implications of this round of reforms. Like in most other military set ups, one of the main issue will be coordination, how the CMC leadership can manage the divergent interests of different formations. The land forces, senior level Army personnel, still holds the maximum top level positions in the new PLA command structure. Professionalization is still a long drawn out process, how the Party leadership can achieve its desired goal of professionalization and tighter Party control is the real challenge.

Role of newly formed Strategic Support Force (SSF) needs special mention, from all accounts this new formation will be coordinating all activities relating to the cyber and space activities. The important role played by these two broader areas in modern warfare is crucial. Lieutenant General Gao Jin, commander of the PLA's new established SSF, has a stronger academic and research background. Gao, 56, has a master's degree from the Second Artillery Engineering University. Before taking up this position Gen Gao was heading the famous Chinese military think tank, Academy of Military Sciences (AMS) in Beijing.

Another second Artillery General Wei Fenghe, 61, who commanded the Second Artillery Corps before it was recently renamed the Rocket Force, is an upcoming military leader of China who must be observed carefully. The Second Artillery corps commands nuclear and conventional strategic missiles and answers directly to the Central Military Command. Gen. Wei is certain to play a key role in the implementation of these round of reforms in PLA. With the new round of reforms the Chinese leadership is trying to shift its focus is to usher in a new and fresh combined use of the various modern forces, in other words the shift in favour of making use of the combined capabilities of space, cyber and nuclear forces.

Most of the new structures created after the new round of reforms are aimed at bringing these advantages together. Some of these areas of jointness and pursuing a cyber-space dominated military command and control system is a highly evolving field. The world is largely aware about the work done in US military command structure. However, this remains highly technology and heavy investment oriented. One need to closely watch the Chinese ability to innovate in the areas of asymmetry related strategies.

Together with this series of reform measures the CMC leadership has appointed Major General Qin Tian, 57, son of former defence minister and revolutionary veteran Qin Jiwei, as chief of staff of the People's Armed Police (PAP). Qin Tian, a well experienced soldier with a research background from AMS, is well known for his views on anti corruption efforts. In the future, the Communist leadership will be mainly relying on police forces to look after the domestic law and order situations. Army will be carrying out its professional duty of guarding the territorial integrity of the nation.

The reduction in the strength and consolidation of logistic services are bound to reduce the expenses of PLA however, this may not have a larger impact on the defence budget of China. PRC is likely to increase its defence budget by around ten percent in this coming financial year too. The official defence budget for China in the last financial year was US$ 142 billion.

Under the new dispensation, India will be looked after by the newly constituted Western Theatre Command (WTC). Geographically, this largest theatre command consists of administrative areas like Sichuan, Tibet Autonomous Region, Yunnan, Shaanxi, Gansu, Ningxia, Qinghai, Xinjiang Autonomous Region and Chongqing Municipal Corporation. Unlike the previous arrangement, wherein India-China border was under the watch of two separate Military Regions, Chengdu MR and Lanzhou MR. Under the new set up only one command authority will be responsible for looking after the entire stretch of India-China boundary. Naturally, the coordination efforts can be expected to be far more sophisticated. Both Indian military establishment and civilian agencies including think tanks in India must enhance their awareness about Chinese military and its affairs.

Keeping in view of the prevailing conditions in the adjoining Afghanistan-Pakistan region, the main focus of China's fight against terrorism and separatism is also likely to be coordinated by WTC. Large scale changes and reforms can be anticipated in the organisational set up of PLA in the near future, hence it need to be watched and studied carefully to safeguard our own security interests.

This latest round of military reforms carefully planned and implemented under the guidance of Xi Jinping at the helm of the Party will have far reaching repercussions on China and its immediate neighbours, especially the one's those share a land border with it, including India. The current cycle of reforms is also equally important for the management of China's internal security issues also.

In recent years the strategic equations among nation states have undergone drastic changes all over the world, relations between nations are no more based on the security aspect alone. Economic and trade relations including personal level contacts in different capacities also have a huge impact on deciding the outcomes of interactions among between different nations and communities of people. Therefore, the ever growing economic factors have become a key factor in deciding the strategic behaviour of nation states. Relationships between nations can no longer be strictly categorised into black and white segments, areas of grey have started spreading enormously.

One major reason for this is the dramatic changes happened in the way the modern wars are fought among nations with comparatively advanced technology and war waging capabilities. The role of asymmetries need more studies. For example, India and China, the two declared nuclear weapon powers cannot think of fighting even a very limited war without thinking seriously about all the repercussions it can have on the two states.

Introductions of nuclear weapons add many different dimensions to war, once nuclear weapons are present the escalation mechanism becomes crucially important. Therefore, both the Asian neighbours have to pay attention to this factor. In India's case this places added responsibility on it on the war preparedness and on the deterrence mechanism.

These kinds of rapid changes would also largely depend on how the strategic scenario across the entire northeast Asia is going to transform from a long term perspective. China's growing military capabilities will certainly impact these equations. In Northeast Asia—Japan and South Korea are the two key allies of USA, with which it has treaty obligations to protect these two powerful countries. After the Second World War and the conclusion of Korean armistice agreement, US have signed formal security agreements with these nations for protecting their territorial integrity and national security. Therefore, USA remains treaty bound to ensure the security and integrity of its allies.

Recently Japanese Prime Minister Abe was the first Asian leader to visit US, after the new President, Donald J Trump took power in White House. The Chinese authorities must be paying special attention to these developments. The age old defence agreements and ties between these two nations are likely to further prosper under the Trump administration.

However, unlike in the cold war era these relations no more remains in a unidimensional mode of security concern alone. Using this opportunity Prime Minister Abe would also try to further his political clout within Japan. One of the issues will be how far Trump will stick to his pre-poll announcement, that United States' allies must enhance their defence spending and contribute more substantially for safeguarding their overall security management system.

Japan will continue to abide by its treaty obligations for the foreseeable future, however, some of the ground realities are changing. The Trump administration's demand for spending more money on its own defence will be taken seriously, this will compel its leadership to see all the options available to it. Unlike some of the European security partners of the US, Japan may be willing to spend more money on its defence efforts, however, will Japan opt for nuclear weapons is a tough question. The existing antipathy towards nuclear weapons as the first victim of nuclear weapons in the hands of USA is still likely to remain as a huge barrier for its weapon programme in the future.

In the meanwhile the economic engagement of some of the business giants of Japan with China directly and with the Chinese diaspora led or influenced business establishment have undergone drastic changes all across Asia and abroad. All these issues complicate the future strategic scenarios in Asia at large. The most likely scenario in Japan-US-China triangular relationship will be somewhat heightened tensions as well as growing, but certainly mellowed down bilateral economic engagement between Japan and China at official levels.

South Korea can be described as the most allied ally of United States of America in Asia after Japan. After the Korean war in early fifties and the signing of the armistice agreement, South Korea came under the security umbrella of USA and it agreed to host US armed forces in its soil. USA has currently stationed a total 28,000 of its serving military personnel in South Korea, as a part of its security arrangements. South Korea's decision to install the US supplied Terminal High Altitude Area Defence (THAAD) anti missile defence system have certainly complicated the scenario. Chinese authorities take this as a direct threat to its deterrence capability in its immediate neighbourhood. Hence China is bound to take necessary precautionary measures to protect its own vital security interests in the region.

Further, the growing military power of China will always be viewed by the North Korean regime with some suspicion and certain level of confidence. Russia and China are two reliable partner nations left for the secluded hermit kingdom. These two nations yet remain as the normal neighbours for by and large ostracised power, North Korea. South Korea's latest move to install the THAAD system in its sovereign territory with the help of United States of America have further complicated the issues. China's ruling Party, the CCP and North Korea's Workers party would naturally like to keep their fraternal relations in good shape despite all the odds. Naturally this will have far reaching consequences to the security interests of all major players in North East Asia region.

At another level one can argue that the real ambition of the North Korean leadership is to engage in direct talks with US. Recently, on 12 February 2017, North Korea conducted a test fire of its medium range Ballistic missile when the Japanese Prime Minister Abe was visiting USA on the invitation of President Trump. Unexpectedly, compared to previous occasions the reaction from the new administrative set up in USA was much muted. This may be an indication for the direct talks between these to nuclear adversaries.

While dealing with the neighbourhood issues, the Association of the South East Asian Nations (ASEAN) established in the late sixties to counter the influence of Communist China in South east Asia still presents some of the severe problems relating to a militarily and economically re-emerged China as a strategic power in Asia. During the post cold war era the ASEAN-China relations have undergone various ups and downs. While trade and economic interactions between China and most of the ASEAN members were on a steady upswing. On the strategic front these relations were never had a very smooth passage. Many of these smaller nations looked at China with suspicion. Some of these nations had traditional border disputes with China.

However, the South China Sea issue remained as a major bone of contention for many countries in this grouping. Five major ASEAN members, the Philippines, Malaysia, Indonesia, Vietnam and Brunei are direct claimant parties in this dispute along with the People's Republic of China and Taiwan (Republic of China), the original 'sole' owners of the region on the basis of the so called "nine dash lines" in the South China Sea region. These nine dash lines were originally drawn by the then Kuomintang government of China in 1947.

China-Philippine relations need to be looked at from different perspectives, during the early cold war era Philippines was a frontline state for US A and its democratic right wing allies. As a result USA started a special relationship with this state. With a formal treaty alliance USA guaranteed the security of Philippines. In June 1978 President Ferdinand Marcos issued a decree declaring Kalayaan island group in north western parts of the Spratly (Nansha) islands of the South China sea as the sovereign territory of Philippines. The discovery of petroleum products in these areas further complicated the ownership issue of these areas. Chinese government claimed all the South China Sea area under its nine dash lines claim over these sea territories. After various twists and turns in 2013 the Philippines decided to take the case against China to the Permanent court of Arbitration at Hague. After three years in July 2016, the court decided in favour of Philippines. As there is no mechanism available for the implementation of the decision, the situation is likely to continue for a long time to come.

Meanwhile the political equations between China and the Philippines have undergone drastic changes. The newly elected president Rodrigo Duterte is not showing any interest in pursuing this vexed time consuming complicated legal issue. He is more interested in exploiting the economic benefits available by improving bilateral relations with the mainland China. Duterte is also trying to make use of the ongoing disputes for reaping possible benefits available from the traditional ally USA. Therefore, any government takes power in Manila would like to continue to keep its good economic relations with China meanwhile keeping its special security relations with USA. How deftly Duterte and his successors can play this delicate diplomatic game needs to watched carefully.

Due to a variety of historical and cultural traditions, China and Vietnam share a long relationship of suspicion and a series of ideologically linked engagement in their neighbourly relations. The long list includes, nearly a one thousand years of occupation of Vietnam by different dynasties that ruled China. This is further complicated by the land border issues and the ever complicated South China Sea (SCS) disputes. The recent ruling by the Permanent Court of Arbitration at the Hague against China's claims in the south China Sea, has further added to the problems of the bilateral relations.

In early January 2017, the Vietnamese Communist Party (VCP) chief, General Secretary Nguyen Phu Trong visited China and met with his counterpart Xi Jinping and reiterated the traditional friendship with China. During the deliberations they agreed to have better relations and reached a better level of understanding on all controversial issues including the South China Sea dispute.

Due to a vertical split, the ASEAN as a group has almost become strategically irrelevant vis-a-vis China, this provides a golden opportunity for China to continue to pursue its own long term security goals in Asia.

Ever since India and China become independent in the mid of last century, the bilateral relations between these two Asian giants have undergone various ups and downs. India was one of the first nations to recognise the newly liberated state, China however, the border dispute and the resultant skirmishes led to a total collapse of mutual trust between these two neighbours. Sadly this cast a long shadow on the traditional friendship and resulted in a comparatively huge spell of gloom over the normal bilateral relations between these two nations. Large sections of Indians still look at any Chinese activities with suspicion.

During the past few decades after China and India launched their economic reform and opening to the outside world and adoption of open trade policies, the level of bilateral trade and other mutually beneficial economic cooperative endeavours have grown steadily. After the economic deceleration in Europe and all over the world in 2008, just like most other nations China had already emerged as India's number one commodity trade partner. But in the case of China, India comes as one of the junior trade partner. This certainly complicates the level of bilateral relations and the scope for competitive security issues.

Further, both India and China are well aware about the futility of an open war for both the nations under the given international scenario. China is very much focussed on emerging as one of the most advanced nations among world. This naturally questions the existing global order, a certain reorder is required. However, in this endeavour both India and China are competitors and collaborators. In certain areas like the climate change, world trade order, global economic management institutions etc both the nations will be cooperating on various issue. On many other issues like the reform of various United Nations institutions and other organisational reforms both India and China would be working at cross purposes.

On the strategic front these rivalries and competitions would be much more fierce and subtle. As India has already declared itself as a nuclear weapon power it must prepare itself to counter any nuclear blackmail. One must be prepared to keep the deterrence mechanism intact. No adversary should be in a position to threaten and blackmail India. This needs to be achieved through a judicious combination of defence capability and shrewd use of diplomatic manoeuvres.

This round of the military modernisation of China provides a good opportunity and a huge challenge for Indian defence establishment. Luckily for India, we are not expecting a major war along the border, therefore, one has an opportunity to understand the broad changes taking place in the weapons, equipments, mode of war, role of cyber and space in the future wars etc, one need to plan and adapt once own resources for waging such a war in the future. In other words India still have time to make one's own responses to the military advances of China in the near future.

India must make use of this opportunity to reorient its own strategic thinking and reform its large and almost unwieldy military establishment, surviving at different levels. We must make use this chance to look at the options available for Indian Military. We need to look at the future wars more seriously and prepare the required human resources urgently. The existing conventional forces are required for time being, in the meanwhile one must plan for the future. We need to look at all available options to reorient our military for the future wars.

In conclusion one can argue that in coming years Indian leadership need to gather its full diplomatic sagacity to mange this complicated relationship for the benefit of Asia and world at large. At one level India need to work with China to achieve its own economic objectives of a sustained development for all its population. In order to achieve this we need to manage the relations between India and China as well as India and its immediate neighbours. We should not allow our smaller neighbours to take advantage of our bilateral relations.

Index